Foundations of
Education

Winga &ell
llye
1985

2ND EDITION

Planning for Competence

Foundations
of
Education

Joseph F. Callahan
Leonard H. Clark

Jersey City State College

MACMILLAN PUBLISHING CO., INC.
New York

COLLIER MACMILLAN PUBLISHERS
London

Copyright © 1983, Macmillan Publishing Co., Inc.

Printed in the United States of America

Earlier edition copyright © 1977 by Macmillan Publishing Co., Inc.

Macmillan Publishing Co., Inc.
866 Third Avenue, New York, New York 10022

Collier Macmillan Canada, Inc.

Library of Congress Cataloging in Publication Data

Main entry under title:

Foundations of education.

(Planning for competence)
Includes bibliographies.
1. Education—Handbooks, manuals, etc.
I. Callahan, Joseph F.   II. Clark, Leonard H.
III. Series.
LB17.F68   1983   370′.973   82-4705
ISBN 0-02-318220-2

Printing: 1 2 3 4 5 6 7 8   Year: 3 4 5 6 7 8 9 0

ISBN   0-02-318220-2

To Jane E. Callahan and Maria A. Clark

Preface

This volume is an attempt to give the student an overview of the theoretical foundations on which pedagogical practice in the United States rests. It begins with the history of education in the United States since colonial times and then turns to matters of philosophy, psychology, the nature of the learner, and sociology, and their implications for educational practice today. The topics are presented in a series of learning modules, each of which stands alone and provides the student with a rationale, behavioral objectives, a self-administered and self-corrected test, and a textual presentation of the topic being considered. In each module the authors have attempted to provide the student with all the information one needs for a basic understanding of the topic and at least some of its implications. Additional readings are suggested for those interested in amplifying their knowledge and understanding.

This format is designed to lend itself to individualized teaching techniques. It thus is a means for providing students with basic knowledge without using up precious class time. Consequently, instructors may wish to use the modules to enable students to acquire basic information outside of class so that they can devote their class time to developing higher learnings and deeper understanding, and to sharpening their skills with follow-up activities such as discussion and seminar classes on the implications for solution of today's educational problems.

Sexist expressions easily find their way into a manuscript. We have tried to avoid them and other marks of prejudice. We have, however, at times used the editorial pronoun "he" to refer to both men and women. This should not be taken as evidence of sexism, but as an effort to facilitate readability.

J. F. C.
L. H. C.

Contents

1. Our Schools: The First Three Centuries

2. Our Schools: The Twentieth Century

3. Philosophical Development of Education: General Background

4. Philosophical Development of Education: Major Approaches

5. Psychological Bases: Major Theories of Learning

6. Psychological Bases: Nature of Learning

7. Psychological Bases: Nature of the Learner

8. Tests and Measurement

9. Social Problems: Culture, Society, and Education

10. Social Problems: Integration, Poverty, Delinquency, Crime, Mobility

11. Social Problems: Political and Social Ideologies

12. Impact of Change

Foundations of
Education

To the Student

Welcome to an adventure in learning.

Now that you have begun to think seriously about a career in teaching, it is our guess that you will find adventures of this sort very helpful in planning to meet the challenges that await you in the classroom. It seems safe to predict that not only will you increase your background in educational theory and methodology as you work your way through these modules, but also you will improve your chances of becoming an effective teacher when the time arrives to put theory learned into practice.

Probably you have not encountered many books organized as this one, calling for such active participation on your part. From this point forward, you are expected to become a sensitive, self-motivated learner engaged in making frequent and sound judgments about your learning. You will be the one to control the rate of progress through the various modules, and you will decide when you have mastered the knowledge presented in each. We have tried to help by (1) listing the objectives of each module; (2) providing a comprehensive set of questions to test your mastery at the end of each module; and (3) providing an answer key for your use in evaluating progress. Those with little time to spend on study can move through the various modules and finish quickly so long as they study attentively and demonstrate the mastery called for on each test. Slower-paced individuals, who wish to ponder and probe various areas and who decide to read extensively from the selected readings listed in each module, can establish a pace that suits their purposes.

It is not intended that any student will be able to prepare for a teaching career solely by completion of this kind of study program. Teaching is a human activity. It deals with people, with children, parents, and fellow professionals. It involves various kinds of knowledge, judgments, and decision making; it requires communications skills, human relations techniques, and a host of other attributes for the cultivation of which human interaction and professional expertise are necessary. But faithful and zealous use of this learning tool will add depth and meaning to your classroom sessions in education courses. Mastery of these modules will carry you beyond the initial steps of preparation so that you may place into context more of the campus lectures about education which you hear, and ask questions about schools and students that go beyond the layman's level of significance.

The sections of the book are called modules, for essentially they are self-contained units that have cognitive values by themselves. Each module contains a rationale, a list of objectives, a post test, an answer key*, and a list of

---

* The answer keys will be found at the end of the last module.

1

selected readings. The rationale attempts to establish the purpose of each module and, in some cases, the link with other aspects of pedagogical knowledge. The objectives inform you very specifically what you should know and be able to do as a consequence of your study of the module. The test and the key inform you of your progress toward module mastery. The general study plan recommended is as follows:

1. Read the rationale to acquaint yourself with the task you are addressing and, if possible, to discover how this module fits among the others that you will study.
2. Examine carefully the module objectives. Find out what will be expected of you upon completion of your study.
3. Read through the module, checking back from time to time to see how well you are mastering the objectives. Review what you do not understand.
4. Take the Post Test. Evaluate your success by using the answer key. Where your answer differs from that of the author, search out the sentence or paragraph in the text that confirms your answer or his.
5. If you score less than 85 per cent on any test, reread and retake the test until your mastery improves.
6. Try out your knowledge by exposing yourself to some of the suggested readings. Your progress should accelerate as you bring more and more knowledge to each book that you read.
7. Engage in interaction with fellow students, professors, and members of your family on the topics studied, whenever possible.
8. Enjoy the experience. The profession needs zealous seekers of knowledge who enjoy learning and who, in the process, develop a capacity for infecting other people with the same "felicitous virus."

In this revised edition, a subsection has been added to each module to help you perform item number seven in the preceding study plan. We have titled the addition *Involvement Experiences* in lieu of the usual end-of-chapter activities, because these lists will require more subtle and more provocative action on your part.

As study exercises to enhance content mastery, the impact of these experiences will, of course, depend upon your desire to learn. If your engagement with the text content has been intense enough, if you have grasped the essence of any or each module well enough, and if your desire to test out your newly acquired mastery is vibrant enough, you will be tempted to perform acts that will help you to develop your professional psyche in a number of ways.

Gauge the breadth of your emerging pedagogical maturity by the number or divergence of the concepts that accompany your participation in the experiences. These are the kinds of activities to which we cannot supply ready-made answers. Actually, these kinds of experiences constitute the pleasure of teaching associated with college classes that no text can supply. We would enjoy engaging in give-and-take about each one with you, but are stymied by the lack of a medium through which to communicate.

Be imaginative. Be creative. Design your own testing devices for the responses that you collect. Begin with the knowledge that there is no one correct answer that will suffice for each of us on all of the experiences. Collect responses avidly from all around you without becoming a crashing bore. Mull them over. Ferret out your own conclusions and experience the satisfaction of watching your own philosophy of education unfold gradually.

MODULE
1

Our Schools: The First Three Centuries

Perspective of History / Generalizations from American Educational History / Educational Consciousness in America (1607–1787) / Major Issues that Shaped the American School System / Universal versus Class Schools / Control of Schools / Public Secondary Education Policy / Public Higher Education Policy / Teacher Education / Summary

The first-edition version of this module was written by William A. Liggitt, Jersey City State College. It has been edited and updated for this edition.

RATIONALE

... first module, we trace the development of education in America from 1600 to 1900.

You will discover from the perspective of history that almost from the date of the first settlements in New England the Colonists were interested in education for their children. Colonial colleges were established to provide for an educated ministry and for training in the law and the professions. The early schools were very much like the seventeenth-century schools in England. They were modified and changed by the demands of the American Colonial society. By the time of the American Revolution, the inhabitants of New England and the Middle Colonies were very much aware of their educational heritage. As in Europe, the schools were training grounds for the socially and economically elite, but, after the Revolution, the Common School (elementary) education and secondary education began to effect a transformation that by 1900 resulted in a unique, distinctly American system of education. The shaping of our school system in the nineteenth century corresponded to what historians have termed the period of "national consciousness" in our history. With the adoption of the Constitution in 1789, new democratic political forms needed to be developed and made to work. An educated citizenry was to be the means by which the American people could participate in the implementation of the Constitution. You will note that common schooling, universal secondary training, and, by the close of the nineteenth century, higher education, were outlined as the educational requirements for participation in American society.

In historical perspective, the American educational system is the result of broad, dynamic, almost revolutionary changes in American society during the nineteenth century. It was in this century that America broke away from the European tradition of separate schools for different classes in society and established a free, tax-supported, nonsectarian system of primary, secondary, and higher education.

In this module we present the broad sweep of social, political, and economic events in America, from early Colonial times to the beginning of the twentieth century, that led to the establishing of the free, tax-supported, nonsectarian, state system of public schools. (In Module 2, we shall trace developments in the structure and organization of the public school systems in the twentieth century.)

SPECIFIC OBJECTIVES

Upon completion of the study of this module you should be able to

1. Cite at least two contributions that the study of educational history makes to the professional education of a teacher.
2. List factors that distinguish the new history of the 1970s and 1980s from previous histories.

3. Identify at least five historical tendencies in education that have had a significant impact on current educational practices.
4. Describe a cycle of change that an educational institution tends to follow.
5. Recognize the major motivating factor in establishing Colonial primary schools and Colonial colleges.
6. Contrast the purpose of the Latin Grammar School with the purpose of the Academy.
7. Describe some of the methods of teaching in a Colonial primary school.
8. Cite some of the components of the curriculum in the Colonial college.
9. Recognize the historical reasons for emphasis on study of ancient languages—Latin and Greek.
10. Identify two leaders who were instrumental in changing the curriculum of Colonial secondary schools.
11. List three nineteenth-century economic and political forces that helped shape American education.
12. Describe three sources of revenue in the early nineteenth century that were used to support elementary and secondary education.
13. Distinguish between the Pauper-School concept and the Free-School concept.
14. Identify the political process that resulted in state supervision of local schools.
15. Assess the significance of the office of State Superintendent of Instruction in shaping the structure of the American school system.
16. Define two implications of the secularization of American schools for the organization and financing of American education.
17. Identify the chief legal bases that required the secularization of American schools.
18. Cite two socioeconomic reasons for the emergence of secular public education in the United States.
19. Recognize two nineteenth-century educational institutions that provided for the education of women.
20. Place, in order of their appearance in the American culture, such institutions as the Academy, Latin Grammar School, high school, and the state university.
21. Evaluate the influence of the various geographical regions of the United States in establishing the high school and the state university.
22. Compare the influence of the city with that of the rural population in the development of the public high school.
23. Define the significance of U.S. Supreme Court decisions in establishing a state university system.
24. Place in historical order some of the strategic battles in the nineteenth century that resulted in the emergence of an uniquely American system of public education.
25. Trace the development of teacher education in the nineteenth century.

MODULE TEXT

Perspective of History

It has been said that one studies the past to understand the present and to project the future. The study of great public events (national elections, wars, civil strife, revolutions), large-scale transformations (the Renaissance, the Industrial Revolution), or great figures in politics, economic life, or the worlds of art and ideas, tells us much about where we have been and where we are at the present time. The historian is concerned with the scope, forms, approach, and assumptions underlying historical events. History is more than a faithful retelling of the "story of the past." The most skillful historians perceive history as both an art and a science. A reconstruction of the past, based on the most reliable valid evidence, is only useful when, through an interpretation of the historical narrative, the reader gains some new insights, some broader understandings, of the forces that shaped society's institutions, and some notions of the future directions of these institutions.

Contemporary historiography, inspired by the work of the *Annales* school in France, is far more comprehensive than the old sociopolitical histories of the past. The new historians concentrate their studies in three principal areas: the first is the basic condition of life, that is, birth, education, marriage, and death, and the fundamental units of social organization—the household, family, and community. The second is the structure of economic and social life, including the modes of production, and social organization in its broadest sense. The third area the new historians are beginning to focus upon is "collective mentalities," that is, the belief-systems and perceptual frameworks that determine the ways people interpret both the routine and the extraordinary events in their lives. The purpose of the new history is to give us explicit insights into the nature of the human condition through time and space. These are insights that enable the student-scholar to acquire a rich perspective on life in the present and upon life in the future. It is for this reason that as a beginning student in education you are urged to study the history of education, and in particular the development of the American public school system.

A comprehensive study of the history of education generally includes some narrative on educational philosophies, aims and purposes, curricula (content); public attitudes and support, teaching-learning process (methods); professional personnel (teachers, administrators, specialists); and a full description of changes in education organization and structure. The historian believes that every event, movement, crisis, political act, and social behavior, has its antecedent. To know the antecedents of your field of study is to have a breadth and depth of understanding that will enable you to appraise the present and approach the future with both confidence and humility.

We must add that the formal study of educational history is not a *sine qua non* for success in teaching, especially when teaching is defined solely as what teachers do in the classroom. But a professional teacher is required to do more than prepare and present daily lessons. There is much that you will do, in collaboration with your colleagues, to change the schools. In the study and implementation of new approaches to teaching, in examining the school structure, and in listening and responding to community groups, you will help your school to continue to be a vital, relevant social force in the community. The wide-awake teacher knows, for example, that although the American tradition of elementary school is more than three hundred years old, the idea of the high school dates back only a little more than one hundred and fifty years, to the Massachusetts Law of 1827; and that the American public school system was finally structured in its modern form by about 1870, which makes it only slightly more than one hundred years old.

American public education is a social institution. A *social* institution is a practice that has become established as a part of the culture or way of thinking and living of a social group. Freedom of speech, marriage, the church, the family, and public education are examples of social institutions. The public school is a community institution: a social institution sometimes supported and sometimes threatened by two other major social institutions—the church and the family.

History tells us that American public education is still in its infancy as a social institution. Its newness as an institution explains much of the confusion about education and schooling. Although humans early incorporated education into their culture, it has been only in recent times that scholars have systematically addressed the study of education as an institution. Today, as you shall soon find out, if you have not already, educators have still not developed a firm terminology generally accepted and understood by all practitioners. Neither have they, nor have the people they serve, yet determined the directions, purposes, and roles of schools in our society. History also reveals the economic and social forces and the philosophic influences that produced the American school system. It shows us how social institutions become obsolete and how new institutions take their place. Basically then, the study of the history of education will help you to discover how American education happens to be what it is, and will assist you in making some tentative judgments as to where it is going and why.

Generalizations From American Educational History

Although history never repeats itself exactly, the history of education does provide data from which one may draw generalizations about education in the past and its probable course in the future. This section will present generalizations that the authors believe apply to the history of American education.

1. On the whole, the American school system has been enormously successful. Years ago it took on a mission never before attempted: to educate *all* the children of *all* the people through the secondary level. Of course, at times its efforts have been fumbling and the schools have gone off course, but, in general, American schools have accomplished this mission with surprising success.
2. The American people are convinced that good schools are a necessity. People are willing to sacrifice to support them. Even though individu-

als are not always sure about what constitutes good education, they are sure that schools are needed to support the American way of life. They expect the schools to teach children and youth to become effective American citizens. They do not want the schools to change society; rather, they want the schools to socialize pupils so that these students will maintain and support society. Therefore, citizens mean school programs to support the *status quo*, the customs and mores of the main social group, and the goals of the community. Disadvantaged citizens support schools with the hope that good schools will make them share more fully in the good things of our present society.

3. The American people have always looked to the schools for aid in solving social problems. They continue to do so. For example, in past decades school programs were expected to Americanize the flood of immigrants from foreign lands. Today society looks to the schools to help solve the problems of racial, ethnic, and class disparities. Because of their faith in the schools' influence on social matters, special-interest and pressure groups continually seek to use the schools to promote their objectives and points of view. As a result, school programs often become a bone of contention between opposing community factions.

4. Most of the basic decisions that affect schools and schooling are not made by educators. Rather, they are the result of social, political, and economic pressures beyond the control of school administrators and teachers.

5. In general, curriculum development follows a spiral pattern consisting of a series of cycles. The first step in each cycle occurs when changes in social and economic life create demands for new services, resulting in a new school being established and/or old schools revitalized. Programs are developed; teachers are prepared; state education departments, colleges, and various professional agencies accredit the school. In the meantime, social and economic conditions continue to change, and there is again a need for new services. However, teachers are not prepared to teach new subjects, and many in the adult population are not ready to accept schools that differ fundamentally from the institutions in which they themselves were educated. Educationally unsound reasons are manufactured to support antiquated practices and requirements. Finally, there is mounting criticism that the school, which was once a "new" school, is no longer functional; this factor forces educational changes, and the cycle begins anew.[1]

In sum, curriculum development has over the years been a matter of action and reaction—periods of vital, relevant curriculum activity alternating with periods of stagnation and retrenchment.

6. Over the years, throughout the nation as a whole, progress in real curriculum change is relatively slow. Although the past century has seen

[1] Although none of the cycles exactly repeats other cycles, they may bring back old practices, usually in a somewhat different form. Thus the schools and their programs change over the years in a zigzag or spiral fashion. Although each cycle may retain much from an earlier cycle, the cycle also explores new ground.

movement after movement—progressivism, individualization, social action, back to basics, the structure of the disciplines, and so on—much of today's teaching and curriculum remains amazingly similar to that of fifty or more years ago. Many of the new exciting innovations of the recent past have disappeared as the schools revert to the old so-called tried and true teaching content and methods of the *status quo ante.*

7. The curriculum cycles are marked by fads. All too frequently, curriculum development is a matter of following the leader. The new curriculum for School X is introduced solely because it seems to work in School Y. One year the fad may be "discovery learning," another year "learning in the community," and in still another year "back to basics." Neither educators nor lay leaders seem to be guided by educational theory. Many of them have not quite decided what a proper education for all boys and girls should be. Nor have they paid much attention to the results of scholarly research concerning students, subject matter, and the educational process, or to the reports of the various commissions and study groups that began to appear just about a hundred years ago.

    Moreover, school people neglect their own history. Consequently, educational innovators constantly reinvent the wheel. Many recent highly touted "educational innovations" were common twenty-five, fifty, or even a hundred years ago. Perhaps if teachers were better informed about the history of their profession, they could build on past successes and avoid past mistakes.

8. Often a social lag develops between what the school teaches and what the pupils need and their parents demand. This lag may exist partly because of the developmental change spiral described in generalization five. Also, educators tend to keep the old curricula and methods of teaching long after these programs have lost their effectiveness. Further, teachers have a knack for formalizing and desiccating lively programs. Academic studies are all too often impractical, irrelevant, out-of-date, and bookish. Despite recurrent efforts to center school learning around creative thinking, discovery, learning by doing, problem solving, and practical experience, the curriculum remains largely a matter of repeating what textbooks say.

9. The role and influence of the school has always been more than merely academic. The attitudes, ideals, prejudices and habits of behavior and thinking taught in school usually have a greater, longer lasting influence on pupils' lives than does the course content. The American society is what it is today partly because of the influence of the American school.

10. Many innovative educational programs and ways of teaching begin in private schools. Being free from some of the restraints that govern public schools, and being dependent on pleasing their clientele for their livelihood, they are more open to experimentation and innovation. When the public schools disappoint them, parents often turn to private schools for the schooling they wish for their children. Then,

frequently, public schools adopt the innovations and programs begun in private schools by incorporating them into the educational mainstream.

Educational Consciousness in America (1607–1787)

Primary and Elementary Schools

The first permanent European settlements in North America included Jamestown (1607), Plymouth (1620), Massachusetts Bay (1630), Maryland (1632), Connecticut (1635), and Providence Plantations (1636). Most of these settlers moved to the New World for religious, economic, and political reasons. The religious motive was very strong in Colonial America, and it dominated Colonial education.

The common public school system, consisting of primary, elementary, and secondary schools, had its origin in the Northern Colonies. In 1642, the General Court of Massachusetts enacted a law that encouraged parental responsibility for education of their children:

> This Co^t, [Court] taking into consideration the great neglect of many parents & masters in training up their children in learning . . . do hereupon order and decree, that in euery towne y chosen men . . . take account from time to time of all parents and masters, and of their children, concerning their . . . ability to read & understand the principles of religion & the capitall lawes of this country . . .

In 1647, five years later, the Massachusetts Court enacted a second law that required towns to provide education for the youth. This law stated:

> It being one cheife project of y ould deluder, Satan, to keepe men from the knowledge of y Scriptures . . . It is therefore orded [ordered], ye evy [every] towneship in this iurisdiction, aft y Lord hath increased y number to 50 houshold, shall then forthw appoint one w [with] in their towne to teach all such children as shall resort to him to write & reade . . . & it is furth ordered y where any towne shall increase to y numb [number] of 100 families or househould, they shall set up a grammer schoole, y m [am] thereof being able to instruct youth so farr as they shall be fited for y university [Harvard] . . .

The Massachusetts school laws of 1642 and 1647 served as models for similar laws that were soon created in other colonies.

The primary schools that emerged from the Massachusetts laws of 1642 and 1647, and similar laws in other American Colonies, were of several different types. They included Dame Schools which were conducted in the home by housewives; Writing Schools, which were concerned chiefly with teaching reading and writing; parochial schools conducted by various religious groups; and charity or Pauper Schools, which were managed by missionary groups. Instruction in all these schools was limited to the basic skills—reading, writing, numbering.

The instructional materials included the Bible and a few other religious books; the hornbook, which consisted of a sheet of paper containing the alphabet, numbers, and some bit of religious verse tacked onto a wooden paddle and covered with a thin sheet of transparent cow's horn; writing imp, ments; and a small amount of paper. Paper was extremely scarce; therefore, some Colonial schools made use of wax tablets. The wax tablets used in America were usually made of two thin pieces of wood, hinged together with leather straps; the wood was hollowed out and filled with wax. Students wrote on the wax with a stylus that had one sharp end for writing and a flat end for smoothing over the wax when something new was to be written. Some appreciation of the nature of the Colonial elementary school can be gained from the following notes of Christopher Dock, a Mennonite school teacher in Pennsylvania in 1750:

> The children arrive as they do because some have a great distance to school, others a short distance, so that the children cannot assemble as punctually as they can in a city. Therefore, when a few children are present, those who can read their Testament sit together on one bench; but the boys and girls occupy separate benches. . . . Those who have read their passage of Scripture without error take their places at the table and write . . .
>
> When all are together, and examined, whether they are washed and combed, they sing a psalm or a morning hymn, and I sing and pray with them. As much as they can understand of the Lord's Prayer and the Ten Commandments (accordingly to the gift God has given them), I exhort and admonish accordingly. . . . After these devotional exercises those who can write resume their work. Those who cannot read the Testament have had time . . . to study their lesson. These are heard recite immediately after prayer. Those who know their lesson receive an O on the hand, traced with crayon. This is a mark of excellence. Those who fail more than three times are sent back to study their lesson again. . . . any one having failed in more than three trials a second time, is called "Lazy" by the entire class and his name is written down. . . .
>
> Whichever child has during the day received the greatest number of marks (good marks), has pointed out the greatest number of letters . . . To him I owe something—a flower drawn on paper or a bird . . . Thus much in answer to his question, how I take the children into school, how school proceeds before and after prayers, and how the inattentive and careless are made attentive and careful, and how the timid are assisted.[2]

The elementary schools that were established in the New England and Middle Colonies prior to the Revolutionary War were patterned after the schools in England. They were founded so that children could read and understand the Bible. The curriculum was limited to teaching of skills, and the subject matter was taken from the Bible. From a reading of Christopher Dock's account, you will note that Colonial school teachers, more than two hundred years ago, were concerned with what to do with the children while waiting for all of them to arrive at school; how to capture their attention; and how to reward the good student and punish the lazy one. Although the methods of education have changed many times during the course of elementary education, the pedagogical problems of teachers remain much the same.

[2] Contained in Edgar W. Knight and Clifton L. Hall, *Readings in American Educational History* (New York: Appleton-Century-Crofts, 1951), pp. 31–35.

Secondary Schools and Colleges

The first type of secondary school in the Colonies was the Latin Grammar School. It was established in Boston in 1635, only five years after the Colonists settled in that area. As we have seen, the Massachusetts Law of 1647 required towns of a certain size (one hundred families or households) to set up a grammar school to prepare youth for college. Within sixteen years after the Massachusetts Bay Colony's school was established, seven or eight other towns in New England had Latin Grammar Schools in operation. These schools, like the Dame Schools and Writing Schools, were replicas of those in England. They were traditional in nature, designed to prepare youngsters for college and "for the service of God, in church and commonwealth."[3]

Harvard was the first Colonial college. It was established in 1636 for the purpose of preparing young men for the ministry. The extent to which the religious motive was dominant is illustrated in one of the 1642 rules governing Harvard College, which stated: "Let every student be plainly instructed, and earnestly pleased to consider well, the main end of his life and studies is, to know God and Jesus Christ . . ." Other early American colleges included William and Mary (1693), Yale (1701), Princeton (1746), and Dartmouth (1769). In all these early colleges, there was a heavy emphasis on theology and the classics, as their aims were to prepare students for the ministry. The Colonial colleges, like their European counterparts, required that students know Latin and Greek as a condition of admission. The entrance requirements to Harvard stated

> When any scholar is able to read Tully,[4] or such like classical Latin author *extempore*, and make and speak true Latin in verse and prose *suo (ut aiunt) Marte*, and decline perfectly the paradigms of nouns and verbs in the Greek tongue, then may he be admitted into the College, nor shall any claim admission before such qualifications.

Admission to Yale in the mid-eighteenth century required that

> None may expect to be admitted into this College unless upon Examination of the President and Tutors, they shall be found able Extempore to Read, Construe, and Parce Tully, Vergil and the Greek Testament; and to write true Latin in Prose and to understand the Rules of Prosodia, and Common Arithmetic, and Shal bring Sufficient Testimony of his Blameless and inoffensive Life.

With these admission requirements for the early Colonial colleges, you can readily understand why the Latin Grammar School concentrated on traditional learning, with heavy emphasis on Latin and Greek, and catered to only a select few—those boys of blameless character (girls were not admitted) who were deemed worthy of admission to study for the ministry.

Our earlier comments about the elitist tendencies of the schools are amply supported by the foregoing. In truth, a very small percentage of children attended these early secondary schools, for not many were interested in going to college. As late as 1785, there were only two Latin Grammar Schools in Boston, and the combined enrollment was only sixty-four boys.

---

[3] James A. Johnson, *et al., Introduction to the Foundations of American Education,* 2nd ed. (Boston: Allyn & Bacon, 1973), pp. 253, 281–282.

[4] The works of Marcus Tullius Cicero, the Roman orator and statesman.

By 1750, it was evident that the Latin Grammar School did not provide a practical secondary program for most youths. In 1749, after an abortive attempt to attract support for a new secondary school in 1743, Benjamin Franklin published *Proposals Relating to the Education of Youth in Pennsylvania.*[5] Although Franklin's views were not particularly novel, they represent the first systematic representation of what became the modern American public high school. Because Franklin perceived that there was considerable need for more and better trained skilled workers, he advocated establishing an Academy "where youth of this Province [Pennsylvania] . . . might receive the accomplishments of a regular education." He invited "those who incline to favour the design with their advice, either as to the Parts of Learning to be taught, the Order of study, the Method of Teaching, the Economy of the school, or any other Matter of Importance to the Success of the Undertaking," to communicate by letter with him as soon as possible.

The purpose and rationale for establishing such an academy were clearly delineated in the introductory paragraphs of Franklin's proposals:

> The good Education of Youth has been esteemed by wise Men in all Ages, as the surest Foundation of the Happiness both of private Families and of Commonwealths. Almost all Governments have therefore made it a principal Object of their Attention, to establish and endow with proper Revenues, such Seminaries of Learning, as might supply the succeeding Age with Men qualified to serve the Publick with Honour to themselves, and to their Country.
>
> Many of the first Settlers of these Provinces, were Men who had received a good Education in *Europe*, and to their Wisdom and good Management we owe much of our present Prosperity. But their Hands were full, and they could not do all Things. The present Race are not thought to be generally of equal Ability: For though the *American* Youth are allow'd not to want Capacity; yet the best Capacities require Cultivation, it being truly with them, as with the best Ground, which unless well tilled and sowed with profitable Seed, produces only ranker Weeds.
>
> That we may obtain the Advantages arising from an Increase of Knowledge, and prevent as much as may be the mischievous Consequences that would attend a general Ignorance among us, the following *Hints* are offered towards forming a Plan for the Education of the Youth of *Pennsylvania.* . . .

Franklin's "hints" on a plan for the education of the youth of Pennsylvania included:

1. The Rector [teacher] be a man of good understanding, good morals, diligent and patient; learn'd in the languages and sciences, and a correct pure speaker and writer of the English tongue;
2. The boarding scholars [students] should be taught everything that is useful: to write a fair hand; arithmetick, accounts and first principles of Geometry and Astronomy; English language to be taught by Grammar, Reading with emphasis on pronouncing properly and distinctly and History to be made a constant part of their reading . . . with the History of Men, Times and Nations, scholars should also

---

[5] Franklin's proposals may be found in Edgar W. Knight, and Clifton L. Hall, *Readings in American Educational History* (New York: Appleton-Century-Crofts, 1951), pp. 74–80.

study Histories of Nature, and History of Commerce. Natural History might be accompanied with some teaching of Gardening, Planting, Grafting, Innoculating etc. The Improvement of Agriculture being useful to all, and skill in it (was) no Disparagement to any.

Although an academy was established in Philadelphia in 1751, Franklin's proposal did not really take. The academy in Philadelphia turned classical in orientation, and finally became the University of Pennsylvania. A quarter century later, the idea of the academy was taken up by such men as Samuel Phillips, Jr., and his uncle John Phillips, who created Phillips Academies in Andover, Massachusetts in 1778 and in Exeter, New Hampshire in 1783. The goal of the Phillipses was to counteract "the prevalence of ignorance and vice, disorder and wickedness" by creating a public free school or academy for the purpose of instructing youth not only in English and Latin Grammar, Writing, Arithmetic, and those Sciences wherein they are commonly taught, but more especially to learn them the great and real business of living."[6] The stated aims of these schools were

1. the promotion of true Piety and Virtue;
2. instruction in the English Latin and Greek languages together with writing, arithmetic, music, and the art of speaking;
3. practical geometry, logic, and geography;
4. the literal arts and sciences as opportunity may hereafter admit and as the trustees shall direct.[7]

The creation of schools of this type evidently fulfilled a public need. In the next twenty years, more than thirty-five other academies were founded, and by mid-century the number had grown to about six thousand.

The academies were private schools. Popular as they were, they and the numerous "private venture schools"[8] were expensive. Because Boston parents objected to this expense, in 1821, the School Committee established what three years later became known as the English High School. This first American high school consisted of a three-year course in English, mathematics, science, and history. Later, the school added philosophy of history, chemistry, intellectual philosophy, linear drawing, logic, trigonometry, French, the United States Constitution, and such practical vocational subjects as bookkeeping and navigation.

Table 1-1 summarizes the characteristics of early American secondary schools, and compares them with twentieth-century high schools.

Major Issues That Shaped the American School System

Social, Economic, and Political Forces

Until the time of the American revolution, education almost everywhere was regarded as an affair of the church. Social, political, and economic influ-

---

[6] Deed of gift for the endowment of Phillips Andover Academy, April 21, 1779.
[7] Ibid.
[8] Special-purpose schools operated by private entrepreneurs. They were similar to modern private business or technical schools.

TABLE 1-1
American Secondary and Middle Schools Compared

Type of School	Purpose	Student Body	Place in the Educational Ladder	Control	Size	Curriculum	Time of Greatest Importance
Latin Grammar School	Preparation for college	Boys only, age 10 to 20	School for the elite. Included upper elementary school, secondary school, and sometimes collegiate levels.	Usually public	Small (25 to 50 pupils)	College preparatory Latin and Classics Math	Colonial period
Academy	Preparation for vocation and for college	Teenaged boys and girls	Post elementary, some collegiate, normal school, and vocational school functions.	Usually private	Small (50 to 150 pupils)	At first practical; later mainly college preparation. Vocational training on demand.	1st three quarters of nineteenth century.
Traditional High School	Preparation for college and vocation	Coeducational 15 to 18 year old boys and girls	Post elementary (grades 9–12)	Usually public or parochial	Usually 500 or fewer pupils	Mainly college preparation. Later business and vocational subjects.	1870s to 1930s
Comprehensive High School	Education for all American youth. Education for complete living	15 to 18 year old boys and girls	Post elementary (grades 10–12, 9–12, 7–12)	Usually public or parochial	500 to 2,000 or more pupils	Broad, general, business, vocational, college preparatory. Education for complete living, and education for all.	1930s to present
Junior High School	Preparation for high school transition from elementary to secondary school. Exploration.	13 to 15 year old boys and girls	Replaced upper elementary and beginning high school grades. Usually grades 7–9.	Usually public	200 to 1,000 pupils	Exploratory, general introduction to disciplines	1920s to 1960s
Middle School	Smooth transition from childhood to adolescence and from elementary to secondary education.	12 to 14 year transescent boys and girls	Replaced upper elementary grades (usually grades 6–8, 7–8 or sometimes 5–8)	Usually public	200 to 800 pupils	Exploratory, general, transition from elementary to secondary. Block of time.	1960s to present

ences after 1800 materially changed the character of American life. These changes made it imperative that Americans examine seriously and critically the nature and functions of schooling, and determine how education might support and contribute to the American society that was emerging in the nineteenth century. The economic, political, and social developments that made America a nation state and world power by 1900 helped to create a public system of education that is truly a remarkable contribution to Western culture. It is a system that visibly demonstrates how universal education serves to maintain a viable democratic society. American education (1) is free to all children and youth; (2) is tax-supported, and nonsectarian; (3) is supervised and controlled by individual states; (4) includes both elementary and secondary education, and, in many states, provides for a free or relatively free education through college and the university.

The growth of city population and manufacturing, the extension of suffrage, and the rise of the working class were significant developments which generated demand and support for the schools.

At the time of the adoption of the Constitution (1789), nearly everyone lived on a farm or in a small village. As late as 1820, there were only thirteen cities with a population of eight thousand or more in the twenty-three states that comprised the United States. Between 1820 and 1850, particularly in the New England states and in New York and Pennsylvania, manufacturing began to develop very rapidly. Cotton spinning and the weaving of wool became a New England industry. Pennsylvania became the center of the iron manufacturing industries. Lowell, Massachusetts, for example, which in 1820 did not exist, had a population of twenty thousand in 1840. In that same period, the number of cities with a population of 8,000 or more increased from thirteen to forty-four, and by 1860 they numbered 141.

As cities developed and much of the country became more city-like in character, several problems, which seem to be indigenous to city life—immorality, crime, juvenile delinquency, drunkenness, and poverty—greatly increased. The church and philanthropic organizations headed by public-spirited citizens, began to pressure for city and state funds and for private donations to be used to educate the children of the poor.

Governor Wolf, in his message to the Legislature of Pennsylvania in 1833, observed that

> Universal education, if it were practical to enforce it everywhere, would operate as a powerful check upon vice, and would do more to diminish the black catalogue of crimes, so generally prevalent, than any other measure, whether for prevention or punishment, that has hitherto been devised; . . .
>
> According to the returns of the last census, we have in Pennsylvania, 581,180 children under the age of 15 years, and 149,080 between the ages of 15 and 20 years, forming an aggregate of 730,269 juvenile persons of both sexes, under the age of 20 years, most of them requiring more or less instruction; . . .
>
> It is time, fellow citizens, . . . that a system should be arranged that would ensure not only an adequate number of schools to be established throughout the State, but would extend its provisions so as to secure the education and instruction of a competent number of active, intelligent teachers, who will not only be prepared, but well qualified, to take upon themselves the government of the schools and to communicate instruction to the scholars.

In Governor Wolf's message, we see not only the concern of the political leaders of Pennsylvania that provisions be made for the education of children and youth, but that a supply of well-trained teachers must also be available if the schools were to be successful.

Extension of Suffrage. Prior to 1815, the right to vote was based on ownership of property. Only four states granted the right to vote to all citizens regardless of property holdings. After 1800, every new state admitted east of the Mississippi River, except Ohio (where the New Englanders predominated) and Louisiana, provided for full manhood suffrage at the time of its admission to statehood. By 1845, seven additional Eastern states had extended full voting privileges to its citizens. The result of this democratic movement, which culminated in the election of Andrew Jackson as President in 1828, was that universal education was encouraged for all citizens. De Witt Clinton, for nine years the governor of New York, when arguing for school support in 1826, said

> The first duty of government, and the surest evidence of good government, is th encouragement of education. A general diffusion of knowledge is a precursor and p tector of republican institutions, and in it we must confide as the conservative p that will watch over our liberties and guard them against fraud, intrigue, corru , and violence. I consider the system of our common schools as the palladium ur freedom, for no reasonable apprehensions can be entertained of its subversio long as the great body of the people are enlightened by education.

The governors in other states echoed the sentiment of Governor Clinton in urging that the success of democratic government depended upon mass education. Governor McArthur of Ohio insisted that "intelligence alone is capable of self-government," and he urged upon every member of the community, as a "solemn duty," attention to common schools. Delaware's governor used the strongest terms in urging the claims of primary education . . . especially the fact that "an enlightened public opinion is the only safeguard of a government like ours."

Labor Unions. After about 1825, many labor unions were formed, and the leaders of these organizations joined in the demand for schools and education. Typical of the many resolutions adopted by labor organizations was one approved at a general meeting of Mechanics and Workingmen in New York City in 1829.

> Resolved, that next to life and liberty, we consider education the greatest blessing bestowed upon mankind;
> Resolved, that the public funds should be appropriated (to a reasonable extent) to the purpose of education upon a regular system that shall insure the opportunity to every individual of obtaining a competent education before he shall arrive at the age of maturity . . .

In 1830, at a City and County Convention of the Working Men of the State, a speaker observed that "it is now forty years since the adoption of the constitution of Pennsylvania, and although that instrument strongly recommends that provision be made for the education of our youth at the public expense, yet during that long period . . . that patriotic obligation has been disregarded by our legislative authority . . . thousands are now suffering the consequences of this disregard to public welfare."

Labor organizations and their leaders were interested in securing public common schooling for all children. They pointed out that the "honest and industrial poor" reject the notion of state schools for their children, although children of the wealthy continue to be educated privately; that such a system violates the spirit of free men in a democratic society and that, in the long run, it would tend to divide Americans into classes, in a pattern reminiscent of English society. It was further argued that without a common school system, compulsory and open to all, the poor would not take advantage of the proffered educational opportunity, because the poor are less attuned to the advantages of education than the more liberal cultured class.

The pressures generated by the growth of cities, the rise in manufacturing, the extension of suffrage, and the development of a distinct working class with special educational needs resulted, in the second quarter of the nineteenth century, in a widespread and bitterly fought movement for universal common education. It has been observed that "excepting the battle for the abolition of slavery, perhaps no public question has ever been before the American people for settlement which caused so much feelings or aroused so much bitter antagonisms . . . The friends of free schools were at first commonly regarded as fanatics, dangerous to the state, and opponents of free schools were considered by them as old-time conservatives or as selfish members of society."[9] However, by 1850, Common schools that were tax-supported, publicly controlled and directed, and nonsectarian, had become an actuality in almost every Northern state.

School Financing. At the beginning of the nineteenth century, a variety of license, occupational, and bank taxes, as well as lotteries, were used to support the schools. Connecticut, for example, turned over all proceeds of liquor licenses to the towns where the money was collected, to be used for schools. New Orleans licensed two theaters on the condition that they paid $3,000 annually for support of schools in the city. New York and New Jersey authorized state lotteries to raise school money. These indirect taxes were an early expression by the several states that levied them that education should be supported by tax revenues.

By 1825, public leaders and many associations interested in Common Schools (public elementary schools) called for general and direct taxation of all property for school support. State legislatures in New York, Delaware, New Jersey, and other states began to provide state aid for public schools from permanent endowment funds (mostly from public lands), state appropriations, or through direct state taxation. The general condition for state aid was that communities receiving aid must also levy a local tax for schools. In some instances, states required a duplication of all state aid received. The Wisconsin Constitution of 1848 required a local tax for schools equal to one-half of the state aid received. Other conditions were soon added by various

[9] Ellwood P. Cubberley, *The History of Education* (Boston: Houghton Mifflin, 1920), p. 672.

legislatures as prerequisites for receiving state aid. The length of the school term (generally fixed at three months), free textbooks, and free heat, were but a few of the requirements written into state educational laws for receiving money from the state for school support. The right of the state to tax directly and to compel local taxation for support of the Common School was the key to the development of the American system of public education.

Universal versus Class Schools

By 1820, it was generally accepted by American society that all children deserved to have a Common School education. However, in the old Central and Southern Colonies, represented by the states of New Jersey, Pennsylvania, Delaware, Virginia, and Georgia, the prevailing thought was that families who could afford it should educate their children in church schools and private academies, and that the state should provide common schooling for children of the poor in what came to be called Pauper Schools.

The Pauper Schools. The Pauper-School idea was fully developed in Pennsylvania, where the Constitution of 1790 provided for a state system of such schools. This provision was implemented in 1802 with the enactment of the Pauper-School law which authorized local taxes for an education poor fund, levied and collected in much the same way as a county-road tax or poor-relief tax. Needless to say, large numbers of families who qualified nevertheless refused to send their children to schools that were only for the children of the poor. The idea of a two-track system of education, one for the affluent and one for the poor, was based on a class system inherited from England and was out of tune with a society founded on the doctrine that "all men are created equal, and endowed by their Creator with certain inalienable rights."

The struggle to eliminate this dual-system concept was spearheaded in Pennsylvania by the Pennsylvania Society for the Promotion of Public Schools. Their efforts, combined with much educational propaganda from various sources, resulted in the Free-School Act of 1834. This law created 987 school districts, and ordered the voters in each district to decide whether to accept the law which provided for establishing one local common school, supported by local taxes and state supplement, or to remain under the educational provisions of the Pauper-School Act. By 1836, the Free-School law had been accepted by 75 per cent of the districts in Pennsylvania, and by 1847 by 88 per cent. The last district in the state accepted the new system in 1873. The Pennsylvania experience in eliminating the Pauper-School concept was replicated in other states which had at first subscribed to the notion that only poor people should be educated at public expense. By 1870, nearly every state had established, either through their constitution or through legislative action, the concept that public money may be used, and must be used, to provide common schooling for the children of all the people.

Free Schools versus Partially Free Schools. The public Common Schools in the 1820s and 1830s were supported by state and local taxes and by a tax on parents for each child they sent to school. This tax, which was generally known as a *rate-bill*, was a charge levied upon the parent to supplement the school revenues. The deficiency in school revenues was charged against the parents and collected as ordinary tax bills. Although the charge was small, parents who could not afford it would not send their children to school. The problem of large numbers of children not attending school was so acute in the cities, and the objections to the special educational tax were so strong, that cities secured special permission from state legislatures to levy a city-wide tax sufficient to provide free education for the children of the city. The issue was whether to have free, public, tax-supported schools or partially free, rate-bill schools.

New York State, largely because of the vigorous action of New York City in contesting the rate-bill system, was a pivotal state in eliminating the rate-bill as a means of financing public schools. A New York State referendum of 1849 showed that 249,872 were in favor of making "the property of the State educate the children of the State," and 91,952 were against this.[10] In 1850, the New York Legislature, although retaining the rate-bill, materially increased the state appropriation for schools and created "union districts" to provide by local taxation free schools where people desired them. In 1867, the rate-bill was abolished in New York and the schools of New York were entirely free. In the older Northern states, Pennsylvania was the first to abolish the rate-bill (1834), and New Jersey was the last (1871).

Control of Schools

State versus Local Control. The first steps toward establishing some form of state control were taken when the state agreed to furnish financial aid and imposed some conditions for receiving such aid. As we said earlier, conditions often included the length of the school term, free textbooks, subjects to be taught, and regulations defining powers of the local board. The first state to create a state officer to exercise supervision over its schools was New York, in 1812. By 1861, there were twenty-eight state school officers in the thirty-four states of the United States.

Another step toward state control was the creation of a state board of education. In 1837, Massachusetts provided for a small, appointed State Board and empowered it to "investigate conditions, report facts, expose defects and make recommendations to the Legislature." Horace Mann (1796–1859), a prominent Brown University graduate and a lawyer, was the first secretary of this Board. In a series of twelve annual reports to the Massachusetts State Board, Mann defined the purposes of education and made the case for a universal, nonsectarian, free, common school education to promote social efficiency, civic virtue, and character.

Under Mann's vigorous and enlightened leadership, the independent Common Schools in the towns of Massachusetts began to be viewed as part of a coordinated state system of education. Henry Barnard (1811–1900), a Yale graduate, as exofficio secretary of the Connecticut State School Board from 1851 to 1855, rewrote the school laws of that state, increased taxation for

---

[10] Ibid., pp. 685–686.

schools, checked the power of local districts, and laid the foundations for a state school system in Connecticut.

The struggle to establish state supervision of schools was characterized by bitter controversy and dispute. Gideon Hawley, New York State's first state school officer, was removed from office in 1821. The Legislature abolished the position and did not recreate it until 1854. The position of State Commissioner of Education (or Superintendent of Public Instruction) has always been a sensitive one, especially since it carries with it the responsibility for administering the state educational law. In most of the states, County superintendents of schools assist the chief state educational officer in supervising the schools in the local communities and municipalities. By 1861, ten states had created the office of County Superintendent, and twenty-five cities had established the position of City Superintendent.

State versus Church Control. In early colonial times, education was in the hands of the church. In New England, for instance, the church provided the education, and the state assisted by donations of land and money. The minister, as a town official, was expected to examine the teacher and evaluate instruction. Schools were established with the needs of the church in mind.

In the early 1800s, the emphasis in education shifted from religious purposes to the industrial, civic, and national needs. Controversy developed over the question of using tax money to support religious schools. This question was settled in Massachusetts in 1855 with the adoption of a constitutional amendment that provided that "all state and town moneys raised or appropriated for education must be expended only on regularly organized and conducted public schools and that no religious sect should ever share in such funds."

Education in New York City in the 1800s was conducted by the Public School Society, a nondenominational organization chartered to teach "the sublime truth of religion and morality contained in the Holy Scriptures." The Society was given authority to levy a local tax to supplement its private donations and the grants received from the State Legislature. When the New York City Council refused to give public money to various religious societies for conduct of their schools, the societies petitioned the State Legislature for a share of state school funds. Instead of voting such monies, the Legislature, in 1842, created for the City of New York a City Board of Education and provided that "no portion of the school funds was in the future to be given to any school in which any religious sectarian doctrine or tenet should be taught, inculcated or practiced." Thus, the real public school system in New York City evolved out of the attempt to divide public funds among the churches for educational purposes.

Following the Massachusetts pattern, the various states adopted constitutional amendments that prohibited use of tax monies for religious educational purposes. All states admitted to the Union after 1858, except West Virginia, had such a provision in their first State Constitution. Presumably the question is settled now. The public school is a secular institution, established as a public institution to meet public needs, and is financed by public funds. Religion may not be taught or practiced in the public school. Private religious schools, under federal and state constitutional prohibitions, are not to be supported by tax dollars.

The separation of church and state in the matter of education is a significant principle in the organization and financing of the public system. In a country where religious freedom is guaranteed as a constitutional right, and which currently has more than fifty religious denominations and sects, any attempt to provide for education by dividing the responsibilities among the various denominations would be likely to lead to educational chaos. Although the principle of separation of church and state was explicitly defined by the middle of the nineteenth century, questions pertaining to this principle continue to be argued and ruled on by the courts.

Public Secondary Education Policy

Most of our narrative has so far been directed toward the development of the elementary school in America and the controversies surrounding the issues of private versus public schools, selective versus universal education, free, tax-supported versus private, charitable support, local versus state control, and the issue of religious influence. By 1850, elementary, or Common Schools, were established in all the states. The last half of the nineteenth century witnessed the struggle to extend free tax-supported education beyond the elementary school to what is now known as the high school and state university.

The antecedents of the American high school were the Latin Grammar Schools, which reached their peak enrollment of a little over a thousand students in the 1700s, and tuition Academies, which had maximum enrollments of six thousand in the 1850s.

As we mentioned earlier, the Latin Grammar School was a free school maintained by the New England towns for those boys who were ministerial candidates. The tuition Academy developed about 1800 in response to the demand for a more practical education for boys of middle-class families who aspired to a career in business and finance. We noted earlier that Benjamin Franklin in Philadelphia outlined a plan for education to meet the needs of this group. Governor DeWitt Clinton of New York State was a strong advocate of locating Academies in the country towns of the state in order to "give a practical scientific education suited to the wants of farmers, merchants, and mechanics, and also to train teachers for the schools of the state." The new subjects to be studied included English Literature, Algebra, Botany, Chemistry, Surveying, and Debating, and emphasis was to be on the "study of real things rather than words about things, and useful things rather than subjects merely preparatory for college." The Academies were independent private institutions and were established for girls as well as for boys. In New York State alone, between 1819 and 1835, thirty-two "Female Academies" were established. For those of you who have a major interest in the current Women's Liberation Movement, you should note that the Troy (New York) Seminary, founded by Emma Willard in 1821, and Mt. Holyoke (Massachusetts) Seminary, founded by Mary Lyon in 1836, made significant contributions to higher education for women. The Academies were a major source of supply for teachers to staff the primary and elementary schools of the nineteenth century.

The first high school in the United States was established in Boston in 1821. It appears in the records as the "English High School." A Massachusetts Law of 1827 required that there be a "high school" in every town containing fifty families, and that in every city or town or district having four thousand or more inhabitants, instruction must be provided in Greek, Latin, history, rhetoric, and logic. By 1850, the high schools competed with the Academies for enrollments: the Academies enrolled six thousand students, the high schools served three thousand students. By 1900, this enrollment pattern had been reversed, and by 1920 the high schools with enrollments totaling twelve thousand, had become the dominant secondary educational institution in the American public school system.

The appearance and demise of the Latin Grammar School and tuition Academy, and the emergence of the American high school, were the products of political, social, and economic forces. The Academy represented the efforts of a few to meet the demands of a rising middle class for a more practical education. Following the Civil War, with an increased emphasis on democracy and the demand of large immigrant populations for educational opportunities, the high school emerged as a cooperative effort of the general population to provide opportunities for themselves.

It was inevitable that the movement to establish the high school as the logical extension of the Common School system should be challenged in the courts. Taxpayers in Michigan, in 1872, questioned the legality of providing public education beyond elementary school; they also challenged the constitutionality of employing school administrators and teaching foreign languages. The Michigan Supreme Court in 1874, in a case known as the "Kalamazoo Case," declared that tax money could be used to provide free public high schools as well as elementary schools; that administrators could be employed to administer a comprehensive system of schools, and that high schools could offer instruction in any branch of knowledge deemed necessary for the education of high school pupils. In handing down this decision, the Michigan Court interpreted the education clause in Michigan's Constitution of 1850—which provided for "the establishment of free schools in every school district for at least three months in each year, and for the university"—to mean that the people of Michigan did not intend to restrict the schools to certain branches of knowledge or to the lower grades.[11]

The Kalamazoo ruling established that free public schools in Michigan were to be schools which taught something more than the rudiments of a common education; they were to give to the poor the advantages of the rich; and would enable both alike to obtain within the state an education broad and liberal as well as practical.

By 1900, the high school was accepted as a part of the common school

---

[11] *Stuart* et al. v. *School District No. 1 of the Village of Kalamazoo*, 30 Michigan 69 (1874).

system by all the states, and the funds and taxation provided originally for the Common Schools were extended to cover the high school as well.

Public Higher Education Policy

At the close of the Colonial period, the Colonies had nine colleges. The earliest college was Harvard, founded in 1636, followed by William and Mary, 1643; Yale, 1701; Princeton, 1746; Pennsylvania (University of Pennsylvania), 1753; Kings College (Columbia), 1754; Brown, 1764; College of New Jersey (Rutgers), 1766; and Dartmouth, 1769. The primary purpose of these colleges was to "train up a learned and godly body of ministers." An advertisement published in the New York newspapers, announcing the opening of King's College (Columbia) in 1754, stated:

> The Chief Thing that is aimed at in this College is, to teach and engage the Children, *to know God in Jesus Christ*, and to love and serve him in all *Sobriety, Godliness*, and *Richness of Life*, with a perfect heart and a Willing Mind: and to train them up in all Virtuous Habits, and all such useful Knowledge as may render them creditable to their Families and Friends, Ornaments to their Country, and useful to the Public Weal in their generation.[12]

The Colonial colleges were all small. For the first fifty years, Harvard's enrollment seldom exceeded twenty students, and the president did all the teaching. From Colonial times to 1870, higher education, as was the case with the Latin Grammar School and the Academy, was selective, open only to those students who could afford the tuition. The Colonial colleges, patterned after two major English universities, Oxford and Cambridge, offered liberal arts education and professional studies in law, medicine, and theology. Higher education in Colonial times was class-based and designed for the elite, not for the masses of population. Of the 246 colleges founded by 1860, only seventeen were state institutions; the rest were founded by various religious denominations for sectarian purposes. Presbyterians, Congregationalists, Roman Catholics, Methodists, Lutherans, Baptists, Quakers, and Mormons were among the sects that founded a number of small liberal arts colleges. These colleges were the result of religious revivals that took place in the country during the 1830s and 1840s. Gerald Gutek[13] comments that two factors operated to involve religious denominations in higher education: first, American Protestants usually valued an "educated ministry"; second, the proliferation of religious groups resulted in competition among them. In order to build a religious commitment to the ministry in the congregation, each denomination began to establish and support new colleges in the towns that were springing up in the Midwest. Thus by 1900, the Presbyterians had founded a number of Presbyterian colleges; the Methodists, Baptists, Lutherans, and others had done likewise. Instruction in these institutions was given in liberal arts and practical education as well as in religion. It was not unusual for many of these small colleges to prepare their own students at the secondary level.

[12] Cubberley, op. cit., p. 703.
[13] Gerald Gutek, *An Historical Introduction to American Education* (New York: Thomas Y. Crowell, 1970), p. 102.

In 1816, the New Hampshire State Legislature sought to change Dartmouth from a private college to a state institution. The U.S. Supreme Court ruled that the charter given to Dartmouth by the Colonial legislature in 1769 was a contract which future legislatures could not change without the consent of Dartmouth. The basis for this decision was Article I, Section 10 of the Constitution, which prohibits states from "passing any law that impairs the obligation of contracts." The effect of this decision was twofold: it encouraged private and denominational efforts to support the old Colonial colleges, and on the other hand, it stimulated state legislatures to create new institutions of higher learning under state control to meet the demand for higher education. States coming into the Union after 1820 provided for a state university in their constitutions. Today all of the states support state universities.

The same aggressive, democratic, nationalistic forces that had created the common school system, by 1870 pressured for public institutions of higher learning. It was argued that colleges were important for molding the future of the nation, and that higher education should not be regarded as a private monopoly. Another argument was that lawyers, judges, and legislators were needed by society and that therefore the question of their education was a matter of public policy. It began to be recognized that the state should not only maintain a system of elementary and secondary schools, but that it should also exercise some control over colleges.

State-established and state-maintained universities appeared in the Midwest in the early nineteenth century. Indiana University was founded in 1820, Michigan in 1837, and Wisconsin in 1848. These universities marked the initial appearance of public higher education on the educational scene. In contrast to the Colonial colleges such as Harvard, Princeton, Rutgers, and others, these institutions were publicly controlled and supported; they emphasized a scientific rather than a classical curriculum, provided for student election of subjects rather than a prescribed curriculum, and were nonsectarian. The Continental Congress, in the Ordinances of 1785 and 1787, had reserved the sixteenth section of each township of the Northwest Territory for education (1785), and had expressed a commitment to encourage schools and the means of education (1787). In addition, the establishment of state universities was further encouraged by the federal land-grant policy, which granted to each state as it entered the Union two townships of land (about twelve square miles) for institutions of higher learning. Ohio was the first to benefit from this policy, and the Ohio Enabling Act, in 1802, which contained a provision for land grants to higher education, set a pattern for other states as they were admitted to the Union and gave a precedent for later land-grant laws. It is of some significance that very early in our history, the federal government vigorously supported public higher education.

In 1860, higher education consisted of eastern colleges that dated from Colonial times, a series of denominational colleges founded by religious sects for their special needs, and some state-established universities. The historical precedent for use of federal lands to support higher education was used in the 1850s as an argument for the development of a system of land-grant colleges and universities by a coalition of farm, labor, and industrialist groups, who saw the need for agricultural and industrial instruction in a developing technological society. The existing liberal arts colleges were unresponsive. The Common School, the Academy, and the high school were unable to meet the demands of a pioneer people for education that would improve their economic condition. The idea of the industrial college was first developed by Jonathan Baldwin Turner, who in the early 1850s outlined a plan for a state industrial university in Illinois, and who asked the federal government for a land grant in order to establish it. Justin S. Morrill, a Vermont Congressman, introduced a land-grant bill into Congress in the late 1850s; it encompassed three broad goals: development of practical instruction at the collegiate level; vocational preparation of the agricultural and industrial classes; and de-emphasis on the classics in higher education.

This Act, known as the First Morrill Act of 1862, and the Second Morrill Act of 1890 laid the foundation for the establishment of land-grant agricultural and mechanical colleges and universities. A number of agricultural and mechanical colleges were established as separate institutions: Purdue University, founded in 1869; the Agricultural and Mechanical College of Texas (Texas A & M), founded in 1871; and the Alaska Agricultural College and School of Mines, founded in 1922, are examples of such institutions. In a number of states, these colleges have become part of the state university. Examples are West Virginia, in 1867, Nebraska, in 1869, Ohio State, in 1870, and Arkansas, in 1871. Seventeen Southern states established separate land-grant colleges for Negroes under the provisions of the Second Morrill Act of 1890. As we have noted in our discussion of purposes and objectives of American education, the land-grant college movement was the response of the federal government to the demand for relevant, practical instruction that was oriented toward improving the scientific and technical skills of the American people.

This movement had its counterpart in the large American cities on the Eastern seaboard. In 1838, the Workingman's Party demanded that a "free" college for the inhabitants of New York City be established. The New York State legislature authorized such a college, and it opened as New York Academy in 1864, with a provision of "free tuition" for those admitted to study. The New York Academy is today the City University of New York (CUNY). It is comprised of twenty colleges, enrolls one-half million students, and has a budget of a one-quarter billion dollars. It was not until more than a century later that the State Legislature ended the mandate of free tuition. In the controversy over whether there should be free tuition in the City University, arguments continue to be advanced: public higher education is a "human right"; the university is a place where young men and women of all ethnic groups may improve their chances of upward mobility by completing a four-year, relatively free education. As some proponents of free tuition have said, meaningful free education is cheaper in the long run than supporting prisons, welfare, and unemployment.

Teacher Education

How to categorize the institutions that prepare teachers in the United States is a complex problem. As we have noted, during the first half of the nineteenth century, the elementary school became a significant social institution. Its success depended upon a body of well-trained teachers. Very early in the nineteenth century, a pattern for preparing teachers for the common schools was adopted. In this pattern, prospective teachers were trained in special schools, called normal schools, that offered courses in pedagogy and placed a unique emphasis on personal character and pedagogical method.

The first institution in America to devote its full attention to teacher training was a private normal school in Concord, Vermont. The Headmaster was a Mr. Samuel Hall, the Congregational minister in Concord, who was interested in the qualifications of teachers for elementary schools. In 1830, Hall became the head of the normal department at Phillips Andover Academy, where he lectured on the "art of teaching." As a minister and a teacher, Hall found time to write on the subject of education. His book, *Lectures on School Keeping*, published in 1829, was in all probability the first professional education book written and published in the United States. This book was widely read and quite influential in the development of elementary teaching training in other institutions. New York State bought ten thousand copies for distribution in its schools. Hall emphasized that education was a science, and that precise application of accepted principles was necessary for success. In his book, he treated such topics as

> competence, character, and usefulness of common schools; obstacles to their usefulness; qualifications of teachers; management and government of a school; teaching of spelling, reading, arithmetic, geography, English grammar, writing, history, and composition; gaining the attention of students; location and construction of school houses; beginning the first day of school.[14]

The movement to provide special training for Common School teachers developed rapidly in the 1830s and 1840s, largely through the efforts of educational leaders like Horace Mann, Secretary to the Massachusetts State Board of Education, and Henry Barnard, Secretary of the Board of Commissioners of Common Schools in Connecticut. These men were joined in their efforts to promote the cause of teacher education by prominent private citizens, state legislators, and governors, who foresaw that the success of the Common School movement depended upon a supply of teachers. The outcome of their effort was the establishment of a special institution—the normal school for the preparation of Common School teachers.

The Massachusetts experience is characteristic of the movement in general. In 1838, Edmund Dwight, a Boston merchant and a member of the newly created State Board of Education, provided a sum of ten thousand dollars for "qualifying Teachers of our Common Schools," on the condition that the Massachusetts Legislature would furnish an equal amount. After some deliberation, the Legislature accepted the gift and proceeded to establish three normal schools: Lexington and Barre in 1839, and Bridgewater in 1840. These were the first state normal schools in the United States.

The admission requirements and course of study for the early normal schools in Massachusetts established precedents and traditions that have had a continuing influence on teacher education and public higher education.

---

[14] Ibid., p. 133.

The following excerpts from the regulations indicate the scope of the requirements.

Admission

As a prerequisite to admission, candidates must declare it to be their intention to qualify themselves to become school teachers. If they belong to the State, or have an intention and a reasonable expectation of keeping school in the State, tuition is gratis. Otherwise, a tuition-fee is charged, which is intended to be about the same as is usually charged at good academies in the same neighborhood. . . .

If males, pupils must have attained the age of seventeen years complete, and of sixteen, if females; and they must be free from any disease or infirmity, which would unfit them for the office of school teachers.

They must undergo an examination, and prove themselves to be well versed in orthography [spelling], reading, writing, English grammar, geography, and arithmetic.

They must furnish satisfactory evidence of good intellectual capacity and of high moral character and principles.

Examinations for admission take place at the commencement of each term, of which there are three in a year.

Term of Study

The minimum of the term of study is one year, and this must be in consecutive terms of the schools.

Course of Study

The studies first to be attended to in the State Normal Schools are those which the law requires to be taught in the district schools, namely, orthography, reading, writing, English grammar, geography and arithmetic. When these are mastered, those of a higher order will be progressively taken.

For those who wish to remain at the school more than one year, and for all belonging to the school, so far as their previous attainments will permit, the following course is arranged:

1. Orthography, reading, grammar, composition, rhetoric, and logic.
2. Writing and drawing.
3. Arithmetic, mental and written, algebra, geometry, bookkeeping, navigation, surveying.
4. Geography, ancient and modern, with chronology, statistics and general history.
5. Human Physiology, and hygiene or the Laws of Health.
6. Mental Philosophy.
7. Music.
8. Constitution and History of Massachusetts and of the United States.
9. Natural Philosophy and Astronomy.
10. Natural History.
11. The principles of piety and morality, common to all sects of Christians.
12. The science and art of teaching, with reference to all the above-named studies.

Religious Exercises

A portion of the Scriptures shall be read daily, in every State Normal School.

James G. Carter, a member of the Massachusetts Legislature, urged that normal schools should be governed by a board of commissioners representing public interests in public education; have a principal as its head; a staff of assistant professors; a library of books on the science of education; and a demonstration school comprised of children of different ages pursuing various studies. Carter stressed the need for a model school to be part of the normal school. Here, the prospective teacher would be guided by experienced and skillful professors of education, in order to gain needed experience in actual teaching. Carter sponsored the legislation that created the Massachusetts State Board of Education, and enthusiastically supported the normal-school concept for the preparation of elementary teachers.

New York authorized a normal school for the "instruction and practice of teachers of common schools," in 1844. The New York State Normal School at Albany, headed by David Perkins Page, stressed training in both theory and practice of education. Page's book, *Theory and Practice of Teaching or the Motives and Methods of Good School Keeping*, published in 1847, became a standard work in teacher education. Practice teaching in the model school was an integral part of the preparation program. Following the example of Massachusetts and New York, seven other states adopted the pattern of the normal school by 1860: Connecticut and Michigan in 1849, Rhode Island in 1852, Iowa in 1855, Illinois in 1857, Minnesota in 1858, and Pennsylvania in 1859. By 1900, all states had made some provision for the training of teachers; and by 1910, all had established normal schools.

You will note that the normal school, in its origin and design, had a very special relationship to elementary education and almost nothing in common with the evolving institutions of higher education in the nineteenth century. It was a special institution where Common School graduates with some academic aptitude and good moral character might receive additional instruction in elementary school subjects, be exposed to principles of teaching, and have some actual practice before being assigned to a Common School. Other Common School graduates might enroll in the Academy for practical training in commercial and business fields, or enter the high school in preparation for university study, but those who were to teach in the Common School applied to the normal school.

In the late nineteenth century, universities began to be interested in teacher-training programs. In 1873, the University of Iowa established the first permanent chair of pedagogy; Wisconsin University followed in 1879, Indiana and Cornell in 1886; and in 1892, Teachers College became a part of Columbia University. The interest of universities stemmed in part from general developments in secondary education—especially from the recognition that the high school was the logical next step in the educational ladder. The universities also recognized that secondary schools would require teachers and administrators with professional preparation not available (and not intended) in the normal schools. President James B. Angell recommended courses in Pedagogy at the University of Michigan in 1874. Angell observed that

> It cannot be doubted that some instruction in Pedagogics would be very helpful to our Senior class. Many of them are called directly from the University to the management of large schools, some of them to the superintendency of the schools of a town. The whole work of organizing schools, the management of primary and grammar schools, the art of teaching and governing a school;—of all this it is desirable that they

know something before they go to their new duties. Experience alone can thoroughly train them. But some familiar lectures on these topics would be of essential service to them.

In 1879, the University of Michigan followed up on Angell's recommendations by establishing a chair of the "History, Theory and Art of Education," and by appointing William H. Payne, former Superintendent of Schools of Adrian, Michigan, as its first occupant. Payne had delivered some lectures in the Normal Department of Adrian College, in which he had expressed his views on the need for a coordinated school system in Michigan—particularly his concerns about the relation between the University and the high schools. In appointing Payne, President Angell said his action would promote the highest interests of education, not only by tempting future teachers to the training of the University, but by apprising the public that teaching is itself an art. Angell acknowledged that the State Normal School was engaged in the same general work, but upon another plane. The action of the University in establishing such a chair, said Angell, again justified its position as the head of the educational system of the State. It is of some general interest that William Payne later became jointly Chancellor of the University of Nashville and President of the Peabody Normal School (now George Peabody College for Teachers of Vanderbilt University) in Nashville.

In these brief excerpts we see the special concern of the university for the training of secondary school teachers and school administrators, and the willingness on the part of the university to leave the preparation of Common School teachers to normal schools and to state teachers colleges. In Payne's joint appointment at Nashville, and in developments at other universities, notably the establishment of the Teachers College in Columbia in 1892, we also note the beginning of a trend to include the normal school and education faculty in the general structure of the university.

SUMMARY

In summary, if you want to make some professional contributions to the field of education beyond the limits of the classroom, it is important to have some grasp of the history of education: the historic social, economic, and political forces; the changes in democratic philosophy; the nature of the early elementary and secondary institutions; and the great leaders in the development of American schools. The American education system was built by such forces, institutions, men, and events. The changes to come in education in the twentieth century will be dictated by similar forces.

With reference to the first two hundred years of America's history (1600–1800), we have noted how the early colonists, almost from the date of their first landing on the shores of the New World, were conscious of the need for schools for children to learn "reading and writing," and for education of youth for training for the ministry. Toward this end, the colonists established some colleges and organized some secondary schools for those who wished to enter the ministry. Ministerial education was based on a knowledge of Greek and Latin and limited to those few who could qualify morally and intellectually for such a profession. The early colonial schools were patterned after existing English schools. The overriding aim of education at all levels was to enable students to read and understand the Bible, to gain salvation, and to spread the Gospel. Practical education on how to provide the basic necessities—food, clothing, and shelter—and how to make a living from the land, was provided through the home and from "on the job" training as apprentice to a master craftsman, farmer, merchant, and others actively engaged in business or commerce.

Toward the end of the Colonial period, men like Benjamin Franklin and others began to see the need for a new type of schooling, broader in program and more available to the youth, and more relevant to the needs of society. The development of a uniquely American system of schools after the Revolutionary War coincided with what historians have termed the National Period of American History, roughly the years 1800 to 1870. It was during this period that the inhabitants of the several states began to think of themselves as citizens of the United States of America, and that the schools began to be looked upon as the means for developing a national unity.

The American secondary school (high school) and the state university became full-fledged units in the American education system in the twentieth century. In the next module, we trace the development of these two educational units in much more detail. By the close of the nineteenth century, the American people had decided to support a free, tax-supported, non-sectarian universal system of common schools, and were vigorously expressing interest in extending the "common-school" concept to the high school and the public university. An in-depth analysis of primary original source materials in American educational history shows that Americans in each historical period from Colonial times to the present have been concerned with certain basic educational principles: public support and control; free, universal, and compulsory education; sectarian influences; the education of teachers; and the extension and expansion of educational opportunities. A study of these documents illustrates not only the "roots" of contemporary educational issues but demonstrates also the persistence of these problems over the years. The American people have characteristically been action-oriented and problem solvers. The story of American education in the nineteenth century and, as you will see, in the twentieth century, is the record of how we Americans expanded and supported a comprehensive public education from primary school through the university. It was through this means that the promise of freedom and dignity for the individual and equal opportunity for all was to be achieved.

SOME MOMENTS TO REMEMBER

1635   Founding of Boston Latin School.
1636   Appropriation of four hundred pounds for founding of Harvard College by the Massachusetts General Court.

1642   Massachusetts law establishing parental responsibility for the education of children.
1643   Founding of William and Mary.
1647   Olde Deluder Law passed by Massachusetts General Court.
1693   Massachusetts Bay law placing school tax on ballot.
1701   Yale College founded.
1749   Publication of Franklin's proposals for the Philadelphia Academy.
1778   Founding of Phillips Andover Academy.
1785   The Ordinance of 1785.
1787   Ordinance of 1787 (The Northwest Ordinance).
1787   Founding of state universities in Georgia and North Carolina.
1802   Pennsylvania's pauper-school law.
1816   The Dartmouth College Case (decided 1819).
1820   Founding of Indiana University.
1821   Boston English High School established.
1821   Founding of Troy (New York) Seminary (for women).
1823   First normal school, Concord, Vermont.
1826   Founding of the first high school for girls, Boston.
1827   Massachusetts law mandates maintenance of high schools.
1834   Pennsylvania law authorizing free elementary education.
1836   Mary Lyons founds Mt. Holyoke (Massachusetts) Seminary (for women).
1837   Establishment of Massachusetts State Board of Education; Horace Mann, first secretary.
1837   Founding of first coeducational college at Oberlin, Ohio.
1839   Founding of first state normal school (Lexington, Massachusetts).
1842   Creation of New York City Board of Education.
1850   Common schools established in all states.
1852   Massachusetts Law stipulates compulsory education.
1855   Massachusetts Law forbids state support of religious schools.
1856   Founding of first coeducational high school in Chicago.
1862   Enactment of The Land Grant College Act (First Morrill Act).
1864   Founding of New York Academy (City University of New York).
1867   Elimination of rate-bills in New York.
1867   Creation of the U.S. Department of Education (later the U.S. Office of Education, and now the Department of Education once again).
1873   Creation of first permanent chair in pedagogy, at the University of Iowa.
1874   The Kalamazoo Decision.
1876   Establishment of first graduate school, Johns Hopkins University.
1884   Founding of first industrial training high school (Baltimore Manual Training Act).
1890   Second Morrill Act.
1892   Committee of Ten on Secondary School Studies.
1892   Establishment of Teachers College, Columbia University.
1895   The Report of the Committee of Fifteen.
1900   Founding of the College Entrance Examination Board.

2. Dip into Clifton Johnson's *Old Time Schools and School Books* (New York: Dover Publications, Inc., 1963, first published by Macmillan Publishing Co., Inc., 1904). Sample some of the lessons and selections. Examine the pictures. Read the descriptions of the schools and programs. What do you think?

3. Look at some of the documents concerning schools and teaching found in such books as Ellwood Cubberley, ed., *Readings in the History of Education* (Boston: Houghton Mifflin Company, 1920), Edgar W. Knight and Clifton L. Hall, eds., *Readings in American Educational History* (New York: Appleton-Century-Crofts, Inc., 1951); Rush Welter, ed., *American Writings on Popular Education: The Nineteenth Century* (Indianapolis, Ind.: The Bobbs-Merrill Co., Inc., 1971). What do you think of the reasoning and positions taken?

4. Read the Phi Delta Kappa Fastback on private schools (Otto F. Kraushaar, *Private Schools: From the Puritans to the Present.* Bloomington, Ind.: Phi Delta Kappa Educational Foundation, 1976). What do you see as the role of private schools in American history? What should it be today? Should persons who send their children to private or parochial schools receive tax credit?

5. Read the Fastbacks describing the contribution to education of Thomas Jefferson, Benjamin Franklin, Benjamin Rush, and Noah Webster. What impact do they have on American education past and present? Do you agree with their positions?

6. If possible, try to find out about the early schools in your home school districts.

7. Talk to older members of your community about their experiences in schools. If possible, get retired school teachers and administrators to talk about the schools they knew as beginners.

8. Try to get the flavor of schools, school life and teaching in the past by reading such novels as Edward Eggleston's *The Hoosier Schoolmaster* (various editions, originally published in 1871) or Dorothy Canfield's *Seasoned Timber* (New York: Harcourt Brace Jovanovich, 1939), or such biographical works as Jesse Stuart's *The Thread That Runs So True* (New York: Charles Scribners' Sons, 1949) and *To Teach To Love* (Cleveland: The World Publishing Co., 1970) or Charles H. Wilson's *A Teacher Is A Person* (New York: Holt, Rinehart & Winston, Inc., 1956). Other books about schools, school life, school children, and school teaching include,

Ashton-Warner, Sylvia, *Spinster* (New York: Bantam, 1961).
———, *Teacher* (New York: Bantam, 1964).
Auchincloss, Lewis, *The Rector of Justin* (Boston: Houghton Mifflin, 1964).
Barzun, Jacques, *Teacher in America* (Boston: Little, Brown and Co., 1945).
Bean, Lura, *He Called Them By the Lightning* (Indianapolis, Ind.: The Bobbs-Merrill Co., Inc., 1967).
Braithwaite, R. R., *To Sir, With Love* (Englewood Cliffs, N. J.: Prentice-Hall, Inc., 1959).
Dickens, Charles, *The Life and Time of Nicholas Nickelby* (various editions).
Ernst, Morris, *The Teacher* (Englewood Cliffs, N. J.: Prentice-Hall, Inc., 1968).
Forster, Margaret, *Miss Owen-Owen* (New York: Simon & Schuster, 1969).
Hilton, James, *Goodbye Mr. Chips* (Boston: Little. Brown and Co., 1966).
Hunter, Evan, *The Blackboard Jungle* (New York: Simon & Schuster, 1954).
Ingle, William, *Good Luck, Miss Wyckoff* (Boston: Little, Brown and Co., 1970).
Kaufman, Bel, *Up the Down Staircase* (Englewood Cliffs, N. J.: Prentice-Hall, Inc., 1965).
Kohl, Herbert, *36 Children* (New York: New American Library, 1967).

Kozol, Jonathon, *Death at an Early Age* (Boston: Houghton Mifflin, 1967).

Marshall, Catherine, *Christy* (New York: McGraw-Hill Book Co., 1967).

Patton, Frances, *Good Morning, Miss Dove* (New York: Dodd Mead, 1954).

Peterson, Houston, ed., *Great Teachers* (New York: Vintage Books, 1946).

Prescott, Peter S., *A World of Our Own* (New York: Coward/McCann, Inc., 1970).

Ross, L. O., *The Education of Hyman Kaplan* (New York: Harcourt Brace Jovanovich, 1937).

Spark, Muriel, *The Prime of Miss Jean Brodie* (Philadelphia: J. B. Lippincott Company, Inc., 1962).

Specht, Robert, *Tesha* (New York: St. Martins Press, 1976).

Sterling, Philip, ed., *The Real Teachers* (New York: Random House, Inc., 1972).

Sutherland, Elizabeth, *Letters From Mississippi* (New York: Signet, 1966).

Updike, John, *The Centaur* (New York: Alfred A. Knopf, Inc., 1974).

VanTil, William, *The Making of a Modern Educator* (Indianapolis: The Bobbs-Merrill Co., 1961).

Weber, Julia, *My Country School Diary* (New York: Harper & Row, Publishers, 1970).

9. As you learn about schools of the past, in what ways do they seem different? In what ways do today's schools seem better than the schools of yesterday to you? Are there ways that the old days seem better?

10. In some communities old school buildings and classrooms have been preserved much as they used to be. If feasible, visit these old schools and try to imagine how it would be to teach in such surroundings with the equipment then used.

MODULE
2

Our Schools: The Twentieth Century

The Aims of American Education / The American Educational Ladder / Elementary and Secondary School Curricula and Methods / Higher Education / Teacher Education

The first-edition version of this module was written by William A. Liggitt, Jersey City State College. It has been revised and updated for this edition.

RATIONALE

In this module, we shall trace developments in public education in the first eighty years of the twentieth century. By 1900, three distinct school units had emerged: elementary school, high school, and college. When questions arose concerning their purposes and relationships to each other, significant attention was given to the clarification of educational aims and objectives, and particular emphasis was placed on articulation between the units. As we know, the idea of a "public" school grew from the demand of the people for common schooling; later, major social and economic changes in the twentieth century dictated the establishment of new educational units and a broad expansion of courses and programs in secondary schools and colleges. Therefore, the history of education from 1900 to 1980 is the record of how the elementary school, high school, college, and university expanded their programs and services, and how and why new units, such as the junior high school and junior college, were established.

SPECIFIC OBJECTIVES

At the completion of this module, it is expected that you will be able to do the following:

1. Give the gist of the reports of the major committees and commissions on educational goals and reforms from the Committee of Ten to the present.
2. Explain the rationale of "Education for Complete Living."
3. Describe the Life-Adjustment Education movement.
4. Describe the movement toward behavioral objectives and its rationale.
5. List conservative objections to life-adjustment education and the education for complete living ideal.
6. Describe the development of the American educational ladder in the twentieth century.
7. Cite the principal characteristics of the various units in the educational ladder: kindergarten, elementary school, middle school, junior high school, and high school.
8. List critical problems that confronted secondary educators in large city schools in the second half of the century.
9. Cite three modifications in city high schools in the sixties and seventies that were related to educational aims and purposes.
10. Describe the direction of the reforms for secondary education recommended by the various commissions during the 1980s.
11. Give the principal reason for the forming of alternative schools.
12. Describe the major curriculum movements during the twentieth century.
13. Trace the major movements in teaching methodology during the twentieth century.

14. Describe at least three movements that stressed making education more socially relevant.
15. Trace the zigzag swings from progressive to conservative curriculum and methods during the twentieth century.
16. Cite curricular results of the civil rights movement.
17. Trace the development of state colleges and universities, private colleges and universities, and junior and community colleges during the twentieth century.
18. Contrast the objectives and purposes of land-grant colleges and universities with private colleges and universities.
19. Cite two problems confronting public higher education in the sixties, and give the sources of these problems.
20. Give at least two reasons for the initiation of the idea of the junior college in the twentieth century.
21. Describe the characteristics of State Master Plans for Higher Education in the seventies.
22. Trace the development of teacher education throughout the century.
23. Describe federal legislation in the past twenty-five years that contributed to the aims and purposes of American education.

MODULE TEXT

The Aims of American Education

In the Northwest Territory, the States of Ohio, Michigan, and Illinois, and others that came into the Union after 1800, wrote into their constitutions and into state law provisions for public education up to and including the state university. The purposes of education were suggested in the Northwest Acts of 1785 and 1787. These Acts encouraged the establishment of education in the Territory by stating, "Religion, morality and knowledge being necessary to good government and the happiness of mankind, schools and the means of education shall forever be encouraged." As states were formed in the Northwest Territory, they were required to set aside the sixteenth section (640 acres) of each township to be used for educational purposes. The Morrill Land-Grant Act, passed by Congress in 1862, provided for the establishment of agricultural and mechanical colleges in the various states. This Act granted each state 30,000 acres of public land for each senator and representative it had in Congress, according to the apportionment of the Census of 1860. The income from this land was to support at least one college, whose primary purpose was agricultural and mechanical instruction. A second Morill Act, passed in 1890, provided for a direct cash grant of $15,000, to be increased annually to a maximum of $25,000, for support of land-grant colleges and universities. Instruction was to be provided in agricultural and mechanical subjects and in military training. The Hatch Act of 1887 established agricultural experimental stations across the coun-

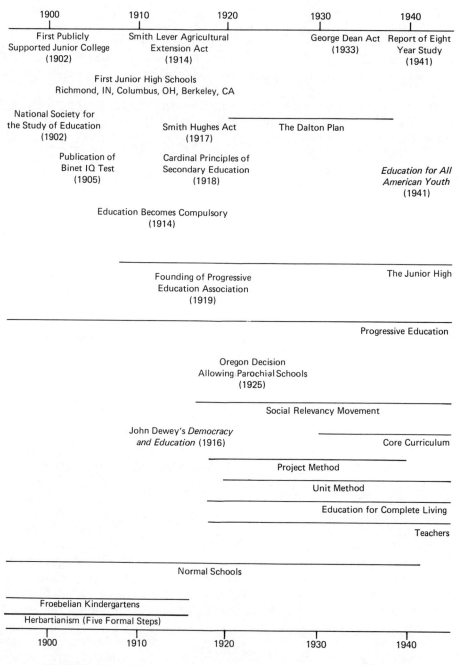

FIGURE 2-1. Education in the Twentieth Century: A Time Chart.

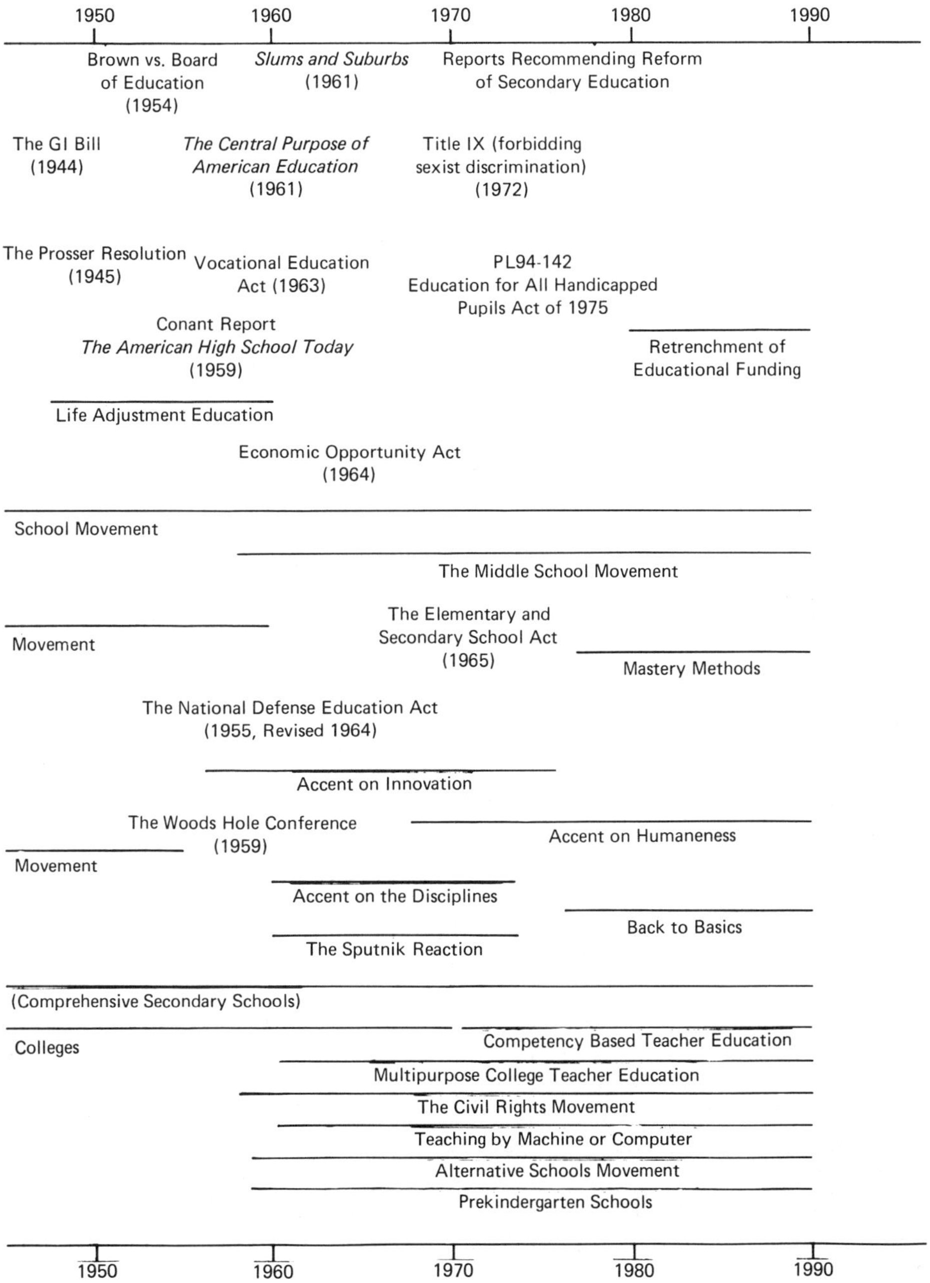

1950	1960	1970	1980	1990

Brown vs. Board
of Education
(1954)

Slums and Suburbs
(1961)

Reports Recommending Reform
of Secondary Education

The GI Bill
(1944)

*The Central Purpose of
American Education*
(1961)

Title IX (forbidding
sexist discrimination)
(1972)

The Prosser Resolution
(1945)

Vocational Education
Act (1963)

PL94-142
Education for All Handicapped
Pupils Act of 1975

Conant Report
The American High School Today
(1959)

Retrenchment of
Educational Funding

Life Adjustment Education

Economic Opportunity Act
(1964)

School Movement

The Middle School Movement

Movement

The Elementary and
Secondary School Act
(1965)

Mastery Methods

The National Defense Education Act
(1955, Revised 1964)

Accent on Innovation

The Woods Hole Conference
(1959)

Accent on Humaneness

Movement

Accent on the Disciplines

Back to Basics

The Sputnik Reaction

(Comprehensive Secondary Schools)

Colleges

Competency Based Teacher Education

Multipurpose College Teacher Education

The Civil Rights Movement

Teaching by Machine or Computer

Alternative Schools Movement

Prekindergarten Schools

1950	1960	1970	1980	1990

FIGURE 2.1. (Continued)

47

try, and the Smith-Lever Agricultural Extension Act of 1914 carried the services of land-grant colleges to the people through extension services.

The aims and purposes of education in the developing period of American education, although not specifically stated, are reflected in the rhetoric over public school issues and in the language of early state and federal legislation. It is evident that, by 1900, the American people were interested in common schooling that provided the basic skills and promoted sound moral behavior. At higher levels, the people demanded technical knowledge suited to the agricultural and industrial economy. The idea that elementary school and high school training should be a preparation for college, and that college should be a preparation for the professions, has always been a persistent theme in American education, but it has never been the most compelling argument for supporting a universal mass-education system.

One of the first efforts to state precisely how high schools should be organized was made in 1892 by a Committee established by the National Education Association (NEA). This Committee, known as the Committee of Ten, recommended, among other things, that

1. High school should consist of grades seven through twelve.
2. Courses should be arranged in sequential order.
3. Students should be given very few electives in high school.
4. Gifted students should be given advanced courses.
5. One unit, later called a Carnegie Unit, should be awarded for each separate course that a student takes each year, providing that the course meets four or five times each week, all year long.

The Committee was composed of representatives from five colleges and universities, one public school principal, two headmasters of private schools, the United States Commissioner of Education, William T. Harris, and Committee Chairman Charles W. Eliot, President of Harvard University. The work of this Committee was oriented primarily toward the college-preparatory function of the high school. Although its report stated that the high school did not exist exclusively for the purpose of college preparation, the Committee's curriculum recommendations were designed chiefly for college entrance. Subjects were to be taught in the same way to both college-preparatory and terminal students. Chairman Eliot was concerned with improving the efficiency of the schools and making economic use of the time that students spent in school. As a consequence, the high school was very early in its history defined as the institution where students studied fundamental subject matter: English, foreign languages, mathematics, natural and physical sciences, and history, in preparation for advanced college study. It was claimed that terminal students could also profit from such study because the mental discipline involved would train their powers of observation, memory, experience, and reasoning.

The definition of aims, purposes, and objectives of American public education in the twentieth century has evolved chiefly from the subsequent efforts of national commissions to describe what American secondary schools should do, and how secondary education is related to higher education. In 1913, the National Education Association established a Commission on the

Reorganization of Secondary Education to re-examine the scope and function of the high school. The Commission was concerned with the articulation of institutions at all levels of education, and although its report issued in 1918 was entitled the Cardinal Principles of Secondary Education, the objectives recommended became a basic set of principles for elementary, secondary, and higher education. The Commission said that a student should receive instruction in the following areas:

1. Health.
2. Command of Fundamental Processes.
3. Worthy Home Membership.
4. Vocation.
5. Civic Education.
6. Worthy Use of Leisure.
7. Ethical Character.

These areas cover most aspects of human life. They make up what we may call "education for complete living."

Since 1918, a number of commissions and associations have published statements outlining the aims and objectives of American education. Many of these statements have been reshapings of the notions behind the "seven cardinal principles" of the Commission on the Reorganization of Secondary Education. The Progressive Education Association, for instance, adopted seven points as its guiding principles: "Freedom to develop naturally"; "Interest, the motive of all work"; "The teacher a guide, not a task master"; "Scientific study of pupil development"; "Greater attention to all that affects the child's physical development"; "Cooperation between home and school to meet the needs of child life"; and "The progressive school as a leader in educational movement."[1]

Although the progressivists were undoubtedly in favor of education for complete living and against rote memorization, meaningless drill, harsh discipline, and regimentation, they were never really united on the major purposes of education. One group, associated with William Heard Kilpatrick, stressed the needs and interests of pupils; another group, associated with George S. Counts, advocated that schools take on an activist role in the study and solution of social problems; a third group, associated with Boyd H. Bode, insisted that the schools use problem-solving methods to study authoritarian and democratic ways of living. Nevertheless, the notions underlying the progressive movement and its various wings were similar to those underlying the Cardinal Principles of Education.

This same type of thinking was evident in the 1938 statement of the Educational Policies Commission of the National Education Association. This Association divided the objectives for complete living into four categories:

The Objectives of Self Realization.
The Objectives of Human Relationships.

[1] The Progressive Education Association, *Progressive Education Journal*. Printed on the inside cover of each issue.

The Objectives of Civic Responsibility.
The Objectives of Economic Responsibility.

Later in World War II, an attempt to outline the ideal education for post-World War II youth, the Educational Policies Commission, recast the objectives into the following needs of youth:

1. All youth need to develop saleable skills and those understandings and attitudes that make the worker an intelligent and productive participant in economic life. To this end, most youth need supervised work experience as well as education in the skills and knowledge of their occupations.
2. All youth need to develop and maintain physical fitness.
3. All youth need to understand the rights and duties of the citizen of a democratic society, and to be diligent and competent in the performance of their obligations as members of the community and citizens of the state and nation.
4. All youth need to understand the significance of the family for the individual and society and the conditions conducive to successful family life.
5. All youth need to know how to purchase and use goods and services intelligently, understanding both the values received by the consumer and the economic consequences of their acts.
6. All youth need to understand the methods of science, the influence of science on human life, and the main scientific facts concerning the nature of the world and of man.
7. All youth need opportunities to develop their capacities to appreciate beauty, in literature, art, music, and nature.
8. All youth need to be able to use their leisure time well and to budget it wisely; balancing activities that yield satisfactions to the individual with those that are socially useful.
9. All youth need to develop respect for other persons, to grow in their insight into ethical values and principles, and to be able to live and work cooperatively with others.
10. All youth need to grow in ability to think rationally, to express their thoughts clearly, and to read and listen with understanding.[2]

Again, these objectives are a reshaping of the cardinal principles, and of the ideal of education for complete living.

The life-adjustment movement following World War II was another reincarnation of the idea of education for complete living. In 1945, at a conference on "Vocational Education in the Years Ahead," Charles Prosser summarized the sense of the conference in the so-called *Prosser Resolution*. In brief, this resolution stated that (1) the schools were preparing 20 per cent of youth for college and another 20 per cent of youth for skilled occupations, but were doing nothing for the 60 per cent of youth who were not training for college entrance or a skilled trade, and (2) school administrators and vocational educators should formulate a program to meet the needs of students neither vocationally nor college bound. This new program was called *life-adjustment education*. As laid out in 1948, the system was de-

[2] Educational Policies Commission, *Education for All American Youth* (Washington, D.C.: National Education Association, 1944), pp. 225–226.

signed to equip "all American youth to live democratically with satisfaction to themselves and profit to society as home members, workers, and citizens."[3] Once again, we have a restatement of the position of the cardinal principles as they were devised in 1918.

During the 1970s, there was a great deal of pressure for schools to emphasize the affective and social aspects of life. In this context, Richard E. Gross reformulated the seven cardinal principles once again. In this reformulation the principles appear as

1. Personal competence and development.
2. Family cohesiveness.
3. Skilled decision making.
4. Moral responsibility and ethical action.
5. Civic interest and participation.
6. Respect for the environment.
7. Global human concern.[4]

Not everyone has accepted the seven cardinal principles and their derivatives—at least not as goals for the schools. Some critics maintain that some of these goals should be reserved for the home, the church, and other agencies. In short, these critics think that the schools are butting in where they have no business. Others believe that by accepting the responsibility for meeting all the needs of all the children, the schools are attempting more than they can possibly accomplish. Schools, they insist, should concentrate on academic knowledge and skills. The watchword of these critics, *back to basics*, has drawn many adherents, both lay and professional, to their fold. Prominent among these critics in the 1950s were Hyman G. Rickover, Arthur E. Bestor, Mortimer Smith, and the members of the Council for Basic Education who were bitter in their denouncements of the schools' alleged failure to recognize the importance of their intellectual role. In the opinion of these critics the concept of education for complete living had so weakened the schools that they were no longer effective. In response to this bitter criticism, the Educational Policies Commission revised its stand. In a 1961 report, they stated that although the schools should educate pupils broadly, the central purpose of schooling should be to teach pupils to think independently.[5] Today the position of these critics continues to be strongly maintained by many powerful and influential citizens and educators.

Nevertheless, on the whole, today the aims and objectives of American education are essentially the all-inclusive aims that were set forth during the first half of the twentieth century (1892–1952). It is clear that in contemporary America public opinion believes the mission of the public school is

[3] *A Look Ahead in Education*, USOE Bulletin #4 (Washington, D.C.: United States Office of Education, 1954), inside cover.

[4] Richard E. Gross, "Seven New Cardinal Principles," *Phi Delta Kappan*, 80:291–93 (December, 1978).

[5] Educational Policies Commission, *The Central Purpose of American Education* (Washington, D.C.: The National Education Association, 1961).

to educate youth in all dimensions of living: personal, economic, social, and aesthetic. In the words of Joe Nathan and Herbert Kohl,

> If we abandon the vision of providing good education for *all* the children of *all* our people, we must then face the frightening realization that we also have abandoned our belief in democracy.[6]

The task of the educator is to translate these goals into concrete programs that will fulfill the educational purposes of American society.

One aspect of the controversy over educational goals and the effectiveness of the schools has led to an attempt to clarify just what the schools are to accomplish. To make the objectives of instruction clear, theorists say that the aims should be stated as behavioral or performance objectives. Such objectives ought to spell out the behavior, performance, or competencies the pupils are supposed to achieve as a result of the instruction. Often they also specify just how well or to what extent the pupils should perform in order to meet the objective. "At the end of the year the pupils will be able to solve exercises in long division in eight out of ten cases" might be an example of such an objective. The rationale behind the use of behavioral objectives is that if education is defined as a "change in behavior," as a result of instruction, a student's behavior will change, and this change can be measured. The stating of objectives in behavioral terms has been utilized to make education more accountable to the public. In requesting monies to support schools, budgets are now being prepared to show how objectives and outcomes are related to costs. This systematic approach to budgeting has been termed *Management by Objectives* (MBO), or *Planning, Programming, Budgeting, Evaluation System* (PPBES). (No doubt, as a teacher, you will be called upon to define your instructional objectives in behavioral terms, and to follow through with evaluations to determine the degree to which your objectives have been met.)

In the attempt to define educational objectives clearly, scholars such as Benjamin S. Bloom have divided them into three domains—cognitive, affective, and psychomotor.[7]

1. Cognitive: Those objectives that are concerned with remembering, recognizing knowledge, and developing intellectual abilities and skills.
2. Affective: Those objectives that are concerned with interests, attitudes, opinions, appreciations, values and emotional sets.
3. Psychomotor: Those objectives that are concerned with the development of muscular and motor skills.

These scholars have also arranged the objectives in each domain into taxonomies or hierarchies according to complexity. These taxonomies are a major contribution both as an aid to communication and as a means for clarifying and developing the meaning of educational objectives.

[6] Joe Nathan and Herbert Kohl, "Public Alternative Schools and the Future of Democracy," *Phi Delta Kappan*, 62:734 (June, 1981).

[7] Benjamin S. Bloom, ed., *Taxonomy of Educational Objectives* (New York: Longman, 1956).

The American Educational Ladder

The term *American educational ladder* is used to describe the single, articulated, and sequential system of schools open to all—regardless of social and economic class or religious affiliation—that became the ideal in American education. This concept is in direct contrast to the European dual system, which provides for separate and discrete educational tracks, with one set of schools for the leadership elite and another set for the large masses of the population.

Originally, the American school system was also a dual system. Early elementary and secondary schools often followed separate tracks. But by 1900, the American educational ladder had become fixed. In this system, the boys and girls can progress sequentially from kindergarten to college without encountering dead ends. Figure 2-2 illustrates this ladder. Basically it follows the K–8–4–4 pattern—kindergarten, eight years of elementary school, four years of high school, and four years of college. Variations to this plan abound. Many contemporary systems include junior high schools or middle schools. Often the breaks between the institutions are determined by fiscal and building considerations rather than by educational ones. In every case, however, the ladder provides pupils with a smooth route from kindergarten through grade twelve and beyond.

Now let us look at some of the institutions of typical school systems.

Early Childhood Education During the Twentieth Century

American kindergartens in the twentieth century were first organized for the children of the well-to-do. Later, in an effort to rescue the children of

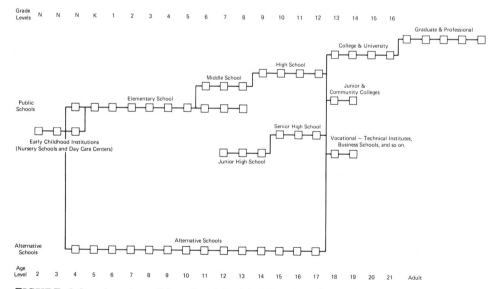

FIGURE 2-2. American Educational Ladder. Public School System 1981. [Reprinted and adapted by permission of the publisher from W. F. Connell, *A History of Education in the Twentieth Century World* (New York: Teachers College Press, © 1980 by Curriculum Development Centre), p. 356.]

the poor from their environment, philanthropic groups supported kindergartens in slums. These kindergartens were private institutions built on the principles advocated by F. W. A. Froebel. Their curricula consisted mostly of carefully programed play activities. At the beginning of the twentieth century, the kindergarten was shedding its role of social reformation to become a downward extension of the elementary school. By the 1920s, it had become a place to help prepare children to enter the first grade. Teachers had discontinued the occupations and games prescribed by Froebel. Instead, following the lead of Teachers College, Columbia University professors Edward Lee Thorndike and William Heard Kilpatrick, they had switched to building social habits and specific skills. Now in the 1980s, the kindergarten seems to be focusing on the readiness skills needed for beginning reading, arithmetic, and primary grade subjects.

The twentieth century has also seen an explosion of pre-kindergarten schools. Today, nursery school programs are not uncommon in public school systems; day-care centers and private nursery schools abound. Often these are sponsored by churches or other philanthropic institutions. Some of these schools are simply custodial institutions. The better ones are more purposeful, however.

The Development of the Elementary School

As the high school began to emerge, considerable discussion took place as to the number of years that should constitute elementary education. In the South, a seven-year span was dominant. In New England, nine years was common. The rest of the country seemed to have settled on an eight-year school. Yet, the issue of whether the eighth and ninth grades were high school or elementary school was a persistent problem to educators. To some extent, this issue was resolved by the establishment of a new unit, the junior high school, and, in rural and small-town America, the six-year junior-senior high school.

Pedagogical methods and content in the elementary school were greatly influenced by educational philosophers such as Pestalozzi, Froebel, and Dewey. Dewey believed that education involves not merely learning, but also play, construction, use of tools, expression, and activity. Furthermore, he believed the school should be a place where children are working rather than listening, learning life by living life, and becoming acquainted with social institutions and industrial processes by studying them at first hand.

The conflict of purpose and program between elememtary school and secondary school has persisted to this day. Elementary schools have modified their course offerings to insure that their graduates will succeed in middle and high school. In much the same fashion, high schools developed a standardized curriculum to meet college admission standards. The internal organization in the elementary school has been revised in a variety of ways to meet the demand for closer articulation between elementary and secondary education. The "self-contained" classroom, in which a teacher is assigned a group of children and is expected to educate the child in the "business of living," epitomizes the application of Deweyan philosophy and the rejection of the notion that elementary school should be a high school in miniature.

The departmental organization provides for elementary teachers to teach specific subjects and for children to move from teacher to teacher for subject-matter instruction. This instructional pattern is found most often in upper elementary grades and in the junior high school. The upper grades of some elementary schools and some junior high schools were semidepartmentalized as a compromise between the two organizations. In this plan, classes stayed together, but moved from teacher to teacher as a group. In another compromise—in the upper grades—was the block-of-time scheduling so popular in middle and junior high schools today in which double or triple period classes combine or replace two or more subjects. Historically, both of these plans were accomodations by the lower schools to the high school point of view about education and teaching. One of the principal thrusts of American educators in the twentieth century has been to close the gap in purposes and programs of the various units on the educational ladder.

The Junior High School

The junior high school commonly consists of Grades Seven, Eight, and Nine. It is organized and administered as a separate unit of the public school system. It was the outcome of a reorganization movement that began as a protest against the long period of elementary schooling, and the insistence of colleges that students be better prepared in academic subjects before admission to college.

The reorganization movement was set in motion in 1888 by President Charles Eliot of Harvard, in an address before the National Education Association. President Eliot pointed out that (1) for the past sixty years, the average age of college admission had steadily risen; (2) the period beyond college graduation required for professional training had lengthened to three or four years; and (3) it would be desirable to condense school courses to gain time and to increase the efficiency of instruction. As we have previously noted, the NEA appointed a Committee of Ten, chaired by President Eliot, to make recommendations on the questions he had raised in his address. The Committee subsequently suggested an academic program for the upper elementary grades and high school grades that would better prepare students for advanced college study.

By 1910, the idea of the junior high school had begun to gather momentum. Junior high schools were started in Richmond, Indiana, Columbus, Ohio, and in Berkeley, California. About 1913, the Board of Regents of the University of Michigan adopted the following two resolutions pertaining to the public-school structure in Michigan:

1. That school authorities be encouraged to incorporate the seventh and eighth grades of the elementary school as an integral part of the high school system, forming a six-year system.
2. That school authorities be recommended to organize the six-year high school system into a Junior High School of three years, and a Senior High School of three years, as soon as local conditions will admit.

The junior high school plan was accepted throughout the nation because it offered a more varied program of instruction for seventh and eighth grade students, and because it appeared to be a rational way to bridge the philosophical differences between the elementary school and the high school.

As the junior high school emerged in the twenties and thirties, it was characterized by flexible promotions, curricula that allowed pupils to explore their interests and talents, provisions for individual differences in pupils, and a limited choice of elective subjects in the upper years. Additional support for this unique unit in the educational ladder was forthcoming from behavioral psychologists, who, through their studies in human development, argued that a special school unit would undoubtedly facilitate the educational development of children during their early adolescent years. The age of puberty, approximately twelve to fourteen, is a difficult time both physically and socially. The American way was to invent a special educational unit to meet this particular problem.

The structure of the junior high school also made it possible to give special emphasis to vocational training and occupational education, in programs that were prescribed for the four-year high school. Because most youth's formal education ended at age fourteen or fifteen, this training fulfilled the public's demand that all children have the opportunity to acquire "saleable skills" prior to leaving school.

The Middle School

During the mid-fifties, a movement critical of the junior high school idea developed. Educators felt that the junior high school was not doing the job that they had hoped it would. They thought it had become too much like the high school in both its curricular and social aspects. The fact that the ninth grade was considered to be a high school grade by many made the 6–3–3 system somewhat awkward. Another fact that concerned educational critics was that youth seemed to be maturing earlier. The advent of junior high school interscholastic sports, and social activities in imitation of the high school extracurriculum program, it was felt, put an unnecessary burden on pupils' normal development. As a result of these and other concerns, educators began to turn to a revival of the four-year high school and, in many systems, to replace the junior high school with a middle school that did not include Grade Nine. It was hoped that this school, by combining the elementary schools and the junior high schools, would provide a more suitable educational program for pupils in Grades Six to Eight (and, in some instances, Grades Five to Eight, or Seven to Eight). Many middle schools have inaugurated successful innovative programs in pursuit of this ideal. Other middle schools are simply truncated junior high schools, renamed.

In order to make the transition from self-contained classes in the elementary school to fully departmentalized classes in the high school, modern middle schools are often built around block-of-time courses. In such organizations, subjects such as mathematics and science, social studies and English are combined to provide large block-of-time courses in which pupils stay together with one teacher for two or three periods.

The High School

The early high schools of the nineteenth century were entirely independent of the elementary schools. Although these schools taught children of the same age as those enrolled in upper elementary grades, they served a special function for a group of students, who were selected through entrance examinations. By the late nineteenth century, high schools began accepting graduation from an elementary school as a satisfactory basis for admission, and the age of entrance to high schools was increased accordingly. Out of this process emerged the twelve-year school system and the prevailing organization pattern of an eight-year graded elementary school and a four-year high school. Historically, the high school was superimposed on the elementary school. The curricula and programs of the two schools were fundamentally different in origin and purpose. Elementary educators saw their tasks as that of providing a "common schooling" that was adjusted to the needs of all the children, and somehow related to the day-to-day living of the students.

The role of the high school was to prepare youth for college and for vocations, but by the end of World War II, because of numerous pressures, it had taken on the job of providing a suitable education for all the youth of all the people. The high school had, in effect, become a common school.

The Comprehensive High School is a distinctly American invention. It is an institution that enrolls adolescents from all kinds of backgrounds and offers a broad range of subjects. It serves to prepare students for college; but it also functions as an agent of social and cultural integration, a place where students participate in a common set of social and intellectual activities. It also provides specialized electives for students with varying interests and backgrounds. The popularity of the high school may be appreciated by looking at some enrollment figures.

1880   110,277
1920   2,382,542
1930   4,427,000
1960   9,619,000.

By 1940, it was well-established that for the American student, the Comprehensive High School was the next step on the educational ladder, perhaps with an intermediate step—the junior high school. Historically, the elementary school was termed the *Common School*. With the acceptance of the idea that secondary education should be available to all youth, and with the introduction into the high school of comprehensive academic, social, and cultural activities, the high school became a part of the American common school system.

The fact that the Comprehensive High School became the prevailing type of secondary education during the period 1920 to 1950 did not automatically eliminate other forms of secondary training. The Latin Grammar School did not immediately disappear with the establishing of the Academy. Likewise, the Academy continued to exist side by side with the high school through the nineteenth century. Some still exist in modified form in New England. Similarly, in the first half of the twentieth century, both college preparatory high schools and specialized high schools (that provided terminal vocational and technical preparation) operated in a number of communities. The Comprehensive High School, in which all students and curricula were contained within one school, was strongest in moderate-size cities and in consolidated rural areas. It was almost nonexistent in large cities.

In 1959, James B. Conant, a former president of Harvard University, published a short book, *The American High School Today*, in which he examined the contemporary condition of the American high school. Conant focused his attention on the conditions of the Comprehensive High School, and made suggestions as to what high schools should do if they were to continue to be viable common-school institutions. The purpose of a Comprehensive High School, said Conant, was to develop a democratic spirit and understanding between students with different intellectual abilities and goals. According to Conant, the high school should achieve three major aims: a general education for all future citizens, good elective programs for terminal students, and a good college preparatory program for the rest. Conant did not reject the idea of a Comprehensive High School. Instead, he sought to improve it by making some recommendations about the curricula and services that must be provided in an institution in which more than half of the students terminate their full-time education upon graduation. The core of the curriculum, said Conant, would include four years of English, three or four years of social studies, and at least one year of mathematics and science. One half of the student's time would be devoted to the core; the remainder could be taken in electives appropriate to student interest and specific needs. Conant was especially interested in diversified programs that would develop marketable skills, and suggested that vocational programs should be offered in Distributive Education, agriculture, trade, and industry—depending upon the nature of the community served by the school. Diversification and supplemental services were two of the major themes of Conant's recommendations. He recommended the scheduling of increased time for English composition, special programs for slow readers, greater challenges for gifted students, more offerings in science and foreign languages, and a strong, fully articulated counseling program to help students choose electives corresponding to their interests, aptitudes, and achievement; all these suggest that Conant was sincerely interested in making the Comprehensive High School viable and relevant for the last half of the twentieth century.

We have noted that between 1920 and 1950, the Comprehensive High School, as an integral unit in the educational ladder, came to be the dominant secondary form in medium-size cities and in consolidated school districts. This was not the case in the large metropolitan areas, particularly not in cities such as New York, Philadelphia, and Boston. Here, specialized high schools were organized according to socioeconomic status. The result was a dual system of education—one track for the privileged children of the upper class and one track for children of the lower class. This duality could result in splitting American society into two radically different groups. Further, such a situation was in direct conflict with the stated aims of American education. New York City may be used to illustrate the depth and seriousness of this problem.

The New York Times, in its June 29, 1975 edition, initiated a series of articles on the city's high schools. According to the articles, the City had undertaken in 1965 to convert virtually all its traditional academic and vocational high schools into comprehensive schools. This policy decision was a major effort to provide a variety of programs and options to meet the diverse needs of the 305,500 children who attended the city's high schools. You will recall that one of the educational trends in the twentieth century has been to be more scientific in assessing the values and outcomes of schooling. New York City school officials in the late sixties were confronted with attendance rates which dropped, at one point, to only 57.8 per cent of the students enrolled; high attrition rates (47 per cent of students dropping out before graduation); and serious problems relating to the quality of high-school education. Many high-school graduates were reading below eighth-grade level. The system, which had not been changed since 1940, provided for traditional academic high schools, including four elite special high schools where admission was by competitive examination only; and vocational schools for preparation for jobs in commerce and industry. These traditional high schools provided three basic unrelated tracks. The academic college preparatory program had its own prestigious diploma. A "general" track enrolled the majority of students, most of whom had no special academic or career goals. The vocational school, with its own diploma, existed separately from the others and was strongly criticized for offering obsolete programs and denigrating the intellectual potential of its students.

The 1973 Fleischmann report on education in New York State noted that this fragmentation was unfair, and according to statistics, the system seemed to be failing. The growing majority of students were ending up in the "general" track, and if they did not drop out, were graduating with no saleable skills or useful credentials. Vocational programs were drawing students who, with a little special help or enlarged opportunities, might have been college material. The elite one third of the students in the academic program were isolated from exposure to "practical skills," and also from the larger society of the schools and city around them.

The New York City secondary-school reforms were directed toward making the city's schools more responsive to the growing dissatisfaction with its traditional system of separate academic and vocational schools, and to the pressures generated by the great social and educational controversies relating to the Civil Rights Movement. (Integrationists point out that vocational schools enrolled most of the minority youngsters and that academic schools had most of the white students.) The concept of the traditional academic high school was revised, beginning in 1965, to a type of high school that would combine the traditional college-preparatory curriculum with a vast array of career- and professional-course offerings; a great variety of electives to enrich the rather rigid academic track; and expanded counseling services: in short, a comprehensive school.

The country went into the 1980s with its faith in the comprehensive schools unshaken. There was some movement toward providing specialized education for youth with specialized goals in specialized schools. Regional and county vocational schools had become popular. Programs in which pupils spent part of the day in comprehensive high schools and part of the day in vocational schools were not unusual. Cities were supporting specialized magnet schools of various types, to entice youths having certain interests and goals to attend them. Educators hoped that such schools would both combat patterns of racial segregation and reduce the number of school dropouts. To give pupils practical experiences with potential careers and community activities, schools were conducting "Learning in the Community" and "Action Learning" programs. In these programs, pupils took part in real community-service projects and had field experiences in various trades and professions.

During the 1970s, various commissions and committees recommended major reforms in secondary education. If their recommendations are followed, the schools of the 1980s

> will become more flexible, move out into the community, adopt more functional curricula, become less formally academic, provide more effectively for the differences in students, and provide for the needs of a much larger clientele. Truly they will become community schools that serve all age and ethnic groups, giving students experiences in such adult activities as work experience, action learning and service with adult groups and institutions. The mamoth, all-purpose high schools will be replaced by smaller institutions with more specialized education and training purposes. In short, education would become a living functional part of the community as a whole—no longer an ivory tower—in which youths have an opportunity to discover and exploit their talents freely in a natural environment.[8]

Alternative Schools

Alternative schools have been common throughout the history of the United States. Usually these schools have been formed to meet a specific need. Two hundred years ago, parents sent their children to private venture schools to procure for them a practical, career-oriented education. In this century, Roman Catholics have built parochial schools because they felt public schools to be too Protestant or anti-religious. Other religious groups have founded schools to combat what they consider the anti-Christian, immoral, and atheistic biases in public schools. In some communities, parents have started independent schools to protest the racial integration of the public schools. In the 1960s, groups founded progressive alternative schools to protest the alleged regimentation and inhumanity of public schools. In the beginning of the 1980s, private and parochial schools were becoming popular because of the belief, aggravated by media reports, that the schools were not delivering academically. Partly to meet the needs of their pupils, and partly in self defense, school systems in many communities are now providing alternative schools within their public school system.

Elementary and Secondary School Curricula and Methods

At the turn of the century, the curriculum in the elementary schools was reading, writing, and 'rithmetic, and in the high school college preparation via the standard academic disciplines. Since that time, the scientific study

---

[8] Leonard H. Clark and Irving S. Starr, *Secondary and Middle School Teaching Methods*, 4th ed. (New York: Macmillan, 1981), p. 9.

of education movement, the progressive movement, movements to make schooling more socially relevant and humane, movements for the return to basics and to make schools more accountable, and the like, have strongly influenced both the organization and content of the curriculum and methods of teaching in the elementary and secondary schools.

At the end of the nineteenth century, educators were beginning an attemp to provide a scientific basis for education. In 1895, Charles DeGarmo, Charles A. McMurry, Frank McMurry, John Dewey, and Nicholas Murray Butler, among others, organized the National Herbart Society for the Scientific Study of Education. This name was changed in 1902 to the National Society for the Scientific Study of Education, and is now the prestigious National Society for the Study of Education. Interest in child study had blossomed and flourished until World War I, when the subject began to be merged with such subjects as tests, measurements, and learning theory, to become educational psychology.

Herbartianism

The first methodological reform of the century was contributed by the Herbartians[9], particularly by Charles DeGarmo and the two brothers Charles A. and Frank McMurry. Central to Herbartianism was the belief that instruction should be conducted according to formal steps. As laid out by Charles A. McMurry, these steps were

1. Preparation.
2. Presentation.
3. Association and Comparison.
4. Generalization or Abstraction.
5. Application.

Vestiges of these steps still persist in good expository teaching. After peaking in the pre-World War I years, however, Herbartianism gradually declined as it became mixed with the theories of the new psychology of John Dewey and other progressive educators.

The Progressive Education Movement

Progressive education has been with us a long time. The father of the progressive education movement in the United States, according to John Dewey, was Colonel Francis W. Parker, superintendent of schools in Quincy, Massachusetts, and later head of Cook County Normal School in Chicago. Basic to Parker's educational philosophy were four principles:

1. Schools should be child-centered.
2. Schools should create a warm democratic community atmosphere.
3. The curriculum should consist of multidiscipline units based on the real practical experiences of the learners.
4. The schools should stress creative art and expression.

[9] After the great German philosopher and educational theorist J. F. Herbart.

John Dewey's description of typical progressive schools in 1915 shows how well they followed Parker's lead:

1. The schools fostered the physical welfare and health of the pupils.
2. The school curriculum centered around activity programs.
3. The learning activities were based on pupil interest in the solving of real problems.
4. The schools fostered democratic values and practices.[10]

Thus we see that progressive educators were committed to child-centered, interested, motivated, problem-solving, activity-programed schooling. This, of course, placed the emphasis on individual pupils. Among plans to individualize schooling was the Dalton (Massachusetts) plan. This plan was built around a series of contracts consisting of a number of assignments that the individual pupils agreed to complete. There was no formal large-group teaching. Instead, pupils worked individually in laboratory fashion, meeting with teachers individually or in small groups as the occasion required. (A similar plan, the Winnetka, Illinois plan, combined self-instruction, self-correction, diagnostic testing, and individual progress with creative and social activities.) Variations of these plans of the 1920s and 1930s surfaced again in the 1960s, and are presently to be found in American elementary, secondary, and tertiary schools.

During the 1920s and 1930s, Harold Rugg and other progressive reformers sought to make education relevant to contemporary society. To this end, Rugg, with the research support of literally thousands of teachers and school administrators, brought out a series of textbooks consisting of integrated social studies units that attempted to present a rounded view of society, stressing scientific and democratic values. Conservative groups were opposed to these texts because of their supposed socialistic bias and because the texts encouraged pupils to examine our society and government critically. In the 1960s and 1970s, similar attempts to make education relevant and to arouse in pupils attitudes of independent critical thinking, were again opposed by patriotic groups. Presently, one of the aims of the proponents of basic education is to make pupils more patriotic and less critical of the American way. Yet, social studies educators, in particular, insist that pupils should examine our society objectively with open minds—much as Rugg advocated.

In the period between the World Wars, a few rural progressive community schools reached near to the ultimate in social relevance. In these schools, the community was the school curriculum, and the school was the center of the community. Examples of the responsibilities assumed by the community schools included the local cooperative market, the fair, the labor exchange, the community canning kitchen, and the local health and fire facilities. During the 1960s and 1970s, this community school idea was revived in both rural and urban areas. Several schools in New Haven, Connecticut, for instance, assumed the role of community centers for both children and adults.[11] Recently, action-learning and learning in the community programs

---

[10] John and Evelyn Dewey, *Schools for Tomorrow* (New York: E. P. Dutton, 1915).

[11] Gregory Farrell, *A Climate of Change: The New Haven Story* (New Brunswick, N.J.: Rutgers Urban Studies Center, 1965).

continue in a similar vein. In such programs, pupils learn about the community in their schools, and acquire real experience in community affairs as well.

Another methodological innovation of the progressives was the project method developed by William Heard Kilpatrick. As visualized by Kilpatrick, projects were purposeful, problem centered, cooperatively planned, interest based, and productive of tangible results. Pupils were to learn not from dictation, but from "purposeful activity" in groups or as individuals.

Somewhat similar to the project was the unit method. In this technique, the learning objectives were specifically delineated by the teacher. Then, after an introduction in which the teacher tried to prepare and motivate the pupils, the pupils performed both required and optional learning activities in a laboratory situation. This laboratory work was followed by "pooling, and sharing," and a final evaluation. The purpose of these activities was to combine rigorous intellectual activity, independent thinking, pupil interest and individualization.

During most of the present century, there has been a movement from separate subjects toward correlation and integration of subject matter. The old studies of orthography, declamation, grammar, literature, and so on, have been fused into "broad fields" English courses. Similarly, various sciences have been combined into general science; history and the social sciences have been blended into social studies; and elements of mathematics integrated into such "broad fields" courses as general mathematics.

One product of this trend was the unified studies core curriculum. Basically, the core curriculum was a multiperiod block-of-time course that replaced or combined certain subjects—often English and social studies. In the ordinary block-of-time core, the subjects were taught as separate but correlated courses. In the unified studies courses, the subjects were fused into one subject. The most sophisticated core curriculum courses consisted of block-of-time units centered around problems of youth or society. Any subject matter or resource that would contribute to the understandings sought was legitimate content for that unit. Such core courses were popular at the junior-high-school level after World War II; block-of-time courses, some of which are essentially core courses, are still popular in middle schools today.

The Sputnik Reaction

After the launching of Sputnik in 1957, a reaction against the alleged faults of progressive education provoked a strong push for rigorous academic basic education. Academicians became interested in public-school teaching. Along with this movement came an interest and commitment to discovery-learning. Jerome Bruner and others were convinced that children could best be taught concepts by arranging for them to experience various manifestations of the concept to be learned and by encouraging them to draw their own generalizations from these experiences. This inductive method of teaching was the basis for many new curriculum programs. Later critics contend that the method is too time consuming to be efficient. Today, the trend seems to be toward the use of more direct methods.

B. F. Skinner popularized one type of direct teaching—programed learning. This technique, based upon the psychological principles of operant conditioning, was the basis of many of the new teaching machines popular a decade or so ago. Lately, such machines have declined in popularity, but other machines and programs are becoming popular. Among them are the computers which are being used to speed, intensify, and individualize instruction. The invention of mini-computers has made it possible to bring computer-programed instruction into every classroom. This appears to be the coming fad of the next decade.

Spurred by the funding from the National Defense Education Acts of 1958 and 1964, the academic specialists who had become interested in elementary and secondary school education introduced new programs in the various disciplines. Among the projects were those of the Physical Science Study Committee, the Biological Sciences Study Group, the Foreign Language in the Elementary School Program, and the High School Geography Project. These projects attempted to revise public school instruction in the disciplines according to the most modern concepts and theories. As a result, schools were flooded with the new mathematics, the new grammar, the new social studies, and similar programs. These programs were buttressed by the Woods Hole Conference of 1959, which stressed the study of the structure of the disciplines—i.e., the major concepts and methods of inquiry of the disciplines. In their report, the conferees advocated a *spiral* curriculum. Because, they said, any subject "can be taught effectively in some intellectually honest form to any child at any stage of development,"[12] they recommended that the concepts of the disciplines be taught with increasing rigor from the bottom to the top of the educational ladder.

The Search for Humaneness

Again there was a reaction. Educators revolted against the emphasis on the disciplines. The stress on the structure of the disciplines had not seemed to pay off, and the general education of pupils seemed to be deteriorating. Critics thought that something should be done to make the schools more humane.

One aspect of the search for humaneness in schooling was the search for relevance to the needs of society and to the lives of pupils. Other concerns were the need

1. to provide more adequately for individual differences.
2. to involve pupils in the planning and managing of their own schooling.
3. to help pupils clarify their values.
4. to make the school more flexible and personal.
5. to make pupils free-inquiry persons.
6. to help pupils fully realize their human potential.[13]

[12] Jerome S. Bruner, *The Process of Education* (Cambridge, Massachusetts: Harvard University Press, 1960), p. 33.

[13] Leonard H. Clark, Raymond L. Klein, and John B. Burks, *The American Secondary School Curriculum*, 2nd ed. (New York: Macmillan, 1972), p. 524.

To accomplish such goals, schools revamped their curricula not only to make them more "relevant," but also to make them more flexible and more responsive to pupils' interests and desires. One approach was to offer many electives and minicourses so as to guarantee pupils a chance to select courses they could "really get something out of." Another approach was to offer increased emphasis on career and vocational (practical) education.

Innovation and Experimentation

The quest for humaneness and relevance was only part of the educational ferment during the past two decades. This ferment, which was a result of Lyndon Johnson's quest for a great society, the civil rights movement, and the Vietnam war, among other things, brought on numerous attempts to revitalize and reorient the schools. As we have already noted, great injections of federal money led to a multitude of projects and innovations. Among the innovations were numerous attempts to make the schools more efficient and effective. The Ford Foundation sponsored large-group television teaching. The National Association of Secondary School Principals sponsored what came to be called the Trump plan. This plan introduced teaching teams and flexible scheduling. The teachers on the teaching teams carried out different roles, some giving large-group lectures, some teaching small groups, and some supervising individual study. The flexible schedules combined short fifteen-minute classes and longer one- or two-hour classes, depending on the time needed for the activity and content. Many middle and junior high schools introduced block-of-time scheduling in which a multidisciplinary team of teachers (English, social studies, science, and mathematics, for example) shared the same pupils. The team members planned together to coordinate and schedule the activities of all the pupils in the block of time.

Simultaneously, school personnel became greatly concerned with individual differences in pupils. Curricular tracks for the talented, college-preparatory, vocational, and general students were common in secondary schools. Some schools adopted non-graded plans in which pupils were placed according to ability rather than by grade level. Others established continuous progress schemes. As a rule, continuous progress courses are made up of pre-planned learning modules or packets which pupils work through independently or in small groups. This method allows pupils to progress through the curriculum at their own speed, as they move from level to level when they are ready. Theoretically, at least, the modules make curricula flexible and personal—especially since they allow pupils to follow their own individual sequences. The Dalton plan of fifty years ago and, to a lesser degree, the mastery plan of the eighties are variations on the module approach basic to the continuous progress plan.

The Civil Rights Movement

The civil rights movement also had direct impact on the curriculum. Courses in black studies, black history and black literature multiplied. So did programs designed to remove the stigmas and disadvantages of urban and rural ghetto life. Among these were compensatory education projects supported by the federal government to bring up to standard the educational skills of pupils who had fallen behind presumably because of past substandard educational opportunities. Another change was the rewriting of textbooks to remove racial bias and to present pictures of life recognizable to young blacks.

The strength of the movement for the improvement of black education caused similar movements in other ethnic groups. Presently, it has become fashionable to speak of the United States as a pluralistic multicultural nation, and to present courses that would support the ethnicity of the various groups in the community. Important in the ethnic programs are the bilingual and English-as-a-second-language courses designed to help pupils adjust to school and to become competent both in English and in their native languages.

Similarly, educators, because of congressional mandates, are attempting to remove sexual bias and discrimination from the schools. Textbooks have been rewritten to present the sexes more equitably. Eligibility rules for both curricular and extracurricular activities have been rewritten to remove sexual prejudice. Federal law also mandates equal treatment to the handicapped in the schools. As a result of PL 94-142 and other laws, schools must now educate handicapped persons in the least restrictive environment. To carry out this mandate, school authorities, with the cooperation of teachers and parents, work out for each handicapped youngster an Individual Educational Program that will allow the child a least restrictive environment, that is, one that gives the child optimum access to a normal education and to the usual school classes, facilities and programs feasible in view of the pupil's handicap.

Back to Basics

At all levels, the schools of the eighties are stressing competence and academic standards. States are beginning to test students to be sure that schools are producing adequate scholarship. Automatic promotion policies have been rejected in favor of forcing unsatisfactory students to repeat grades. Schools are setting up and enforcing competency-based teaching goals. Throughout the nation, schools are moving toward conservative tradition-based programs. The slogan of the eighties so far has been "back to basics."

Nevertheless, if this writer is any prophet, the overall trend throughout the eighties will be toward

> more humane, responsive schools in which the curriculum will be much more down to earth and the needs of the community and of youth will be better and more democratically served then in the past.[14]

Higher Education

Colleges and Universities

Module 1 describes some of the early movements in higher education. One of the uniquely American forms of higher education appeared in the early

---

[14] Leonard H. Clark, and Irving S. Starr, *op. cit.*, p. 20.

nineteenth century, with the founding of denominational colleges. This pattern of secondary and higher education institutions, initiated and nourished by the churches in the nineteenth century, continues to this day. It is said that Ohio and Pennsylvania have more small liberal arts colleges of denominational origins than any other two states in the Union. The public high school, to a large extent, has replaced the college preparatory school as a source of students for denominational and church-related colleges. However, private secondary schools and academies still flourish as college-preparatory institutions for private denominational colleges.

The twentieth century has also seen a marked development in public-supported colleges and universities. Many land-grant universities have developed a full complex of graduate and professional schools. The University of California at Berkeley, the University of Wisconsin, and the University of Illinois are major research centers that include distinguished scholars and scientists on their faculty. In contrast, the Negro land-grant colleges have continued to concentrate much of their effort on vocational, technical, and remedial instruction. The land-grant colleges and universities in each state serve the particular needs of the people, and, in general, each has been responsive to the changing demands of its constituency.

Questions of admissions, costs, and programs have been particularly troublesome to these instutitions since the sixties. In contract to the private colleges and universities, land-grant colleges had always been open to all high school graduates, at little or no cost, and were expected to offer programs of study required by contemporary society. Except for the New England and Middle Atlantic states, nearly all state legislatures had made these provisions for high school graduates. In most instances, this meant that the student who did not, by reason of preference, expense, or academic ability, choose to attend a private college or university, could enroll in the state university.

In the period from 1920 to 1940, state facilities (if one includes the normal schools) were adequate to accommodate those students who chose the state college or university. Tuition fees were minimal or nonexistent, and enrollments did not place much of a strain on state budgets. Because of a number of reasons associated with the ideal of equality of educational opportunity, there was enormous pressure on higher education—public and private alike—to admit all students who sought a college education. During this period, state legislatures authorized the state university to expand its physical facilities and broaden its programs to provide for the many thousands of students who were being denied admission for lack of space. Following World War I, a comparable pressure had forced the expansion of secondary education, resulting in the integration of the high school into the educational ladder of American education.

Although the state university, by the close of the nineteenth century, had been accepted, in principle, as the capstone of the American educational system, it was not until the 1950s that the various states, in their legislative and administrative actions, began fully to define a state system of education that included higher education.

Even the Eastern states, where higher education had traditionally served only a limited number of high school graduates in private institutions were compelled to recognize the mounting student and parental pressures for college-education opportunities. For example, New Jersey—which was notorious for its lack of public higher education opportunities, and known as the "Cuckoo" state to college and university leaders in other states[15]— enacted, after much controversy, the Higher Education Act of 1966. This legislation provided for a Board of Higher Education, a State Department of Higher Education, and a Chancellor for a state system of higher education. Prior to 1966, New Jersey funded six state teachers colleges. By 1975, the six state teachers colleges had been transformed into multipurpose colleges, two new state colleges had been added, seventeen junior colleges had been established; moreover, pressures were on the state university (which had been a private university until 1947) to introduce a broader range of programs.

The New Jersey experience, although occurring ten to fifteen years later than most other states, is typical of what happened to higher education following World War II. Although the principle of open admission has been retained, because of the acceleration in capital and operating costs to support more students and more programs, state legislatures have gradually increased the state college and university tuition and fees for both in-state and out-of-state residents. The state universities and colleges are viewed as state institutions. State legislatures have traditionally reserved the right to assess out-of-state residents higher fees than those charged to in-state students. In some instances, the differential is quite significant.

For the flood of students applying for admission in the fifties and early sixties, the maintenance of an open admission policy generated serious questions about the nature and quality of programs that should be offered in the public institutions. The traditional liberal parts pattern of private higher education—a four-year program of general and liberal studies followed by enrollment in the university for study in the professions—did not appear to have relevance for many students who were seeking admission. Many of the land-grant colleges and universities, whose historic mission had been to provide scientific and technical preparation for special categories of students, had by 1950 settled into college programs that were comparable to the patterns in private colleges and universities. Faculty members in land-grant institutions believed that their courses required as much intellectual rigor as any liberal arts program in the private colleges, and they were reluctant to modify their teaching—either content or method—to accommodate a "new" student body. The problem of admissions and programs was further exacerbated in the sixties by the demand of minority groups—Blacks, Hispanics, and Chicanos—for admission to the university.

The public higher-education faculties in the fifties and sixties, as were the high school faculties in the forties, were confronted with a changing student population. The population was heterogeneous rather than homogeneous, more demanding, more insistent on their right to a higher education, and

[15] The Cuckoo is a bird that hatches its eggs in the nests of other birds. The great majority of New Jersey high school graduates, until 1960, were required to enroll in colleges out of state, for lack of public education institutions in New Jersey.

more critical of the content and teaching methods, which they deemed inadequate for the times. The state institutions responded by providing "remedial instruction" and special counseling for those students who were not deemed fully prepared for college study. A variety of new courses and new programs were introduced into the traditional curricula. New emphasis was on the responsibility of a college instructor for teaching, and less emphasis on his activity as a researcher and producer of knowledge. Problems pertaining to physical facilities and the mission of the state university have been resolved to some extent by two major movements: the junior college, and the transformation of the normal school to a four-year multipurpose college.

The advent of the 1980s brought considerable retrenchment to the colleges and universities of the nation. Declining enrollments, restricted financing, and the pervasive conservative atmosphere of the times led to the reexamination of policies and programs. In a reaction against the openness of the past two decades, colleges, led by such prestigious schools as Harvard, attempted to make college curricula more orderly and rigorous. Relatively free choice of electives was being replaced with less flexible requirements. Because of prodding by legislatures, critics of education, the press, and educational agencies, entrance requirements were being upgraded. In order to maintain higher standards of academic and scholarly work, many colleges were reviewing their policies for providing remedial instruction. Evidently, the college of the near future will be more formal and academic, and perhaps more scholarly than in the recent past.

Junior and Community Colleges

The junior college or community college is an institution that furnishes the thirteenth and fourteenth year of education to high-school graduates. The idea of a junior college dates back to the late nineteenth century, when the heads of several universities argued that the first two years of undergraduate education should be offered elsewhere than in the existing four-year college. These university leaders were not so much interested in initiating a new institution as they were in freeing their universities from what they considered secondary education in order to devote more time to graduate instruction and research. President Harper, of the University of Chicago, in 1892 separated the first two and last two years of instruction into what were called the Academic College and the University College. In 1896, these titles were changed to the Junior College and the Senior College. For Harper, the junior college was essentially an extension of the high school. The initial venture in the junior college as a separate institution was made in 1901, in Joliet, Illinois. Joliet Junior College encouraged high school students to take post-graduate work without tuition. Although the principal aim was to enable high school students to take sufficient courses to acquire advanced standing in four-year colleges, terminal courses quickly became part of the program.

Another impetus for the junior college sprang from the desire of communities sincerely interested in the educational welfare of their youth to sponsor vocational and technical courses beyond high school for their high school graduates. In 1925, the American Association of Junior Colleges defined the nature of this institution by stating that its member institutions would offer two years of collegiate instruction of a quality equivalent to the first two years of a four-year college. In addition, the junior college curriculum would serve the social, civic, religious, and vocational needs of the community in which the college was located. In the late 1920s, and in the 1930s, junior colleges tended to place greater emphasis on vocational and technical training programs than on the liberal arts. One of the most extensive programs of terminal education—terminal because it was the final formal education experience of the student—was introduced at the Los Angeles Junior College in 1929 in its inaugural year. The College offered fourteen separate technical and semiprofessional programs.

This emphasis on terminal programs was the result of several factors. The Smith–Hughes Act of 1917 provided federal aid for vocational education. In states that recognized junior colleges as an extension of secondary education, this aid was available to support vocational programs.

The Great Depression of the thirties was another factor that stimulated vocational programs. Graduates of traditional academic high schools, jobless, and financially unable to enroll in four-year colleges, sought in the junior colleges specific job training to make them more employable. Following World War II, the demand for technical skills in such fields as computer sciences, communications, and health encouraged community colleges to branch out into a large number of specific, job-related, technically-oriented programs. These programs were viewed as terminal, leading to skilled jobs upon completion. Since World War II and until 1970, one of the principal responsibilities of the two-year college was to relieve the four-year colleges and universities of the academic and financial burdens associated with the tremendous increase in students seeking admission to college. Another purpose, as first defined by the Association of Junior Colleges—that of offering both terminal programs and two-year academic programs for transfer to senior colleges—has been realized.

In order that educational opportunities could be made available to large numbers of people at a reasonable cost, and without reducing educational quality, some states turned to master-planning a completely articulated system of public education, from primary school through the university. In most master plans, extensive systems of junior colleges were included to handle the increasing student population.

California was one of the first states to devise such a plan (1959).

> The state system of higher education in California consists of junior colleges, state colleges and the University of California. The junior colleges offer instruction through but not beyond the fourteenth year in courses that can be used for transfer to higher institutions, in vocational and technical fields, and in general arts courses.
>
> The state colleges provide undergraduate and graduate instruction through the master's degree in liberal arts and sciences, in applied fields, in teaching and in the professions.
>
> The University of California is the primary state-supported academic agency for research. It provides undergraduate and graduate instruction in liberal arts and sci-

ences, teaching and the professions. The University has sole jurisdiction in law, medicine, dentistry, veterinary medicine and architecture. It has sole authority to award the doctorate in all fields of learning, with the exception that in some areas it may award a joint doctorate with the state colleges.[16]

The first legislation in California for the establishment of junior colleges came in 1907, when the State Legislature authorized high school districts to offer post-graduate courses. In 1921, the Legislature authorized the formation of junior college districts. The California Master Plan for Higher Education (1960–1975) proposed that as many as fifty thousand students, who would otherwise enter the state colleges and the university in 1975, be diverted to the junior colleges. The result of the California plan is that it created in California the largest junior college system in the country. In a period of intense pressure for admission to California colleges and universities, the plan provided that no California student would be denied an opportunity for higher education; at the same time, it insured the maintenance of selective admission to the four-year college and university. The California model, with modification, was replicated in a number of other states (Illinois, Texas, Florida), and appears to be accepted as a rational, educationally sound means of fulfilling the promise of equal educational opportunity for all students.

The junior college is a distinctly American social institution, which reached its full promise in the middle of the twentieth century, for the reasons just described. It is a multifunctional institution. It provides the first years of collegiate study for transfer to senior institutions, and it offers training in technical and subprofessional services. The student living at home and working part time may thus obtain a relatively inexpensive education. As a community college, it offers educational services to adults, and is often the cultural, educational, and civic center for the people in the area which it serves. With its policy of open admissions, and its diversified programs, the junior college has taken its place alongside the elementary school, junior high school, and high school—another rung in the American educational ladder.

As they enter the 1980s, most junior colleges have become true community colleges. Open to senior citizens who hope to fulfill old dreams; to adults who hope to update their skills, to prepare for new vocations, or to expand their horizons; and to youths who hope to prepare for admission to liberal arts colleges, or semi-professional occupations, the colleges are in session days, evenings, and weekends, summer and winter, doing their best to provide education, training, and service to the entire community.

Teacher Education

By 1900, it began to be recognized that a mere review of elementary school subject matter and exposure to teaching methods was not an adequate

---

[16] T. R. McConnell, *A General Pattern for American Public Higher Education* (New York: McGraw-Hill Book Co., 1962), pp. 155–156.

foundation for teaching at any level. Critics of the normal-school curriculum wanted psychology, philosophy, history, and advanced educational methodology to be included in the professional preparation of teachers, in order that teachers might have the same broad perspectives and scholarship base as that afforded the graduates of denominational colleges and state universities. Normal-school leaders responded by requiring a high-school diploma for admission, increasing the term of study from two years to three or four years, and introducing those subjects that would provide for a general education. The Normal School was renamed the State Teachers College, and in place of a normal-school diploma a college degree was awarded, usually a Bachelor of Science (to denote the science of education). With the emergence of the high school in the 1920s and 1930s, a great many states authorized these "new" state teachers colleges to devise curricula for the preparation of secondary school teachers. This action encouraged the offering of courses in the sciences (biology, zoology, physics, chemistry); social sciences (economics, political science, sociology); and the humanities (English literature, art, music, languages).

State teachers colleges, as special-purpose schools for teacher preparation, continued to be very closely associated with public education. Their faculty members, most of whom have had some teaching experience in the public schools, have been one of the significant forces in the development of teaching as a profession. Although the liberal arts subjects now taught in these institutions correspond to those taught in liberal arts colleges, their orientation is often toward the usefulness and relevancy of such subjects for students who are preparing for teaching in elementary or secondary education.

By 1930, the extent of elementary-teacher preparation can best be appreciated by an examination of some statistics from the *National Survey of the Education of Teachers*, Vol. VI, Bulletin, 1933, No. 10. In response to the question of how much schooling American teachers had in 1930–1931, it was reported that

> Approximately 1 out of every 20 elementary teachers in the United States in 1930–31 had no schooling beyond high school.
> About half (46.2 per cent) of the elementary teachers had had 2 years' work above high school in a normal school, teachers college, junior college, college, or university.
> Not 1 in every 200 rural school teachers had done a year's graduate work . . . in the largest cities, only 1 elementary teacher in each 20 reported a year or more of graduate work.

In 1938, the American Council on Education, an organization consisting of the major colleges and universities in the country, appointed a commission to conduct a comprehensive study of teacher education. Their recommendations have had a significant impact on upgrading teacher preparation through the master's level. One of the major tasks of the state teachers college in the period 1940 to 1960 was to provide the necessary courses to enable normal-school graduates and others with less than four years of study to complete the bachelor's degree. In recent years, state teachers colleges in some states were encouraged to begin offering applied educational work at the master's level. The degree was generally the Master of Science in Education, corresponding to the Bachelor of Science in Education degree at the undergraduate level.

There have been in the history of teacher education two distinct preparation tracks: primary and elementary teachers were prepared in normal schools and state teachers colleges; and secondary teachers in colleges and universities. These tracks emerged as a result of the unique origin of the elementary and secondary school. The two institutions continue to be notably different in philosophy and programs, because of differences in teacher preparation. In teacher education in the twentieth century, the trend has been to transform normal schools into state teachers colleges and state teachers colleges into general purpose or multipurpose state colleges. The latter change was partly the result of the pressures of increased college enrollments in the forties and fifties, and partly because of the theory that teachers could be better prepared for teaching in comprehensive heterogeneous American schools if training programs were offered in multipurpose colleges and universities. In a number of states, the old normal schools and teachers colleges have become regional state universities which offer a wide variety of liberal arts and professional programs, as well as other services for people of their region. The education faculty in these institutions is located in a School of Education within the university.

The result of these institutional changes has been to increase the academic preparation of teachers and to decrease the emphasis on methodology, and on what educators have termed *professionalized subject matter*—academic courses whose content is particularly relevant to the elementary or secondary school. Today, the young person graduating from high school may enroll in a public higher education institution and is permitted to select a major from a wide variety of programs. The teacher-education major will be likely to have two years of general education followed by two years of specialized training, including some work in "methods" and "practice teaching." The nomenclature of the degree awarded to teacher-education graduates—a Bachelor of Arts or a Bachelor of Science—is the same as that awarded to the graduates in other programs of the college or university. With these developments, one might say that by 1970 institutions that once-specialized only in teacher-education programs had joined the mainstream of American higher education.

During the 1970s many teacher educators turned to competency-based teacher education. A survey in 1980 indicates that more than half of the institutions accredited for the education of teachers were involved in competency-based teacher education programs of one sort or another.[17] In brief, competency-based teacher education teaching is divided into a series of tasks or competencies that the students learn to perform. Students are then tested to see if they can perform the tasks adequately. Students who can perform these competencies when evaluated are presumed to be effective. Whether or not the premises underlying competency-based teacher education are really valid is questionable at present. Nevertheless, competency-based teacher education represents an aspect of the movement to make

[17] Walter S. Sandefur III, and Willis L. Nicklas, "Competency-Based Teacher Education in AACTE Institutions: An Update," *Phi Delta Kappan*, 62:747–748 (June, 1981).

teachers accountable for pupil learning and to ensure that teachers are masters of the techniques of teaching.

Another current development in the education of teachers is an emphasis on in-service education. Traditionally in-service education has consisted of lectures, workshops, and courses offered by professors at teachers colleges or universities. Presently, much in-service work is offered by teachers teaching other teachers, local school system supervisory personnel, and in teacher centers maintained by state educational agencies, colleges, and universities,[18] large school systems, and by teachers' unions and professional organizations.

In Conclusion

The history of education in the twentieth century has been to clarify and to define more precisely the aims and purposes of American education. By 1930, it was clear that the American people viewed educational aims as the responsibility of all units in the educational system. Much energy was directed toward identifying relationships between elementary, secondary and higher education, the outcome of which was a fully articulated system of common-school education Grades One through Twelve, and a powerful trend toward extending free public education an additional four years—through Grade Sixteen. In this process, some new units were established, notably the junior high school and the junior college. In addition, specialized units known as teachers colleges were transformed into multipurpose state colleges and regional state universities.

The purposes, aims, and the emerging organizational structure of education in the twentieth century was a product of social, economic, and political factors. It has always been true that social institutions are modified and changed by such pressures, and education is no exception. We would like to comment on two general factors that had an impact upon education in the period from 1900 to 1970.

Child-Labor Laws and Compulsory-Attendance Legislation

Child-labor laws in the first three decades of the twentieth century took adolescents out of the factories and the mills and placed them in schools. By 1914, nearly all the states in the Union had enacted compulsory-attendance legislation requiring that "parents and guardians having control or charge of any child or children between the ages of seven and fourteen years" have their child sent to a public, private, denominational, or parochial school taught by a competent instructor; and that "such child or children shall attend school for at least sixty days during each and every scholastic year."[19] These laws were gradually changed to require compulsory attendance until the age of sixteen, and extended the school year to 180 days. One of the outcomes of these twin movements was the tremendous expansion of high-school enrollments, school physical facilities, and the development of broad comprehensive programs to meet the needs of a heterogeneous secondary school population.

---

[18] These go by a number of names, such as Educational Improvement Centers, Board of Cooperative Educational Services, and Resource Centers.
[19] Mississippi's Initial Law on Compulsory Attendance at School.

Shift from Rural-Agrarian Society to Urban-Industrial Society

America in 1900 was a rural society. Most persons lived on farms and in small villages. The land-grant college movement was directed toward the improvement of agriculture and the mechanical arts. The development of urban America, accompanied by major industrial and technological changes, required new types of institutions and new programs. The American high school and junior college were to become the means through which American youth could acquire vocational and occupational skills, and become contributing members of the emerging industrial society. Rapid societal changes occurred as a result of scientific developments in such fields as transportation—the automobile and the airplane; communications—the radio and television; and more recently, the computer. Advanced technical knowledge, and skills far above the level that schools of the early 1900s could offer, were required for this new industrial scientific era.

Following World War II, the federal government began to appropriate large sums of money to support public education. The Servicemen's Readjustment Act, known as the G.I. Bill, was passed in 1944 to provide education for the returning veterans. World War II veterans, numbering 7,800,000, received benefits at a cost totaling 14.5 billion dollars. The benefits were extended to veterans of the Korean and Viet Nam wars. In 1958, the National Defense Education Act (NDEA) was passed to stimulate studies in science, foreign languages, and mathematics. An extension of this Act in 1964 made loans available to college students; financially assisted improvements in science, mathematics, and foreign language instruction; supported guidance, counseling, and testing programs, as well as vocational education; and encouraged research and experimentation in educational media.

The Vocational Act of 1963 and the Manpower Development and Training Act of 1963 concentrated on providing opportunities to train people for gainful employment. The Elementary and Secondary Education Act of 1965 (ESEA) was a landmark among the federal acts designed to aid education. The basic purpose of ESEA was to equalize educational opportunities. It had five titles:

Title   I: Financial Assistance to Local Educational Agencies for Education of Children of Low Income Families.

Title II: Funds for School Library Resources, Textbooks and Other Instructional Materials.

Title III: Purchase of Textbooks as well as Library Books.

Title IV: Funds for Educational Research and Training.

Title V: Grants for Strengthening State Departments of Education.

The eighty-eighth and eighty-ninth Congresses (1964–65) enacted twenty-four major pieces of legislation. These laws provided billions of federal tax dollars for elementary schools, high schools, vocational schools, colleges, and universities. In 1963, the U.S. Office of Education budget was $700 million; in 1966, it was about $3,3 billion.

Although these congressional actions were based on the general recognition that American society required a high level of professional and technical skills, the immediate impetus for this legislation was the Civil Rights movement of the sixties. The funds were provided as categorical aid to improve and equalize educational opportunities for the educationally and economically deprived children in urban and rural areas of the country. It is significant that 170 years after the Ordinance of 1787, our federal government once again, in enacting this legislation, affirmed the historic principle that education is to be encouraged as "necessary to good government and the happiness of mankind."

The American public school system, with its graded structure from elementary school through the university, as conceived in the nineteenth century, became fully developed in the first seventy years of the twentieth century. The system continues to have the same characteristics the early educational leaders envisioned: it is tax-supported, free, nonsectarian, and open to all children and youth. It is a single-ladder system, with many options on each step of the ladder. It is a system that fits the American concept of what the well-known educational philosopher, Harry S. Broudy, has termed a "single-ladder" society.

In a single-ladder society, with its many rungs, there is competition and struggle, but there is also some unity of outlook, some integration of the value system. In such a society, says Broudy, the same kind of schooling—however much it differs in amount and depth—will have to be provided for all citizens, on whatever rung of the ladder they happen to perch.

SUGGESTED READING

Beck, Robert H., "A History of Issues in Secondary Education," in William Van Til, ed., *Issues in Secondary Education*, The Seventy-fifth Yearbook of the National Society for the Study of Education, Part II. Chicago: The University of Chicago Press, 1976.

Becker, Richard J., "Education and Work: A Historical Perspective," in Harry F. Silberman, ed., *Education and Work*, The Eighty-first Yearbook of the National Society for the Study of Education, Part II. Chicago: The University of Chicago Press, 1982.

Brown, Hugh S., and Lewis B. Mayhew, *American Higher Education*. New York: The Center for Applied Social Research in Education, 1965.

Butts, R. Freeman, *Public Education in the United States: From Revolution to Reform*. New York: Holt, Reinhart & Winston, Inc., 1978.

Conant, James B., *The American High School Today*. New York: McGraw-Hill Book Co., 1959.

Connell, W. F., *A History of Education in the Twentieth Century World*. New York: Teachers College Press, 1980.

Cremin, Lawrence, *The Transformation of the School*. New York: Alfred A. Knopf, Inc., 1961.

Gabert, Glen, *The Public Community College: The People's University*, Fastback 162. Bloomington, Indiana: The Phi Delta Kappa Educational Foundation, 1981.

Goodlad, John I., and Harold G. Shane, eds., *The Elementary School in the United States*, The Seventy-second Yearbook of the National Society for the Study of Education, Part II. Chicago: The University of Chicago Press, 1973, Section I, The Elementary School in Perspective.

Gutek, Gerald L., *Basic Education: A Historical Perspective*, Fastback 167. Bloomington, Indiana: Phi Delta Kappa Educational Foundation, 1981.

Karier, Clarence J., ed., *Shaping the American Educational State: 1900 to the Present*. New York: The Free Press, 1975.

MODULE
3
Philosophical Development of Education: General Background

Meaning and Relationship of Philosophy and Education / Epistemology / Metaphysics / Value Theory in Education

The first-edition version of this module was written by Leo Charles Daley, Jersey City State College. It has been revised and updated for this edition.

RATIONALE

In the age of visual immediacy, any effort to transfix and hold spellbound a student reading and studying a module entitled "Philosophical Development of Education" seems doomed at the very outset. Unfortunately, the average person is convinced that philosophy, whatever it might be, is every bit as dull as it is deep, and as useless as it is serious. Adding the world *education* merely compounds the problem. Sometimes people use the word *philosopher* as a social compliment because they consider the activity of philosophy to be so abstruse that it is beyond ordinary understanding. However profound the philosopher might be in examining and evaluating the educational scene, the work is often viewed as somewhat impractical because of the negative misconception about the educational philosopher.

Philosophy in its literal sense means *love of wisdom*. Love ought to imply pleasure, and wisdom certainly should suggest usefulness. In *As You Like It*, Shakespeare has Touchstone ask, "Hast any philosophy in thee, Shepherd?" Perhaps this question assumes that the philosopher is someone unconcerned with everyday practical affairs of life. In a sense, it is a fact that the philosopher is not concerned with the operations of the school boiler, the preparation of football posters, the quantification of the budget, or the working effectiveness of the sewerage system. However, the enormous power of education to form opinions, belief, and character is based upon some conception of what constitutes the values necessary to the achievement of a good life in a democratic society. The philosopher deals with the practical issues of human values: justice and peace, crime and violence, love and hate, freedom and happiness. He examines the prescriptions of democracy, fascism, and communism. The philosopher's evaluation includes every area of human thought and even encompasses the techniques of reasoning and the analysis of what is knowable. These activities form the basis for any educational enterprise. They determine the direction a school takes in producing an educated person.

Although it is relatively easy to demonstrate the practical value of educational philosophy, proving that its activity is pleasurable is another matter. However, keep in mind that the philosopher brings us to the essential questions which many may never have considered, or, may have considered but have forgotten about in the pursuit of living: Why are we alive? How shall we organize our brief lives to maximize our happiness? How may we contribute to the happiness of others? How should we enjoy life? How can one live a noble life in a society that often rewards corruption? There is pleasure, at least for this writer, in examining the perennial questions that have perplexed mankind in every age, for they lead to an understanding of one's existence and to self-knowledge. The educational philosopher applies these questions to education in order to determine the goals, curriculum, and methodology best designed to achieve a philosophical evaluation.

In this module we shall examine the basic problems of philosophy—the nature of knowledge and the problem of truth; the nature of man and his relationship to the universe; the meaning and organization of values; the criteria of moral values; the nature of beauty and art—in terms of educational implications and practices.

In so doing, we shall discuss five major areas of philosophy. Each area has important implications for the goals and practices of education.

1. Epistemology: branch of philosophy concerned with the problem of truth.
2. Metaphysics: branch of philosophy concerned with the nature of ultimate reality.
3. Axiology: branch of philosophy concerned with the problems ·of values, which includes
4. Ethics: branch of philosophy concerned with the problems of morality.
5. Aesthetics: branch of philosophy concerned with the problems of beauty and art.

The importance of these areas of philosophical problems stems from the fact that they do more than identify the content of philosophy itself. They have much to do with the resolution of educational standards, the content of education, the organization of the curriculum, teacher education, academic freedom, the nature of discipline and student expression, the aims of the school and its social relationships, and the teaching-learning process.

The general goal in studying this module should be to discover and understand the essential relationship between educational activities and the content problems of philosophy. Beyond this, it is hoped that your understanding of the content of the module will form the foundation for your future analysis of educational assumptions and problems within the school system where you are employed.

SPECIFIC OBJECTIVES

At the conclusion of your study of this module, it is expected that you will be able to

1. Define the following terms: *epistemology, intuition, authority, common sense, reason, controlled experience, necessary propositions, analytic propositions, synthetic propositions, a priori propositions, a posteriori propositions, coherence, correspondence, skepticism, pragmatism, perennialism, essentialism, progressivism, metaphysics, axiology, naturalism, instrumentalism, ethics,* and *aesthetics.*
2. Identify applications of perennialism and essentialism from the implications of epistemological thought.
3. Identify applications of progressivism from the implications of epistemological thought.
4. Identify the essential differences of idealism and naturalism on the mind-body problem and on the problem of human freedom.
5. Explain applications to education of the Idealist theory of man.
6. Explain applications to education of Materialistic theories of man.

7. Identify and explain applications of intrinsic-value theorists to educational activities.
8. Identify and explain applications of instrumental-value theorists to educational activities.

MODULE TEXT

Meaning and Relationship of Philosophy and Education

Literally, philosophy means the love of wisdom. The remarkable feature of philosophy is its effort to evaluate the sum total of human experience. Unlike any of the specific sciences, philosophy adds no new facts. It examines the facts provided by the scientist and analyzes the meaning, interpretation, significance, and value these facts hold for life. As the philosopher synthesizes the data of this examination, he formulates a meaningful picture that enables him to evaluate human experience. Therefore, most will accept the idea that philosophy is a systematic and logical examination of life so as to frame a system of general ideas by which the sum total of human experience may be evaluated in such a manner as to make the world more understandable. Thus, it becomes obvious that every rational person evaluates his life experiences. But the philosopher's search is systematic and determined. Conclusions must meet the rigid test of logic. The philosopher's findings provide a comprehensive interpretation of knowledge and truth; of the nature of man and man's relationship to the universe; of the significance of the ultimate constituency of the universe as it relates to the meaning of life; of consciousness; of freedom; and of the meaning of value, mortality, beauty, and art. These findings provide the educator with guidance in selecting goals, methods, curriculum, and the role of the school in society.

Although most educational theorists are content to view educational philosophy as an applied discipline, many regard philosophy more as an activity than as a statement of content propositions. John Dewey believed that philosophy is both a method of identifying problems and a source of suggestions about ways to handle these problems. This view increases the importance of philosophy to education. It reminds the philosopher that nothing is exempt from philosophical scrutiny, and it encourages us to remember that in this atmosphere of healthy philosophic doubt, conclusions must never be accepted dogmatically.

Epistemology

Epistemology is the branch of philosophy that inquires into the nature of knowledge and truth. The problems raised in this area are "What are the sources of knowledge?"; "How reliable are these sources?"; "What can one know?"; and "What is the nature of truth?"

If this is your first excursion into the realm of philosophy, it is highly possible that you have never seriously wrestled with questions such as these. Knowledge, for you, has just been there. Where it all came from and how you happen to have as much of it as you do has never seriously concerned you. You studied and learned what was presented in school. As you matured, you experienced other things on your own, and all of these things together constituted explanation enough for you about knowledge. It came in handy when you had it; frustration was rampant when it was lacking.

The reality of the situation about knowledge, however, is simple enough to grasp. While it "always has been there," it has come to us in a number of ways, and exists for us in its present form because of a tremendous amount of effort on the part of generations of thinkers and doers.

Sources of Knowledge

The sources of knowledge are (1) authority; (2) common sense; (3) intuition; (4) reason; (5) controlled experience.

Authority. A great amount of our knowledge is derived from the testimony of some authority. Such knowledge as we find in encyclopedias or in our best textbooks written by experts is usually regarded as authoritative. In school practice, we accept without question formulas for solving certain mathematical problems, and we memorize tables for decimalizing English measurements. We could check the accuracy of these formulas personally, but we elect to accept them in order to save time and effort. After all, they have been vouched for by authorities in mathematics for a long time. Modern civilization would be unable to function without authoritative knowledge of this sort. Yet philosophical problems arise concerning the validity of the information upon which we base our conclusions. These problems tend to become more complex as factual information proliferates. One must ask, what are the criteria by which an authority exists? On whose say-so is this source of information authoritative? Thus, the act of suspending one's critical faculties in accepting the veracity of an authoritative source becomes a matter of serious concern.

When the authority is religious in nature, this problem becomes unique. If faith is the basis of knowledge, many additional questions arise. What assurance has one that the assertion or revelation is indeed from God and not from a human source? Even when one assumes that God did reveal something, we are left with the problem of interpretation: How can we be certain that God's message is understood; and if it is understood, how can we be certain it is communicated accurately?

In education there are many who stress the importance of authority in learning. In their view, a student who is left to his own interests and felt problems may neglect the essential knowledge derived from past authorities. They insist that this knowledge ought to be organized and presented to students by the teacher. Those who oppose this viewpoint stress the limitations of knowledge derived from an authority, because an authority can only provide one with information that must be tested before it can be accepted as truth.

Common Sense. The second source of knowledge we shall discuss is common sense. Common-sense knowledge is bound directly to the customs and the traditions with which one is associated. One should not confuse common sense with good sense. Every system of educational philosophy agrees that the development of good sense—clear thinking and sound judgment—is one of the most important achievements of a good teacher. Common knowledge in this context consists of that which everybody in a given society knows: for example, to walk under a ladder is bad luck; "If you stuff a cold, you'll starve a fever"; or, "You can't lick city hall!" Such knowledge may be dangerous because, in the philosophical sense, these beliefs and assertions have not been verified in a way which warrants the conclusion that they are accurate and dependable.

Intuition. Our third source of knowledge is intuition. It occurs on what psychologists call the *subliminal level*, beneath the "threshold of consciousness." It is connected intimately with feeling and emotion, and constrasts with the logical processes usually associated with thinking at the conscious level. As people, we see "in a sudden flash of insight" that something is the case. Intuition is defined as "the direct and immediate apprehension by a knowing subject of itself, of its conscious state, of other minds, of an external world, of universals, of values or of rational truths."[1]

Through intuition, a person makes sudden moves and arrives at accurate conclusions without having had either previous exposure to a topic or experience in the area.

The role of intuition as a source of knowledge is debated hotly among philosophers. The proposition that one can grasp with immediate certainty conscious knowledge of the things, events, and people of the external world, the values and universal rational truths of reality, without utilizing the senses, implies the existence of a nonphysical experience that gives direct insight to truth. This immediate knowledge carries with it an absolute conviction of truth. According to this view, the intellect apprehends the knowledge. It does not think or reflect to reach a conclusion. A belief in intuition causes many philosophical problems regarding its interpretation and usefulness.

Many think intuition is acceptable as a source of knowledge if it is viewed as a subconscious process in a person who intuits in a field in which he is well experienced. Philosophers with a mystical inclination root intuition in the higher levels of the soul. To them, intuition, then, is seen as the source of absolute truth. It is obvious that one's position on this question affects one's views of human nature and learning, and as a consequence it must affect the aims of education and the values stressed by the teacher.

Reason. When knowledge is derived through a series of inferences that connect ideas consciously so as to arrive at judgments or conclusions, the process is called *discursive reasoning*. Sometimes we call it *logical thinking*,

---

[1] Dagobert D. Runes, ed., *Dictionary of Philosophy* (New York: Philosophical Library, 1961), p. 149.

even though it involves more than the form employed in the thinking process. Through reasoning, we derive universally valid judgments that are consistent with one another. When regarding theories about the nature of reason, we are faced with a philosophical problem. One group of philosophers, the Rationalists, insists that reason reveals a capacity (or faculty) of the mind itself to know the truth. To these philosophers, the source of knowledge is in the mind and not in the senses. They acknowledge the contribution of the senses to knowledge in the form of bare facts and isolated impressions. But they believe that the intellect interprets and organizes these bits and pieces of information into what we can call reliable and significant knowledge. Empiricists oppose this view. They believe that the reasoning process is only the way in which a person directs and organizes his sensations. According to this position, the source of knowledge is found in the senses, not in the mind. Without the senses, the intellect could do nothing. By seeing, hearing, smelling, feeling, and tasting, we form our composite of the world around us.

The Rationalist rejects the idea that the mind is passive, a blank slate receiving sensed impressions. This viewpoint considers that the mind is the active agent which selects, organizes, synthesizes, and then conceptualizes what is known. For instance, hearing the song of a mockingbird does not augment or diminish one's knowledge. The sound is not knowledge but the raw material of knowledge. It is only in the internal mental processes, where knowledge is derived, that one can distinguish the song of the mockingbird from the clang of the school gong. The mind then, is a thing in itself.

Empiricists insist that knowledge cannot exist in the reason; it is found in sense experience alone. Reason is merely the way one thinks about one's sensations. No reality beyond experience exists. The mind is functional. It is a special activity of an organism that selects and organizes experiences to resolve problems.

The conflict between rationalism and empiricism has far-reaching effects in education. Rationalists demand that the mind be developed. They insist that we "think things through." Therefore, education must have content or essential knowledge, and the child must learn to reason properly in a teacher-centered school. Generally, the Empiricists consider it more important for the pupil to know *how* to think than to know *what* to think. They caution us to "look and see." Education must relate to the experiences of the child. It should be centered on the individual, whole child, for knowledge is simply a by-product of the educational experience.

Controlled Experience. Science has grown rapidly. By means of critical, exact, and precise analyses of sense observations, it has advanced knowledge by accumulating a body of facts in a variety of fields. Scientists employ a variety of methods consistent with the aims and limits of their respective fields of inquiry. Moreover, the success of the procedures for controlling experimentation has especially recommended their use in education. These procedures involve the following elements:

1. Identify the problem.
2. Gather data that are relevant to the resolution of the problem.

3. Reason, organize, analyze, and infer suitable solutions.
4. Formulate a testable hypothesis.
5. Test: analyze and classify in a controlled design that is precise, complete, predictable, useful, and effective.
6. Solution arrived at that is reproducible, accurate, open, and precise.

Types of Propositions

In analyzing the nature of knowing, philosophers distinguish four types of propositions. Once clarified, these propositions provide us with an intelligent basis for examining the question, "can we know anything that can be said to be true without sense experience?" They are (1) necessary or analytic propositions; (2) synthetic propositions; (3) a priori propositions; (4) a posteriori propositions.

Necessary Propositions. Necessary propositions consist of statements that become immediately evident when asserted. Early philosophers called them *self-evident.* Immanuel Kant called then *analytic*, because the statement produces no new knowledge. In a necessary proposition, the predicate of the statement is already contained in the subject. "Things equal to the same thing are equal to each other," is an example of a necessary proposition.

Synthetic Propositions. Synthetic propositions consist of statements that contain predicates related to the subject through empirical verification; their truth is not internal to themselves but is discovered afterwards; for example, "The teacher carries an umbrella." This statement produces knowledge. It can be verified empirically by looking at the teacher.

A Priori Propositions. A priori propositions consist of statements that are asserted prior to or before the predicate is verified empirically. These propositions contain knowledge that is self-evident. They are principles which, once understood, are recognized to be true (such as $2 + 2 = 4$; the old maid is a woman) and do not require proof through observation, experience, or experiment. When we grasp the truth of these types of propositions, our minds make a jump from the actual instances in which the truth of the propositions has been verified to the realization of the truth of all instances both verified and unverified. Some rationalists consider such statements valid when they are derived through intuition.

A Posteriori Propositions. A posteriori propositions consist of statements containing predicates that are related to the subject after empirical verification. They are very similar to synthetic propositions, and the terms may be used synonymously. A posteriori propositions contain knowledge that is based upon experience and observation. A statement such as, "The air is calm today," is not true by virtue of the meaning of the terms "air," "calm," and "today"; it is true only if the statement asserts what is the case.

Rationalists versus Empiricists. The significance of the types of propositions may be seen in the conflict between Rationalists and Empiricists. The resolution of this conflict is essential to the development of a consistent philosophy of education. The Rationalist will argue that some assertions can be accepted as true prior to any empirical verification, and that these assertions provide us with knowledge. Some of these assertions form the basis by which one may reason to additional truths; an example is, "I think; therefore, I am." Empiricists reject this type of thinking. They state that if an assertion cannot be verified empirically, it is without meaning. Furthermore, they insist that such propositions produce no new knowledge. A "self-evident" statement is merely a tautology; that is, it says the same thing twice.

Theories of Truth

There are four major theories concerning the nature of truth: (1) coherence; (2) correspondence; (3) pragmatism; (4) skepticism.

Coherence. The theory of coherence (or logical consistency) asserts that truth is a property of a body of ideas. Any individual idea is true when it is consistent with—that is, coheres with—this whole body of propositions. Each particular idea, when true, forms a fragmentary part of a vast whole that embodies every truth. The nature of this whole is mind-like and therefore nonphysical. This is the position of *idealism*, a system of philosophy that describes ultimate reality as thought or spirit. According to Idealists, the entire universe is an expression of intelligence and will. The ultimate substance must be Mind. In the act of knowing, one thinks the thoughts and purposes of this absolute, eternal, spiritual reality. One cannot have knowledge in and of oneself alone.

It is, according to this view, the *mind* and not *matter* that thinks, perceives, experiences, and has meanings. These meanings are true if they stand the test of logical consistency. A school ought to be "idea centered." The aim of education must be to increase knowledge of the truth and to achieve wisdom in applying truth so as to develop the pupil's will to perfection and to cultivate personal total growth.

Correspondence. The theory of correspondence proposes the notion that truth exists when the idea in a subject's mind is in accord (corresponds) with the object it describes. *Realism* is the system of philosophy affirming this theory. Realists assume that a subject's sense experience reports a true description of the objects of nature, once this correspondence is verified. Thus, truth is discoverable. Realists generally tend to stress the importance of factual information in education.

Pragmatism. Pragmatism affirms that the meaning or truth of anything is found in its consequences. Every meaningful assertion can be tested. If the idea proves worthwhile, then the external facts agree with the idea. Truth, then, is something that happens to an idea. It is created, not discovered. No absolute or unchanging truth exists. Truth is relative and changing, for it is related to individual problems and experiences in a changing environment. Charles Peirce and William James developed the theory of pragmatism. Subsequently, John Dewey modified it to what is known as *Instrumentalism*, which stresses the social consequences of experimentally verifying the consequences of an idea. As a theory, pragmatism has had a far-reaching impact on American public education. Our current accent on individualism, problem solving, and democracy are largely attributable to pragmatism and instrumentalism.

Skepticism. Skepticism denies the possibility of ever achieving truth. Because our knowledge is confined to sense information, it is never possible to obtain a complete, true knowledge of the objective world. Most skeptics insist on following scientific procedures in the search for knowledge. This knowledge, they believe, is probable, but never absolutely certain.

Educational Implications

The question of inquiry and learning is central to the educational enterprise. Epistemological differences lead to two general but extremely important differences among educators. Some consider knowledge to be power, and others view knowledge as a by-product of thinking.

Knowledge as Power. According to those who view knowledge as power, the fundamental purpose of education is to achieve knowledge. Teaching in order to impart knowledge is essential if the teacher is ever to make it possible for pupils to discover truth. In short, the subject matter is of value in itself. It contains the body of knowledge that enables the pupil to discover the truth of the natural environment, and it provides the basis for the cultural and personal growth of the ideal person.

Generally, this view has represented the thinking of the majority of traditional thinkers, and has been known as Essentialism and Perennialism.

Knowledge As a By-product. Instrumentalists, on the other hand, believe that knowledge is only a by-product of thinking. To them, the sole aim of education is to enable the pupil to know how to think. What the student thinks, they say, is not essential to the educational task. According to their position, all thinking begins when an individual *feels* a problem. It is then that the person formulates plans of actions or ideas to determine what may solve the problem. Therefore, lessons should be designed to solve problems. Knowledge has no value in itself. It merely provides the data in the problem-solving process. This is the position of the school of educational theory called *Progressivism.*

Position of Perennialism and Essentialism. The Perennialist and Essentialist tradition is a long one in the history of education. It includes the philosophical systems of realism, idealism, and scholasticism. Although many major differences exist between these giant systems of thought, the labels *Perennialism* and *Essentialism* are useful in evaluating the educational implications arising out of a consideration of epistemology. Perennialism assumes an innate mental power that is developed by reflecting upon reoccurring intellectual problems of man. Essentialism assumes that it is the chief responsibility of the school to transmit the cultural heritage of the past.

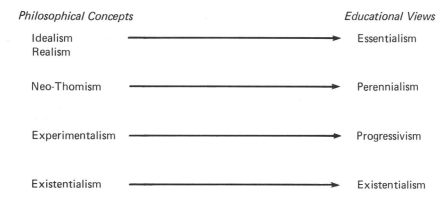

Philosophical Concepts   Educational Views

Idealism ————————————————————————▶ Essentialism
Realism

Neo-Thomism ————————————————————▶ Perennialism

Experimentalism ————————————————▶ Progressivism

Existentialism —————————————————▶ Existentialism

FIGURE 3-1. Relationships Between Philosophical Concepts and Educational Views.

Adult Interest. In Perennialist dogma, although the good teacher must not ignore the psychological factor of motivation in learning, the task in motivation is to raise the level of interest and induce the pupil to study the intellectual content of education. It is a mistake to assume, as Progressivists do, that the child should determine the content of education.

Teacher-Centered. Perennialists and Essentialists assume the schooling should be teacher-centered. The essential duties of the teacher in the teacher-centered classroom, according to their belief, consist in organizing materials, knowing the subject, directing clearly, stimulating interest, providing opportunities for students to achieve success, giving encouragement, controlling behavior, demonstrating necessary facts, transmitting knowledge, and evaluating pupils' learning.

Discipline. Because they believe pupils to be immature and ignorant of the value of essential knowledge, Perennialists and Essentialists stress the need for discipline. Because the learning process involves efforts that are difficult at times, demanding of the pupil perseverance, control, and self-discipline, the teacher must encourage desirable work habits and a sense of responsibility on the part of the pupil. Using the best methods available, the teacher must serve as an example to the pupils, and hold pupils always to the need of disciplined effort.

Authority. Perennialists and Essentialists insist that the immature pupil needs adult instruction to gain essential knowledge. If the pupils are left to their own interests, and if, because of following the pupils' whims, lessons are allowed to become disorganized rap sessions, the pupils will remain ignorant and immature. A lesson must be highly structured and lead to a conclusion in order to be productive.

Essential Knowledge. Perennialists and Essentialists reject the notion that truth is something determined by each individual. Soliciting random opinions from ignorant pupils only adds to this misconception of truth, in their opinion. Because they believe that truth does exist in nature and in the universe, they assume that it is our task to discover and to pass on this truth. Consequently, they insist that the repository of truths accumulated throughout civilized history provides the content of education. It is our cultural heritage.

Rational Thinking. In the Perennialist-Essentialist view, thinking occurs in an orderly and systematic manner. Therefore, it is the duty of the teacher to organize the subject material in such a way as to foster good habits of thought. Effective thought, they say, is never haphazard. It is facilitated by a body of content that stimulates reasoning. Because this is so, the teacher must stress recall, observation, effective reasoning, comparison of ideas, and the inference of new possibilities. In their thinking, "Observe, Remember, and Compare" is an excellent educational motto. Finally, they assert that curriculum content must be arranged sequentially so as to provide the pupil with a logical development of knowledge.

Position of Progressivism and Social Reconstructionism. Progressivism in education is a phenomenon of the twentieth century influenced largely by the philosophy of John Dewey. Epistemological thought is the foundation of their philosophy. Progressivists include the important systems of pragmatism, instrumentalism or experimentalism, and reconstructionism. Although little has been written by Existentialists and Analytic philosophers in education, their philosophies have some similarities in their respective emphasis upon individual experience and the relativity of truth.

In general, we can say that as applied to education, progressivism emphasizes (1) child-centered education; (2) human thinking as the core of education; (3) socialization and democratization; (4) the method of problem solving; (5) individual differences; and (6) self-discipline.

Child-Centered Education. Progressivists stress the importance of each child's learning how to think as a whole human being. One's social-emotional character and intellectual development are both of equal importance in natural growth. The school ought not to stress any one area of development at the expense of another. Progressivists criticize Essentialists for their alleged overemphasis upon intellectual matters. As the person improves in thinking, effectiveness is increased as an adapting organism in a changing environment.

Human Thinking. In Progressivist dogma, thinking is the process by which man adjusts to a changing environment. It involves felt needs, recognition of a problem, plans of action, the collection of information or data, sense-verification, and individual and social utility. Human ideas arise in experience and are nothing more than plans of action which enable the organism to adjust satisfactorily to the environment. Because this is so, Progressivists hold that education must relate to the experiences of the child. Experiential background is the beginning point fundamental to future learning.

All knowledge, they insist, is derived through experience. This experience is more than mere activity. It involves aspects of doing and undergoing. While experiencing, the pupil must both act upon and enjoy the consequences of the activity. The connection between the active and passive elements in experience is the measure of the experiential value. Therefore, to be effective, schools must avoid passive and inflexible methods of teaching. They must make provision for individual differences based upon each child's different experiences, needs, and goals.

Socialization and Democratization. According to Progressivists, when experiencing, the pupil interacts with the environment. In one sense, the individual *is* the environment. In another sense, the person affects and modifies the environment through interaction. In still another sense, this interaction with the environment modifies him. The consequences of the person's actions have important implications for social improvement. Socialization is therefore an important educational goal in Progressivist thinking.

Briefly, their argument is that the democratic form of government contributes to individual and social growth. Each person is improved through the interaction of free and equal citizens. Therefore, the school should organize its curriculum in an individualized, problem-centered, need-related program so as to foster individual growth; and the school should also relate curriculum-content to current social problems, and thus socialize education. By making the school democratic, Progressivists hope to give pupils experience in democratic living so that they will be good citizens of our democracy now and in the future.

The Method of Problem Solving. According to the Progressivists, the subject matter and the content of education have no value in themselves; these serve only to provide information and data to the pupils who may find some need or use of them in solving problems. In their scheme, the methods or processes—that is, the experiences—are what matter. Consequently, because one learns by solving problems, teaching method should be based on the solving of individual problems. The subject matter is merely a means to be used in solving problems, and knowledge of the subject results only as a by-product of the problem-solving experience.

Individual Differences. Each pupil is an individual with unique differences. It follows then, Progressivists tell us, that an essential task of the school is to provide for these differences. The educator must realize that experiential backgrounds vary in each pupil. Opportunities must be provided to assist individual growth. Pupils should proceed at their own rates, as determined by their maturation, intelligence,· and needs, toward their own personal goals.

Discipline. Because Progressivists believe that truth is determined by its consequences and verified in social interaction, they deny the existence of any ultimate or absolute standard by which to guide or judge human actions. In their thinking, no standard ought to be imposed upon the pupil. Instead, discipline should always be internal or subjective. In other words, discipline exists when the pupil understands what must be done and is moved to undertake the action quickly, using the requisite means necessary. The teacher ought to encourage the pupil to undertake actions only after careful deliberation of the consequences of the actions. Discipline includes the willingness of the pupil to endure in an intelligently induced course of action, even in the face of obstacles.

Educational Innovation

It does not follow logically that any system of philosophy must be applied to education in a specific way. Rather, a philosophic system gives the individual a frame of reference by which to evaluate education. Certainly the psychological outlook of a teacher on the nature of man and reality must have some consistent consequences in his approach to teaching, and, to some degree, the outlook must have been influenced by his philosophic position. Although proponents of various philosophies may view the goals of education differently, they may all agree, with varying degrees of emphasis and enthusiasm, that certain innovative methods are acceptable if they seem to be effective in producing learning.

Metaphysics

Metaphysics is the branch of philosophy that examines the problems of ultimate reality. It asks, "What is the nature of the universe, of life, of mind and its products, the freedom of mankind, the existence of God?" Two major points of difference emerge in education as a consequence of metaphysical positions: (1) man is essentially spiritual in nature; and (2) man is a material organism that is one with nature.

Man is Essentially Spiritual in Nature

Philosophers who affirm the spiritual nature of man usually rest their case on the idea that the mind is substantially different from matter. Although they do not all agree on just what *mind* is, proponents of the position have usually concluded that mind is an active, immaterial something that receives and uses sensation, images, ideas, and so on, in order to form concepts and ideas, to remember, and so forth. To many philosophers the *mind* is synonymous with the *soul*. Others agree that all of reality is reducible to mental states, and they therefore assume that the reality basic to all entities is immaterial. Thus Bishop Berkeley, the eighteenth-century English Idealist, inferred that objects and events were actually ideas. Of course, although they would not all accept Berkeley's idea, generally Idealists and Scholastics, and some Realists, agree on the basic immateriality of reality.

Educational Implications. This position—that man is essentially a spiritual being—has numerous implications for education and educators. On the whole, philosophers supporting this position agree that education affects eternity. Furthermore, they hold that because man is essentially spiritual, human nature is unchanging and the mind is free. Their beliefs have caused them to take rather definite positions on such matters as the aim of education, standards, the curriculum, mental discipline, higher education, academic freedom, and educational opportunity.

Aim of Education. There can be only one basic educational aim if one accepts this position. Whereas the principle which underlies and unifies all education is the spiritual nature of man, education must aim at self-realization, self-knowledge, and self-development. The ultimate goal of all education must, of course, be self-knowledge, which is the beginning of wisdom.

Absolute Standards. Wisdom and virtue are that part of human nature constituting the ultimate aim of a person. Educators who hold this position are inclined to see values as absolute, fixed, objective qualities intrinsic in what is being valued. According to this way of looking at values, a thing is right or it is wrong; it is good or bad; it is up to standard or not up to standard. Values do not change. Value judgments are as true today as they were in centuries past, and no truer. Thus, to study the classics has value because their authors' clarification of values and standards of behavior is as valid today as it was in the past; moreover, these values and standards are presented in inimitable literary style. In teaching, the unchangeable ideals of intellectual and moral development must never for any reason be sacrificed.

Curriculum. In accordance with the spiritual nature of man, the curriculum ought to be designed so that it liberates the mind and prepares one for his ultimate end. A knowledge of essential subjects is necessary. The fundamentals of reading, writing, and arithmetic are instrumental in the development of the individual. The fundamental subjects dealing with human values ought to be the ultimate goal of education. These subjects are what we have come to call the liberal, or liberating, arts. Such a curriculum is superior to vocational curricula. Vocational subjects aim at training and ought not to be called educational, because the term *educational* should be reserved for subjects that are liberating. Consequently, philosophers of this persuasion are inclined to favor a traditional, unchanging curriculum for everyone.

Mental Discipline. Although the mind is an active spiritual "something," it is subject to discipline. Evidently the mind can be trained, and some subjects can train it better than others.

The habits educational leaders must foster in pupils are forethought, concentration, industry, alertness, observation, memory, comparison ability, and self-discipline. Certain disciplines help to develop these desirable intellectual and moral habits. According to this position, curriculum-builders should select those studies that provide the most vigorous training for the mind.

Higher Education. As one might expect, theorists of the spiritual persuasion have been particuarly interested in higher education. In their view, the college must be completely free of all vested interests. The administration should be in the hands of scholars and professionals who are not controlled by public whim, political pressures, or monetary interests. The curriculum must include the humanities, the arts, and sciences, because they believe mathematics and science lead the individual to understand nature, the arts enrich life, and the humanities are the most liberating of all studies in the curriculum. Vocational skills, including teacher training, ought therefore to be based upon a solid education in the humanities, arts, and sciences.

Academic Freedom. Because of their belief that mind is spiritual, these thinkers are very concerned about academic freedom. In their judgment, freedom in teaching and learning is essential to the free development of the individual. It must exist at every level of education.

Educational Opportunity. Because they believe that it is important to train the mind as vigorously as possible, these educators insist that everyone ought to be provided with the opportunity to develop his potential through education. It is evident that individuals vary in abilities. When it is evident that a student has arrived at the highest level of his ability, it is time to train him in some useful vocational skill. Education must never be watered down to the lowest common denominator.

Man As a Material Organism

Naturalists, Materialists, Experimentalists, Pragmatists, and some Realists believe that man is a material organism that is one with nature. They find no evidence for the existence of anything spiritual in man or nature. Man has evolved as a material part of nature; an organism that must make satisfactory adjustments in order to survive. Obviously, their beliefs about education are in many respects different from those we have just discussed.

Education for Living. To these educators the nature of man can be understood only in the context of nature. His welfare and happiness in a changing material world are the starting point of education. One must educate pupils for a happy material existence. "Education for living" is one of the catch phrases common with this type of educator.

Empirical Method. According to educational theorists of this persuasion, there exists no set of absolutes to guide man. Truth is determined in the test of life. The educational approach must not confine itself to any preconceived set of subjects that are supposed to contain essential truths. Individuals must be taught to think creatively and critically.

Whereas these educators hold that there is no set of absolutes to guide man, they maintain that truth can be determined only in the test of life. It may even be that truth is changeable. What is true today may not be true tomorrow—because of changes in the circumstances. One cannot really tell what is true until one has tested it empirically, and so one cannot specify any subject matter as being essential to the curriculum. Certainly the educational approach must not confine itself to any preconceived set of subjects that are supposed to contain essential truths. Perhaps the best curriculum is one that is continually being revised. In any case, as we have already pointed out, the curriculum and methods should be so arranged that individuals are taught to think creatively and critically.

Social Communication. According to the beliefs of educators in this camp, the matter of social isolation is pivotal. An individual cannot be isolated from society. One may be changed by society and in turn affect the society of which one is a part. Education must concern itself with social goals. Education must aim at socialization as well as thinking skills. Its role as a socializing agent is one of the things that makes the school a necessary part of society.

Science. Advocates of this position assign science a greater role in education than do those who think of man as essentially spiritual. In their view, science enables man to manipulate and control the environment. It contributes greatly to the improvement of his physical comfort and social needs by increasing knowledge of the physical world. The sciences are extremely valuable areas of knowledge and should be given higher priority than other subjects.

Curriculum. Pragmatists stress the practical importance of science. So much do they value it that they give it a high place in the curriculum. To them it provides an opportunity for the individual to experience for himself how things appear to work. Realists, however, give science a more central place in education. They stress as ends rather than means the logical, systematic mastery of the facts of the physical world. Not only do Realists and

Pragmatists plan more emphasis on science than do Idealists, but they are more likely to emphasize the practical, useful realms of education. Furthermore, they tend to believe that the curriculum should be flexible rather than fixed; and should emphasize provisions for individual differences rather than common content for all students.

Relativity. In the Pragmatists' view, almost everything is relative—not absolute, and not fixed. Man is capable of knowing and appreciating beauty and of arriving at a satisfactory and worthwhile system of ethical relationships with his fellow man through living and experiencing. Human experience, and not an absolute code, is the basis of ethical and aesthetic values. Schools, therefore, should help their pupils develop their own aesthetic and moral appreciation and understanding so that each one can formulate his own code by which to live.

Aims of Education. In this pragmatic view, the central aim of education should be to teach pupils to think rationally, independently, and well. Because the function of human intelligence is to solve problems and to guide one's behavior in order to satisfy needs and aspirations, education must stress the student's development of thinking skills and effectiveness in social interaction.

Value Theory in Education

The branch of philosophy concerned with the general problem of values—that is, the nature, origin, and permanence of values—is called *Axiology*. Most philosophers include, as subdivisions of Axiology, *Ethics*, the branch of philosophy that is concerned with morals; and *Aesthetics*, the branch that is concerned with the problems of beauty and art. We shall do so in this module and discuss them all under the heading of *value theory*.

Value theory underlies every single educational activity. Any statement of aims constitutes a statement of what its authors consider to be of value in life as applied to the educational process. Manifestly, the content of education in any society is derived from a belief of what is good in education. The curricula, methods, and materials that school administrators and teachers choose to introduce into their schools and classes are all determined by their value outlook.

In order to understand the educational conflict in value theory, especially as it affects moral behavior and the role of art appreciation in education, we arbitrarily divide the groups of theorists into two camps: (1) those who affirm that values are *intrinsic*, that is, absolute and permanent, and that values are arranged in an order from highest to lowest—the higher values being determined and discovered by human reasons; and (2) those who affirm that all values are *instrumental* in nature, that is, values are useful, constantly changing, equal, and nonfactual.

Theory of Intrinsic Values

Let us now look more closely at the theorists' view that values are intrinsic, especially as this viewpoint pertains to educational aims, the curriculum, teaching-learning, and the role of the school in society.

Education Aims.   If values are intrinsic, they must reside in the nature of man. The aim of the school, then, should be to provide pupils with the essential knowledge that will enable them to live a successful natural and spiritual lives. To meet this aim, education must give supreme priority to the development of the rational potential within each pupil. Educators must stress the importance of the development of both the intellect and the will. Properly developed, the will will enable one to act habitually in controlling his emotions and passions, according to this view.

Curriculum.   Whereas the goal of education is the development of the rational potential of the pupil, education must include those subjects that assist in the intellectual development of the pupil. Because they contain the accumulated wisdom of civilized man, the humanities ought to be given pre-eminence. However, science and mathematics must not be neglected. Although they are less important as instrumental subjects (serving a useful purpose), they are important in preparing the individual for the practical concerns of life. Vocational training becomes an important concern only after one has been educated.

Teaching-Learning.   Lessons should be taught as realistically as possible. The teacher ought to provide as many real experiences as possible, and follow the principles of the psychology of learning. The factual content must be organized systematically, proceeding from the simple to the more complex. The pupil is expected individually to understand, memorize, recite, and, in group drills, to explain, compare, and discuss. Habits of study, concentration, and perseverance must be encouraged consistently. Because man is imitative, the teacher ought to provide opportunities to discuss virtuous acts and lives.

Role of School in Society. Proponents of the position that values are intrinsic insist that the role of the school is to interpret and pass on to young people the accumulated knowledge, wisdom, and tradition of the society; it is not the function of the schools to change society. To fulfill its role, pupils must be educated to live within the values held important in their society. It must be understood that the school must remain aloof from politics. The task of the school is to educate its pupils. It is not the only agent of society, and it should leave other roles to the other agents.

Theory of Instrumental Values

In many ways, the educational views of the proponents of the instrumental nature of values are diametrically opposed to those we have just presented. We shall now examine the same aspects of education—educational aims, curriculum, teaching-learning, and the role of the school in society—from this new point of view.

Educators who hold that values are instrumental are likely to be what have come to be called *progressive educators*. The Progressivists consider values in terms of their social results. To them, values are determined by an ever changing society; therefore, values are not fixed. Ethical behavior is based upon social agreements and law, and may change as the society changes. The criteria for a society's values are the standards of the majority in that society. Behavior is evaluated in terms of the conventions of the society. There is no such thing as an absolute standard of right or wrong, or good or bad. What seems to work in a society is considered to be good or valuable—at least for now, or for a particular purpose. What does not work is considered to be bad or worthless.

Educational Aims.   From the Progressivist standpoint, the major aim of the school should be to teach pupils how to think. Knowing how to think in order to make good decisions will make it possible for students to cope with life's problems and to steer themselves onto the course for the good life. To carry out this objective, schools must reorganize pupils' experiences in order to enhance their meaning, thereby enabling them to direct more fully and more competently the course of their own future experiences.

Curriculum.   Progressivist theory tells us that knowledge has *instrumental* value, that it is useful for the pupils to resolve problems arising as a result of their felt needs. Problem solving is not an end in itself; it is a process by which pupils learn how to think clearly. The primary educational objective (to learn how to think) is not really an end; it is a means by which the individual learns to live intelligently. In fact, there are actually no ends in education, because education *is* effective living. And so, the aims of education are not ends but means to effective living. Education is life itself; therefore, the curriculum too must be life itself. It cannot be limited to the academic. A problem-centered, pupil-centered, experienced-centered curriculum featuring such approaches as shared activities, critical evaluations, pupil involvement in decision making, community service projects, and the like, in which the school is, in effect, a miniature society, may bring about the desired result.

Teaching-Learning.   The heart of the progressive approach to teaching and learning is problem solving. For this method to be successful, it is essential that each pupil accept a problem as his own. If pupils are to learn, they must have an active role in selecting, defining, working on, and evaluating their activities in resolving the problem. The teacher must never impose solutions. Neither should the teacher impose ethical codes or standards of behavior; these should arise out of the social situation and the pupil's evaluating of his own behavior.

Role of the School in Society.   The school as seen by Progressivists is an integral part of society; it reflects all the social problems. The school must therefore emphasize social living and must assume an active role in improving society. Both within the schoolroom and without, it should face up to the problems that society too must face. In short, the progressive school must not be an ivory tower; it must take an active role in community affairs.

Many educators who view the nature of value as being instrumental are inclined to agree with George S. Counts[2], who, when he was asked, "Can the schools build a new social order?" replied, "Yes," Progressivist educators think the school should dare at least to do its share in building the social order.

Conclusion

Philosophy is a systematic and logical examination of life so as to frame a system of general ideas by which to evaluate the sum total of human experience. It is useful for providing educators with a basis for selecting educational goals, methods and materials of teaching, curricula, and the school's role in society. Philosophy is divided into five branches: *Epistemology,* the study of the nature of knowledge and truth; *Metaphysics*, the study of the nature of reality; *Axiology*, the study of values; *Ethics*, the study of morality and right conduct; and *Aesthetics*, the study of the beautiful in art and nature.

In each of these fields philosophers have divided into camps promoting specific theoretical positions.

From the educational point of view, these camps can be divided into two categories, Essentialist-Perennialists and Progressivists. In general, the Essentialist-Perennialists favor the traditional subject-centered approach to education; the Progressivists, the liberal pupil-centered approach.

Any individual who enters education must recognize that in the pluralistic American society, there will be many views regarding what constitutes sound educational practice. The criticisms made of certain educational programs need not necessarily be taken as evidence that something is basically "wrong" with the practice. Rather, they should be analyzed to determine if the objection stems only from the fact that the critic comes from a different philosophical orientation from those who support the existing school program. When objections to programs result in changes, it suggests that the philosophical orientation of a former minority has captured the support of a great many people and now represents a majority position. Professional educators need some understanding of the various philosophical orientations, not only to supply support for the positions they take in programs and policy changes, but also so that they can understand the points of departure of critics calling for change.

As you add to your knowledge about the various schools of educational thought, you will find that your ability to cope with the various kinds of criticism of the school will be considerably enlarged.

SUGGESTED READING

Barrow, Robin, *The Philosophy of Schooling*. Somerset, New Jersey: The Halsted Press, 1981.

[2] George S. Counts, *Dare the School Build a New Social Order?* (New York: The John Day Company, Inc., 1932).

erally? Is this the same reason that some teachers are so in favor of these views? Are you? Will you be able to pick and choose among the views when you begin your career? How will you do so without confusing those around you and perhaps yourself?

3. It is often claimed that schools try to do (or are forced to try) too much and that, as a result, they do a poor job of doing what they are really supposed to do. Another view is that schools as institutions of society do not do nearly enough in the way of social service, and that they could reasonably be expected to greatly expand their sphere of concern in meeting human needs at the local community level. Where do you stand on this issue? Prepare a rationale for your position, and try it out on your friends.

4. Can "how to do it" in-service workshops ever be very effective with teachers who do not embrace the educational philosophy on which they are based? Prepare several dilemmas based on this concept (that is, methods and practices used by teachers that are incompatible with their philosophical position, and pose them for resolution to your group. Can you resolve these contradictory positions for yourself?

5. Schools are often intimidated by parents and others who wish to censor instructional material. Should schools remove from the library books that some parents find objectionable? Do the same principles apply in selecting material for required reading (that is, textbooks) as apply in selecting optional reading such as library books? How would you resolve the conflict of values inherent in the parents' right—and responsibility—to guide the lives of their children, and the child's right to learn, and the teacher's right—and responsibility—to teach?

6. Much has been written urging schools to serve as agents of social change. Yet schools were created by society to transmit the cultural heritage. These two missions appear to be in conflict with each other. Can you provide some insights as to how—or if—schools can function in these two roles?

7. How do you account for discipline and punishment being so severe in Colonial schools? Did your teachers in high school appear to be functioning on the same wavelength as the more moderate Colonial teachers? Which "wavelength" will you opt for in your classroom?

8. List some of the ways in which early concepts of education have influenced educational practices today. Do you endorse their use in contemporary schools? Which ones, if any, will you make efforts to change when you start your career?

MODULE
4

Philosophical Development of Education: Major Approaches

Idealism / Realism / Experimentalism and Pragmatism / Scholasticism / Perennialism, Essentialism and Progressivism / Logical Analysis / Existentialism / Communism / Democracy and Education / Problems of Excellence in Education

The first-edition version of this module was written by Leo Charles Daley, Jersey City State College. It has been revised and updated for this edition.

RATIONALE

As John Dewey said, philisophy can never be defined in terms of subject matter. His position makes sense, because the purpose of philosophy is to identify problems and suggest ways of handling these problems. Because education is not distinct from the total life situation, the educational philosopher cannot be bound by the limitations of subject content; he must be free to examine any problem that has social significance. The educational philosopher must explain education, criticize its practice, and offer suggested solutions to problems by means of critical and reflective thought.

In this module, the philosophers are grouped for convenience into systems of philosophy. Although there are many differences among philosophers in any given system, basically they tend to agree in general on questions dealing with the good life, the nature of man, the nature of truth, and the role of social institutions in society. These agreements may be applied to the problems confronting the educator: the objectives of education, the nature of the learner, the curriculum, and the role of the school in society.

We shall limit our philosophical inquiry to the foregoing problems, and shall study the solutions proposed by different schools or systems of philosophies. Underlying the solutions are assumptions that were included in the prior module.

Finally, this module will focus upon the important matter of excellence in education. This is designed for the student's review and evaluation of the significance of the various systems of thought.

This module contains eight major systems of philosophy. It examines the points of emphasis stressed by each in resolving the problems of education. The general goal is to discover the meaning of each system and the point of view that is stressed. Your understanding of this module should contribute considerably to the development of your own frame of reference as you think about the problems in your educational experiences.

SPECIFIC OBJECTIVES

Specifically, upon completing your study of this module, you should be able to

1. Explain the philosophical assumptions basic to the systems of *Idealism, Realism, Experimentalism, Pragmatism, Communism, Scholasticism, Logical Analysis*, and *Existentialism.*
2. Identify the general viewpoint of each system as it is applied to education.
3. Identify the essential differences between these various systems of philosophy.
4. Identify the applications of each system to the educational problems of the aims, curriculum, teaching-learning process, methods, and discipline.

5. Identify ten different interpretations of the meaning of *excellence* in education.
6. Identify seven essential values basic to democratic education in the United States.
7. Point out the social factors that affect the problem of excellence in education.
8. Identify seven major tasks in the education of any school.

MODULE TEXT

Idealism

Idealism is the oldest system of philosophy known to man. Its origins go back to ancient India in the East, and to Plato in the West. Its basic viewpoint stresses the human spirit as the most important element in life. The universe is viewed as essentially nonmaterial in its ultimate nature. Although Idealist philosophers vary enormously on many specifics, they agree on the following points: (1) *the human spirit is the most important element in life*; and (2) *the universe is essentially nonmaterial in its ultimate nature*. Idealism should not be confused with the notion of high aspirations—that is not what philosophers mean when they speak of *Idealism*. In the philosophic sense, Idealism is a system that emphasizes the pre-eminent importance of mind, soul, or spirit. It is possible to separate Idealism into different schools, but for our purposes we shall be content to identify only the most general assumptions of the Idealists in metaphysics, epistemology, and value theory, without regard to the idiosyncrasies of the various schools.

Basic Metaphysics of Idealism

In Idealism, all of reality is reducible to one fundamental substance—spirit. (You may better understand the nature of *spirit* in this context if you think of it as the total absence of materiality.) Matter is not real; rather, it is a notion, an abstraction of the mind. It is only the mind that is real. Therefore, all material things that seem to be real are reducible to mind or spirit. The chair you are sitting on is not material; it only *seems* material. Its essential nature is spirit. On the universal level, finite minds live in a purposeful world produced by an infinite mind. It is as though the entire universe is made up of an infinite mind or spirit, which is, in effect, everything, and we are small bits and pieces of that mind. Because man is a part of this purposeful universe, he is an intelligent and purposeful being.

Epistemology of Idealism

Idealists believe that all knowledge is independent of sense experience. The act of knowing takes place within the mind. The mind is active and contains innate capacities for organizing and synthesizing the data derived through sensations. Man can know *intuitively*; that is to say, he can apprehend immediately some truth without utilizing any of his senses. Man can also know truth through the acts of reason by which an individual examines the logical consistency of his ideas. Some Idealists believe that all knowledge is a matter of recall. Plato was one who held this notion. He based this conclusion upon the assumption that the spirit of man is eternal. Whatever he knows is already contained within his spirit. *Objective Idealists*, such as Plato, think that ideas are essences which have an independent existence. *Subjective Idealists*, such as George Berkeley, reason that man is able to know only what he perceives. His only knowledge is of his mental states. Existence depends upon mind. Every stimulus received by the mind is derived ultimately from God. God is the Infinite Spirit.

Idealistic Value Theory

Idealists generally root all values either in a personal God or in an impersonal spiritual force of nature. They all agree that values are eternal. *Theistic Idealists* assert that eternal values exist in God. Good and evil, beauty and ugliness, are known to the extent that the idea of *good* and the idea of *beauty* are consistent with the absolute good and the absolute beauty found in God. *Pantheistic Idealists* identify God with nature. Values are absolute and unchanging because they are a part of the determined order of nature.

Educational Theory of Modern Idealism

Aims of Education. The purpose of education is to contribute to the development of the *mind* and *self* of the pupil. The school should emphasize intellectual activities, moral judgments, aesthetic judgments, self-realization, individual freedom, individual responsibility, and self-control in order to achieve this development.

Curriculum. The curriculum is based upon the idea or assumption of the spiritual nature of man. This idea in turn leads to an idea of the nature of the larger units of family, community, state, earth, the universe, and infinity. In preserving the subject-matter content which is essential for the development of the individual mind, the curriculum must include those subjects essential for the realization of mental and moral development. These subjects provide one with culture, and they should be mandated for all pupils. Moreover, the subject matter should be kept constant for all.

The Teaching-Learning Process. Idealists have high expectations of the teacher. The teacher must be excellent, in order to serve as an example for the student, both intellectually and morally. No other single element in the school system is more important than the teacher. The teacher must excel in knowledge and in human insight into the needs and capacities of the pupils; and must demonstrate moral excellence in personal conduct and convictions. The teacher must also exercise great creative skill in providing opportunities for the pupils' minds to discover, analyze, unify, synthesize, and create applications of knowledge to life and behavior.

Methods of Teaching. The classroom structure and atmosphere should provide the pupil with opportunities to think, and to apply the criteria of moral evaluation to concrete situations within the context of the subjects.

The teaching methods must encourage the acquisition of facts, as well as skill in reflecting on these facts. It is not sufficient to teach pupils how to think. It is very important that what pupils *think about* be factual; otherwise, they will simply compound their ignorance.

Teaching methods should encourage pupils to enlarge their horizons; stimulate reflective thinking; encourage personal moral choices; provide skills in logical thinking; provide opportunities to apply knowledge to moral and social problems; stimulate interest in the subject content; and encourage pupils to accept the values of human civilization.

Realism

There are many differences among philosophers classified as Realists, but with the exclusion of the Scholastic Realists, they generally agree upon the following philosophical assumptions:

Metaphysics of Realism

The world is made of real, substantial, material entities. In material nature there are natural laws which determine and regulate the existence of every entity in the world of nature.

Realistic Epistemology

At birth, the mind of man is blank. As soon as he is born, and throughout the rest of his life, a variety of sensations are impressed in his brain. It is thus that man learns. Knowledge, then, is derived through sense experience. However, man can capitalize on this knowledge by using reason to discover objects and relationships which he does not or cannot perceive. That this is so is proved by common sense, for common sense shows that it is reasonable to assume that objects exist independent of one's mind, and that man can discover these things by using his senses. Whereas reality is material, the test of truth for Realists is whether or not a proposition within the mind is in accord with the material object or condition outside the mind. Thus, if through reasoning one deducts that *A* must be equal to *B,* the proposition is true only if *A* is equal to *B* in the material world.

Realistic Value Theory

If follows, then, that anything consistent with nature is valuable. Standards of value are found (determined) by means of the act of reason. However, a value judgment is never considered to be factual; it is a subjective judgment based on feeling. Acceptable individual values are values that conform to the values of the prevailing opinion of society. The prevailing opinion of society reflects the *status quo* of social reality; and because the social reality represents the truth that is out there, beyond the mind, it is useful as a standard for testing the validity of individual values.

Educational Theory of Modern Realism

Aims of Education. The basic purpose of education, in Realist educational theory, is to provide the pupil with the essential knowledge required for survival in the natural world. Such knowledge will provide the skills necessary to achieve a secure and happy life.

Curriculum. Realists believe that the curriculum is best organized according to subject matter—that is, it should be subject-centered. These subjects should be organized according to the psychological principles of learning, which teach that the subjects should proceed from the simple to the more complex. Subjects must include (1) science and mathematics; (2) humanities and social science; and (3) values.

Science and mathematics should be emphasized, because the Realist considers these to be the most important area of learning. Knowledge of our natural world enables mankind to adjust to and progress in his natural environment.

The humanities are not as important as science and mathematics. However, they must never be ignored. Because it is important for each individual to adjust to the social environment, the curriculum should emphasize the effects of the social environment on the individual's life. By knowing the forces that determine our lives, we are in a position to control them.

Values of scientific objectivity and critical examination should be stressed. When teaching values, one should not use normative methods but critical analysis. To encourage desirable learning habits, rewards should be given when required.

Teaching-Learning Process. The Realist classroom is teacher-centered; subjects are taught by a teacher who is impersonal and objective, and who knows the subject fully. The teacher must utilize pupil interest by relating the material to the pupil's experiences, and by making the subject matter as concrete as possible. He or she maintains discipline by rewarding efforts and achievements, controlling the attention of the child, and keeping the pupil active.

Methods of Teaching. The teaching methods recommended by the Realist are authoritative. The teacher must require that the pupil be able to recall, explain, and compare facts; to interpret relationships, and to infer new meanings. Evaluation is an essential aspect of teaching, according to this view. The teacher must use objective methods by evaluating and giving the type of test that lends itself to accurate measurement of the pupil's understanding of the essential material. Frequent tests are highly desirable. For motivational purposes, Realists stress that it is important for the teacher always to reward the success of each pupil. When the teacher reports the accomplishments of his pupils, he reinforces what has been learned.

Experimentalism and Pragmatism

We are grouping together Experimentalism with Pragmatism in this module, partly for convenience, but more especially to avoid duplication. As a matter of fact, we could group the philosophies of Pragmatism, Positivism, Instrumentalism, Empiricism, Reconstructionism, and Progressivism under the general name "Experimentalism," without doing violence to any of them. Although these philosophies differ in particulars, their position follows the line delineated in the following paragraphs.

Metaphysics, Experimentalism, and Pragmatism

Uniformly, all Experimentalists reject metaphysics as a legitimate area of philosophical inquiry. Reality, they argue, is determined by an individual's sense experience. Man can know nothing beyond his experience. Therefore, questions pertaining to the ultimate nature of man and the universe simply cannot be answered because these problems transcend one's experience. For example, there is no way for any living being to determine whether there is life after death, because life after death cannot be experienced while one is living. Any conclusion we make about life after death is merely conjecture. Unless we can experience the phenomenon in question, it is impossible to verify any solution suggested for such problems. Therefore, Experimentalists hold that the philosopher who attempts to think through such problems is wasting time, because the conclusions would be meaningless. Attempts to answer metaphysical questions are little more than guessing games, in their opinion.

Epistemology in Experimentalism and Pragmatism

The Experimentalist rejects the dualism that separates the perceiver from the object that is perceived. Man is both *in* the world of his perception and *of* the world of his perception. All that can be known is dependent upon experience. This experiencing of phenomena determines knowledge. Because the phenomena are constantly changing, it follows that knowledge and truth must similarly be changing. Truth is something that happens to an idea. Whatever is considered true today must also be considered as possibly changing tomorrow. Circumstances do alter cases: To a starving sailor, marooned on a desert island, a moldy loaf of bread that a suburban parent would throw into the garbage would be worth more than its weight in gold.

Value Theory in Experimentalism and Pragmatism

In Experimentalist theory, values derive from the human condition. Because man is a part of his society, the consequences of his actions are either good or bad, according to their results. If the consequences prove worthwhile socially, then the value of the action is proven to be good. Thus, value in ethics and aesthetics depends upon the relative circumstances of the situation as it arises. Ultimate values cannot exist, for truth is always relative and conditional. Nevertheless, value judgments are useful as a means to an intelligent life that is successful, productive, and happy.

Educational Theory of Experimentalism

Aims of Education. Education must teach one how to think so that one can adjust to an ever changing society. The school must aim at developing those experiences that will enable one to lead a good life. These objectives include

1. Good health.
2. Vocational skills.
3. Interests and hobbies for leisure living.
4. Preparation for parenthood.
5. Ability to deal effectively with social problems.

Additional specific goals must include an understanding of the importance of democracy. Democratic government enables each citizen to grow and live through the social interaction that takes place with other citizens. Education must help its students become excellent citizens in the democracy.

Curriculum. According to the Experimentalists, the democratic tradition is a self-correcting tradition. As such, the social heritage of the past is not the focus of educational interest. Rather, the focus is for the good life now and in the future. The standard of social good is constantly being tested and verified through changing experiences; therefore, education must work to preserve democracy. The nature of this democracy is dynamic and changing as a result of its continually undergoing reconstructive experiences. However, this reconstruction does not demand or include total change. Only the serious social problems of society are re-examined in order to arrive at new solutions.

In the Experimentalist view, the curriculum of the school must not exist apart from the social context. The subject matter of education is the tool for solving individual problems, and as the individual pupil is improved or reconstructed, society is improved in similar fashion. Therefore, the problems of democratic society must form the basis of the curriculum; and the means to resolve the problems of democratic institutions must also be included in the curriculum. Therefore, there must be

1. A social basis to the curriculum.
2. Opportunity to practice democratic ideals.
3. Democratic planning at every level of education.
4. Group definition of common social goals.
5. Creative means to develop new skills.
6. Activity-centered and pupil-centered curriculum.

The Teaching-Learning Process. In Experimentalism, learning is always considered to be an individual matter. Teachers ought not to try to pour the knowledge they have into the pupil, because such efforts are fruitless. What each pupil learns depends upon his own personal needs, interests, and problems. In other words, the content of knowledge is not an end in itself but a means to an end. Thus, a pupil who is faced by a problem may be able to reconstruct his environment so as to solve this felt need. To help him *the teacher must*

1. Provide experiences that will excite motivation. Field trips, films, rec-

ords, and guest experts are examples of activities designed to awaken pupil interest in an important problem.

2. Guide the pupil into formulating a specific definition of the problem. Because each pupil approaches the problem from his own experiential background, the teacher should encourage the pupils to formulate their own aims and goals.
3. Plan with the class the individual and group objectives to be used in solving the problem.
4. Assist the pupils in collecting the information pertaining to the problem. Essentially, the teacher serves as a guide by introducing skills, understandings, knowledge, and appreciations through the use of books, compositions, letters, resource speakers, films, field trips, television, or anything else that may be appropriate.
5. Evaluate with the class what was learned; how they learned it; what new information occurred; what each pupil discovered for himself.

Methods of Teaching. The teaching-learning method just described is the method of problem solving. Experimentalists are committed to the use of the problem-solving inquiry and discovery method. This approach to teaching requires that a teacher be

1. Permissive.
2. Friendly.
3. A guide.
4. Open-minded.
5. Enthusiastic.

6. Creative.
7. Socially aware.
8. Alert.
9. Patient.
10. Cooperative and sincere.

Scholasticism

The philosophy of St. Thomas Aquinas is the official philosophy of the Roman Catholic Church. This philosophy is sometimes called *Scholasticism*. Scholasticism arose during the Middle Ages and reflects a synthesis of the philosophy of Aristotle and Medieval Church doctrine. However, in the thinking of most Scholastics, philosophy is given a role subordinate to theology. "I believe in order that I may know" characterizes this relationship.

Scholastic Metaphysics

Scholastic metaphysics holds that the universe is a creation of God, whose existence can be known through reason. Man, according to their definition, is a rational animal, possessing a soul as well as a body. Human nature is, therefore, everywhere the same, and because of his spiritual nature, man's destiny is eternal. A person achieves eternal happiness through leading a good life as defined by the Catholic Church.

Scholastic Epistemology

Scholastics believe that *absolute truth* is found in faith. Man can achieve truth through the use of his reason, but this reason is clouded because of the sin of Adam. Man can also know things through intuition; this is the source of knowledge following the death of the body. It resides in the higher faculties of the soul.

Scholastic Value Theory

Reason dominates Scholastic philosophy. Man must first know the good in order to will to be good, for although every man is inclined toward good, his judgment may lead him toward evil. Because of faulty knowledge, he may choose evil under the mistaken notion that it is good. In this sense, evil is error; therefore, man must develop the habit of good action so that he will consistently choose the good, in his ethical actions. Because God is the ultimate good, and the final end of man, man must live a life in which he passes the test of goodness in fulfilling his moral responsibility to himself, to humanity. and to God.

Educational Theory of Scholasticism

Aims of Education. Education must aim for the development of the full potentiality of man, according to Scholastic doctrine. Because man is a rational animal, his full potentialities include the intellectual as well as the physical, the volitional as well as the vocational. Consequently, the school must provide opportunities for every student to develop his reason and to strengthen his will. Education is complete only if its aims include mankind's future existence in heaven as well as his material existence on earth. Obviously, the care of the soul and the future eternal destiny of mankind are of greater importance than what happens to the body during its short stay on earth.

Curriculum. The content of education must include religion and the humanities. A liberating education includes the development of the instrumental subjects necessary for life and for the study of the fundamental subjects that deal with human values.

Methods of Teaching. The teacher must be a good example to the pupils. The classroom is teacher-centered; here, the teacher structures lessons so as to provide the development of knowledge, skill in reasoning, and opportunities to act virtuously.

In the decades since World War II, the positions of Thomas Aquinas have been renewed, especially by lay thinkers, under the heading of Neo-Thomism. A number of intellectuals who adhered to the thinking that the basic beliefs and knowledge of ancient cultures applied as well in our lives today shared many common educational views with the ecclesiastics of the Scholastic school, even though their views on religion differed vastly. These lay thinkers endorsed the studying of subject matter of a disciplinary and spiritual nature such as mathematics, languages, logic, and great books. They assumed the learner to be a rational and spiritual person, and considered the subjects to be disciplines for the mind. Difficult mental calisthenics such as reading, writing, drill, rote memory, and computations were important in training the intellect. Learning to reason was very important and was attainable only be vigorous exercise in grammar, logic, and rhetoric. While the clerical Neo-Thomists continued to insist that all programs give priority to the study of theology, some of the lay group favored the studying of great books, while others endorsed other contemporary sources of knowledge such as trade and skill training for the less gifted. Because there is much to be learned, youngsters must work very hard. Assignments, it is felt, should be rigorous and students should be pushed to develop their intellectual powers.

Perennialism, Essentialism and Progressivism

The three major streams of philosophic thought just discussed are represented in each of the several educational theories upon which instruction is based in the school: Perennialism, Progressivism, and Essentialism. Perennialism reflects those streams that maintain that universal truths and values do exist and that education should consist of a search for and the dissemination of these truths and values. Progressivism reflects those that hold that knowledge is ever-changing and that the best approach to knowledge is through scientific experimentation. The focus of Essentialism is on those streams that stress the practicality of knowledge essential or useful for individuals who will play productive roles in society as adult citizens. Teachers are expected to provide this kind of knowledge to learners and to take a leadership role in guiding them toward its mastery. *Reconstructionism* is a variation of Progressivism that suggests that the role of the school is to teach learners how to remake society in such a fashion that the general human condition will be improved.

In general these educational orientations correspond with the philosophical schools as follows.

Philosophic Concept	*Educational Orientation*
Idealism	Essentialism
Realism	
Scholasticism (Neo Thomism)	Perennialism
Experimentalism	Progressivism
Existentialism	Existentialism

Table 4-1 outlines these philosophic conditions and the corresponding educational orientations. When studying this table please remember that Idealism and Realism are associated with Essentialism, Scholasticism (Neo Thomism) with Perennialism, and Experimentalism (including Reconstructionism) with Progressivism.

Logical Analysis

The phrase *logical analysis* describes all the current philosophies that assert that the function of philosophy is basically a type of logical and linguistic analysis. Sometimes this is described as *Analytic Philosophy*. The term includes such schools as *Logical Positivism, Logical Empiricism, Scientific Empiricism, Logical Atomism, Cambridge Analysis, Oxford Analysis, Opera-*

TABLE 4-1
Schematic Summary of Views*

	Definition	Comparative Philosophies					
		Idealism	Realism	Neo-Thomism	Experimentalism	Existentialism	
Metaphysics	The study of of reality: What is real?	A world of mind	A world of things	A world of Reason and Being/God	A world of experience	A world of existing	⇨
Epistemology	The study of knowing and knowledge: What is true?	Seeing with the "mind's eye"— consistency of ideas	Spectator Theory: sensation and correspondence	Intuition, logical reasoning, and revelation	Testing to see what works	Subjective choice, personal appropriation	⇨
Axiology	The study of valuing and values: What is good? — **Ethics**	The imitation of the Absolute Self	The law of nature	The rational act	The public test	The anguish of freedom	⇨
	What is beautiful? — **Aesthetics**	Reflection of the Ideal	Reflection of nature	Creative intuition	The public taste	Revolt from the public norm	

* Van Cleve Morris and Young Pai, *Philosophy and the American School*, 2nd edition. Copyright © 1976 by Houghton Mifflin Company. Used by permission. (pp. 294–295).

tionism, and *Modern Pragmatism*. The areas of philosophical agreement among these philosophies are described briefly in the following paragraphs.

Metaphysics and Analytic Philosophy

In logical analysis, reality consists of what is knowable; that is to say, what is verified by experience. All questions that transcend the knowable are not the proper concern of philosophy. Speculation upon these matters is meaningless and a waste of time. Man is distinct from the other representatives of the animal kingdom because of the degree to which he is able to learn. The complexity of this learning is evident in man's ingenious employment of symbolic behavior in language and other media. The use of language serves to represent, express, and appeal to the thoughts of the individual and to other human beings. Man is also different from other animals in that he has the capacity to engage in critical reflection. The use of symbols is valu-

Educational Implications					
	Idealism	*Realism*	*Neo-Thomism*	*Experimentalism*	*Existentialism*
Curricular Emphasis	Subject matter of the mind: literature, intellectual history, philosophy, religion	Subject matter of the physical world: mathematics and science	Subject matter of intellect and spirit: disciplinary subjects: mathematics and language and Doctrine	Subject matter of social experience: the social studies	Subject matter of choice: art, ethics, moral philosophy, religion
Preferred Method	Teaching for the handling of ideas: lecture, discussion	Teaching for mastery of factual information and basic skills: demonstration, recitation	Disciplining the mind: formal drill— readying the spirit: Catechism	Problem solving: project method	Arousing personal response: Socratic questioning
Character Education	Imitating exemplars, heroes	Training in rules of conduct	Disciplining behavior to reason	Making group decisions in light of consequences	Awakening the self to responsibility
Developing Taste	Studying the masterworks	Studying design in nature	Finding beauty in reason	Participating in art projects	Composing a personal art work

able to the extent that man can assign meaning to each symbol, and that he can be guided by reason to an interpretation of the message implied.

Epistemology and Analytic Philosophy

Analytic philosophers assert that the method of science must be the method of philosophy. Things are knowable only through experience, that verifies the truth that is apprehended. The scientific attitude of open-mindedness, objectivity, and critical reflection in thinking is necessary for correct thinking. The reasoning function is without doubt the most important function of the animal, man.

Value Theory and Logical Analysis

All values are relative to the needs of the individual man and to humanity. The social values of justice and benevolence are outcomes that follow the natural intercourse between human beings. A democratic government provides, through social interaction, the best possibility for individual growth, and it is therefore the best form of political rule.

Educational Implications of Analytic Philosophy

Aims of Education. The purpose of education is to promote the intellectual and social development of the individual.

Method of Teaching. The teacher must encourage in each pupil the scientific attitude of open-mindedness and objectivity. The ability to withhold one's judgment until all the relevant data are collected reflects the goal of mature judgment and is valuable for the growth of the individual person. Education must be based upon the experiences of the learner. In this regard, this system of philosophy differs little from that of Experimentalism.

Existentialism

This system of philosophy is the newest to appear upon the intellectual scene. The important Existentialist thinkers repudiate the very label which classifies them as belonging to this or any other group of philosophers. Obviously, it is a philosophy of extreme individualism. Yet there are some very important areas of common agreement which enable us to classify, in general, Existential thinkers.

Existential Metaphysics

Reality is a matter of individual existence. *Existence* precedes *essence* in individual development: One exists, and then becomes. Each human being exists in a world that is without purpose; and life is fundamentally absurd because of this. The only significance discovered in living is that found in the meaning that each individual human being authentically—that is, freely—chooses for himself. The decisions and commitments one makes determine the kind of person one becomes. This is his *essence*, which is continually becoming (that is, developing). When a person is aware of his identity as an individual, realizes his contingent nature (he is not the reason for his own existence, and will eventually die), he suffers a sense of anguish, despair, and loneliness. Yet, man, alone in an indifferent universe, can and must choose what is significant and what is meaningful for him.

Existential Epistemology

A person knows only through experiences. However, there are levels of experience. When one is aware of the existence of things and beings in themselves, one is functioning upon the highest level of human experience—the level of *awareness*. Truth is always relative to an individual's judgment. Absolute truths are nonexistent. Each person must decide what is true and what is significant for him.

Existentialist Value Theory

Existentialists contend that values are neither absolute nor determined by outside criteria. Rather, each value is determined by the free choice of the individual person. Existence is the basic value for any person. The values that are significant for each individual are relative to one's individual circumstances. One must not conform to the social values and norms of his society for the sake of conformity; if one permits society or any institution of society to impose values, then one loses authenticity and humanity. Human freedom demands that a person decide, freely, his own commitment; this is what provides significance and meaning for him, and this is the source of moral and social responsibility. In short, value is a completely personal, individual matter.

Educational Implications of Existentialism

Aim of Education. The major purpose of education, according to Existentialist philosophers, is to serve the individual human being. It ought to guide him into an awareness of his condition and to promote his successful commitment to a significant and meaningful existence. Important specific goals are

1. To develop individual awareness.
2. To provide opportunity for free, ethical choices.
3. To encourage the development of self-knowledge.
4. To develop a sense of self-responsibility.
5. To awaken a sense of individual commitment.

Curriculum. Existential educators do not favor a subject-centered curriculum. To them, subject matter has no value in itself. Whatever is studied is an instrument by which the person develops self-knowledge and self-responsibility. If one were existentially oriented, the humanities would be most important in the subject-centered curriculum, but the ideal curriculum for the Extentialist would stress

1. An activity curriculum.
2. Pupil interest as the basis of planning and activity.
3. Complete freedom for the pupil to work in groups or alone.
4. A curriculum based on immediate needs.
5. Recognition of individual differences in experiences.

Methods of Teaching. The Existential teacher must be democratic and must utilize a nondirective technique.

Democratic. The teacher never imposes his personal goals upon the pupil; his function is to guide the pupil. The teacher is a resource person, and must therefore make plans along with the pupils (democratically), on the basis of their individual needs and goals.

Nondirective. Exact and detailed lesson plans are unnecessary; this would be imposing adult interests and values on the pupil. With the teacher as a guide, each individual must be free to develop his own purposes and work out his own learning. Problems the individual pupil directs to the teacher should be reflected back in such a way as to arouse the pupil's insight into the nature of the problem.

Communism

Communism explains the past, present, and future of man in terms of economic determinism. Because roughly a third of all humanity lives under a communist form of government, an understanding of such views is essential for the educator. The democratic theory of education fosters and preserves the freedom to think, to inquire, to disagree, and to choose, as one sees fit. This theory assumes that individuals have rights apart from the society in which one lives. The communist view is different.

Communistic Metaphysics

Communist philosophy derives from the theories of Karl Marx, who interpreted the universe in terms of materialism. According to Marxist dogma, whatever exists must be material in its ultimate nature. Man must strive for a life of material happiness, which can be achieved only on a collective, rather than on an individual, basis. Thus, all rights are social. The individual has no rights apart from society; one's rights, duties, and economic well-being derive from the State.

The nature of government is determined by the owners of property. The best form of government will eliminate all property rights. Because all private property rights will be abolished, rights will exist only in the government. Such a government is communistic. Communists believe that it is inevitable that communist states will develop everywhere in the world. They accept the predictions of Karl Marx, who used the dialectic theory of an Idealist philosopher, George Hegel, to support his belief that societies must necessarily evolve toward communism.

Communistic Epistemology

Communists believe that absolute truth exists and that it exists in the ideal of communism. Therefore, they hold that whatever is useful in the promotion of the Communist State contains truth. This notion of *Proletarian Utilitarianism*, i.e., that propositions useful to the party are true, explains changes in Communist-Party positions. As political circumstances change, the ideas that promoted communism in the past may be discarded, and new, quite different ideas may be accepted as truth because they promote the ideal of communism.

Communistic Value Theory

The ultimate value exists in the idea of communism as embodied in the communist State. The communist does not think in terms of *man* but in terms of *men*. He accepts the labor theory of value: the laborer cannot possess the product of his labor apart from society. In the communist society, the ideal is to give everyone what he needs and take from him what he is able to contribute to the whole. The communist rejects the idea that an individual person possesses individual inalienable rights. Because all rights are social, all people must be viewed as creatures of society. Everything serves this end; for instance, art must serve the state. Thus, if an individual artist writes anything critical of the government, he is viewed as an enemy to society, his individual right of free speech notwithstanding.

Communism and Democracy

The communist gives the illusion that he alone is concerned with oppression and economic injustice. Yet he does not describe the condition of the worker who labors under the absolute control of the Communisty Party leaders. The right to dissent, the right of following one's conscience, is a privilege notably absent in the communist society. Communists cannot speak legitimately of the human rights of mankind when they justify, philosophically, regimentation, thought control, subversion, assassination, and slavery to the State. Communist theory is inconsistent with human happiness, because it considers human life to be inferior to political ideology.

Educational Theory in a Communist Society

Aims of Education. The ultimate aim of education in a communist society is to provide for the success of the communist state. The school is and must be a creature of society. It can have no goals inconsistent with the government. Rather, its role is to prepare ideal servants for the communist society. To carry out this mission, the school aims at developing an attitude of obedience to authority and an awareness of one's responsibility to promote the common good of the State.

The development of vocational skills is also an important goal, as the school must provide future workers for the State. Academic skills and understandings are essential for those capable of intellectual progress. It is expected that these students will be trained by the school to be potential future leaders of the State. The curriculum for these future leaders stresses mathematics, science, and communist social studies.

Curriculum. In communist countries, the curriculum is subject-centered. The essential subjects are social science, the natural sciences, mathematics, and literature. Vocational training is provided for those unable or unwilling to undertake secondary education. Higher education is extremely competitive and is reserved only for the best students. There is no room for dilettantes in communist higher education.

Methods of Teaching. In the communist school, the teacher is the leader in a classroom where the lessons are carefully structured. Much stress is put on discipline and control. In his teaching, the communist teacher is expected to employ scientific principles of learning to impart both knowledge of the factual material and political orthodoxy. In fact, the teacher is quite authoritarian.

Democracy and Education

Whatever their philosophical frame of reference, American school teachers have a basic area of agreement simply because they are teachers in this democracy of the United States. Certain aims and principles follow as a result of teaching in such a democracy.

Critical Thinking. The democratic way of life excludes a "conditioned-reflex" type of loyalty. We must develop citizens who are free to think and to express criticism.

Indoctrination. The kind of indoctrination that instructs individuals in what to think has no legitimate place in American schools. The school must create a climate where the pupil is free of any thought control by the teacher.

Freedom and Responsibility. The school ought to develop citizens capable of enjoying the benefits of freedom, and who know the responsibilities inherent in protecting the rights of freedom.

Material Well-Being. Education in a democracy must foster the development of vocational skills to insure each citizen the opportunity of living a productive life, free from the enslavement and bitterness of poverty.

Personality. The education of citizens ought not to be restricted to vocational concerns alone. Education must be concerned with the development of aesthetic and ethical values, to insure that each person becomes capable of realizing his full potential as an individual personality.

Concerned Citizen. The school should encourage attitudes of social responsibility and concern for the social problems of human society. Education must aim toward the development of a citizenry who will actively seek intelligent remedies through the democratic institutions.

Problems of Excellence in Education

The meaning of *excellence* is always a problem when it is applied to education. The problem, stated as a question, is "What kinds of educational experiences constitute an excellent education?" The response is complicated by the different philosophical positions of our educators, and by the ever changing forces affecting our society—urbanization, technology, changing human values, economic prosperity, and international problems. Excellence may be viewed in any one or more of the following ways:

1. Education is intellectual, and ought to produce well-informed citizens.
2. Education ought to produce cultured citizens.
3. Education ought to produce skilled workers.
4. Education ought to produce socially concerned citizens.
5. Education ought to produce highly trained specialists.
6. Education ought to produce self-disciplined individuals.
7. Education ought to produce persons capable of enjoying life.
8. Education ought to produce thinking citizens.
9. Education ought to produce individuals capable of living successfully.
10. Education ought to produce persons whose moral, social, emotional, and intellectual well-being is developed to the extent that they are capable of living successfully in a democratic social order.

Common Agreement

Fortunately, we have considerable agreement on some of the answers to the problem of education and excellence. All agree that education that fails to develop those democratic values basic to life in the United States has failed in its essential task. Of course, of all the institutions that exist in American society, it is the school that is considered to be the important agent for the continuance of these crucial social values. What these values are, then, is of great consequence to public education, in particular, and

MODULE

5

Psychological Bases: Major Theories of Learning

Historical Theories of Learning / Faculty Psychology / Apperception / Modern Theories of Learning / Associationism / Stimulus-Response / Cognitive Theories / Application of Learning Theory / A Theoretical Framework / Understanding the Learner

The first-edition version of this module was written by W. Ralph McCaw, Jersey City State College. It has been revised and updated for this edition.

RATIONALE

Psychology As a Science

The study of mankind has intrigued people throughout history. The motives, thoughts, and behavior of man have always stirred the curiosity of his fellow men. The ancient inscriptions on the walls of caves are a permanent testimony of early man's interest in such activities. The concern with human behavior has not been limited by time or place. Today, newspapers and magazines are eagerly read daily by millions of people who want to know what others are doing and thinking, what concerns and worries others have, and what causes some people to behave in strange and uncommon ways.

Psychology, which is also interested in human behavior, belongs to a group of studies known as the *behavioral sciences*. The behavioral sciences, including anthropology, sociology, psychiatry, psychology, economics, history, and political science, are concerned with the systematic pursuit of knowledge about human activity but from different points of view. The study of humans, however, is not limited to the behavioral sciences. Literature concerns itself with what people do and what people are like, though of course it is not limited to reality.

Psychology, the behavioral science which is the main concern of this module, endeavors to study human behavior in a scientific manner. Psychology is a science concerned with understanding, predicting, and controlling the actions, feelings, and thoughts of people. As a science, psychology must conform to the limitations and requirements of science as it studies people. *Science* refers to an exact and systematic statement or classification of knowledge about some subject in which the results of investigations have been systematized in the form of hypotheses and general laws, which are subject to verification. In short, science is knowledge in the form of facts, phenomena, laws, and causes which have been gained and verified by exact observation, organized experiments, and accurate thinking. Whether human behavior is studied directly or by inference from the study of animal behavior, the accuracy, objectivity, and the logic of the conclusions must be maintained.

Psychology uses many procedures to assemble an ever increasing record of the knowledge of human behavior. Rats are run through mazes, and monkeys are assigned tasks of skill and insight. In an attempt to reap the reward of a few kernels of grain, pigeons are put into a situation where they will peck persistently at disks—to satisfy the scientific curiosity of a stealthy observer. Other scientists must be content to collect useless poker chips for their labor. Men and women tackle puzzles, or fly mock airplanes under the surveillance of the white-coated observers. Each year the scope and pace of scientific experimentation increase, and yet man and his behavior still conceal many secrets from the scientist.

Psychology versus Common Sense

There are many who confuse the scientific findings of psychology with common-sense information. According to them, the content of psychology is common knowledge to "the man on the street." They claim that psychologists are compiling information that everybody already knows. In a sense, this is partly so. Although the main concern of psychology is the adding of original knowledge of human behavior, one of its functions is to verify beliefs that previously have been accepted only on the basis of folkwisdom or to prove their fallaciousness. The difference between the facts produced by psychology and the "facts" of common-sense beliefs can be demonstrated by the following exercise.

Are the following statements true or false?

1. Long slender hands indicate an artistic temperament.
2. The number of one's senses is limited to five.
3. The color red is especially exciting to bulls.
4. Coffee in small amounts decreases efficiency in learning.
5. A slow reader understands and retains what he has read better than a fast reader.

These five common-sense statements were selected from a collection of one hundred such items. They are all incorrect, as shown by scientific study. A study by McKeachie (1960) involved giving a test with the one hundred statements to 513 students in six colleges. The average score on the test, given before an elementary course in psychology, ranged from 60.4 to 68.8 per cent. The test was readministered after the course in psychology. Although there were gains in the average in all cases, the typical student continued to hold about 85 per cent of the misconceptions he had held before the course began. This study reveals that common-sense beliefs lingered, even after the students who held them were exposed to scientific evidence to the contrary. Beliefs adopted at an early age show resistance to change, even though the beliefs are inadequate and inaccurate.

Psychologists must always remember that psychology is a science. To understand their own behavior and that of their fellow men, psychologists must not trust their own opinions. Even a psychologist's strongest beliefs must be set aside. Science demands accuracy, honesty, a healthy skepticism, and the willingness to accept results, whether favorable or adverse. The laboratory will not tolerate whimsy or prejudice, carelessness or quackery.

One branch of psychology has concerned itself with the problems of the schools, and is known as *educational psychology*. It is the application of psychological principles to the problems of learning and teaching. You, the student who uses this module, have been involved in learning, consciously or unconsciously, all of your life. In spite of your long acquaintance with your own learning and your observations of the behavior of others in learning situations, much of what you know about the learning process is undoubtedly fragmentary, unsystematized, and sometimes contrary to scientifically derived principles. If this is the case and your understanding of the learning process is limited, you are probably an inefficient learner. (Module 6 is concerned, in part, with recent discoveries about learning.)

SPECIFIC OBJECTIVES

Upon completion of your study of this module, it is expected that you will be able to

1. Describe the concept of faculty psychology.
2. Explain how faculty psychology leads to the doctrine of formal discipline.
3. Cite the major disadvantages of the doctrine of formal discipline.
4. Cite the experimental evidence which discredited the theory of formal discipline.
5. Defend yourself against the argument that mathematics is the only subject to teach logical thinking.
6. Show how the philosophy of John Locke helped to counteract the influence of the concept of formal discipline.
7. Cite the major contributions of Herbart to education.
8. Explain the terms *mental state*, *sense impressions* and *apperceptive mass*.
9. Cite the two principles of apperception proposed by Herbart.
10. Cite the three levels of learning proposed by Herbart.
11. Explain what influences were responsible for the demise of Herbartian principles of teaching and learning.
12. Relate the event that contributed most to the development of psychology as a science.
13. Explain the term *introspection*, and why it fell from favor during the heyday of behaviorism.
14. Cite the major characteristics of behaviorism.
15. Cite the contributions of Pavlov, E. L. Thorndike, and B. F. Skinner to what is currently known about learning.
16. Explain the differences between classical conditioning and operant conditioning.
17. Explain shaping and reinforcement in the learning of complex behavior.
18. Name and explain the four major forms of cognitive theory.
19. Explain the term *Gestalt*.
20. Demonstrate that you are aware of the evaluation of psychological theories in relation to learning.

MODULE TEXT

Historical Theories of Learning

Although the formal study of psychology as a science began relatively recently, the study of human learning has intrigued philosophers since early times. (Some of the classical theories of ancient and medieval thinkers have been touched on in the modules dealing with philosophy.) As scientific studies of psychology began toward the end of the nineteenth century, two theories of how we learn were developed: *faculty psychology* and *appercep-tion.* These commonly held theories have still not been given up entirely by laymen.

Faculty Psychology

Historically, faculty psychology was a theory that held that the mind was composed of a number of mental faculties such as reasoning, memory, atten-tion, will, judgment, and observation. It was believed that the process of education was directed toward developing and strengthening these faculties. Based on faculty psychology was the doctrine of *formal discipline*, which considered the faculties of the mind to be much like muscles—capable of being developed and enlarged by exercise.

For this reason, the classical curriculum consisted of the study of Latin, Euclidian geometry, and other rigorous intellectual and abstract exercises. Vestiges of this outmoded theory are still evident in some school curricula, and in the reasons often cited for the inclusion of some subjects therein.

Whether or not the mind can be improved by rigorous exercise was first scientifically examined by William James in 1890. James and his associates memorized a section of the poem, "Satyr," by Victor Hugo. Everyday for a month they exercised their memories for twenty minutes by memorizing another poem. As a final test, they memorized other passages by Hugo. Although the other passages were learned a little faster than the first one, James saw the difference as so insignificant that he concluded that one's retentiveness is not improved by exercise.

Studies by Edward L. Thorndike and Robert S. Woodworth at Columbia University led them to believe that the theory of formal discipline was scientifically untenable. In their experimental work, using drills and training for certain tasks, the "faculties" for performing those tasks were not im-proved by practice.

Further studies were done by A. G. Wesman to determine if some school subjects contributed more to intelligence than others. He found that no one school subject was superior to another insofar as its contribution to intelli-gence in any of the general achievement areas was concerned. In 1913, T. H. Briggs tested a longstanding belief that vigorous training in formal grammar would transfer to improved abilities in other fields. His careful experiment, using two groups of elementary school students over a three-month period, did not demonstrate that grammar contributed to improved abilities in other areas.

Apperception

J. F. Herbart, an early nineteenth-century German philosopher and teacher, developed a systematic psychology which was in accord with the eighteenth-century *tabula rasa* theory of John Locke. Locke, an English philosopher, had been a leader in shifting the conception of education from mental discipline and faculty psychology to *habit formation.* According to the *tabula rasa* theory, the mind was a blank slate upon which the experiences of life were recorded. The mind was therefore the product of life experiences.

Herbart saw morality as the greatest goal of education, and assumed that the purpose of education was to make children good. To obtain this objective, he developed a system known as the *psychology of mental states.* Herbart saw a mental state as a nonspatial mental reality which is experienced at firsthand. Mental states have three forms: sense impressions, images or copies of previous sense impressions, and the affective elements of pleasure and pain. These mental states are the only source of mental energy, and one's stock of mental states at any time is one's apperceptive mass.

In Herbartian theory, until a presentation takes place, the mind is completely empty, inert, and passive. New things are learned only as they are related to what is in the apperceptive mass. The combination of ideas present in one's mind at any one time determines what the center of one's attention is, and what will maintain one's attention. According to this system, ideas either attract or repel one another. Each idea in one's mind has at one time been the center of one's consciousness, and it seeks to return. The idea also seeks self-preservation; it tries to conserve itself and to form relations with other ideas.

All perception, Herbart believed, is *apperception*, a process of relating new ideas to the store of already held mental states. A mind contains much that is not at the conscious level. Memories, for instance, are stored in the subconscious and are useful in the interpretation of current experiences. Ideas only have meaning in terms of previous experience. At any one time, several ideas may be in the range of consciousness, but only one will be at the focus of attention; some will be dropping below the threshold of consciousness, and others will be attempting to rise from the subconscious to the realm of consciousness.

In apperception, Herbart saw two principles: The first, the principle of *frequency*, means that the more often an idea or concept is brought to consciousness, the easier it is for it to return; the second, the principle of *association*, means that whenever a number of presentations or ideas associate to form a mass, the combination so formed will determine which ideas are allowed to enter the consciousness. Herbart therefore proposed three levels or stages of learning. The first stage is primarily that of *sensory activity*. This stage is followed by the *memory* stage, which involves the exact reproduction of previously formed ideas. The third stage is that of *conceptual thinking* or *understanding*, which includes generalizations and the demonstration of rules, principles, or laws from a study of particulars—an inductive process.

Herbart, who was himself a teacher, laid out precise instructions for teachers to follow in building a student's store of knowledge. According to his plan, instruction should follow five steps: preparation, presentation, association, generalization, and application. This Herbartian plan, known as the five formal steps, became the model for teacher training for several generations.

Herbart's methods were widely accepted in Europe and soon were adopted in the United States. Many educators found them practical and effective. With the new ascendancy of science over philosophy and the beginnings of progressive movement at the turn of the century, Herbartianism lost favor and was gradually replaced by the child-centered classroom approach advocated by John Dewey. Dewey himself vigorously attacked both Herbart's conception of the human mind and human learning, and his five formal steps of teaching. Thus, new movements rejected the mechanical associationism of Herbart's thinking and the mindless execution of the five formal steps. Still, Herbartian techniques were favored well into the twentieth century in some circles. They were used successfully for military training in the U.S. Army well into the post-World War II years.

Meanwhile, other developments in the application of psychology to learning were taking place. Apperception was being replaced by stimulus-response relationships.

Modern Theories of Learning

Contemporary theories of learning can be classified into two categories or systems: *associative* or *stimulus-response*, and *cognitive* or *field theories*.

Associationism

The history of associationism began with Aristotle, who was concerned with the association of ideas through similarity, contrast, and contiguity.

As psychology began to be more scientific, particularly from the time when Wilhelm Max Wundt established the first psychological laboratory in Leipzig, Germany, in 1879, learning was a prime concern. In the beginning, associationism was the only scientific theory concerning the nature of learning, and the method of study was introspection. This method involved the psychologist's observing the workings of his own mind. As psychologists began to realize the subjective nature of introspection, a reaction arose against it. This resulted in an attempt to find more objective data. This reaction, in turn, resulted in a new theory, known as *behaviorism*, of which the leading exponent was John B. Watson.

Although somewhat mechanistic in nature, behaviorism was confined to the study of those aspects of behavior that were sufficiently overt to enable the psychologist to make objective observations. Because of its reliance on verifiable evidence, behaviorism was not able to account for such psychological phenomena as purposive behavior. As a result, this theory of behaviorism was abandoned, although the effects of it are still discernible in some of the current theories.

Stimulus-Response

Classical Conditioning. A major breakthrough in the study of learning was the theory of conditioning developed by the Russian Nobel Prize-winner Ivan P. Pavlov during the first quarter of the present century. The method of his original experiment, now known as *classical conditioning*, involved the association between the sound of a bell and salivation, which normally occurred in the presence of food. In his experiment, the ringing of a bell was accompanied by the repeated presentation of meat (the unconditioned stimulus) to a hungry dog. Eventually, the dog responded by salivation (the conditioned response) to the sound of the bell alone. By repeated pairings, the association was strengthened. After the use of only the conditioned stimulus over a period of time, the salivation eventually stopped. Evidently the conditioned response had been extinguished because the dog no longer associated the sound with food. It is in this way, through classical conditioning, that much incidental learning takes place—for example, the learning of fears, attitudes, and preferences.

Pavlov also found that when stimuli similar to the conditioned stimulus were presented, the dog tended to generalize the stimulus, and responded to it as well as to the conditioned stimulus. By selective reinforcement and extinction, the dog learned to discriminate between similar, but not identical, stimuli.

Instrumental Conditioning. E. L. Thorndike (1874–1949), an American associationist, contributed much to the theory of learning and had a great influence in the application of his findings on instructional practice. In working with animals, such as a cat, in a puzzle box with food outside, Thorndike noticed the trial-and-error characteristic of the behavior, which persisted until the door-releasing lever was accidentally touched. As the trials continued, the cat's behavior became more and more refined as useless movements were eliminated and the animal could immediately trip the door and escape. Thorndike concluded that learning was a matter of "stamping in" correct responses and eliminating incorrect responses because of their rewarding or annoying consequences.

As a result of these experiments, Thorndike postulated the *law of effect* to indicate the relationship between stimulus and response. In effect, the law stated that there was a connection or bond between these two events (stimulus and response), and that when a response was followed by satisfying consequences, the subject was likely to repeat that response in a similar situation. Learning, then, was a matter of trying various approaches until the right one was found, then practicing that response until it was stamped in.

Operant Conditioning. A concept introduced in 1938 by B. F. Skinner, operant conditioning, refers to the learning of voluntary or emitted behavior. Classical conditioning refers to the learning of reflexive or elicited behavior. This latter behavior, called *respondent behavior* by Skinner, is under the control of a stimulus, and the learning involves relating the behavior to other stimuli. In operant conditioning, the behavior is rewarded after it occurs; it does not cause the behavior. That the reward or reinforcement occurs after the behavior takes place makes the repetition of the behavior more probable in the future, according to Skinner. Any event, including one that satisfies a drive, is a reinforcing one if it strengthens the behavior that precedes it. Skinner maintains that a great deal of our everyday behavior is operant, that is, it operates on the environment, and often it is strengthened by reinforcement. Turning a key in a lock and being able to open the door is an example of operant behavior and reinforcement.

Skinner found that after the initial learning period, partial reinforcement was more effective in maintaining the learned behavior than was constant reinforcement. Accordingly, he developed four schedules for providing reinforcement: (1) fixed ratio, where reward occurs after a fixed number of responses; (2) fixed interval, where the reward occurs after a set period of time; (3) variable ratios, where the number of responses between reinforcements varies from one reinforcement to the next; and (4) variable interval, where the time between reinforcements varies from one reinforcement to the next.

By reinforcing successive approximations to a desired behavior, it is possible to shape the behavior of an animal into the mold one wishes. In this way, Skinner was able to teach pigeons to bowl; others have used shaping to teach porpoises rather elaborate behaviors.

Operant-conditioning techniques are applied to human behavior in what is known as *behavior modification*. Behavior modification involves the use of both shaping and reinforcement in changing a person's behavior.

Cognitive Theories

In contrast to the foregoing theories, which were based on association or stimulus-response sequences of behavior, are the theories based on cognitive processes such as perception and knowledge. There are several kinds of cognitive theories: Gestalt theory, topological theory, sign learning, and the phenomenological approach to learning.

Gestalt Theory. Gestalt theory is interested in large patterns of behavior called *molar behavior*. As applied to learning, Gestalt theory considers the learner as already having a complex of attitudes and skills from his learning. The learner perceives the learning situation as a whole, or a gestalt,[1] and responds to elements of the whole that seem to be significant. In so doing, the learner organizes the stimuli in the learning situation into a meaningful pattern or gestalt. Learning also takes place through insight, which involves going from a stage of confusion to one of organization and insight by the discovery of order. Thus, the learner uses organization and reorganization of experience to make sense of his world. A famous example is that of Sultan, the chimpanzee, who was in a cage with two sticks, neither of which was long enough to reach a bunch of bananas outside. After a time he saw the pattern, then fitted the two sticks together to reach the fruit.

Lewin's Topological Theory. Kurt Lewin's topological theory (1952) was an attempt to explain human behavior in terms of responses to environmental forces, especially social environmental forces. This theory features the *field* or *life space*, which is the environment as perceived by the individual; it emphasizes the need for empathy or sensitivity in order to understand the feelings and attitudes of the learner. One's life space is the psychological world in which one lives. It contains all those aspects of the environment—persons, objects, ideas—with which one has psychological contact. One's life space changes from moment to moment, and by restructuring the forces of attraction and repulsion, called *vector forces*, one can fulfill a need and reassess the situation. One can then perceive new and more effective ways to achieve one's purposes. In learning, a change in the valence or strength of the

---

[1] *Gestalt* = form, figure, or shape in German. Presumably, this is what the layman means when he speaks of "getting the picture."

importance of the goals results from reappraisal and clarification of the life space.

Tolman's Sign Learning. The sign-learning theory of Edward C. Tolman (1886–1959) involves the realization that behavior is goal-directed. Learning is the acquired expectation that one stimulus will be followed by another in a certain situation. These expectancies, or means-end readinesses, may be in the form of a cognitive map rather than specific responses; thus, learning is concerned with understanding rather than with conditioning.

The existence of cognitive representation was supported by Tolman's experiments on latent learning, wherein nonrewarded rats learned as much in the first day of reward as the other rats had learned in eleven days of reward. Evidently, while in the maze, although not rewarded, the first group had learned a cognitive map of the maze, but until reward was offered had no opportunity to show by performance what they had learned.

Phenomenological Theory. The phenomenological theory of Snygg and Combs views the person as being in a state of *dynamic equilibrium* and emphasizes the phenomenological nature of perception. According to Snygg and Combs, what determines behavior is psychological or phenomenological reality rather than objective reality—that is, what *appears* to one to be so, rather than what *is* so. It is the environment, as it is perceived by the learner, to which the learner reacts. Thus, a child may be frightened by an innocent, playful puppy because to childish eyes it appears to be a dreadful animal. Evidently, my reality is what appears real to me, and your reality is what appears real to you. Learning is conceived as a natural and normal process for children—a dimension of growth and development. Learning is a result of changes in the way we perceive ourselves and our environment. This theory has had much support from educationists in the 1960s and 1970s.

Application of Learning Theory

Sometimes a theory offers us a clearly defined path to follow, but more often, particularly in education, it only offers us opportunities to develop new and better methods as solutions to old problems. In the following pages, several examples demonstrate how a theoretical framework may guide a teacher in using more effective and efficient teaching procedures. In accordance with much modern theory, understanding the learner and involving him in his own learning will also be discussed in some detail.

The approach used in this module is an attempt to harness a psychological theory. Perhaps you have already recognized that this module is intended as an application of the operant-conditioning approach of Skinner.

Similarly, modern techniques of mastery learning, which are popular now, are an expression of John B. Carroll's theory that learning effectiveness is a function of student "time on task." In this type of teaching, pupils keep at a topic long enough to master it before moving on to the next one.[2]

[2] John B. Carroll, "A Model of School Learning," *Teacher's College Record* 64:723–33 (May, 1963).

A Theoretical Framework

Educational psychology has made it possible for a student to use a theoretical framework for solving problems that arise in the teacher-learner situation. The benefit of using one theory as a frame of reference is that it enables the teacher to devise a technique consistent with that theory in order to remedy a particular situation. It is not uncommon for the beginning teacher to rely on a "bag of tricks," those miscellaneous devices that may have been collected from other teachers, from courses in the teacher-education institution, or from books which purport to supply specific solutions for all problems. These often simple and expedient techniques usually specify what action to take in specific kinds of misbehavior, or they specify the manner in which a learning situation should be handled. Sometimes a "trick" involves the use of detention at the end of the school day for almost any kind of misdemeanor. Students have often been required to write statements about their behavior as many as one hundred times. Solutions such as these usually fail to take into account the variability of human nature. Some teachers are more successful than others in a particular technique; and some methods of teaching are more successful with one student than with another.

The result of these "tricks" may be the arousal of antagonism on the part of the student, more resistance to learning, or negative learning. Also, the teacher usually finds that these haphazard techniques are very inefficient: some methods work some of the time, and some never work. When no consistent behavior pattern emerges from the trial-and-error approach, the teacher is confused; he or she has no means of knowing which "trick" to try in any given situation. Moreover, a teacher who has used a particular technique to prevent recurrence of an undesirable behavior may be unaware of what actually has happened. For instance, the teacher may believe that a disruptive boy who now appears submissive has learned self-control from a disciplinary experience, when actually the boy has only learned to fear the teacher and to respond to external control without learning anything positive about self-control. The following examples illustrate the point.

> Miss Jones sat amid her second-grade reading group. Each student in turn read one or two paragraphs from the three pages of text that comprised the lesson for the day. Billy, who had read first, realizing that his task was completed, entertained himself by poking the boy who sat next to him. As Miss Jones' eyes perceived the mischief, she arose, escorted Billy to the hallway, and resumed her place. In a few minutes she noticed that Jimmy had closed his book and was busy making faces at the girl across the circle. Miss Jones, having precluded the possibility of isolating him in the hallway because of Billy's being there, again dug into her "bag of tricks." She sent Jimmy to his seat, with the prescription of writing out the entire lesson before he left school that afternoon.

Miss Jones was imitating a teacher she had observed while in training, but had not evaluated the effectiveness of "round-robin" reading, nor had she investigated the purpose of the activity she had so readily adopted. Moreover, when the attention of two students wandered from an apparently uninteresting activity, she had not availed herself of a generalized question: "Why are they not attending to the matter at hand?" She had merely dug into her "bag of tricks" to deal with the offenders and deter others from similar acts. When dealing with student misdemeanors, the most efficient procedure is to attempt to determine the source of the unwanted behavior as in the following example:

> Miss Eden had asked her second-grade reading group to read through the selection in order to find the answer to a question which had been carefully planned. After the group had completed the silent reading and an answer to the question obtained, Miss Eden continued to question the class to determine how well they understood what they had read. Sometimes the questions required an answer in the child's own words; sometimes the answer had to be proven by reading from the book.
>
> As the session continued, Michael became restless and attempted to engage the boy next to him in conversation, thus taking his attention from the lesson. Miss Eden recognized that perhaps Michael had become fatigued. After involving him again by asking him a question, she returned the class to their seats, and swung them into a new activity.

A theoretical framework, although sufficient to provide a basis for dealing with many situations, will not be able to prescribe the exact manner in which to manage each particular situation. Instead, its virtue lies in permitting the teacher to utilize the unique characteristics of each situation, and to arrange them in conformance with the theoretical framework. The choice of a theoretical framework that is psychologically sound can provide the teacher with an appropriate basis for making sound decisions and for taking effective actions.

Not all theories have equal validity. Knowledge of psychological principles can assist the teacher in choosing between a sound theory and an unsound or ineffective theory. Our previous examples show that Miss Jones and Miss Eden operated from different theoretical conceptions regarding the nature of reading. Let us now look at two more examples to see the difference between a psychologically sound theoretical position and an inferior one.

> In planning the fifth-grade arithmetic lesson, Mr. Case had decided to demonstrate the relationship between the circumference and the diameter of a circle. He began the lesson by giving the pupils the formula $C = \pi D$ or $C = 22/7$ D. Next, he showed them how to work several examples, using the formula. Then Mr. Case assigned the class a number of examples to complete by themselves in the time that remained.
>
> In giving the general rule first and the specific uses of it later, Mr. Case had used the *deductive* method of teaching.
>
> Mr. Egan was also teaching the relationship between the circumference and the diameter of a circle to a fifth-grade class. He had provided himself with a tape measure and a number of circular objects—a waste basket, a cup, a pail, and several cardboard circles. After the measurements of these objects had been taken and checked by the pupils, and they had done some figuring, they came to the conclusion that multiplying the diameter by 22/7 would give them approximately the circumference of the circle.
>
> Mr. Egan had allowed the students to use several particular examples to arrive at a general rule. This is referred to as the *inductive* method of teaching.

The superiority of using an inductive theoretical framework rather than a deductive one has been demonstrated in the research of Kersh and Colville. In the Kersh experiment, three comparable groups of college students were used. Each was given a series of problems involving arithmetical and geometrical relationships. The methods used by each group were different. In one of the groups the students were given no help at all: in another they were given instructional but no other help, forcing them to learn inductively; and in yet another they were given the rules for solving the problem so that they learned deductively. A test given to the three groups four to six weeks later demonstrated that those who had been given instructional aids but no other help (inductive method) were superior to those who had received no help. The poorest results were achieved by those who had first been given the rules (deductive method). This experiment implies that the inductive method is superior to the deductive method in learning to solve problems, and in learning to use the ability to solve similar problems later on. Similarly, Colville was able to demonstrate that the learning of simple physical skills was best learned inductively from experience, and that learning the skills was not aided by first learning the physical principles involved. These findings do not prove that the inductive method is preferable to all other methods for all instructional purposes, however. The efficacy of a method for a particular situation is contingent upon the characteristics of the situation!

Learning practices often consist of a collection of untested and poorly conceived methods. A common practice is to continue to read material over and over until it is memorized. For example,

> Glen's history teacher had suggested that he learn the list of presidents of the United States. This was to be a framework to which the sequence of facts in American history could be attached. Glen tried reading the list over and over again, so that he would be familiar with it for the history test at the end of the course.

Psychology, through research, has shown that the majority of time spent in learning should be spent in recitation. After reading the list twice, Glen should have tried listing the names without the list, or writing them down in order. The importance of recitation in memorization was demonstrated in a study by Gates. A more detailed study by Forlano showed the superiority of recitation over rereading. His data showed that up to 80 per cent of the time should be spent in recitation, especially for delayed recall.

Educational psychology has made it possible for the teacher in training to adopt a sound theoretical framework on which to base teaching, and thus avoid the pitfalls of unsound practices in the teacher-learner situation.

Understanding the Learner

Another way in which psychology contributes to education is in providing a better understanding of the learner. The fact that each individual is different is, of course, not new. As long ago as 400 B.C., the Greek philosopher, Plato, wrote about the differences in the natural endowment of children. One of his recommendations was that the "better" children be raised much more carefully than "inferior" children.

What *is* new about individual differences is the psychological investigation of these differences. This investigation is concerned with how children differ and what significance these differences have for educational practice. The behavior of each child is more complex than most people realize, and only through familiarity with what psychologists have discovered in their research is the teacher able to come closer to understanding the child. A teacher who fails to understand the child's behavior may cause severe damage to the self-concept of the child, and may actually cause the student to learn negative attitudes toward education.

Psychology has provided a wealth of information concerning the characteristics of children, and every student preparing for the teaching field ought to avail himself of this scientific material. Knowing how personality is developed, how it can be warped, distorted, or inhibited, is of extreme importance in the teacher-learner situation. A teacher who does not realize how an adaptive personality can be fostered may unwittingly be guilty of damaging the personal fulfillment of the individual. An awareness of the characteristics of the developmental stages of children is also necessary. This knowledge enables the teacher to know what performance to expect of a child, what is normal behavior at a certain age, and how to evaluate the development of the child according to the norms of this developmental stage.

Each child is a product of a unique environment. A child's personality becomes what it becomes because environmental forces cause it to grow in certain directions. Thus if a girl's social environment is one in which education is not highly valued, the teacher may find that she has become resistant to learning. The values acceptable to a pupil's social group may be alien to those of the teacher, and may thus interfere with the teacher's management of a particular learning situation. All of this must be taken into consideration.

Learners are changing organisms. As they learn, they change. Not all that pupils learn will be agreeable to their teachers, nor will the students necessarily learn the things the teachers want them to learn. Teachers must familiarize themselves with those psychological factors that are related to success and failure for the learners. It is important for the teacher to understand, for example, that psychologists have discovered that when the introduction of formal reading is attempted before children are ready for it, a majority of the children will fail, and that early training that results in failure may be harmful. After many experiences of learning failure, a child may refuse to try, or may even become emotionally disturbed.

The more understanding the teacher has of an individual student, the more the teacher is able to guide the learning of that student. The interests, abilities, deficiencies, state of health, family background, aspirations, past experience, and the current outlook of the learner all contribute positively or negatively to the learner's attempt to cope with the learning situation.

The child's behavior must be viewed in terms of its arousal. The teacher must be conditioned to think *causally* in order to refrain from reacting to how the behavior affects him. Miss Jones, in our example, reacted to the effect of the child's behavior on herself, whereas Miss Eden viewed the behavior in a causal manner.

Teachers who have a thorough and sound understanding of children and their behavior will be able to predict the behavior of children. This ability depends on the insights and sensitivity teachers have developed from the study of psychological findings and from their own empathy with children.

Summary

Psychology is a behavioral science in which scholars ascertain facts and principles through the application of the scientific method rather than by gut feelings or by conventional wisdom. Educational psychology is the application of psychological principles to the problems of learning and teaching. During the course of history, thinkers have developed many psychological theories, most of which, such as the faculty psychology and apperception theories of the past centuries, are pretty much discredited. Present day theories still in vogue can be divided into (1) associative or stimulus-response theories, and (2) cognitive or field theories. The associative theories, which began with Aristotle, include the modern theories of conditioning. These theories have led to the modern techniques of behavior modification in which human behavior is shaped through the use of operant conditioning and reinforcement.

The cognitive or field theories differ from the associative theories in that they are based on the cognitive processes. Among these theories are *Gestalt*, *topological theory*, *sign learning* and the *phenomenological approach* to learning. According to Gestalt theory, learners learn by organizing the stimuli of the learning situation into meaningful patterns which yield insight. In short, the learner organizes and reorganizes exercises until he gets the picture, or the *Gestalt*. Lewin's topological theory, on the other hand, supposes that learning results from a restructuring of one's life space. According to the sign-learning theory, all behavior is goal directed, and learning is the acquired expectation that one stimulus will be followed by another in a given situation. Learning, according to this theory, results from understanding rather than from conditioning. Phenomenological theory indicates that as people grow, they learn naturally from their perceptions of the situations in which they live.

Knowledge of these theories of learning can help one to develop rational teaching strategies and tactics suitable to the teaching-learning situations one faces. Theories relieve teachers from having to rely on a box of pedagogical tricks; give a basis for judging which type of teaching approach will be most productive in a given situation; and also give a basis for understanding both the common and individual aspects of pupils. These understandings will help teachers not only to predict pupil behavior, but also to adapt their own behavior so as to make their teaching more productive.

SUGGESTED READING

Ausubel, D. P., *Educational Psychology: A Cognitive View.* New York: Holt, Rinehart & Winston, 1968.

Bigge, Morris L., *Learning Theory for Teachers*, 4th ed. New York: Harper & Row, Publishers, 1982.

Bogelski, B. R., *An Introduction to the Principles of Psychology*. Indianapolis, Indiana: The Bobbs-Merrill Co., Inc., 1973.

Charles, C. M., *Educational Psychology*, 3rd ed. St. Louis, Missouri: The C. V. Mosby Company, 1982.

Furth, H. G., *Piaget for Teachers*. Englewood Cliffs, New Jersey: Prentice-Hall, Inc., 1970.

Gagné, R. M., *The Conditions of Learning*, 2nd ed. New York: Holt, Rinehart & Winston, 1970.

Hilgard, Ernest R., ed., *Theories of Learning and Instruction*, The Sixty-third Yearbook of the National Study of Education. Chicago: University of Illinois Press, 1964.

Hill, Winfred, F., *Learning: A Survey of Psychological Interpretations*, 3rd ed. San Francisco: Chandler Press, 1977.

Linskie, Rosella, *The Learning Process: Theory and Practice*. New York: D. Van Nostrand Company, 1977.

Neel, Ann F., *Theories of Psychology: A Handbook*, revised. Cambridge, Mass.: Schenkman Publishing Co., Inc., 1969.

Peterson, Lloyd R., *Learning*. Glenview, Illinois: Scott, Foresman and Company, 1975.

Reilly, Robert and Ernest Lewis, *Educational Psychology: Applications for Classroom Learning and Instruction*. New York: Macmillan Publishing Co., Inc., 1983.

Skinner, B. F., *About Behaviorism*. New York: Alfred A. Knopf, Inc., 1974.

Snelbecker, Glenn E., *Learning Theory and Psych-educational Design*. New York: McGraw-Hill Book Company, 1974.

Staats, A., *Child Learning, Intelligence and Personality*. New York: Harper & Row, Publishers, 1971.

Tarpy, Roger M., *Basic Principles of Learning*. Glenview, Illinois: Scott, Foresman and Company, 1975.

POST TEST

Multiple Choice (*Circle one.*)

1. Psychology as a science is concerned with
   a. studying behavior through literature.
   b. the study of the beliefs of ancient people.
   c. finding out what the man in the street knows.
   d. understanding, predicting, and controlling behavior.

2. Psychology differs from common sense in that
   a. the subject matter is different.
   b. the former is interested in scientific evidence.
   c. the latter is interested in scientific evidence.
   d. both concern information that everybody already knows.

3. The study of McKeachie on the common-sense items, with college students, demonstrated that
   a. college students are subject to prejudice.
   b. college students learn about the same as the man on the street.
   c. college students hang on to common-sense beliefs after exposure to contrary evidence.
   d. none of the students profited from an elementary course in psychology because of resistance to change.

4. The main contention of the doctrine of formal discipline is that
   a. minds are plastic and must be molded in order for learning to occur.
   b. minds are like muscles and improve with rigorous exercise.
   c. minds are incapable of being improved, so we must compensate by developing strong bodies.
   d. no one should have to learn Latin or Euclidean geometry.

5. Faculty psychology resulted in the doctrine of formal discipline because
   a. they both occurred at the same period in the history of education.
   b. the classical curriculum was in the zenith of its development.
   c. the mind was considered to be made up of mental faculties that could be improved by practice.
   d. some subjects needed to be included in the school program, and this was the best way to account for it.

6. The major disadvantage of the doctrine of formal discipline is that
   a. it was responsible for some of the instruction in school today.
   b. it was based on a false assumption that mental faculties improve with exercise.
   c. it was responsible for teachers' insisting that students memorize poetry.
   d. it was responsible for making Latin and mathematics more practical than history and literature.

7. The theory of formal discipline was largely discredited by the
   a. experimental work of William James on memory.
   b. work on Ebbinghaus on memory.
   c. rise of behaviorism.
   d. philosophy of John Dewey.

8. Herbart developed a form of psychology involving habit formation, which was based on
   a. John Locke's theory of *tabula rasa*.
   b. the doctrine of formal discipline.
   c. rigorous exercise of mental faculties.
   d. the theory that all subjects were equal in developing logical analysis.

9. One of the positive contributions of Herbart to education was
   a. to discredit faculty psychology.
   b. to define the purpose of education in moral terms.
   c. to make minds become *tabula rasa*.
   d. to place the child at the center of the curriculum.

10. According to Herbartian psychology, the apperceptive mass was
    a. the same as a mental state.
    b. the total stock of one's mental states at any one time.
    c. images or copies of previous sense impressions, occurring in various stages of awareness.
    d. the completely empty, inert, and passive mind.

11. One of the two principles of apperception proposed by Herbart was that
    a. all perception is apperception.
    b. ideas either attract or repel one another.
    c. most activity is sensory activity, memory activity, and conceptual thinking.
    d. the ease with which an idea enters consciousness is determined by the number of times it is brought into consciousness.

12. Herbart's system lost its influence in education even though vestiges of it are seen in present day educational practices. The reason for its decline was that
    a. it became widespread throughout Europe and the United States but not in Germany.
    b. many educators became concerned because his system was too mechanical, and because John Dewey attacked the system.
    c. John Dewey approved of the five steps, and John Dewey, the apostle of progressive education, was scorned by most educators.
    d. it was based on John Locke's theory that the mind was the product of life experiences.

13. One of the major characteristics of behaviorism is
    a. its opposition to conditioning.
    b. its acceptance of Gestalt principles.
    c. its denial of the apperceptive mass as representing one's total mental states.
    d. its insistence on observable behavior as the essential content of psychology.

14. The first major thrust of psychology as a science resulted from the work of
    a. John Locke and his *tabula rasa* theory.
    b. Wundt and his experimental laboratory in Leipzig.
    c. Pavlov and his conditioned dog.
    d. John Dewey and the child-centered curriculum.

15. Which of the following statements is *not* characteristic of behaviorism?
    a. A rat runs a maze in thirty seconds.
    b. A monkey raised in isolation will not associate with normal monkeys.
    c. A pigeon pecked a disc seventy times in a minute.
    d. John told the psychologist how it felt to receive a shock of seventy-five volts.

16. In the experiment performed by Pavlov in conditioning a dog,
    a. the unconditioned response was the meat.
    b. the conditioned response was the bell.
    c. the unconditioned stimulus was the bell.
    d. the conditioned response was salivation.

17. Because of his work with the cat in the puzzle box, Thorndike concluded that
    a. all learning is trial and error.
    b. learning consists of reinforcing correct responses and eliminating incorrect responses.
    c. operant conditioning is essentially the same as classical conditioning but is useful mainly with lower animals.
    d. there was not much his theory of learning could offer the school.

18. The main difference between classical conditioning and operant conditioning is that
    a. the former is used with animals and the latter with people.
    b. the law of effect implies that operant conditioning is inferior to classical conditioning.
    c. classical conditioning works on elicited or reflexive behavior, and operant conditioning on voluntary behavior.
    d. there is no major difference between classical conditioning and operant conditioning.

19. When a worker in a factory is paid by the piece rate, which schedule of reinforcement is being used?
    a. Fixed interval.
    b. Variable interval.
    c. Fixed ratio.
    d. Variable ratio.

20. "Learning occurs through insight, which happens after traversing a period of confusion to one of organization and this discovery of order is insight." This statement refers to
    a. Gestalt theory.
    b. Tolman's sign-learning theory.
    c. Lewin's topological theory.
    d. Snygg and Combs' phenomenological theory.

21. If behavior is being "shaped" under conditioning, the process referred to is
    a. behavior elicited by the subject under reinforcement.
    b. successive approximations to some goal-behavior under reinforcement.
    c. behavior occurring without reinforcement.
    d. behavior emitted after reinforcement has taken place.

22. Seeing the learning situation as a whole, and responding to elements that he sees as significant , refers to which type of theory?
    a. Behaviorism.
    b. Topological.
    c. Gestalt.
    d. Sign-learning.

23. A theory dealing with behavior as responses to environmental forces within the life space is
    a. behaviorism.
    b. topological.
    c. Gestalt.
    d. sign-learning.

24. When behavior is considered to be the result of psychological reality rather than objective reality, and the learner reacts to the environment as he perceives it, we are discussing
    a. Gestalt theory.

    b. topological theory.

    c. sign-learning theory.

    d. phenomenological theory.

25. When teachers start with a number of examples and from them develop a general law, they are using

    a. inductive reasoning.

    b. deductive reasoning.

    c. shaping behavior.

    d. topological theory.

INVOLVEMENT EXPERIENCES

    1. Talk to teachers about their teaching. What types of teaching method do they recommend? Why do they think these teaching methods are effective? Do they base their teaching approaches on theoretical considerations, practical experience, or hunches? Do they subscribe to overall theories about teaching method? If so, what theories do they believe most valid?

    2. Talk to lay people about learning. Do they, unconsciously perhaps, seem to lean toward certain learning theories? Do you see evidence that they hold beliefs about learning no longer held by the profession?

    3. Ask teachers about tricks they use in their teaching. In your experience as a student, how did you react to such tricks?

    4. Think back over your own school career. What tricks did your teachers use? Can you think of any teacher tricks that had undesirable effects; for example, disciplinary techniques that made you dislike school, the class, or the subject? Can you think of tricks your teacher used that caused you to enjoy school and your subjects, that made you study harder, or learn better?

    5. Compare the stimulation-response theories to the cognitive-learning theories. Do you see any difference in the teaching method implied by these learning theories?

    6. Consider the deductive and inductive methods of teaching described in this module. Can you think of instances in which you would prefer to use the inductive method. Can you think of situations in which you think the deductive method might be preferable? Remember, the effectiveness of a teaching method is contingent upon the teaching-learning situation.

    7. The module recommends one method for memorization over another. Try a little experiment. Study a lesson by the rereading technique. Study another lesson by the recitation technique, by asking yourself questions, or repeating to yourself what seem to be the important facts or ideas. Which approach seems to pay off better?

    8. Observe a class. If you were to teach this class, what would you wish to know about the students as a group? What would you want to know about individual students? How would this knowledge help you in your teaching?

    9. Study a student. Does the student have special characteristics or traits one should consider when selecting one's teaching approach or teaching material?

    10. Think about yourself. What things about you would it be helpful for a teacher to know in order to encourage you to do your best?

MODULE

6

Psychological Bases: Nature of Learning

Process of Learning / Readiness / Intelligence / Motivation / Memory / Transfer

The first-edition version of this module was written by W. Ralph McCaw, Jersey City State College. It has been revised and updated for this edition.

RATIONALE

Learning is not unfamiliar to you. You have been involved in it consciously or unconsciously since birth, or even before. You perhaps became particularly aware of it when you became a college student responsible for your own learning for the first time. Then probably you were unsure of yourself and asked yourself such questions as, "Am I allowing enough time for study?" "Am I being an efficient learner?" "How much time should I spend on recitation?" "Is memorization the only way to learn?" "How can I remember the material for a whole semester?" "Why do I forget?" The study of educational psychology should help you answer such questions both for yourself and for your future pupils. It provides experimental evidence that reveals which learning techniques are superior. For example, scientific studies demonstrate that cramming on the night before a test is not the best way to prepare for an examination. By showing how learning takes place and how to extend retention time and that learning is more than the accumulation of information, the study of learning theory gives a basis for developing more effective learning habits and practices.

When you become a teacher, understanding educational psychology will help you see whether or not the educational practices being used are sound. Because you will be aware of the nature of learning and the learning process, you will probably be more alert for indications of learning difficulty and be better able to modify your procedures day by day. You will thus be able to solve problems before they become major obstacles. As a knowledgeable, problem-oriented teacher, you should be able to clear the way for more effective learning for your pupils.

Associated with the learning process are many interdependent topics. They are motivation, readiness, intelligence, retention, and transfer; all of these topics will be treated in this module. Our intention is to give you some insight into what happens when one learns, why learning occurs, and what factors may enhance or hinder each pupil's fulfillment according to his unique interests and needs.

SPECIFIC OBJECTIVES

Upon completion of your study of this module, you should be able to
1. Explain the nature of learning.
2. List factors affecting learning.
3. Explain the need for determining students' readiness to learn no matter what their age.
4. Tell what is involved when learning takes place.
5. Explain why it is necessary to diagnose a problem before prescribing a remedy.
6. Explain the influence of *early training*.
7. Explain Havighurst's developmental tasks.
8. Define the terms *motive, drive, need, incentive*.
9. Demonstrate that motives lie within the person, and are not something *done* to him.

10. List the main motives related to achievement.
11. Explain how levels of aspiration are set.
12. Explain what a psychological construct is.
13. Describe the contributions to the study of intelligence made by Binet, Terman, Spearman, Galton, Thorndike, Thurstone, Gates, and Wechsler.
14. Explain how J. P. Guilford perceives intelligence.
15. Describe the several aspects of mental growth.
16. Describe the position of Piaget and Bruner in regard to intellectual development.
17. Describe the contributions of Ebbinghaus to the study of memory.
18. Describe the theories of forgetting.
19. Explain the terms *primary effect, recency effect,* and *rehearsal buffer.*
20. Explain the difference between retroactive inhibition and proactive inhibition.
21. List and explain each of the kinds of remembering.
22. Explain the difference between STM and LTM, and the functions of each.
23. Explain positive transfer, negative transfer, vertical transfer, and lateral transfer.
24. Compare and contrast the six theories used to explain transfer.
25. Describe at least some of the principles regarding the use of transfer in the classroom.

MODULE TEXT

Process of Learning

Learning is a continuous process that changes the learner in many ways. As one develops skills and habits, one also learns attitudes. And one learns to be the kind of person that one becomes. In school, students sometimes learn because of the teacher's guidance, and sometimes in spite of it. Some of their learning may be irrelevant to the goals chosen by the teacher; and some learning may be in opposition to the social order.

Educational psychologists point out that pupils are most likely to learn what they think they need to learn. These beliefs do not, however, necessarily match what parents and teachers think pupils ought to learn. How well children learn something depends largely on their convictions concerning the importance of learning it. These convictions are closely related to the motivation, goals, and aspirations of the students. In short, we tend to learn what we feel we need to learn and want to learn. As Dewey pointed out, interest yields effort and action that result in learning.

Educational psychology attempts to assist the teacher in managing the learning situation by showing what happens when learning takes place; it emphasizes learning rather than teaching. What happens to the learner is important regardless of what kind of guidance or assistance is provided by the teacher. This does not mean that the teacher is not essential; it means that the teacher's role is that of guiding and directing learning rather than that of manipulating the learner.

Factors Affecting Learning

Problems occur frequently in the learning situation; they may range from a lack of a desire to learn to emotional disturbances resulting from a failure to learn. Some teachers have a tendency to treat these problems in traditional ways; that is, to follow the same procedures they have seen their own teachers use. Frequently, traditional procedures fail to deal with the essential aspects of the problem, and the situation remains unimproved. Most problems are not as simple as they appear, because many factors underlying the cause are not readily apparent to the observer. Also, sometimes what appears to be a cause is merely a symptom.

Too often, remedies are attempted before a diagnosis is made. To deal effectively with any educational problem, all relevant factors must be taken into account. A learning problem is usually a result of more than one cause. If, for example, a child fails to succeed in his early attempt in formal reading, the following factors should be investigated before recommending treatment.

1. Scholastic ability, which sets the limit for scholastic achievement and can be a severe limiting factor but is not often the cause of a failure to learn to read.
2. Past achievement, which includes readiness to learn. (Methods used to teach him in the past may have affected his attitude toward a learning situation.)
3. Aptitudes and disabilities, which may either increase or interfere with his ability to cope with a learning situation.
4. Interests, which are useful in leading him back to areas where he has had difficulty, and may also be the key to motivate his learning.
5. Personality adjustment; that is, emotional and social development, which are closely related to success, particularly in social or group situations.
6. Health, including sight and hearing, which are important factors that are frequently overlooked.
7. Family background, which is pregnant with sources of difficulty— family relationships, discipline, aspirations and goals.

It is not sufficient to assign a simple and inadequate cause, such as laziness or stubbornness, for a failure to learn. A thorough diagnosis usually reveals much more; and though time-consuming, such a diagnosis may pay rich dividends in the excitement of success, rather than having a demoralizing experience of failure.

Awareness of Environmental Factors

When we talk about learning situations, we are referring to the conditions, physical or psychological, that make a situation favorable or unfavorable to learning. The amount of noise, the amount of light, the adequacy of ventilation, and temperature, for example, are physical factors which have an effect on learning. Educational psychology provides evidence that these and many other factors originating in the environment do affect the rate of learning. Other conditions, such as the state of health, sufficiency or lack of nutrition, and harmony or lack of harmony in the home, are also related to the ability to learn.

Other factors which affect the learning situation include the behavior, morale, and attitudes of the teacher, and the emotional tone of the school. The academic aspirations of the community, according to research evidence, are also part of this learning situation. When the learning situation is organized so that the physical and psychological factors are optimal, learning should proceed more efficiently.

Evaluation of Learning

Evaluation is a very important aspect of the learning situation. It mainly involves two processes. The first is the evaluation of the learner's progress; the second is the evaluation of educational practices.

In the evaluation of learning, psychology is useful in the development of principles for test-construction, in standardizing tests to measure scholastic ability or aptitude, and in developing tests to measure growth in specific subject areas. A test of scholastic aptitude enables the teacher to predict the amount and rate of learning for the student, for example.

Psychology also offers suggestions about practices that should be avoided, such as the memorizing of meaningless mathematical formulas or the purposeless diagramming of sentences. Also to be avoided is the use of threats and detentions as punishment for failing grades or to deter misbehavior. Psychology points out that such measures are at best stop-gap measures, and may actually interfere with the learning process by developing negative attitudes in students.

Readiness

In educational shop talk, *readiness* refers to the student's state of being ready to undertake an educational venture. Readiness has cognitive, emotional, attitudinal, and physical aspects. Thus, for instance, one's readiness for a particular learning task may depend on one's prior learning attitude toward the subject or teacher, one's feelings of confidence, physical strength and agility, and so on.

Although readiness is often discussed in terms of a specific subject, such as readiness for reading, it is more appropriate to talk of readiness in terms of a total learning situation. One of the most important factors in learning efficiency is the time when a particular learning experience should begin.

Much disagreement exists in regard to the optimal *age* at which to introduce particular experiences—for example, the introduction of formal instruction in reading. There is agreement, however, on the need for determining readiness. There are, of course, several indications of readiness, and the teacher must be aware of them. In order to recognize readiness, the teacher must understand the ways in which children develop, what readiness for any activity involves, and how to determine when the pupils have sufficient readiness for success with an activity. This is one of the reasons why the teacher needs to have a thorough understanding of the learners, as well as insight into the behavior they exhibit. This will assist the teacher in looking for the causes of unusual or different behavior, and enable him to make more accurate predictions about future behavior.

Development and Readiness

Psychology attempts to show, on the basis of scientific study, the characteristics and criteria for determining readiness. This knowledge enables the teacher to understand the meaning of various stages in the emotional, social, physical, and intellectual growth of the child, and how this is related to academic progress.

If there is an optimal time for learning to begin, it would seem necessary to capitalize on that factor. The order in which behavior occurs in the developing individual appears to indicate that there is a priority in terms of what one is able to do. For example, without prior experience in walking, a child is not prepared to run. Without prior experience in standing erect, one is unlikely to be ready for walking.

A certain degree of biological maturation must first occur in order to provide a child with a reservoir of responses, which he is then able to use in appropriate circumstances. Readiness, however, is not dependent solely upon the maturation of the inherited traits, important as they are. Two other important ingredients in readiness are (1) past experience, which provides a repertoire of responses; and (2) motivation, which causes him to utilize these responses in new ways and in new circumstances.

It is never true that readiness is totally lacking, because a child is always ready for some learning. Even though a very young child is not ready for the traditional approach to formal reading instruction, for instance, recent research shows that some other methods may produce results at a very early age. Maturational factors, however, such as the coordination of the eyes in vision, mental development, the ability to attend to symbols, and favorable attitudes, as well as maturation in the social and emotional areas, are essential factors in readiness for reading.

Readiness is not only a preparation for the early school experiences; it is also a matter of concern at every level of learning. Whenever a new subject or topic is introduced, the teacher should consider the readiness of each class member for the learning experience that is being provided.

At times, readiness refers to the *preparation* of the child for the learning experience. In this case, one must sometimes wait for the required maturation to take place. It is important to remember that a child is always ready for some kind of learning. Rather than waiting for maturation to take place, it may be better to adjust the program so that the learning experiences encountered are suited to the level of maturation. Failure to take into account the readiness of a child for a particular learning experience may lead to much failure and frustration for the child. Repeated failure has a tendency to provide negative attitudes toward learning, which makes the child less ready for further learning situations. Attempts to ignore readiness, or to promote learning without regard to preparation for it, is often called *early training*.

Physical Maturity As Basis for Readiness

Learning is dependent to a considerable degree on maturation. A child walks when he has acquired sufficient physical development. In normal development, learning to walk occurs spontaneously sometime around the end of the first year, the average being approximately fourteen months. *Early training* refers to the provision of special efforts to train a child to develop behavior at an earlier age than that at which it occurs spontaneously, that is, from environmental stimulation. With special training, for instance, children may learn to walk several months before they would without this training. Whether providing extra effort to speed up the appearance of certain learned behavior is advantageous or not is a matter of concern to both parents and teachers.

Fortunately, there is some research related to this problem. Studies involving identical twins demonstrate that learning can be speeded up when one twin is given special training and the other one is not. Such studies were undertaken by S. Gesell and H. Thompson, and by McGraw. The often-cited McGraw study, reported in 1935, concerned two fraternal twins who had been at first thought to be identical twins when the study took place. From the age of twenty-one days to twenty-two months, attempts were made to stimulate the performance of one twin in sitting alone, creeping, walking, reaching, and grasping. This twin soon outdistanced his twin brother and other untrained children in such activities as swimming, diving, climbing inclines, roller skating, and jumping off boxes. But he failed to learn faster the skills more dependent on maturation, such as crawling, sitting, standing, and walking.

Another study by McGraw involved bladder training of twin boys. The training of one was begun when he was about fifty days old: he was placed on the toilet every hour. The first six hundred days showed little learning, but from this point on, the training was more successful; when seven hundred days had elapsed, success was nearly 100 per cent. The training of the other twin was not begun until he was seven hundred days old. His performance was immediately almost as satisfactory as that of the twin with the longer period of training.[1]

Numerous studies on record show that maturation will occur and skills will be developed in spite of lack of formal training, or when practice is inhibited. Dennis and Dennis found that among Hopi papooses, learning to walk was not delayed even though the babies were cradled so that their legs could not move.

Because certain skills can be learned earlier when special training is provided, and because other skills are dependent on maturation, it is imperative

---

[1] Myrtle B. McGraw, *Growth: A Study of Johnny and Jimmy* (New York: Appleton-Century-Crofts, 1935).

to consider where and when early training should be encouraged or discouraged. Research appears to support some of the following generalizations:

1. When early training results in early positive attitudes of confidence (which give a successful flavor to all learning experiences) such early training might well be encouraged. The early development of Handel's musical talent for instance, gave him an early start toward a productive and successful musical career. Early training in touch typing will result in more efficient learning of the skill, provided, of course, that training is begun before the individual has developed bad typing habits that must be unlearned.

2. It is possible for early training to be harmful. The enforcement of early skill-learning before there is adequate maturation, motivation, or background is likely to result in failure, with concomitant attitudes of discouragement and negative attitudes toward learning in general. Sometimes this frustrating experience is sufficiently severe to interfere with adaptive personality development.

3. When early training involves the expenditure of a great deal of effort to learn what would eventually be acquired spontaneously, it appears that its inefficiency may make it a questionable practice. For example, if toilet training can as easily be acquired at the end of seven hundred days without prior practice as it can in 650 days with practice, then the use of early training is foolish. Probably the wise procedure would be to consider each case individually, weighing the advantages and disadvantages before deciding whether or not to go ahead with early training. In making such decisions it is important to consider the collateral learning of attitudes, which may be rather difficult to alter at a later time. (These are sometimes overlooked in the appraisal of the learning process.) Once the decision to train early has been made, the manner in which the training is given and how it is being received by the child need constant evaluation in order to determine whether early training should be continued. If the early training is accompanied by concomitant learning of poor attitudes, early training may do more harm than good.

It is also possible for learning experiences to be too long delayed. When learning experiences are offered after the optimal time for peak efficiency, there may be a lack of interest and undesirable collateral learning. In order to determine the most appropriate time at which to introduce learning experience, educators should become familiar with the concept of developmental tasks.

Havighurst's Developmental Tasks

Robert Havighurst has conceived of a system involving a set of problems or tasks which the individual must solve at each level of his life. If he is successful at solving the appropriate tasks at one level of learning, he will experience happiness, according to Havighurst, and this success will make it possible for him to cope with more difficult problems at later levels. If he fails to solve the problems at a particular level, he experiences unhappiness, the disapproval of society, and difficulty with later tasks. Following is a list of developmental tasks for infancy and early childhood, the middle years, and adolescence. These stages cover the individual from infancy through secondary school.

Developmental Tasks of Infancy and Early Childhood (birth to 6 years)
Learning to walk.
Learning to take solid food.
Learning to talk.
Learning to control the elimination of body wastes.
Learning sex differences and sexual modesty.
Achieving physiological stability.
Forming simple concepts of social and physical reality.
Learning to relate oneself emotionally to parents, siblings, and other people.
Learning to distinguish right from wrong, and developing a conscience.

Developmental Tasks for Middle Childhood (6 to 12 years)
Learning physical skills necessary for ordinary games.
Building wholesome attitudes toward oneself as a growing organism.
Learning to get along with age-mates.
Learning an appropriate masculine or feminine social role.
Developing fundamental skills in reading, writing, and calculating.
Developing concepts necessary for everyday living.
Developing conscience, morality, and a scale of values.
Developing personal independence.
Developing attitudes toward social groups and institutions.

Developmental Tasks for Adolescence (12 to 18 years)
Achieving new and more mature relations with age-mates of both sexes.
Achieving a masculine or feminine social role.
Accepting one's physique, and using the body effectively.
Achieving emotional independence of parents and other adults.
Achieving assurance of economic independence.
Selecting and preparing for an occupation.
Preparing for marriage and family life.
Developing intellectual skills and concepts necessary for civic competence.
Desiring and achieving socially responsible behavior.
Acquiring a set of values and an ethical system as a guide to behavior.[2]

Although not included as one of Havighurst's developmental tasks, the development of perception is one of the tasks of infancy. Renée Spitz's account of the work of Von Senden on the results of removal of cataracts from the eyes of persons between the ages of three and forty-three gives a dramatic portrayal of the failure to master a "task" at the proper time. Even though sight had been provided for these sixty-three subjects, they were unable to organize their perception.

[2] Robert J. Havighurst, *Developmental Tasks and Education*, 2nd ed. (New York: Longmans, Green & Company, 1952).

Von Senden reports that their reaction to the "blessing" conferred on them, namely the gift of sight, was to say the least, unexpected. None of them experienced their gain as a blessing. It turned out that, though they had *vision*, they could not see. Literally, they had to learn how to see in a long, drawn out, laborious and painful process causing them endless mental anguish. When we say "long, drawn-out-process" we mean months and years; many of them never learned to see—some of them actually expressed the wish to be blind again.[3]

Countless examples may be found to confirm the hypothesis that failure of individuals to master particular tasks at the appropriate time leads to difficulty with more advanced tasks. Typical is the failure of children to develop the common skills of walking and talking because their development has been interfered with by psychotic disorders, or by the deprivation of maternal care. An example of severe failure to learn most of the developmental tasks of childhood is Kamala, the girl who was raised by a she-wolf. Kamala had learned to walk on all fours, but after her rescue at the age of eight, until her death at seventeen, she never learned to walk gracefully, and when in a hurry would drop down on all fours. She had failed to learn any human language, and attempts to teach her to speak were not very fruitful. In the first year after her rescue she learned thirty words, and only fifteen more during the second year.

An example of the application of the principle of developmental tasks is the St. Louis curriculum for the primary division of the St. Louis schools. Within this division, a number of levels have been established. For each level, criteria have been determined for successful achievement of the experiences at this level. When a child successfully meets the criteria for this level, he is then ready to deal with the experience of the next level.

This arrangement is similar to W. C. Olson's idea of pacing, which posits that the individual child should be allowed to proceed at his own rate. According to Olson's plan, learners select their own learning experiences and, consequently, are almost inevitably successful in completing their tasks, because the child selects what he feels he can master. Although Olson's pacing does not involve the definitive criteria of Havighurst, it does conform to the principles of developmental tasks.

Intelligence

Learning, which has been defined as a change in behavior resulting from experience, is dependent on the intellectual capacity of the individual to respond. No other area of development is as crucial to readiness for learning as the intellectual development of the learner.

The state of intellectual development at any one time is called *intelligence*. Today, psychologists tend to deny the existence of intelligence as an entity which is present in some degree or at some stage of development; they regard it as a psychological construct. In other words, they regard the term *intelligence* as a verbal invention that we use to represent something that we can know about only by its effect—that is, a concept that must be defined in

[3] Renée Spitz, *The First Year of Life* (New York: International Universities Press, 1965), p. 10.

terms of observable behavior. For instance, we might draw conclusions about the intelligence of two persons by observing and comparing their effectiveness in solving the same problem, for example, "In what way are a mountain and a lake alike?"

Intelligence varies from individual to individual. There are numerous statements in the writings of our earliest civilizations that attest to the differing degrees of human ability. Centuries later, one of the clearest statements about this variability was made in a prediction by Sir Francis Galton, before we had learned how to measure intelligence. Galton, a nineteenth-century English psychologist, said that if the intelligence of humans could be measured, it would be found to range in almost imperceptible degrees from very low levels of intelligence to very high levels, with the majority falling near the middle of the range. This prediction was essentially correct.

Now, we shall limit our discussion to the time since intelligence has been considered a measurable quality.

Early Positions

A few years after the prediction of Galton, Alfred Binet was commissioned by the French government to devise a means of excluding from the schools children incapable of profiting from instruction. Binet, an experimental psychologist, was determined to do this job in as scientific a manner as possible. He rejected the kinds of measurements that were current at that time, and after fifteen years of labor developed a scale built upon the everyday experiences of children; he published his findings in 1905. After many revisions, this scale has become one of the most widely used measures of the intelligence of children today—the Stanford-Binet Intelligence Scale.

The following quotation seems to represent Binet's perception of intelligence, which guided him in producing the first measure of intelligence.

> [Intelligence includes the] ability to give and sustain attention to achieve certain ends, the power of ready and appropriate adaptation, and the tendency to employ autocriticism . . .
>
> It seems to us that in intelligence there is a fundamental faculty the alteration or the lack of which is of the utmost importance for practical life. This faculty is judgment, otherwise called good sense, practical sense, initiative, the faculty of adjusting one's self to the circumstances. To judge well, to comprehend well, to reason well, these are the essential activities of intelligence. A person may be a moron or an imbecile if he is lacking in judgment; but with good judgment he can never be either. Indeed, the rest of the intellectual faculties seem of little importance in comparison with judgment.[4]

As might be expected, many psychologists agreed with Binet's definition, but because intelligence is difficult to define, many developed their own ways of describing it.

L. M. Terman. Terman is the psychologist who was responsible for the American revision of the Binet scale. His version is the one used in this coun-

---

[4] A. Binet and V. Henri, "La Psychologie Individuelle," *Année Psychologique*, 2 (1895), pp. 411–463.

try today. Terman expressed the idea that a person is intelligent in proportion to his ability to carry on abstract thinking.

H. H. Goddard. Goddard was responsible for bringing the original Binet scale to America. He defined intelligence as "the degree of availability of one's experience for the solution of immediate problems and the anticipation of future ones."

Carl Spearman. Spearman, who had been a student of Galton, in 1904 postulated that there is a general factor, g, underlying all mental functions, and a large number of factors that are specific to particular mental functions, s. Individual differences can be explained according to this proposition: as being the result of either different amounts of g or different amounts of s for any task being considered. However, because the g factor is a general one affecting all functions, a deficiency in this factor would make it highly unlikely that a person would be exceptional in any special area. On the other hand, a person with an above-average quality, or g factor, might be high in one specific area and low in another. On the basis of such observations, Spearman concluded that the most important factor determining individual differences is the g or general factor. Spearman's theory is referred to as a *multiple-factor* theory since it includes both a general factor and a number of specific factors.

E. L. Thorndike. Thorndike believed that intelligence is composed of peoples' many specific abilities. As a result of his observations of intelligent behavior and from his research, he classified intelligence as (1) abstract intelligence: the ability to deal with abstract ideas and symbols, (2) mechanical intelligence: the ability to deal with mechanics and things; and (3) social intelligence: the ability to deal with people.

Thorndike further theorized that intelligence could be characterized by the following dimensions: *altitude* or level, which refers to the difficulty of the problems in any one field that the individual can master; *range*, which refers to the number of fields in which one is competent; *area*, which is the product of level and range and the speed at which one is able to complete given problems. On the basis of his theory and research, Thorndike developed an intelligence test, known as the CAVD, composed of a number of items classified as sentence completion, arithmetic reasoning, vocabulary, and following directions.

L. L. Thurstone. Thurstone rejected the idea of a general factor in intelligence. He conceived of intelligence as being composed of a number of primary abilities which are used to solve problems relating to these abilities. The primary abilities that he identified were verbal, numerical, spatial, word fluency, inductive reasoning, deductive reasoning, and memory. Using these factors, he composed the *Chicago Primary Abilities Tests*. In later editions of these tests, now called the *SRA Primary Abilities Tests*, the number of factors have been reduced to five: verbal, numerical, space, reasoning, and word fluency.

Contemporary Conceptions of Intelligence

Recent research has resulted in new theories that are not of the multiple-factor type. In the following paragraphs, we shall look at some of these theories. Although these theories, on the whole, represent recent thinking about learning, some of them were conceived before some of the multiple-factor theories. They are included here because they do represent a contemporary point of view and do not fall directly into the multiple-factor conceptualization.

Arthur Gates. Gates who is best known for his work in the field of reading, has given us a very comprehensive definition of intelligence:

> a composite or organization of abilities to learn, to grasp broad and subtle facts, especially abstract facts, with alertness and accuracy, to exercise mental control, and to display flexibility and ingenuity in seeking the solution to problems.[5]

David Wechsler. Wechsler's intelligence scales for adults and children have become widely used, as was his first test for older children and adults, the *Wechsler-Bellevue Scale*. In 1958, he defined intelligence as "the global or aggregate capacity for the individual to act purposefully, think rationally, and to deal effectively with his environment."

J. P. Guilford. Guilford has been interested in the areas of intelligence and creativity, and has developed an expanded theory of multiple factors of intelligence. He has used factor-analysis statistical techniques to sort out factors, and has developed a model in which the factors are three-dimensional. In 1967, he described the dimensions in terms of (1) the kinds of operations or processes performed by the individual—for example, memory; (2) the kinds of material involved—for example, language symbols; and (3) the kind of products involved—for example, units or relations. The total system, of which these abilities are the parts, is called the *structure of intellect.*

Functional Descriptions. In 1921, Edward Boring declared that intelligence is what intelligence tests measure. The implications of this statement are that if one examines the functions performed by a significant intelligence test, such as the Stanford-Binet, one would be able to describe intelligence from a functional point of view. The functions evident in the Stanford-Binet are manipulation of objects and eye-hand coordination; observation and identification of common objects, perceiving similarities and differences; practical judgment or common sense, memory, spatial orientation, numerical functions, and verbal functions. Presumably, these may be considered to be the components of intelligence, according to the point of view of the test builders.

Summation. Although much thought and much research has been done on the subject, there is still much disagreement about the nature of intelligence. As we have noted, some psychologists see intelligence as a global capacity; others see it as composed of many primary abilities. At this point, it is probably of most value to you, as a beginning teacher, to think of intelligence as the ability to see relationships and make evaluations, and to deal with symbolic material in the form of verbal or abstract terms, because these qualities are relevant to learning and thinking. Having considered the many

---

[5] Arthur Gates, et al., *Educational Psychology*, 3rd ed. (New York: Macmillan, 1948).

concepts of intelligence, we shall consider now some characteristics of mental growth.

Mental Growth

As mental growth takes place, some characteristics are obvious. One of the most noticeable changes is the lengthening of the attention span. In an infant, the ability to concentrate is still very limited, but, as children grow older, the length of time they can apply their concentrative powers increases, until as college students they can pursue problems for hours.

The attention span is not uniform at any stage of development, nor does it change in a gradual, constant manner. The appeal of the situation or material, one's physical condition, one's success in dealing with the situation, one's ability to work independently, one's past experience, and the kind of incentives offered are some of the factors that seem to determine one's temporary ability to focus one's attention for a period of time.

In the educational situation, the inability of a child to attend to a task for as long as other children may be an indication of lack of readiness for that task, or the existence of some other interfering factor. The length of the attention span is both a measure of mental growth and of readiness for particular experiences.

Another aspect of mental growth is the ability of the child to deal with stimuli that are remote in time and space. This includes the ability to deal with current, past, and future events. As Jean Piaget, the noted Swiss biologist and student of mental growth, has pointed out, children have difficulty in perceiving time data and in organizing the data to develop time concepts. If Piaget is correct in his analysis, the concept of past versus present is not understood until a child is eight years old; that understanding the measurement of time is not reached until a child is eleven years old; and that a child is not able to understand time zones until adolescence.

As children's mental abilities grow, they also become progressively more able to deal with material that is not present; as with the abstract as well as the concrete; with directions and placement in space in reference to themselves; and with the spatial distance between two or more external objects.

With the continuing growth of their mental abilities, children tend to become less involved in daydreams and make-believe. They gradually exchange the world of fantasy for one of reality. Although they perceive the real experiences more concretely and more naively than adults do—neither looking for hidden meanings nor seeking ulterior motives—they thrive on them. They also become interested in vicarious experiences as revealed through the media of moving pictures, storybooks, and television. Finally, after sufficient mental development, they become able to distinguish between fantasy and reality. In all of these aspects, their progress in orienting with reality is related to their progress in developing the ability to deal with language.

Until grade six at least, children make marvelous progress in their ability to cope with language. They greatly increase both their understood and spoken vocabulary (with the former outstripping the latter), improve the clarity of their articulation, exhibit greater skill in integrating words into sentences, use longer verbal responses, and show increased facility in the use of the various parts of speech. The amount of change and the language patterns resulting vary greatly from individual to individual, of course, according to the impact of such factors as psychological reinforcement and practice, sex, intellectual capacity, economic circumstances, travel, child-rearing practices, number of children in the family, and the amount of environmental stimulation. As Watson pointed out, "changes are a matter of maturation and learning concomittant with age, not age itself".[6]

A form of mental growth which is of great importance to the school is the increase in the ability to reason. This growth too is subject to individual differences in ability and application. Reasoning ability is dependent on the acquisition of experience and perceptual development. It increases in proportion to the capacity of the child and the opportunities which are provided where this process can be utilized. There is variety in the nature of reasoning, from the early manipulation of the environment by the infant to achieve some end, to the manipulation of data of an abstract quality to develop ideas, gather evidence, and establish proof.

The ability to remember or memorize is another corollary of mental growth. Memory is dependent on the development of language, which provides a medium in which memory can take place. It is very helpful to have a large stock of words and phrases with which to express ideas and tabulate experience for storage in the memory. Memory is useful in integrating the experiences of the individual; to this fund of stored material the new experiences, ideas, and thoughts are connected. Memory functions more fully when the ideas, information, and experiences are clearly perceived and sufficiently understood. Material that has personal relevance becomes especially important to the individual, and therefore is not easily forgotten.

The relative rates of development in individuals tend to remain constant from infancy to maturity, although the rate of development is subject to a number of influences which may cause its alteration. The child's pattern of development in general, owing to the correlation of traits—for example, the quality of nutrition and conditions of health, the various psychological and social forces in the environment, such as social class, emotional climate of the home, and child-rearing practices—affects the rate of development.

In the study of mental growth, some attempts have been made to establish a theory or system to describe, in detail, the order in which various aspects of mental growth take place. The most elaborate system is that of Jean Piaget.

Position of Piaget

That Piaget is basically a biologist is very evident in his theory of cognitive development. He regards intellectual functioning as a special form of biological activity, and sees man as the inheritor of a biological structure with limited perceptive powers. Because our perceptive powers are limited, not all phenomena of the world are available to our sensory and perceptual equip-

---

[6] R. I. Watson, *Psychology of the Child* (New York: John Wiley & Sons, 1965), p. 331.

ment. Thus, our ability to construct fundamental concepts is restricted by our biological limitations, according to Piaget. Although our eyes receive sensations from certain wavelengths, and our ears respond to other wavelengths, we are not equipped to receive directly the wavelengths for x-ray, infrared, or radio, for example.

Cognitive Structure. Intelligence transcends these biologically-imposed limitations by making it possible for us to think about and hypothesize regarding perceptions that are not actually available for our analysis. Piaget also believes that we inherit biological structure and a mode of intellectual functioning by which we adapt to the environment. According to Piaget, cognitive structures are the organizational features of intelligence, and are inferable from the behavioral content, whose nature they determine. For example, young children are regarded as phenomenistic because their cognitive structures are so organized that the surface appearance of objects is their central concern. Their thought is dominated by environmental features, because these are what they perceive first and what they perceive most vividly.

Assimilation and Accommodation. In Piaget's thinking, an act of intelligence becomes an intellectual adaptation when the processes of assimilation and accommodation are in balance. *Assimilation* refers to the restructuring of an environmental object in accordance with the existing structure of the organism. In other words, when we perceive an object, we change its reality in order to make it compatible with our own current structure. In effect, in *assimilation*, one adjusts one's perception to one's preconception.

An intellectual adaptation is one that is accommodative. The organism must make some adjustments, through sensory or perceptual alterations, to the events and objects of reality. The interaction of assimilation and accommodation can best be understood when examined in a context of human behavior. For instance, let us suppose that an infant is presented with a ring suspended from a string. This is a new object to the infant, but because of his past experience with other objects, the infant already possesses structures for accommodating behavior such as touching, swinging, and grasping. The child's behavior is, simultaneously, the *accommodation* of these structures to the shape of the ring and the *assimilation* of this new object to these structures.

Cognitive progress takes place as the accommodatory process is extended to new and different aspects of the environment, but only when it is possible for the new aspects to be assimilated in a meaningful relationship to the existing structure. The functional characteristics of the assimilatory and accommodatory mechanisms are such that the possibility of cognitive change or growth is assured, but the size of any change is always limited. Each accommodation, however, makes it easier for the next one to take place.

Schemata. The structural units in Piaget's system are called *schemata*. A *schema*[7] is a cognitive structure referring to a class of similar action sequences. Schemata are created and modified by intellectual functioning.

---

[7] *Schema*, singular; *schemata*, plural.

They are limited to the behavior patterns that recur many times in the development of cognitive functioning, and, once formed, they apply themselves to aspects of the environment that lend themselves to assimilation. Schemata are characterized by repetition, stabilization, and preparation for change; generalization, to extend the range of application; differentiation, to change a schema into other sharply-focused schemata; and reciprocal assimilation of two schemata. Piaget points out that assimilation is the dominant component in intelligence.

Having provided some background in Piaget's theory of intelligence, we now go on to his description of mental development from birth to maturity. The major developmental epochs in the life of the individual are called *periods*; the smaller subdivisions are called *stages*.

Period of Sensory Motor Intelligence. Piaget's first developmental period is called the *period of sensory motor intelligence*, and covers the first two years of life. During this two-year period, which is broken down into six major stages, the children move from the neonatal state, in which their motor actions are quite indifferentiated and haphazard, to a period in which their actions have not only become differentiated but also relatively well-organized, controlled, and coordinated. Although a baby's control and organization of sensory motor actions become relatively sophisticated during this period, the child is not able to manage environmental objects symbolically. Let us now examine each of the six stages that make up this period.

Reflex Stage. The first stage involves the first month of life, or the neonatal stage. The infant has an extremely limited repertoire of responses, most of which are uncoordinated reflex activities such as sucking, and only a minimal contact with an undifferentiated outer reality.

Primary Circular-Reaction Stage. The second stage, which covers the period from the first month to the fourth, is the time when the first acquired adaptations and the primary circular reaction occur. This begins as the neonatal reflexes begin to alter their form as a result of experiences. Habits, in the form of elementary sensory-motor developments, begin to emerge, but they are still too primitive to be considered controlled actions to deal with the environment. At this stage, there is some development toward a differentiation between accommodation and assimilation, which in the reflex stage were undistinguishable. As a result of experience, the schemata of the child begin to undergo changes. In this stage there is a coordination of reflexes and responses—coordination of eye and hand movements. Children in this stage respond to sounds by looking in the direction from which they come; this is the *orienting* reflex. They also look in the proper direction as they reach for objects to grasp and suck.

Secondary Circular-Reaction Stage. The third stage is called the *secondary circular-reaction stage* and includes procedures for prolonging interesting sights. The secondary circular reaction is a new and higher form of assimilation wherein repetition consolidates motor responses that have interesting results on the environment. One feature of this stage is recognitory assimilation in which children recognize and classify things and change their reaction to familiar objects by adopting schemata that merely show recognition of the thing instead of the real action of earlier schemata. For instance, a four-month-old boy when presented with a rattle he is in the habit of striking, might merely look at it without relinquishing the toy he has in his hand, outline with his hand the movement of striking, and go back to his playing with his toy. Evidently he recognizes the toy, but plans to take no action with it. As they become more interested in the objective world, the children begin to look for objects of which they have lost sight. Piaget views this third stage as a transitional stage in the evolution from nonintentionality to intentionality, the latter being an indication of intelligence.

Coordination of Secondary Schemata Stage. Stage four is labeled the *coordination of secondary schemata and their application to new situations stage*. This stage covers the period between eight and twelve months of age, and its most important characteristics are the differentiation of means from ends and the intercoordination of two or more independent schemata in a means-goal relationship. Two of the intercoordinations of schemata are (1) a behavior sequence, removing an obstacle in order to reach a desired object; and (2) the use of an object as an instrument to reach a goal. It should be noted that in the case of removing an obstacle, at this stage, a part of the hidden object must be visible. To Piaget, this behavior seems to be the first definitely intentional behavior.

It is also during this stage that the child is able to anticipate events independent of the action. Piaget illustrated this in the example of an adult getting up from a chair. The child anticipates the adult's imminent departure by crying. In dealing with new and unfamiliar objects, the child at stage four tries out each schema, in turn. The implication of this behavior is that the child is making an experiment (an attempt to understand it) rather than generalizing his behavior patterns.

Tertiary Circular-Reaction Stage. Stage five, covering the period from twelve through eighteen months, Piaget labeled this stage *tertiary circular reaction and the discovery of new means by active experimentation stage*. The teriary circular reaction is concerned with the pursuit of the novel (the new): those features of an object that are less assimilable to the usual schema. The implications of the child's pursuing the novel are that (1) assimilation and accommodation become differentiated from each other so that the accommodation can prepare the schema for the next encounter; and (2) the child moves from an autocentric action orientation to an orientation wherein he distinctly separates the act from the object and accommodates the act to the object.

At this stage, the children are able to solve problems by using new and unfamiliar means. Much trial and error—which involves experimentation, exploration, variation, and modification of behavior—are necessary before the child can locate the new instrumental techniques to solve the problem effectively. The most important aspect of intellectual development during this fifth stage is that children evaluate the potentialities of the object, and vary their behavior toward the object in order to discover what effect different behaviors have on the object. At this point, the child has learned to perceive the object as part of the environment rather than as a part of himself.

Invention of New Means Stage. The sixth stage, occurring between eighteen months and two years of age, is labeled the *invention of new means through mental combinations stage.* This stage is marked by the emergence of the capacity to respond to, or think about, objects and events that are not immediately observable. Piaget uses the terms *representation* and *invention* to indicate that the various schemata that make up the pattern of the adaptation are internally represented by the child before they are acted out in reality. Through mental combinations of images and ideas, or as Piaget calls them, *symbolic images*, the child is able to perform some limited internal manipulations of reality. Through the process of reciprocal assimilation, the child is able to combine internally the representations of the various schemata of the act to be undertaken.

Piaget applies the adaptations of the sensory-motor period to the processes and concepts of imitation, play, objects, space, causality, and time.

Preoperational-Thought Period. The sensory-motor period is followed by the preoperational-thought period. The first part of this period covers the second to fourth years, and is referred to as the *preconceptual stage.* Its prime characteristic is the development of representational intelligence. Piaget calls this the *symbolic function.* During this stage, the child gains more facility in language and engages in symbolic play. For example, a stick becomes a "gun" and a blanket becomes a "royal robe." At this stage children are still egocentric with respect to representation. They are unable to take the role of the other person, and fail to adapt their speech to the needs of the listener. They feel no necessity to justify their reasoning to others; nor are they able to consider their own thought processes objectively.

The second part of this period is the *intuitional phase*, which occurs between the ages of four through seven. At this stage, children are more able to attend to specific tasks and to apply adapted intelligence to them, in contrast to the earlier phase wherein they would have assimilated tasks to an egocentric play schema. Their thought structures become more flexible, mobile, decentered, and reversible in their operation. *Decentering* refers to paying attention to more than one salient feature of an object.

Period of Concrete Operations. The period of concrete operations occurs between the ages of seven and eleven. During this time, children develop coherent and integrated cognitive systems with which they organize and manipulate their environment. The processes of accommodation and assimilation appear to be functioning in a balanced manner as the children deal with tasks. The cognitive actions are organized into totalities, each of which has a definite and strong structure. These totalities are called *cognitive operations.* An operation is any representational act that is part of an organized network of acts. Included are actions such as the logical operations of addition, subtraction, multiplication, division, and the setting of terms into correspondence. It is in this period of concrete operations that the reasoning processes become evident, and when the concepts of conservation and reversibility are acquired. *Reversibility* refers to the ability to retrace steps of thought or to cancel actions. At this time, children also develop the logic of class and are able to classify objects and to manipulate these classes through addition or subtraction. They can also place objects in order of their value. Because of interaction with their peers, they have moved from an egocentric position to a condition of many perspectives and reversibility, which is typical of the grouping structure of cognition.

Formal Operational Period. The *formal operations period* includes the years from eleven to fifteen, when maturity begins. At this stage of cognitive development, the adolescent tries to perceive all the possible relationships that can be formed from the data at hand, and then, through experimentation and logical analysis, attempts to determine which relationships do exist in reality. Here there is a reversal of the role of reality, which is now something to be considered as a hypothesis, and must be discovered by the adolescent rather than accommodated to, as in the case of the concrete operational stage. At this formal operational stage, the adolescent makes use of the hypothetico-deductive procedure of logical thought to determine reality within the context of possibility. The possibility is a set of hypotheses that are successively confirmed or repudiated in discovering reality.

Formal thinking is propositional thinking. When reasoning, an adolescent manipulates propositions *about* the data, rather than the data per se. Formal operations involve the performance of operations concerning the results of prior concrete operations. This new orientation toward the possible and the hypothetical is shown by systematic isolation of all the individual variables and by an assessment of all the possible combinations of these variables. The combinations are treated as hypotheses to be confirmed or denied by empirical investigation. At this stage, adolescents can follow the form of an argument while ignoring the content. They are capable of cognitive reflection, and can evaluate and criticize the logic of their own thinking. They are capable of both inductive and deductive thinking.

Piaget's Theory of Perception. Piaget has also developed a theory of developmental perception. However, his conception of perception is much narrower than that held by most psychologists: He views it as a form of adaptation which is developmentally subordinate and structurally inferior to intelligence. He believes that perception is not an autonomous mode of adaptation but a dependent subsystem within the sensory-motor intellectual development.

Criticism of Piaget's Theories. Although Piaget continues to be the leader in the field, his theory of the development of intelligence has not had universal acceptance by American psychologists. His work has been criticized because of the small number and nonrepresentativeness of his samples, the methodology used in collecting the data, the lack of evidence to verify ideas, the failure of attempts to replicate his studies, and a lack of concern for the effects of training on the type of operations used. Piaget's discrete stages in intellectual development, particularly, have been the targets of much criticism. Deutsch found discrepancies in the age at which certain types of thinking occurred. In fact, Deutsch found that each type of thinking was found at each stage studied. Piaget's later studies seem to indicate that intellectual functioning is affected by personality, experience, training, and by the form of the question used to elicit the data, not just by development alone.

Position of Jerome Bruner

Another position, which is not antagonistic to that of Piaget, has been established by Jerome Bruner. Bruner sees the development of intellectual functioning in terms of a series of technological advances in the use of mind. Development consists of the mastery of techniques or skills that are transmitted via the society's culture in a more or less successful fashion. Bruner sees the human being who is in the process of cognitive development as attempting to represent the world in a meaningful fashion by using three systems of information-processing: through action, through imagery, and through language. His theory is also concerned with the integration of acts into patterns or organizations so that the larger units of information are available for the solution of problems. Thus, representation and integration are the ways in which growing children link together the past, present, and future recurrent regularities or environmental experience.

In Bruner's thinking, evolution in man has been accomplished through the use of implement systems in the form of amplifiers of sensory capacities, motor capacities, and human ratiocinative capacities, which produce internal skills to organize these capacities and to match them to appropriate tasks. These internal skills or capacities have been gradually selected out in evolution and have, along with the human's particular structure, made it possible for human survival. The integration is a result of mastering the patterned nature of a social environment which has been internalized. According to Bruner, the only way in which environmental experience can remain useful is in the form of representation. In other words, it must be so coded and processed that it may be retrieved at any time, for the solution of relevant problems.

The environmental experience can be represented in three ways. (1) *Enactive* representation refers to a mode of representing past experience through appropriate motor response. (2) *Iconic* representation summarizes events of precepts and images by the spatial and temporal qualitative structures of the perceptual field, and by their transformed images. (3) *Symbolic* representation defines things by design features that include remoteness and arbitrariness.

In middle childhood, ages four to eight, cognitive development is largely a language process. Bruner has been able to show, in experiments at this age, how children's earlier methods of processing information have been increased, shaped, and surpassed. Both enactive and iconic representation are tied to experiences that are in the immediate present. Enactive representation is limited to percepts dependent on action. When experience becomes represented symbolically by language, it can then be dealt with in new, remote, and arbitrary ways. Language permits various operations to take place in the absence of the experience represented by it. It is not limited to the immediate, but can deal with the past and future.

Bruner speculates that the internalizing of language as a program for ordering experience is dependent on interaction with others, and emphasizes the necessity for corresponding categories and transformations for those who work on a common project. He views the development of cognitive functioning as the unlocking of capacities by techniques that have been environmentally shaped—that is, shaped by a culture.

Motivation

Behavior occurs not as a matter of chance but usually as a result of many complex causes. Most of the time these causes are related to the desire to satisfy a need.

Needs and Drives

Needs are states of deprivation within the organism. A need may be physiological or psychological. Regardless of its source, the need gives rise to a psychological consequence which is called a *drive*.

A drive is a pattern of persistent stimulation that tends to evoke sustained activity. A drive also involves a state of tension and goal-directed activity. The goal-directed activity involves searching for some environmental object or situation that will satisfy the need. A positive incentive, consisting of a need-reducing object or situation, attracts the organism to itself, and when the need is satisfied, the motivated behavior sequence is terminated.

Motivation is usually considered to have two main characteristics: (1) energizing or exciting the organism to action; and (2) giving some direction to the activity it has initiated.

Learning is a typical behavior that is subject to the influence of motivation. As in the case of hunger, thirst, or any of the maintenance drives, the motivation to learn involves incitement to action, direction, and goal-seeking behavior. In learning, the incentives are different, but their role is the same— that of satisfying needs.

It is important to note that motivation is not something that is done to the student, or something that is applied to the student. Motivation lies within the person. It may be, for instance, that the need to know will prompt a pupil to study in order to discover the answers to his questions. It is the job of the teacher to ascertain and then utilize each pupil's source of motivation. Also, part of the teacher's job is to provide positive incentives that satisfy the pupil's needs; often, these are in terms of educational goals.

Some student behavior consists of motivational dispositions, i.e., one has motives not currently being used to produce a specific behavior. Motivational dispositions can be transformed into aroused motives, which initiate, sustain, and direct behavior.

Achievement Motivation

David McClelland and his associates, shortly after the close of World War II, decided to explore a long-known fact: that man has a strong achievement motive—a desire to achieve, to produce, and to develop skills. McClelland measured achievement motives by the number of references to achievement-themes in the fantasies of college students. Although his method was based on the assumption that everyone has unconscious motives that denote a strong desire to achieve, the study showed that some people have dispositions with high levels of achievement motivation and some have dispositions with low levels.

In education, especially where instruction is of the individualized type, it is important that the teacher be aware of different levels of achievement motivation. It is also imperative to understand that learning may satisfy many other needs besides the need to achieve, such as the need to belong, the need for approval, and the need for self-esteem. When people find that their previously learned responses are no longer adequate to satisfy their needs, they learn new ways of behaving. If these new patterns of behavior offer sufficient satisfaction, then the people may find that the change is desirable enough to incorporate into future behavior.

Although teachers do not actually motivate, they must see that their students derive satisfaction from activities that are educationally worthwhile, that satisfactions are regulated, and that incentives are manipulated in such a manner as to adjust the activity level and maintain motivation at an optimal level. Too little motivation results in too little learning; too much will result in the disorganization of behavior and interference with learning.

Aspiration

Another matter closely related to motivation is the level of aspiration. *Aspiration* refers to the level of achievement or to the standard a person sets for himself in any area of performance. The height of the level of aspiration refers to the difficulty in achieving the goals the person has set. One's level of aspiration grows out of experience.

Ordinarily, a person sets his level of aspiration in accordance with the level of other people, or in accordance with his past experience. However, some people seem motivated by the pleasure of success, and others by the fear of failure. Studies have shown that children with a history of success are likely to set realistic goals, and children who have a history of many failures tend to set unrealistic goals. The latter set goals that are either too low, so that they feel they do not risk failure, or too high, so that they do not feel humiliated by failure.

Level of aspiration is also related to factors other than success and failure. The standards of their peers, the expectations of parents, the rewards and punishments the school provides, and the social class of the student are all important variables.

A thorough understanding of education, of psychology, and of the student is necessary if the teacher is to provide learning experiences that can be related to the student's goals and purposes. The student who fails to learn in accord with his capacity is often the one for whom the school program or the teaching method is inadequate. The same generalization may also apply to those who continually create a disturbance in the classroom. Teachers do not need to create motivation in these students, nor can they. The motivation is in the student. What the teacher needs to do is to utilize the child's inherent urges to obtain the desirable objectives. When the learning enables the child to enhance his self-concept, he usually participates willingly.

The goals connected with schoolwork are not always as urgent or as enticing as the personal goals of the student. When this is the case, the task of the teacher is to make the schoolwork meaningful in terms of the student goals. The goals may need to be broken down into more immediately attainable subgoals, and these goals often need to be reinforced by satisfaction of the student's needs.

Habit motives, such as punctuality, neatness, and accuracy, are important. Although these habits are usually formed in connection with the satisfaction of some need, they continue to function independently of the original need. For instance, a student may do good work as a means of satisfying a need for recognition and approval, and then because of habit continue to perform well when this need no longer exists. This is called the *functional autonomy* of a motive. In such cases, behavior functions as its own motive, and may become more powerful than the need with which it was originally connected. Unfortunately, the same principle applies when the habit is not a desirable one.

Memory

Memory, the process involved in the retention of material, is very closely interwoven with the process of learning; sometimes it is difficult to separate the one process from the other. Rote learning, for example, means learning something by repeating the words, not attending to their meaning until it is memorized or can be repeated without reference to the copy. In schools, the learning of poetry "by heart," often called memory work, illustrates the process of rote learning. Undoubtedly, much too much of the learning that takes place at all levels of education consists of memorizing—usually as preparation for tests—rather than genuine attempts to understand, to discover principles, and to make applications of learning.

In spite of its misuse by some educators, memory is vital to the learning process. Indeed, it would be impossible to learn anything new if there were not some background of remembered facts, thoughts, or ideas from past experience. The only hold on the past is through memory.

Retention

Retention, the memory process by which past learnings persist, is a complementary process to forgetting. After learning occurs, the concomitant change in behavior is either retained or forgotten. In other words, what is not remembered is forgotten; what is not forgotten is retained.

Studies have shown retention losses of from ten to fifteen per cent between the end of one school year and the beginning of another. The amount of the loss is related to such factors as the functionality of the course content— that is, its practical use, the appeal of the course content, the method of learning, the method of teaching, and the characteristics of the learner, such as intelligence, age, and so forth.

Herman Ebbinghaus, the German psychologist, was the first scientist to investigate the rate and extent of forgetting and retaining nonsense syllables by memorization. He conducted the experiments on himself, using a chance order of materials (a vowel between two constants) in a series. The complete series was used, from beginning to end. The reading and recitation was done at a constant rate, as measured by a metronome at 150 strokes per minute. After learning each series, a uniform pause of fifteen seconds was made. Concentration of attitude on the task was maintained insofar as possible, and care was taken to control objective conditions during the period of testing.

Testing was done by the *savings method.* First, Ebbinghaus calculated the number of repetitions necessary for complete reproduction of the series. After an interval of time, the series was relearned, and the amount of time saved in relearning was the difference in time between that required for the original learning and that required for the second learning. Ebbinghaus found that after one day, less than half the learning was retained. He found that thirty-eight repetitions, made over three days preceding the test, were equal to sixty-eight repetitions made on the day preceding the test.

For the student, the immediate implication of the Ebbinghaus study is that distributed practice is a more efficient way of preparing for an examination than cramming (or massed learning) the night before a test. The long-term effect of Ebbinghaus' research was that he established a pattern for further research on memory, using nonsense syllables and the savings method.

Forgetting

There are several theories to account for forgetting. One of the oldest is the theory of *disuse*, which proposes that forgetting is the result of the passage of time. This theory, however, does not explain selectiveness in forgetting, where some aspects of an experience are remembered and other aspects are forgotten; and it does not explain reminiscence, wherein retention improves after a period of time. If this theory of disuse were correct, additional practice would improve retention, but experiments on memory extinction show that responses are eliminated when they are practised in the absence of reinforcement.

There are records of excellent retention over a long period of time. Some skills seem to be resistant to the passage of time even when no practice occurs. Any of the functional skills, such as riding a bicycle or driving a car, once learned, are not soon forgotten.

A more satisfactory explanation for forgetting is the theory of *interference*, which explains forgetting as being a result of the active interference of subsequent learning. When later learning interferes with the recall of previous learning, the process is called *retroactive inhibition.* When previous learning interferes with the recall of subsequent learning, it is called *proactive inhibition.*

The magnitude of effect resulting from placement of the interference has been researched by many. Although some of the findings are controversial, many of the studies agree that interference is greatest immediately after the learning or directly before the recall. New learning that occurs midway between the original learning and its recall seems to have less interference effect.

Interference Factors. Perhaps more important than the temporal position of interference is the amount of similarity or difference between the original learning and the interfering effect of interpolated learning. Here the term *interference* refers to the effect of learning that occurs between the learning and recall; and interpolated learning refers to the process of learning that takes place in that interval.

According to the Scagg–Robinson hypothesis, the more similar the original and interpolated learning, the greater the interference, up to a point. As these learnings become more nearly identical, the interference effect is lost and the interpolated learning tends to reinforce the original learning. The point at which this support takes place depends on the intelligence, perceptiveness, and background of the learner, as well as the meaningfulness to the learner of the material learned.

Another related factor is the degree of mastery of the interpolated and original learnings. When learning is adequately understood, and if it attains functionality in terms of relationships, applications, generalizations, interpretations, and implications, it is less easily affected by either previous or subsequent learning. In other words, the more thorough the original learning, the less impact other learning will have upon it.

Repression. A third theory of forgetting, proposed by Sigmund Freud, is that of *motivated forgetting*, or repression. According to this theory, memories may be lost to conscious control and stored in the unconscious. This is more likely to happen if the experience is painful or repulsive. Similarly, functional amnesia, where the memory of personal identity is lost, usually results from an experience too painful to remember. In this way, by the loss of memory, one can escape from an anguished condition. This should not be confused with other amnesias, such as *retrograde amnesia*, wherein the patient has no memory of what happened for a short period preceding an injury.

Other kinds of forgetting are related to physical conditions such as senility, arteriosclerosis, toxic conditions, and injuries to the head.

Remembering

Some studies of memory have involved the serial-position effect of learning upon remembering. When subjects were required to learn a list of words in which each word provided a stimulus for the next word, in a fixed-order sequence, it was found that certain words were learned earlier than others. The first words on the list were learned first, a phenomenon called the *primary effect*. The next words learned were the last words, a phenomenon known as the *recency effect*, and the middle items were learned last. Thus, the serial-position effect demonstrates that a list of words is not learned in order; the words at the ends of the list are learned first, and the remaining words are learned later.

Although we have already mentioned meaningfulnesss, perhaps it should be mentioned here as it relates to connectedness. *Connectedness* refers to the fact that verbal material is easiest to learn and remember if it forms a unified whole. Poetry is easier to learn than isolated words, for example. In one study by D. O. Lyon (1914), it was found that a two-hundred-word passage of poetry was learned in ten minutes but a two-hundred-item list of nonsense syllables required ninety-three minutes. Connectedness depends on meaningfulness, redundancy, the predictability of later items because of inclusion of earlier ones, grammatical order, and, in the case of poetry, rhyming and rhythmic structure.

Because memory essentially consists of the association of items, words, ideas, and generalizations, the more associations produced by any of these verbal items the easier it is to remember them. Some words are highly meaningful, for instance, *any*, and others are low in meaning, for instance, *matrix*.

Memory sometimes depends on imagery. In simple experiments done by the writer, Ralph McCaw, some students remember better by imagery and some remember better by repeating words. Of course, not all words are evocative of imagery.

Kinds of Remembering. There are several kinds of remembering.

1. *Redintegrative* memory refers to remembering, on the basis of partial cues, the whole of an earlier experience. An example is: witnesses in a courtroom trying to remember all the details connected with a crime they had not seen committed.
2. *Recall* is often used to measure the amount remembered. It refers to the simple reproduction of material learned. Completion-type items utilize recall.
3. *Recognition*, used in multiple-choice test items, involves selecting from several possibilities the answer that conforms to the demands of the stem of the question, or recognizing from a list the remembered words or syllables.
4. *Relearning* refers to the savings method referred to earlier; the material is learned according to some criterion of mastery, and later is relearned to the same criterion. The savings are expressed as a percentage of the original number of trials.
5. *Written reproduction* refers to writing memorized verbal material, usually in an organized form, as in essay tests.
6. *Serial anticipation*, as discussed earlier in serial-order position, is the recollection of succeeding words or syllables in response to the preceding one, which is used as a stimulus.

If memory is not lost through disuse, it may be considered to be permanent. If the memory trace should decay, the memory would be lost. However, it appears that very often the remembered material is in the mind, but we are unable to retrieve it because we lack the proper cues. Cue-dependent forgetting is illustrated in the TOT (tip of the tongue) state, when a cue permits sudden access to a name or a word previously unrecalled. That memories do remain, even though at present the evidence is inconclusive, is seen in the recovery of material from memory under hypnosis, free recall in psychotherapy, and from the brain-stimulation studies of Wilder Penfield and others. In the case of brain stimulation, weak electrical current is applied to the temporal lobe of the exposed brain, in a conscious person. This procedure elicits vivid memories of material that the individual cannot otherwise recall.

Because of the as yet inadequate explanations for forgetting, many theorists have adopted the idea of a two-process theory of memory. According to this theory, memory is stored in two ways, via a short-term memory (STM) and a long-term memory (LTM). In the former, information is fed in, but it soon begins to fade. It can be maintained by rehearsing it, as when one repeats a telephone number over and over from the time it is found in the directory until it is dialed. The set of traces being maintained in the STM at any one time is called the *rehearsal buffer*; the amount of material that can be maintained in the rehearsal buffer is limited. While the material is in the rehearsal buffer it may become coded in some way and transferred to the LTM, which appears to have unlimited storage.

Aids to Remembering. Sometimes retrieval from the LTM is difficult because the critical cues are lacking. One way that material is coded is through the use of a mnemonic device, a method to improve memory by substituting symbols for the material to be remembered. For instance, to remember the number of days in the months we have all learned the rhyme, "Thirty days hath September, April, June, and November," and so on.

Memory can be assisted in other ways, such as by the organization of the material to be learned. One way, for instance, is to lump together discrete bits of information; another way is to organize the material into clusters, using categorization of items.

Review is the best way of maintaining retention above the threshold of reaction. A sufficient number of reviews will keep it above the threshold. It is important that the first review come within twenty-four hours after the learning, inasmuch as 80 per cent of the learning is lost within this period. In one study, it was found that there was more forgetting in one day without review than in sixty-three days with two review periods. Periodic review, to be effective, should involve reorganization, systematization, and the development of new insights, understandings, and relationships, This kind of activity provides for more functionality and permanency than other methods.

Overlearning, that is, learning more than is necessary for one period of reproduction, has been shown to extend retention. Excessive overlearning is uneconomical, but up to 50 per cent might be considered a wise investment of time and effort if long-term recall is important.

Inasmuch as learning and remembering are affected by many of the same factors, effective learning promotes efficient retention.

Transfer

Transfer of training, or transfer of learning, refers to ways we use past learning to meet the demands of new situations. The programs offered by any school are based on the assumption that transfer of learning is a reality. Because it is not possible to prepare students for all situations they meet, the aim of educators is to provide them with a particular variety of experiences which will enable them to deal with a greater number of other similar events. Much of the learning that takes place within the school is expected to prepare the student for many similar circumstances outside the school, and throughout the life of the individual.

Kinds of Transfer

Transfer can be positive or negative. Positive transfer occurs when learning one task assists in the learning of another. For example, being proficient in playing the piano might assist one in learning to type. Negative transfer occurs when learning one task interferes with learning another. Negative transfer is, in its effect, similar to retroactive inhibition. Transfer may also be considered to be lateral or vertical. In lateral transfer, one is able to perform a different yet similar task at the same level of difficulty as in the original learning. Vertical transfer refers to performing different but similar tasks at a higher level of difficulty than in the original learning.

The schools are interested in promoting both lateral and vertical transfer of a positive nature, and they must provide opportunities to apply principles learned in one situation to another similar situation.

Among the misconceptions about transfer is the idea that specific facts and definite identities are the only elements that are transferable. This view leads to the construction of a curriculum in which subjects are learned for their immediate value; consequently, much rote memorization and skill-learning is provided. Transfer tends to be minimized, and principles, generalizations, and understanding are underused and undervalued in such curricula.

Another misconception about transfer is that it occurs automatically. To prepare for this conception of transfer, the curriculum is structured so that subject matter is arranged in sequential order, and at the right level of difficulty. Unfortunately, unless it is pointed out to them, many students fail to see the relationship between what they know and what they are expected to do. There is no guarantee that a student with a large fund of information will be able to apply it when an appropriate occasion arises.

Some people view transfer and learning as separate and different processes. Transfer, however, is a part of the learning process, giving purpose to much of what occurs in schools. Only when students understand this process are they able to apply the principles learned in new but similar situations at the same (or higher) level of difficulty. But where drill precedes understanding, transfer is unlikely to occur.

Theories of Transfer

A number of theories have been used to explain *transfer* of learning. The first of these is the old-fashioned theory of formal discipline. Based on faculty psychology, this theory proposes that separate elements of the mind can be improved by practice, and the value of the curriculum lies in its providing a means to improve the mind. The more difficult the subjects studied and the more painful the learning experience, the more the mind is improved. Nowadays, this theory has been thoroughly discredited. Scientific studies have provided evidence to deny that one subject is better than another for improving the mind, and these studies indicate that the mind, unlike a muscle, cannot be improved by rigorous exercise.

Another theory, proposed by E. L. Thorndike, is that of identical components. This theory states that transfer from one situation to another occurs because the situations have identical components. The components may be in the form of skills, generalizations, information, procedures, principles, or attitudes. For example, the learning of addition facts can be transferred to subtraction, division, and multiplication, as well as to the use of these skills in fractions, percentages, and elementary algebra.

The Gestalt school of psychology proposed the theory of transposability. According to this theory, a pattern is composed of identical components. The pattern, not its parts, is the important element. Transposing a melody from one key to another is a good illustration. Although the transposed melody starts on a higher or lower note, the melody pattern is unchanged. According to the Gestaltists, facts and skills are not transferred; it is the perception of the relationship of the facts, skills, principles, and generalizations that is transferred.

A fourth theory of transfer, formulated by C. H. Judd in 1908, is called *generalization*. This theory explains transfer in terms of the application of principles and generalizations to different and varied situations. Generalizations and relationships are the components that are transferred. According to this theory, which is supported by experimental evidence, the schools might do well to concentrate on teaching concepts and principles, and spend less time on daily drills on specific facts, skills, and attitudes.

A fifth theory, supported by Robert M. Gagné, Leo Postman, and other contemporary psychologists, explains transfer through the formulation of ideals or generalized attitudes. This theory, developed mostly in the last quarter century, explains transfer in terms of abilities. An ability, sometimes referred to as a skill or strategy, can be developed in solving one problem and then applied to similar problems, either at the same level (lateral transfer) or at higher levels (vertical transfer). According to this theory, this ability is also known by the following terms: *learning to learn, learning how to approach problem situations,* and *learning how to use previous experience to permit insight into newly encountered events.*

Principles of Transfer

The following are principles regarding transfer which apply to the teaching-learning situation.

1. One of the aims of instruction should be teaching for transfer.
2. The lesson that never reaches the stage of generalization provides little that can be transferred. The learning is likely to consist of facts and details which have limited applicability elsewhere.
3. Students should be provided with opportunities for discovering generalizations. The generalizations students discover on their own are more precious, are retained longer, and are applied more widely than otherwise.
4. If the material taught is meaningful to the student, transfer is more

likely to occur. When the student realizes the purpose of learning, both immediate and eventual, the possibility of transfer is increased.

5. The teacher needs to seek out opportunities for transfer, and to be sure that the students are aware of the instances when transfer occurs. The application of understanding in a novel situation is a sounder measure of achievement than a formal test. When the application is followed by satisfying consequences in terms of verbal rewards or feelings of success, operant conditioning tells us this will happen again when the circumstances reappear. The instructional material that is chosen should be appropriate for making relationships vividly apparent. When concepts of a broad and abstract nature are being taught, the use of many examples will enhance the meaningfulness of the situation, encourage transfer, and increase retention.

Retention and transfer are two aspects of learning. Learning, although efficient, is inconsequential if retention is constricted. The application of learning will be limited if it finds no employment other than the one in which it was acquired. For the student, effective learning, efficient retention, and optimum transfer are the greatest of assets for realizing goals.

Summary

Learning is a continuous process that shapes each of us all our lives in school and out, with or without formal instruction. Basically, we learn those things that we feel we need or want to learn. Many factors affect one's learning processes and what one learns. Teachers therefore should carefully diagnose both their pupils and the learning situations so as to select the teaching strategies and tactics best suited to the teaching-learning situations they encounter. In this process, knowledge of psychological principles can give one many clues as to the status of the individual and the types of instructional procedures that would be profitable.

One of the factors in the teaching-learning situation is *readiness*. Readiness to learn is the result of a combination of many elements. Among these are one's age, one's physical development, one's health and vigor, one's prior knowledge and training, one's emotional climate, one's goals, one's interests, and the like. Many of these characteristics develop naturally, but others can be cultivated and sometimes even forced upon an individual. In other words, sometimes a person who is not yet ready can be made ready in certain respects.

In order to introduce learning experiences at the most propitious time, one can use the concepts of developmental tasks. These are the tasks that one must solve at certain stages in life in order to develop normally and successfully. People who do not accomplish their developmental tasks at the normal stage of development find life more difficult in later years.

Learning is also dependent upon intelligence. Unfortunately, psychologists cannot seem to agree on what intelligence is. It may be dominated by an overall global capacity, or it may be made up of a number of specific primary abilities. For our purposes, it is enough to think of intelligence as the ability to see relations, make evaluations, and deal with symbolic material. The better pupils can cope with materials of these sorts, the better they can cope with learning in school.

In any case, mental abilities grow during childhood and youth. Evidently this growth follows a rather definite general pattern, although the pattern may be modified somewhat by the learners' life and life experiences. At the moment the pattern of growth most accepted by educators is that proposed by Jean Piaget. This pattern assumes that children develop first through a period of sensory motor intelligence (ages one–two), next through a period of preoperational thought (ages two–seven), next through a period of concrete operations (ages seven–eleven), and finally through a period of formal operations (age eleven plus). Although these stages follow in order, the rate of development ordinarily varies from individual to individual. Some persons never make it to the formal operations stages. Jerome Bruner has developed a somewhat similar theoretical scheme of mental growth, in which development is largely dependent on language process and cultural shaping.

School learning is dependent upon pupil motivation. Although motivation is part of the pupils' makeup, it is possible for teachers to influence pupil behavior by utilizing their present motives, providing incentives and arousing motivational dispositions. By harnessing pupils' needs to achieve, and such other needs as the need for self-approval, the need to belong, and the need for self-esteem, and by adapting learning to pupils' levels of aspiration so that the tasks are neither too boring nor too frightening, one can often use pupils' present motives to achieve teachers' instructional goals.

Learning that is not retained or transferred is of little practical value. Although the process of remembering has been studied, it is still not perfectly understood. Evidently the memory can be stimulated by mnemonic devices, by careful organization of the material to be learned, and by over-learning. Probably the best method to insure retention is periodic review. Similarly, transfer can be enhanced by thorough learning in which the material is made meaningful, and in which generalizations and transfer values are pointed out.

SUGGESTED READING

Biehler, Robert F., and Jack Snowman, *Psychology Applied to Teaching*, 4th ed. Boston: Houghton Mifflin Co., 1982.

Charles, C. M., *Educational Psychology*, 3rd ed. St. Louis, Missouri: The C. V. Mosby Co., 1982.

Dentler, Robert, and Bernard Shapiro, eds., *Readings in Educational Psychology: Contemporary Perspectives.* New York: Harper & Row, Publishers, 1976.

Gage, N. L., and David C. Berliner, *Educational Psychology*, 2nd ed. Chicago: Rand McNally & Co., 1979.

Galloway, Charles, *Psychology for Learning and Teaching.* New York: McGraw-Hill Book Co., 1976.

Gibson, Janice, *Psychology for the Classroom*, 2nd ed. Englewood Cliffs, New Jersey: Prentice-Hall, Inc., 1981.

Hamachek, Don E., *Psychology in Teaching, Learning, and Growth*, 2nd ed. Boston: Allyn & Bacon, Inc., 1979.

LeFrancois, Guy R., *Psychology for Teaching*, 4th ed. Belmont, California: Wadsworth Publishing Co., 1982.

Reilly, Robert and Ernest Lewis, *Educational Psychology: Applications for Classroom Learning and Instruction.* New York: Macmillan Publishing Co., Inc., 1983.

Smith, M. Daniel, *Educational Psychology and Its Classroom Applications*, 2nd ed. Boston: Allyn & Bacon, Inc., 1978.

Sprinthall, Richard C., and Norman A. Sprinthall, *Educational Psychology: A Developmental Approach*, 3rd ed. Reading, Massachusetts: Addison-Wesley Publishing Co., Inc., 1981.

Strom, Robert D., and Harold W. Bernard, *Educational Psychology.* Belmont, California: Brooks/Cole Publishing Co., 1982.

Travers, R. M. W., *Essentials of Learning*, 5th ed. New York: Macmillan Publishing Co., Inc., 1982.

Wittrock, M. C., *Learning and Instruction.* St. Louis, Missouri: C. B. Mosby Co., 1977.

POST TEST

Multiple Choice (*Circle one.*)

1. Which statement is *not* correct?
   a. Educational psychology places the emphasis on learning rather than on teaching.
   b. Learning is a continuous process which changes the behavior of the learner.
   c. Learning proceeds best when the teacher decides what the student should learn.
   d. The effectiveness with which a student learns depends both on the intensity of his needs and the degree to which the learning satisfies these needs.

2. Which statement refers to one of the factors involving learning?
   a. Most problems are simpler than they appear.
   b. Trial and error is the best method in the long run.
   c. All relevant factors must be taken into account when dealing with an educational problem.
   d. The first step in dealing with a problem is to deal with the symptoms.

3. In dealing with problems, whether they are intellectual or behavioral, the first step to be taken by the teacher is to
   a. decide on the treatment.
   b. treat all students the same.
   c. write a prescriptive program for each student.
   d. make a diagnosis of the problem.

4. Learning is
   a. directly in proportion to the teaching.
   b. dependent on the goals set by the teacher.
   c. the manipulation of the learner by the teacher.
   d. a relatively permanent change in behavior as a result of experience.

5. When a student shows that he is prepared, psychologically, emotionally, intellectually, and physically, to begin a certain activity, this state is called

    a. optimal age.
    b. effectiveness.
    c. assimilation.
    d. readiness.

6. The experimental results of early training have demonstrated that
    a. early training works best on physical functions, such as bladder training.
    b. early training has no affect on learning.
    c. early training has little affect on skills dependent on maturation.
    d. early training is a wise investment of time, and is necessary for full development of motor skills.

7. A system of learning wherein problems are set for each level of learning, and progress to higher levels is dependent on solving the problems at lower levels, is referred to as
    a. effectance.
    b. developmental tasks.
    c. maternal deprivation.
    d. marasmus.

8. A pattern of persistent stimulation resulting from a deprivation within the organism is known as
    a. drive.
    b. motivation.
    c. need.
    d. incentive.

9. In utilizing motivation in the pursuit of learning, it is important for the teacher to
    a. motivate the students to learn.
    b. deprive the students so that they have unfulfilled needs.
    c. utilize the motivation that already exists, or provide enticing incentives.
    d. realize that students will not learn unless someone puts pressure on them to do so.

10. Which is *not* related to the achievement motive?
    a. The need to belong.
    b. The need for approval.
    c. The need for self-esteem.
    d. The need for safety.

11. Which is *not* ordinarily used by the student in setting a realistic level of aspiration?
    a. Past experience.
    b. The behavior of other people.
    c. Success in prior attempts.
    d. Repeated failure.

12. "A verbal invention used to stand for something which is known only by its effect" is a definition of
    a. motivation.

    b. a psychological need.

    c. a psychological construct.

    d. fantasy production.

13. "Intelligence is the global or aggregate capacity for the individual to act purposefully, think rationally and to deal effectively with his environment" is a definition used by

    a. Alfred Binet.   **b.** Lewis Terman.

    c. Carl Spearman.   **d.** David Wechsler.

14. J. P. Guilford, who, like Spearman and Thurstone was interested in the multiple factors of intelligence, developed a model involving the following three dimensions:

    a. operations, memory, and content.

    b. operations, content, and product.

    c. operations, content, and relations.

    d. memory, language symbols, and units.

15. Which is *not* considered an aspect of mental growth?

    a. The visual-cliff avoidance.

    b. Increased attention span.

    c. Ability to work independently.

    d. Grasp of time, words, and dates.

16. In his conception of intelligence, Jean Piaget is chiefly concerned with two intellectual processes that interact at each stage of development. These processes are

    a. organization and adaptation.

    b. systems and relationships.

    c. biological limitations and hypothetical perceptions.

    d. assimilation and accommodation.

17. The main contribution made to the study of memory by Herman Ebbinghaus, and of practical importance to the student, is that

    a. memory can be studied experimentally.

    b. distributed practice is more efficient than cramming for long-term retention.

    c. nonsense syllables are more difficult to learn than words.

    d. relearning something after a lengthy interval allows one to calculate the savings made because of having learned it before.

18. Several theories of forgetting were discussed in the text of this module. Forgetting may be explained in terms of Freudian psychology as

    a. theory of disuse.

    b. interference.

    c. retroactive inhibition.

    d. represssion.

19. In learning a serial-order list of words, the

    a. primacy effect is greater than the recency effect.

    b. recency effect is greater than the primacy effect.

    c. primacy and recency effects are equal in magnitude.

    d. primacy effect is the same as retroactive inhibition.

20. When learning one list of names interferes with the later learning of a second list of names, this is an example of
    a. proactive inhibition.
    b. serial-position effect.
    c. retroactive inhibition.
    d. redundancy.

21. Which term is *not* a type of remembering?
    a. Recall.
    b. Recognition.
    c. Redundancy.
    d. Relearning.

22. The main difference between LTM and STM, besides the length of time that material is remembered, is that
    a. material in the LTM remains in the rehearsal buffer.
    b. material in the LTM must be coded.
    c. LTM must precede STM.
    d. LTM works only on material that is reproduced in writing.

23. A student learns to play the piano. Later he finds that he learns to type more easily than those who had not learned to play the piano. If this is true, it is an example of
    a. positive transfer.
    b. negative transfer.
    c. negative and vertical transfer.
    d. retroactive inhibition.

24. Which theory of transfer has proven to be untenable?
    a. Identical components.
    b. Transposability.
    c. Generalization.
    d. Formal discipline.

25. Which generalization regarding the use of transfer in the classroom is erroneous?
    a. The material taught must be meaningful to the student.
    b. The teacher must teach for transfer and not expect it to happen spontaneously.
    c. The application of understanding in a new situation is an excellent measure of achievement.
    d. Lessons do not need to reach a stage of generalization.

INVOLVEMENT EXPERIENCES

1. Look around at your own classmates. How do they differ in interests, aptitudes, abilities, appearance, and personality? How do these differences affect their learning or how they react to teaching? Talk to them about how

they feel about their classes, the teaching methods used, the material studied, and so on.

2. Observe a public school class. What differences do you see among the various individuals in such things as appearance, physical development, size, evident maturity, behavior, interests, ability, and personality? What range of differences do you notice?

3. Visit classes at different grade levels. Note how the behavior of early childhood, elementary, middle school, and high school boys and girls differs.

4. Talk to some teachers. Ask them:

What do they do to motivate pupils?

What do they do to ensure transfer?

How do they determine if pupils are "ready"? What do they do to help pupils become ready?

What techniques do they use to help pupils to remember the content of lessons?

What do they do to fit their teaching to individual pupils?

5. In classes you have attended, what have teachers done to carry out the tasks mentioned in Question 4. How effective have their techniques been? Discuss with your colleagues techniques you think you should use.

6. Of all the subjects you had studied in secondary school and college, which did you like the best? Why? Of all the courses you have taken, which was the best? What did the teacher do that made this course stand out? What motivates you to study now? How might you use this information about yourself to interest students in the course you will teach?

7. Talk to some high school pupils about their school life—especially their classes. What have teachers done to make them interesting? Which classes seem most worthwhile to them?

8. Are you aware of any developmental tasks confronting you? As you look back over your secondary school years, were there developmental tasks (of which you may or may not have been aware at the time) that affected the priorities in your life?

9. Observe school students. Are there evidences that their behavior represents attempts to fulfill developmental tasks or basic needs?

10. What seem to you to be the implications for teaching methods and curriculum of Jean Piaget's theory of stages?

Psychological Bases: Nature of the Learner

General Nature of the Learner / What Is Learning? / How We Learn / The Elementary School Child As a Learner / The Adolescent Learner

The first-edition version of this module was written by Janice R. Boone, Jersey City State College. It has been revised and updated for this edition.

RATIONALE

It seems so obvious that one almost hesitates to mention it, but sometimes teachers forget that any curriculum or teaching method that conflicts with the nature of the learner and the ways in which people learn is bound to be ineffective. In order to be a truly effective teacher, you must have a thorough knowledge and appreciation of the nature of the pupil. In this module, we shall examine the nature of the learner in general, and certain characteristics of elementary and secondary pupils in particular.

While studying this module, it is important that you realize that human life is developmental. Although the characteristics we describe may be typical of kindergartners or junior high-school pupils, they may not all apply to a particular individual. Some people grow up faster than others. Also, development is uneven. Therefore, a third-grade child might possibly be much further advanced in at least one aspect—perhaps in most aspects—than a fourth grader. Furthermore, children do not become different people just because they move from one age category or stage of life to another. In spite of her many changes in physical form and mental outlook, the adolescent girl is still the same girl she was as a primary-grade child, and, though it may not appear so, she will still be the same girl at sixty! The seeds of the adolescent's character are planted in childhood. In spite of seemingly sudden shifts in character, changes build up gradually. The process is something like bringing cold water to boil in a whistling tea kettle. The cold water gets hotter and hotter, until it finally reaches one hundred degrees, and starts to steam. Then it builds up pressure until, bingo! it starts, suddenly, to whistle. The whistling starts in an instant, but we who have been waiting for our tea know that it has been building up for some time. Therefore, to understand the adult learner or the adolescent learner, it is necessary to know something of the child.

Now let us turn to a general consideration of the nature of learners, and then to some generalizations concerning the nature of the learner in the kindergarten, elementary, and secondary schools.

Growing up is not an easy task. Young people must seek to establish themselves physically, socially, mentally, and emotionally. You, as the teacher, are charged with the responsibility for dealing with whatever stress, tension, or maladaptive behavior may occur in this process, and to help each student in the quest for independence, affection, self-actualization, security, knowledge, and so forth. In order to do this, you need a basic knowledge and understanding of physical, social, and intellectual development. In addition, you should be aware of the factors that influence these developmental processes.

The general purpose of this module is to acquaint you with the characteristics of learners so that you will have a base for developing your understanding of educational theory, teaching strategies, and curriculum. Its primary aim is to increase your sensitivity to the problems encountered by learners. An additional goal is to provide background information about the causes of these problems. In some cases, we shall make general suggestions for coping with behavioral problems and individual differences.

SPECIFIC OBJECTIVES

Specifically, it is expected that upon completing your study of this module, you will be able to

1. Describe and explain the significance of each of the features of the average learner, and their implications:

   Uniqueness.   Developmental tasks.
   Common characteristics.   Needs.
   Different selves.   General tendencies.
   Total organism.   Goals.
   Readiness.   How learners learn.

2. Describe the important physical, social, emotional, mental, and moral characteristics of kindergarten and elementary school children.
3. In your own words, describe the pertinent physical characteristics of both middle and high school students.
4. Describe in your own words the social characteristics of both middle and high school students.
5. Describe in your own words the emotional characteristics of both middle and high school students.
6. Describe in your own words the intellectual characteristics of both middle and high school students.
7. Name the major developmental tasks of adolescence.
8. Name at least two problems associated with physiological change that are pertinent to adolescents.
9. Describe the typical adjustment problems most commonly associated with very early or very late maturation.
10. Name the major determiners of adolescent behavior.
11. Describe some of the common parental practices or attitudes that may contribute to problems with adolescents.
12. Formulate a set of guidelines for your teaching behavior which includes suggestions for rewarding pupils in keeping with your expectations of them.
13. Describe at least three specific methods of teaching you will use in an attempt to provide for differences in the operational level of your students.

MODULE TEXT

General Nature of the Learner

Uniqueness of Each Individual

Each individual person is unique. No one is a duplicate of anyone else who has ever lived or ever will live. Every individual has a peculiar genetic makeup and has undergone a distinctive set of life experiences. Not even identical (monozygotic) twins have identical experiences, even though they have grown from the same cell. Brothers and sisters, fathers and sons, mothers and daughters, and grandparents and grandchildren share characteristics, yet they are all very different from one another. This is why it is unwise to make judgments about pupils on the basis of their inheritance, or the performance of their ancestors or siblings. It is also why no curriculum, lesson, or teaching tactic can be equally effective for all the pupils in a class. What one pupil may enjoy, another may hate; what may be exciting to one, may be boring to another; what one may find too easy, another may find too difficult. As the old folks put it, "One man's meat is another man's poison."

Learners differ in many ways: in aptitudes, abilities, tastes, likes and dislikes, knowledge, strength, ideals, attitudes, appreciations, stamina, sex, and so on. Some of these differences are innate, the result of inheritance; some are the result of experience; and some are the result of both inheritance and experience. For instance, if one is a blue-eyed boy, it is because of his genetic make-up, that is, heredity; if one is frightened by heights, it is probably a result of experience; but if one is an excellent mathematician, it is probably a result of innate intellectual potential (i.e., aptitude), plus experience.

All these differences in the characteristics of learners have important implications for us teachers. The differences in aptitudes and abilities are especially significant. By aptitude we mean potential. If you are endowed by nature with an excellent singing voice, perfect pitch, and the other attributes of a potentially great singer, you have an aptitude. If you take advantage of this aptitude and learn to sing and interpret classical operatic parts *con brio*, then you have developed an ability. *Aptitudes are potentials*, but *abilities are the levels at which one is able to perform*.

Pupils come to school with many aptitudes and many abilities. Some have more aptitude for academic studies than others, for instance. This aptitude is what most people mean by "intelligence." Other pupils may have more potential in art, or music, or crafts. Some pupils may rate high in all these aptitudes; others may rate low in all of them. Similarly, pupils' abilities differ. Some children can read better than others; some can play the guitar, or the harmonica; some are good at multiplication; some can type, or write poetry, or play the piano, and some cannot. Perhaps the pupils who cannot do these things could learn to do them, but until they learn, they do not have the abilities. Teachers have to accept pupils as they find them—with a great variety of aptitudes and abilities. This also holds true for the other characteristics of learners. There is no limit to the ways in which pupils differ from each other. No two pupils have the same assortment of aptitudes, abilities, and other characteristics.

More Like than Unlike

Although each is unique, learners have much in common. In many ways they are more alike than they are different. Both the genetic pool and the culture tend to perpetuate similarities and resemblances in any society. Perhaps the most easily understood examples of our tendency to perpetuate similarity can be seen in the family resemblances so common to all of us. In our nation, our culture confronts all youth with such similar problems that learned societies speak of the "common needs of all American youth."

Because pupils resemble each other and are yet very different, if our educational programs are to be sound, these programs must provide both for individual differences and for individual resemblances. In designing educational programs, educators should first consider the resemblances. Then, after they have made adequate provision for the commonalities in pupils, they should set about making provision for the differences in individuals. To be at all adequate, provisions for individual differences should fall within the general framework mandated by the commonalities of the learners.

Several Selves

We are each of us at least four persons: the person we really are, the person we think we are, the person others think we are, and the person we would like to be.

Theoretically, one's real self is the sum of one's traits. To identify and describe the real self of any individual is almost impossible, because no person's traits are constant or consistent—or even compatible. Seemingly, we are not today what we were yesterday, or even a few hours ago. This afternoon's virago may be sweet and charming tonight. We seem to change our personalities to meet the circumstances. In situation X, we exhibit trait A; in situation Y, we show the opposite, incompatible, trait B. To piece together one's real self from such a hodge-podge is what one must do to identify one's real self. If these parts of the self fit together nicely, so much the better for one's personality and mental health, but very few of us can integrate all the parts of our personalities into a smoothly jointed whole.

What we are is usually quite different from what we think we are. As a rule, we—each of us—see ourselves in a much more flattering light than we have any right to do. Few of us view our faults objectively; when we do recognize them, we tend to excuse them. (After all, are we not the only ones who know all the mitigating circumstances and who truly sympathize with our conditions?) Those of us who do look at ourselves realistically, and who accept ourselves as we really are, are not only exceptional, but most probably are also better off mentally than are most others.

What other people think of us is usually quite different from what we really are or what we think of ourselves. One's concepts of others stem from many things: interpersonal relationships, taste, values, understandings, and so on. Your friend's view of you is quite different from that of your enemy.

Similarly, your concept of what you would like to be may differ greatly from what you really are, or what you think you are. This concept is one's ideal, one's conscience, one's goal, and one's dream. It tends to keep us going in the way we should like to go, but when it verges too far from reality, or what we think is reality, it can smash our egos.

As we have seen, each of us has a basic self that is made up of our major allegiances and values, and which, if we are fortunate, provides us with the harmony and continuity necessary for mental health. It follows, then, that the education we need should make each of our individual selves function fully. To achieve this goal, we need school programs that allow pupils to become themselves, in order to foster the growth of the affective, creative, cognitive, and intellectual aspects of their personalities—in other words, we need curricula and teaching methods that are self-actualizing.

A Total Organism

We human beings are total organisms. Our physical, cognitive, and affective aspects cannot be separated. For instance, whatever we do physically is affectively toned—for instance, a thing is either pleasant or unpleasant. So are understanding and learning. The learning situation never consists of the intellectual alone. The physical aspects of the classroom may be encouraging or depressing. The pupils may be excited or lethargic. The learning process may be encouraging or discouraging. The knowledge we acquire may be pleasant or disagreeable. Teachers must remember that the learner is not just a brain but a living, breathing human being, and must adjust their teaching methods and content accordingly. Opening the window in a stuffy classroom may not only make the classroom's atmosphere more pleasant; it may also stimulate learning.

Readiness

The fact that we are total organisms is particularly important to remember when creating readiness to learn. Students are always in one state or another of readiness for learning, and for learning particular things. As Module 6 points out, this state of readiness, however, may be favorable or unfavorable. For example, the learner may or may not have the necessary background, may or may not feel well, may or may not be interested, and so on. A person who is emotionally upset, irritable, sluggish, restless, tired, indifferent, or sick is usually not so ready to learn as one who is interested, well-prepared, and feeling in the pink. In general we can say that pupils are ready to learn when

1. They are healthy.
2. They are well-adjusted.
3. They have favorable attitudes.
4. They are mature enough.
5. They have suitable background abilities and knowledge.

If these conditions do not obtain, pupils will learn better if the teacher is able to make the conditions more favorable.

Developmental Tasks

Not only are there times when pupils are ready to learn, but there also seem to be specific times when they must learn certain things if they are ever to learn them easily and well. For instance, the young person who does not learn how to carry out the appropriate sex role at the proper time may remain in an arrested state of development for the rest of his or her life. These important learnings that one should master at specific periods of one's life are what Havighurst has called *developmental tasks*. They are discussed more fully in Module 6.

To expect everyone to complete all the developmental tasks fully and on schedule is to expect too much. Some people are early maturers; some are late bloomers; and some never make it at all. As Clark, Klein, and Burks point out,

> no one ever achieves perfection in these tasks. Rather each person achieves in some areas at the expense of other areas, and makes progress in different areas at different

times. Nevertheless, each person who does not successfully complete a particular developmental task remains stunted in this respect, even though he may have attained adulthood in other ways ... The young man who does not succeed in freeing himself from his mother's apron strings in his youth may find it doubly hard to do so in later life.... The importance of completing one's developmental tasks can hardly be exaggerated. Presumably, finishing them is more important than learning any list of French irregular verbs or geometric propositions. To what extent the school should accept the responsibility for seeing to it that boys and girls accomplish these developmental tasks is probably moot, but it seems obvious that the school should do nothing to make the completing of these tasks unnecessarily difficult. In any case curriculum makers must also understand that boys and girls will spend much of their time trying to complete their developmental tasks whether the school provides for them or not, for these matters are really important to the boys and girls. The curriculum worker needs to bear this fact in mind when building a curriculum.[1]

Needs

In addition to developmental tasks, all learners have needs. Needs are just what the word suggests—things required for one's proper functioning. Need may be caused by our biology, or by the environment, or by our own psychic make-up. By and large, they determine what we do and what we are.

Everyone has many different kinds of needs. Maslow has placed them in six categories, ranked according to strength.

1. Physiological.
2. Safety.
3. Love and affection.
4. Self-esteem.
5. Prestige.
6. Self-actualization.[2]

The fact that there are such needs, and that they can be ranked into such a hierarchy, has several implications for teaching: They provide one basis for determining what should be included and emphasized in the curriculum. They also provide a basis for determining which sort of teaching strategies should be used.

General Tendencies in Behavior

These needs are encompassed in general tendencies to behave in certain ways. According to Roy O. Billett, these general tendencies can be grouped into ten categories.

1. To go on living (self-preservation).
2. To seek the company of one's fellows (social gregariousness).
3. To achieve social status.
4. To achieve economic independence.
5. To play (recreation).

[1] Leonard H. Clark, Raymond L. Klein, and John B. Burks, *The American Secondary School Curriculum*, 2nd ed. (New York: Macmillan, 1972), pp. 60–62.

[2] A. H. Maslow, "A Theory of Human Motivation," *Psychological Review*, **50**:370–396, 1943.

6. To mate.
7. To succeed or excel.
8. To receive and bestow sympathy.
9. To relieve suffering.
10. To collect and hoard.[3]

Other lists of general tendencies may differ from this one, but probably most of a person's general tendencies can be encompassed within these ten categories. These general tendencies are, of course, the broad motives from which one's specific goals stem. They seem to be the result of the confluence of one's innate drives and learning. What seems to happen is that one's experiences cause learning, which modifies innate drives, which then form general tendencies. Then, new learning integrates with the general tendencies again to modify one's personality and one's general tendencies to behavior. In this way, one's general tendencies to behavior and one's personality are modified time and again. For example, although you have an innate drive for food, your learning over the years may have so modified your behavior that you tend to be abstemious and to avoid highly spiced food, because you have learned that overeating and highly spiced foods upset you.

Because learning continues throughout life, general behavioral tendencies also change throughout life. The middle-aged man who learns that he is diabetic may adopt a quite new outlook on eating and socializing as he integrates this new knowledge into his general tendencies to keep on living, to relieve his suffering, and to seek the company of others. As a rule, the general tendencies of pupils one sees in schools have been so modified by experience that their behaviors are almost entirely learned, rather than innate.

Educationally speaking, the facts about people's general tendencies in behavior have two extremely important implications: (1) Because learning has such a large part to play in the formation of a person's general tendencies, it follows that education can change one's general tendencies; and (2) a pupil's general tendencies play a major role in determining the pupil's motivation for school work, the pupil's attention in class, and interest in the subjects being studied. Just what effect a general behavioral tendency may have on one's behavior in a specific situation is somewhat difficult to predict, however, because at times the influence of two or more general tendencies may conflict.

Specific Goals

In general, it is safe to say that all conscious behavior is goal-related behavior. We all select specific goals and then behave in ways that we think will bring about their realization. Of course, one cannot tell, merely from a person's choice of a goal, just what that pupil will do in a given situation, because there may be, and usually are, a number of ways to achieve the goal. One may choose an alternative to one's usual behavior because it may seem to be the most appropriate behavior under the circumstances; or one may choose the first alternative one thinks of. Also, one's behavior may be influ-

---

[3] Roy O. Billett, *Fundamentals of Secondary School Teaching* (Boston: Houghton Mifflin, 1940), p. 79.

enced by other goals. Everyone has a multitude of specific goals; at any one instant, several of them may be competing with each other. Nevertheless, there are two things one may be sure of: (1) one's specific goals will be related to one or more of one's general behavioral tendencies; and (2) one will select one's own goals.

No one can select specific goals for anyone else. What this means is that because one's specific goals pretty much determine one's conscious behavior, and because we all select our own goals, all people are self-motivators. As the teacher, you may be able to influence a pupil's goal-selection, and thus his or her motivation, but you cannot, strictly speaking, motivate any pupil. (When, in pedagese, we speak of motivating pupils, what we really mean is *influencing* pupils to select goals compatible with what we hope they will do.) Of course, the specific goals the teacher selects should always be related to the pupil's general tendencies of behavior.

Self-Motivators

Learners, then, are self-motivators. They are naturally active. They operate on their own energy. Whether you as a teacher have any effect on your pupils or not, the pupils will always be motivated and will always be doing something. All you can do is to try to direct their behavior into the desired paths by controlling the teaching-learning environment. Critics sometimes say that teachers and others manipulate pupils; but, to speak accurately: teachers cannot manipulate pupils; they can only manipulate the environment. The pupils then manipulate themselves. The goals pupils select, and their general tendencies of behavior, including their basic drives coupled with their perception of the situation, determine what they will do. Of course, the pupil whose motivation points toward desiring the learning tends to learn best.

Teachers can manipulate the environment by means of praise, rewards, punishments, threats, promises, and the like. But no matter what they do, it is the results of what the learner does that have the most effect. Good results tend to encourage the learner and to reinforce the behavior. Bad results tend to discourage the learner and to weaken the behavior. So do no results at all. If you, as teacher, can arrange for pupils to feel that their good efforts have been rewarded by good results, their motivation and learning will probably be strengthened, but it is their actions, their perceptions of results, rather than yours, that will make the difference.

What Is Learning?

Learning is a result of experience—that is, interaction with the environment. After any action, whatever its result, the person is never quite the same again—even though the resulting change may mean that one is more of the same—that is, a habit is more deeply entrenched, or a prejudice a little stronger. Nevertheless, not all experience results in appreciable learning. It may prove valueless because the learner is not ready, or has gone stale. There are propitious times for learning things. (We have already mentioned the developmental tasks that individuals must accomplish at certain times of life.)

Also, learning is integrative; new learning builds on previous learning. We have seen this building process in the development of general behavioral tendencies and in Piaget's theory of developmental stages.

The processes of learning, understanding, and feeling are pretty much the same throughout one's life. A baby learns in much the same way as an adult; the same principles of learning apply to both. However, the adult's learning techniques are more sophisticated because the adult has learned to learn and has obtained more background. But when faced with a completely new and strange situation to which the old procedures do not apply, the adult will undoubtedly find it necessary to revert to quite babyish methods of coping. There is no reason why a child should not understand relatively adult concepts if these concepts can be presented at a level commensurate with that of the child. When otherwise difficult concepts are presented in very concrete terms, children frequently do understand them. Unfortunately, many concepts are dependent upon vocabulary and background understandings far beyond those in a child's repertory. In such cases, the child cannot understand the concept without first learning the vocabulary and acquiring the background—unless a substitute for them is found. In this the child is no different from an adult, except for lack of experience and motivation.

How We Learn

Human beings are highly adaptive animals. Because we are not particularly specialized, we can cope with almost any situation. In individual cases, the methods used to cope with situations may be unfortunate, but on the whole the race has done pretty well.

Our conscious behavior consists of attempts to adapt, in accordance with our goals, to situations we perceive ourselves to be in. Conscious behavior, then, is always goal-related. It is, in effect, very much the same as purposeful behavior or problem-solving behavior. Conscious learning is such behavior.

Of course, not all learning is conscious learning. Much of our learning is serendipitous. Some of it is sheer conditioning. But we do not always have to go through the same type of routines to learn. We can all learn in many ways, evidently—via simple conditioning, operant conditioning, meditation, sleep learning, and suggestion, for example. School-learning, however, is primarily *conscious* learning.

Conscious learning is done primarily through problem solving. Even when one tries to learn a poem "by heart," one uses a problem-solving approach—in this case, the problem is to learn the poem, and the solution is that of memorization. Problem solving is always goal-directed. When faced with difficult problems, we run through the process that Dewey called the *complete thought*. Basically this is a six-step process in which the learner

1. Becomes aware of the problem.
2. Defines and delimits the problem.
3. Gathers evidence that may help him solve the problem.
4. Forms a hypothesis of what the solution to the problem is.
5. Tests the hypothesis.

6. Successfully solves the problem, or repeats steps 3, 4, and 5, or 4 and 5, until the problem is solved, or gives up.

There are other models for this process, but in the final analysis they are essentially the same. The essentials in learning by problem solving are that the learner

1. Must understand what the goal is.
2. Must be sufficiently motivated to persist until the goal has been reached.
3. Must have time enough to do what has to be done.

All too frequently, school learning is only superficial (or nonexistent) because teachers do not see to it that these conditions are met.

The Elementary School Child As a Learner

At one time children were considered to be miniature adults. We now know that that notion was a mistake; children are adults in the making. The child is father to the man: he is not the man. The maturation and learning processes, by stages, change the infant into an adult—a person somewhat different physically, intellectually, emotionally, and socially. It is important to remember this fact: *one should not expect children to behave as adults.* In the following pages we shall examine some of the characteristics of children.

Physical Characteristics

Kindergarten children are not babies, but are quite well-developed young people. Usually the development of the girls is a little more advanced than that of the boys. Be that as it may, both boys and girls of kindergarten age are an active bunch. They enjoy activity for the sake of activity, so much so that they frequently do not know when to stop, and so tire themselves out. This is why frequent rest periods are necessary in the kindergarten.

On the whole, kindergartners are well coordinated physically. They have already become either right-handed or left-handed. Their large muscles are usually well-developed and under control. Their small muscles, however, are not so well-developed. Consequently, they may have trouble buttoning and tying. They also have trouble focusing their eyes on small objects and in coordinating their eye-hand movements. That is why books for little tots should have large print.

As a rule, kindergartners are hardy. However, their bones are still growing; the soft skull bones of babyhood have not completely hardened; therefore, blows on the head are quite dangerous.

As kindergartners move into the primary grades their physical development continues much as it was. They seem to be somewhat less hardy, perhaps, (this is the age when childhood illnesses are common), but they continue to be very active. Sitting still may be quite an ordeal for them. They also continue to tire easily. Frequent rest periods are still desirable. All in all, however, their coordination and body control are excellent.

The middle graders' physical development has progressed considerably.

The small muscles have developed to the point where the children's fine-motor coordination is excellent, and the eye muscles now allow proper focusing. Bone growth is still not complete. Contact sports such as football can cause serious injuries, particularly of the joints. Nevertheless, boys have become stronger and tougher and have acquired much greater powers of endurance, and so enjoy rowdy behavior and rough games. They are beginning to try to show off their manliness. In spite of all this manly growth, the girls are usually heavier, taller, and more developed than the boys. Most of them shoot up in a preadolescent growth spurt. Some of them achieve puberty. (Although the average age for girls at puberty is about twelve or thirteen years, puberty may come as early as age nine and as late as sixteen for normal girls.) Consequently, girls are likely to become very interested in sex—an interest shared not nearly to the same extent by the boys in their age group. Some boys may start their preadolescent growth spurt during their middle-grade years, but, as a rule, they do not reach puberty until later. (The average age for puberty in boys is fourteen; normal boys may reach puberty as early as eleven or as late as eighteen.) At this stage in life, boys and girls seem to have gotten over the tendency to be ill frequently that seems to plague primary grade children. As a rule they are a healthy lot.

Social Development

The social development of children, from the preschool to adolescent years, tends, when all is considered, to be somewhat spectacular. In the kindergarten, boys and girls seem to have quite similar interests. Their play groups are small and haphazardly organized. Usually the kindergartner has one or two good friends. These friends may or may not be of the same sex. Most kindergartners are willing and able to play with almost any one, but ordinarily they tend to pick as their friends children of the same sex. These friendships and their play groups tend to be quite transient.

As children get older, their friendships usually become more permanent and more selective. Primary-grade youngsters are likely to have a favorite friend, and sometimes an enemy. Their friendships are, as a rule, longer lasting than kindergartners, though they are still transient. In their play groups, children begin to become more organized. They like organized games, yet their games are likely to be interrupted by frequent attempts to establish their independence. Their attempts to assert themselves lead to competition with other children, boasting, and frequent quarrels.

This striving to assert oneself as an individual becomes even more noticeable during the middle grades. Preadolescence (age eight to twelve, approximately) is not an easy time of life. Children of this age can be particularly trying to adults who have to deal with them. In the words of Mary Jane Loomis,

> Many adults, teachers and parents especially, are inclined to view with alarm and varying degrees of rejection the antics of the nine-to-twelve-year-olds. Their ventures and adventures with assertive independence are often construed as open defiance and disobedience. Their peer-group standards are deemed to be of questionable value and are viewed with suspicion. Their often revolting habits of uncleanliness and attire, their table manners, and language idiosyncrasies create innumerable conflicts with adults.

Their reversion to extremely childish behavior on occasion evokes impatience and harsh disciplinary measures. But most intolerable of all, as has been observed, are their rejection of adults as such in favor of their peer-group and sex-group companions, and their adherence to codes of behavior that win the approval and esteem of age mates in utter disregard of the rationalizations or conventions adult guidance may attempt to impose.[4]

In their attempts to establish themselves as individuals, preadolescents turn from the domination of parents and other adults to domination by their peers. It is here that the generation gap we have heard so much about begins. As they turn to their peers, peer groups and peer-group standards and ideas become important elements in their lives. They need the peer group as a medium for establishing social skill and freeing themselves from the home, and as a touchstone by which to appraise their own worth. It is by their acceptance in the group and their success as group members that they judge their own worth. To be an isolate, not accepted by the group, is always hard; it is particularly so at this time of life.

During the preadolescent period, peer groups are usually sex-segregated. As a matter of fact, relations between boys and girls at this stage are likely to be stormy. This seeming dislike of persons of the opposite sex and the exclusiveness of their groups is probably a sign of sexual awakening. Through these mechanisms, boys and girls learn to behave as males and females. That the girls are not so distasteful to the boys as they pretend, for instance, is demonstrated by the fact that boys are loudest in their protests when the girls are in hearing distance, and it is the most attractive of the girls whom they torment most. It was not without reason that Freud called preadolescence the latency period. It is the beginning of what school people now call *transescence*[5] —the period in which a person changes from a child to a full-fledged adolescent or young adult. The group-orientation of children at this age creates interest in team games, clan functions, club activities, and so on. This is the period of the Little League, Cub Scouts, Brownies, and so on.

Mental Development

The astounding feature about early childhood is how, in the period of a few short years, children learn to talk so fluently. Kindergartners are great talkers. They like to talk, and they are good with language. Although their understandings are concrete rather than abstract, they are inventive, imaginative, and eager to learn. These characteristics continue throughout the primary grades. Primary-grade level children love to recite in class, even when they do not know the answers. Although they continue to be imaginative and inventive, they still cannot deal with the abstract.

During the middle grades, children do make the shift from the concrete to the abstract. By the sixth grade, they can deal with formal mental operations, abstractions and symbols, as well as with the concrete. Because they

---

[4] Mary Jane Loomis, *The Pre-adolescent: Three Major Concerns* (New York: Appleton-Century-Crofts, 1959), p. 3.

[5] A word coined by Donald H. Eichorn, in his *The Middle School* (New York: Center for Applied Research in Education, 1966), p. 3.

are able to perform rather high-level thinking tasks, they should learn, and have plenty of experience in, the techniques of inquiry. Children at this stage of development usually have many interests, although often the interests are of short duration. Their curiosity is well developed. Many are avid collectors—bottle caps, McDonald patches, cereal give-aways, anything—is likely to be grist for their collections. Frequently they set too high standards for themselves, then become frustrated and feel guilty when they find that they cannot deliver. They may also be frustrated because at this age they would usually prefer to be physically active, for example, making things, working with their hands, or playing, but they are restricted to such sedentary occupations as writing, thinking, and reading in school.

Emotional Characteristics

Elementary school children are emotional characters. Kindergartners are likely to express their emotions very freely. Tantrums and expressions of anger are common. So is weeping. Children of this age are often fearful. They need encouragement and support. They also tend to become jealous easily. One can put a kindergartner's nose out of joint without really trying.

As kindergartners move into the primary and middle grades, they continue to be sensitive. They want to please, to do well, and to be appreciated. They like to accept responsibility. They are eager for praise. In short, they want to feel worthy. This is one reason why they sometimes misbehave and show off. They hope that by such behavior they will draw attention to themselves, and be appreciated. Sometimes middle graders' attempts to prove themselves lead to juvenile delinquency. Despite this desire to assert themselves independently, they are very dependent. They need support. This dependency, coupled with their desire to be somebody, plus the conflict between peer values and parental values, may cause confusion and mental instability. This insecurity is one reason why they are so sensitive to criticism and ridicule. On the other hand, they are alert to the feelings of others, and consequently are able to be sympathetic or to hurt others' feelings.

In preadolescence youths attempt to achieve mastery over their environment. They greatly need to make some mark on the world, to be somebody, because they gain a sense of identity from their perception of what they can do. Therefore, it is important that they prove themselves competent in at least several ways. This period is sometimes called the "sense of industry" stage. As we have just noted, in their search for independence and for making their mark, preadolescents may be quite ambivalent. They want to be independent but they are quite unsure of themselves and need support. However, they resent heavy-handed help and directions; they would rather do it themselves, without adult interference. This presents the parent or teacher with a delicate problem: how to give the preadolescents the support they need indirectly, without upsetting them by seeming to interfere.

At this stage young people need love and affection, and are very willing to share it. This is the stage of life characterized by hero worship and crushes. The ability of preadolescents to love is tremendous, and their sensitivity and vulnerability to hurts and to the seeming withholding of love, is equally great. The adult teacher or club leader who becomes the love-object of a preadolescent faces a situation that requires delicate handling.

Moral Development

The elementary school years are the period in life when children begin to throw off the yoke of parental values and begin to develop values and a moral code of their own. Preschool and primary grade children have little real sense of right and wrong. They usually believe that something is right or wrong because the parent or teacher said so, or because they have learned a rule. Some of the children in Piaget's experiments evidently thought that the rules for playing marbles were set by God Himself! Furthermore, they see right and wrong as applying only to specifics. They cannot generalize or transfer the concepts from one case to another. This period in life Piaget has called that of moral realism.

At the ages of seven and eight a change in moral development begins. The child no longer accepts unquestioningly adult judgments of the infallibility of rules. As chilren become aware that standards and values differ, they move from a state of moral realism to a state of moral relativism or moral cooperation. When they are in this state, children realize that there may be more than one set of values or more than one concept of right and wrong, and that values may be determined by results rather than by authority. At this stage they take things less literally. They realize that there may be such things as extenuating circumstances, and that rules may be guidelines rather than absolutes. In fact, they learn that rules may be negotiated and that they and their friends can cooperatively make up their own rules for their games and other activities. It is at this period of life that children tend to turn to their peers for values and to reject adult values. This period can be fraught with danger, for when preadolescents reject adult standards, there is no guarantee that they will substitute anything good.

Thus we see that during the preadolescent period young people make two important shifts in their moral development:

1. From the authority of superiors to the authority of their peers.
2. From the morality of restraint by authority to the morality of cooperation with their peers.

Nature of the Adolescent Learner

The Middle School Years

Middle school pupils are either in the last (preadolescent) stages of childhood or in the beginning stages of adolescence. This period of life, which bridges preadolescent childhood and adolescence, is now frequently called *transescense*, to differentiate it from either childhood or adolescence. It is a period of which we know little and of which much we think we know is not so. Nevertheless, we can say flatly that it is a period of great change in everyone's life. The body changes, and the individual must change to meet the demands and needs of the new body and the new life role attendant on these body changes. Sometimes these changes and adjustments are stormy. One often hears this period described as one of storm and stress, although perhaps the storms and stresses are not as prevalent as psychologists once thought. Still, it is one of the more difficult periods of life, and it is one that makes teaching in the middle school grades difficult.

A major reason for this difficulty is the heterogeneity of the age group. It is, for instance, not so very unusual to find a six-year difference between slowly developing boys and rapidly developing girls in the same classroom. Not only is there extreme variability in physical development, but there are similar differences in social, emotional, and intellectual growth as well. These factors are so important that to say that a pupil is thirteen is almost meaningless as an indicator of the person's biological, physical, intellectual, emotional, or social development. In addition, transescents vary intra-individually. A transescent's intellectual, social or emotional development may not, and probably does not, match his or her biological growth. A well developed, mature looking "young woman" may be, and probably is, still a child socially, emotionally, and intellectually.

The High School Years

High school students have, for the most part, completed the physical changes associated with transescence, although some boys and girls do not achieve puberty until grades eleven or twelve, or even later. Having become more or less accustomed to physical changes, these students can now concentrate on becoming adults—intellectually, socially, emotionally, morally, vocationally, and economically. This task, if it is ever completed, will probably be finished during the mid-twenties. (Some people seem never to achieve true adulthood, no matter how long they live!) High school students, therefore, need an education somewhat different from that of middle school transescents. In some respects, older students are more stable and need less support. On the other hand, they are ready for instruction leading toward their particular roles as adults.

Age-Level Characteristics of Adolescence

The phenomenon that dominates both middle and high school education is adolescence. Adolescence is one of the most difficult and trying periods of life. As we have seen, it is accompanied by significant physiological, social, emotional, and intellectual changes. It is the teacher's primary objective to help guide students through this difficult and trying period, and to aid students in their quest for self-determination. Simultaneously, the teacher is faced with the task of preparing students to function within and upon the world they must soon face.

We shall now examine the period of adolescence in more detail. As we do so, you should remember that transescence is the period in which pupils move from late childhood to beginning adolescence, and that early adolescence and transescence overlap. One must also remember that adolescent-development varies not only from individual to individual, but also intra-individually. Although we shall divide adolescents into two groups—the twelve–fifteen-year olds and the fifteen–eighteen-year olds—there is considerable overlap between the two age groups.[6]

[6] Transenscence, the period of change from childhood to adolescence, is usually considered to include ages ten–fourteen; early adolescence, ages twelve–fifteen; adolescence, ages fifteen–eighteen; youth or protracted adolescence, eighteen–twenty-four. Adulthood

Twelve- to Fifteen-Year Age Group

Physical Characteristics

1. The growth spurt for females is usually completed early in this period. Male students tend to finish their growth spurt late in this period.
2. Puberty is reached by almost all females and many of the males.
3. There is some adolescent awkwardness caused by both the rapid growth and by self-consciousness.
4. Young adolescents are often concerned about their physical appearance.
5. At this age, both the physical and mental endurance of boys and girls may be limited.

Social Characteristics

1. The peer group is the arbiter of social behavior.
2. Conformity is a primary social goal.
3. Females tend to mature, socially, earlier than males.
4. Friendships and quarrels are likely to be quite intense.

Emotional Characteristics

1. Moodiness and unpredictability are common, and they are the result of both physical changes and conflicting expectations of different groups.
2. Students may become loud and vociferous in order to conceal insecurity and lack of self-confidence.
3. Youth of this age group tend to be intolerant, opinionated, and critical of adults.

Intellectual Characteristics

1. Students begin to understand abstract concepts and to think abstractly.
2. The attention span of the student lengthens.

The High School Student

Physical Characteristics

1. Most students attain physical maturity, although many males will continue to grow and change, even after graduation.

Social Characteristics

1. The peer group continues to dominate the behavioral code of the adolescent. Some severe conflicts may occur between adult expectations and peer-group expectations. Most adolescents try to solve this conflict by conforming to peer group standards.
2. There is a heightened interest in the opposite sex.

---

is considered to begin at about age twenty-four, although some people never really achieve it. Robert J. Havighurst and Philip H. Dreyer, eds., *Youth*, The Seventy-Fourth Yearbook of the National Society for the Study of Education (Chicago: The University of Chicago Press, 1975), pp. viii, 3–8.

Emotional Characteristics

1. Frequent conflicts occur between parent and child.
2. Moodiness and daydreaming still occur with great frequency.

Intellectual Characteristics

1. In late adolescence, intellectual efficiency peaks.
2. At this time youth form their value systems, their moral and ethical standards, and their philosophy of life.

Typical developmental tasks associated with those age levels are listed in Module 6.

Physical Changes of Adolescence

Adolescence is usually considered to begin with the onset of puberty, that is, the beginning of sexual maturity, which is initiated by an increase of the gonadotropic hormones produced in the pituitary gland. These hormones in turn stimulate the production of the male sexual hormone, testosterone, and the female sexual hormone, estrogen. Both of these hormones are produced in both males and females, but the proportions, which differ according to sex, are genetically determined. Males begin to produce mature sperm and females begin to produce eggs or ova that are capable of being fertilized. The secondary sex characteristics begin to appear. In females, the bone structure of the pelvis increases in depth and width, breasts begin to enlarge, and pubic and axillary hair begins to appear. In males, pubic, axillary, facial, and bodily hair begins to appear and the voice begins to change.

Simultaneously, the height and weight begin to increase rapidly. The proportions of the body change rapidly. Females, as a rule, display these bodily changes a year or two before males.

The changes that take place during this period of change are bound to have some psychological repercussions. At a time when the adolescent male wants to be very mature and sophisticated, his voice is likely to crack, or he is likely to stumble or to knock something over. At a time when he wants to be attractive to the opposite sex, acne occurs, or his hair and scalp become very oily.

The problems connected with the growth spurt and with the advent of puberty are complicated when these changes are early or late. Most females undergo puberty around the age of twelve or thirteen, and males usually around the age of fourteen or fifteen. The range for females however, is from the age of ten to the age of seventeen, and for males it is from eleven to eighteen. The early maturer will probably be somewhat of an outsider. The early maturing girl, for example, who matures a year or two before most of her female companions, will have matured three or four years before her male age-mates. Her interest in the opposite sex will not be shared by her female age-mates, and yet she will probably not be accepted by older girls who share the same interests in the opposite sex.

As a rule, adolescents are very age conscious. Early-maturing boys, however, do not have quite so many problems as the girls. They may not share the same interests as their male age-mates, but they are able to take advantage of the social opportunities afforded by girls who appreciate their interest in the opposite sex. Late-maturers are likely to be excluded because of their lack of interest in the opposite sex, or, even where the interest is present, by lack of the physical attributes deemed desirable or attractive by the age-mates. If an adolescent is excluded because of either of these, he or she is denied the opportunity to practice and develop many of the social skills that are so important in our culture. When the teenager finally does catch up, in interest in sex and level of physical development, he or she is frequently far behind in social development.

Physical development is directly and vitally related to other aspects of development. Social and emotional development, and the development of a healthy self-image, are greatly facilitated by such physical assets as attractiveness, size, and strength. Equally important is that the adolescent be at approximately the same level of development as one's peers.

Adolescent Behavior

The behavior of the adolescent is determined largely by individual needs, environmental influences, the expectations of others, the changes (intellectual, social, emotional, and physical) resulting from growth, and by the interaction of all these factors. It is the teacher's task to be aware of all these influences, and to be knowledgeable about their effects. By acquiring this knowledge and awareness, a teacher can make a conscious provision for them in teaching-style and method, and thus possibly avoid some behavioral problems.

Needs of the Adolescent

All students, and particularly adolescents, have basic needs which must be met. Paramount among them are the needs for approval, affection, security, and belonging. The manifestation of these most often includes a strong desire to conform to the peer group and a strong desire to maintain close ties with the home and family (even though, superficially, this may not appear to be the case), or, where this is difficult at home, a strong desire to form intense relationships outside the home in order to gain affection and security. Teachers who understand these needs heighten their ability to establish rapport and sound modes of communication with students.

Environmental Influences

The environment, particularly the home environment, has a considerable effect on adolescent behavior. For example, parental domination of an extreme form may cause a great deal of instability or aggression. A tension-filled home life may, and probably will, result in a great deal of tension in the student, resulting in disruptive behavior in the classroom.

The sociocultural environment, too, has considerable bearing on adolescent behavior. Those students who come from culturally enriched environments, or who have families that are at the upper end of the socioeconomic scale, are generally more concerned with self-development, creativity, and self-expression than with achievement. The reverse is generally true of those students who lack these enriched environments. Severe problems can occur if teachers have no understanding of the goals of the students with whom they are involved, or of the subculture with which they deal.

Adolescents are also expected to perform in ways that are acceptable to their parents, their peer group, their teachers, society in general, and to themselves. It is conceivable that these expectations may differ and, in fact, may be in direct conflict.

Parental Expectations

Many parents view their children as extensions of themselves and seek to live their own lives through their children. We are all familiar with the father who, from the day of birth, visualizes his child as a doctor, lawyer, or Indian chief. It may never enter the parent's mind that the children might have some ideas of their own about their destiny, or that the child may be gifted in a field that the parent has never considered. Parents frequently forget that our culture changes constantly, and that behavior that they remember as appropriate in their own adolescence may not be appropriate in today's world. The parent's thwarted ambitions and recollection of acceptable behavior may have an adverse effect on the adolescent. It is the teacher's task to intercede on the part of the student where necessary, always being careful to avoid creating a greater problem for the student.

Teacher Expectations

A teacher's expectations of an adolescent's behavior can also sometimes be unrealistic. Teachers frequently forget that not all students live just to go to school and to learn. They forget that the adolescent has a great number of interests outside the school. Many teachers expect that adolescents will always study hard and perform well in the classroom, that they will always be interested in every subject on every day, and that they will always be polite, neat, and well-mannered. By adhering to unrealistic demands and expectations that are unnecessarily rigid, teachers create problems for themselves. To be truly effective, teachers should take into consideration the learnng capacity, the past achievement, the home environment, the personal motivation, and the factors in the social-cultural environment that may affect the performance of each student. On the basis of such essential information, effective teachers try to *adapt* their method and their subject-matter content to fit the students, both as individuals and as a group. It is therefore important to include a variety of techniques which can be related to the child's experiential background.

The adult society with which adolescents most frequently come in contact is composed of their own parents, the parents of friends, and their teachers and school administrators. All components of this adult society expect or demand that adolescents behave in an adult fashion. This adult society is, however, extremely reluctant to provide the privileges and benefits of that society for adolescents. This apparent contradiction between demands and rewards is a sore point with many adolescents. For the classroom teacher, this has many implications. Perhaps the most important of these is that, when students are expected to perform in an adult fashion, and consequently do so, it is important that they receive the respect they have rightly earned.

Peer-Group Expectations

The expectations of the peer group are extremely important for the adolescent. The major expectations or demands of the peer group are conformity and loyalty. Conformity extends to language, dress, in- and out-of-class behavior, music, philosophy, and so forth. A breach of the etiquette of the peer group is grounds for immediate and sometimes permanent ostracism. You should not assume that the adolescent period is the only time in the life of an individual when conformity to group standards is important. We are all subject to the whim of the fashion arbiter, and we generally express opinions that are in keeping with the opinions of other members of our group. Some groups, of course, permit greater latitude than others for self-expression, and this is also true for adolescent groups.

Self-expectations are largely the expectations of the peer group. An individual's behavior will generally fall within the range of behaviors acceptable to the peer group, even though no overt pressure may be applied. It appears that individuals select groups, and are selected by groups, where behaviors and expectations are compatible.

Adolescent Social and Emotional Relationships

Allegiance is usually transferred gradually from home and parents during late childhood, to one's peers during early adolescence. During the adolescent period, social expansion occurs because children are given a little more freedom and mobility and therefore are exposed to a broader segment of the population. Some social constriction occurs as adolescents become more selective about their associates. Generally, the adolescents affiliate in cliques or relatively small, tightly knit groups in order to satisfy their needs for "belongingness." It is through this group affiliation that adolescents gain an opportunity to develop and practice social skills and to evaluate their own performance in social situations.

Friendships become very intense and more stable during the adolescent period. Especially in early adolescence, friends are usually of the same sex. By middle adolescence some cross-sexual friendships will occur, and by late adolescence some very intense cross-sexual relationships will appear. These are not usually relationships of the "buddy," "pal," or "best friend" type, however. Friendships are not made solely on the basis of personal likes and dislikes. The selected friend is usually a member of the same clique, and the "friends" usually have a high degree of similarity in interests and values.

Adolescent crushes occur frequently. They range from intense same-age, same-sex relationships to same-age, opposite-sex relationships, and to crushes on adults of the same or opposite sex. In their transescent years, particularly, students frequently pattern themselves after a favorite teacher and may attempt to find out all there is to know about that teacher. (Perhaps this is where the idea of teaching as "life in a fishbowl" originates.) Both male and female students may develop intense romantic attractions to teachers of the opposite sex. Adolescents display these same reactions to their idols, that is, to television and movie stars, rock stars, and sports figures.

With increasing age, the adolescent turns more and more to dating one person, or at least only a very few people. Dating serves a number of very important functions. Two of the most important of these are to develop the social skills and to become aware of the problems associated with marriage, such as compromise, adjustment, and sharing. In addition, dating also provides an opportunity to define and refine ideals and standards related to the selection of a marital partner.

Intellectual Abilities of the Adolescent

A number of very general statements can be made about the intellectual abilities of adolescents.

1. As a rule, verbal and mathematical abilities appear to reach a peak during the adolescent years.
2. Generally, sex differences in intellectual ability become most prominent during adolescence. Boys are usually superior to girls in mathematics and in spatial relationships; girls are usually superior to boys in verbal ability. (It will be interesting to see whether or not these differences according to sex persist or diminish as our society's view of woman's role continues to change.)
3. Generally, intelligence remains relatively constant from childhood through adolescence. There is no evidence of a mental growth spurt with the onset of adolescence. In fact, during transescence there seems to be a plateau at which both the growth of the brain and of mental ability remain suspended for a year or so. As a general rule, intellectual ability appears to remain relatively constant until the mid-twenties or early thirties, when it begins to decrease slightly. The change is minor, however. Changes in intellectual ability do appear if a great deal of environmental enrichment occurs.
4. There is considerable evidence to suggest that the mode of thinking does change sometimes during early adolescence. Usually, there is, at this time, an increased ability to organize knowledge into meaningful units, and an increased ability to synthesize and to generalize. According to Piaget, most preadolescents perform in ways that are closely tied to their direct personal experiences. At about the age of eleven or twelve, children begin to think and perform much as adults do, in terms of abstractions and generalities.

   The teacher of transescents must take great pains to provide examples, materials, and demonstrations of a concrete nature for children who function only on this abstract level, and also to provide "discovery"-type materials and exercises for children who function on the formal-operational level. In addition, Piaget suggests that the change from performing at the concrete level to the formal level can be instigated and enhanced by the introduction of inquiry-type materials.
5. As a general rule, attitudes, motives, and incentives for achievement in any given situation interact with intellectual ability and skill in the production of success or failure. Social approval rather than intrinsic satisfaction motivates the achievement of many adolescents; others are motivated to achieve solely by intrinsic characteristics. For these reasons it is imperative for the teacher to provide many and diverse opportunities for students to demonstrate their intellectual ability and skill.

Coping Strategies

There is considerable evidence of the presence of a heightened emotionality and of vulnerability to stress during the teen years. Although the heightened emotionality may be based on the physiological changes that are occurring, the vulnerability to stress does not appear to be an inherent trait. Rather, it has been suggested that the adolescent's vulnerability to stress is evoked by adults who *expect* maladaptive behavior on the part of the teenager. This maladaptive behavior may be encouraged by prolonging the immaturity of the teenager and by providing incomplete or inconsistent models for the formation of values and attitudes. The adolescent is soon to enter an uncertain, complicated and troubled world. The fact that many adults are baffled by this same world, and have difficulty functioning in it, and yet expect their own children to be stable, clearheaded, and efficient, is contradictory, to say the least.

A number of changes have occurred in our society which have had considerable effect on youth in general and on adolescents in particular. One of the most obvious of these societal changes is that the extended family of the past is on the wane. Increasingly, we find nuclear families, consisting of parents and young children, far removed from other family contact. More and more families consist of single parents and their children, or of "mixed" families of remarried parents with "yours," "mine," and "ours" offsprings. In addition, the number of working mothers has increased sharply since World War II. These changes, that is, geographic mobility or transience, loss or decline of the extended family, single parent and "mixed"families, and decreased parental contact, may cause adolescents to go outside the home to form relationships which provide some degree of stability and permanence. The practice of "going steady" and the increase of social institutions such as communes may be manifestations or solutions to the problems mentioned earlier.

The school assumes a new level of importance as a resut of these societal changes. Previously, the school functioned in a role that was supplemental to family activities. In recent years there has been a reversal, and young people have increasingly turned to the school and relationships formed within the school to find the permanence or stability that was apparently lacking at home.

Summary

All pupils are unique. No two are exactly alike. Yet, on the whole, they are more alike than they are different. Otherwise we could have no schools, no classes, and no educational programs. To be effective, schools must provide for both the common needs of boys and girls and for their individual differences. To this end, one must adjust the instruction to pupils' readiness, to their developmental tasks, and to their needs. These are reflected in general tendencies of behavior that determine one's specific goals and so one's motivation and subsequent individual behavior, for all behavior is problem-solving and related to accomplishing the individual specific personal goals. Other individuals can influence the behavior of pupils, but in the end one's behavior is self-determined and self-motivated.

Learning results from experience. It may be conscious or unconscious. However, school learning is primarily conscious learning accomplished principally through problem-solving of one sort or another. When learners' problems are difficult, they fall back on the problem-solving process that Dewey called the *complete thought.*

Elementary school children are adults in the making. They develop fairly rapidly in physical, social, mental, and emotional growth. They develop strength and, less rapidly, skill, in using their small muscles. However, their bone structure is still not complete, and they are thus liable to sustain serious injury in contact sports. Although their social and mental development runs on apace, they do not progress to heterosexual roles nor to abstract thinking. Their behavior in these spheres is, in short, childish. Emotionally they need love, affection, support, and praise.

The later years of childhood, the preadolescent phase, and the first years of adolescence, make up the transescent phase of development. During this period of change, puberty and attendant physical changes take place.

Before puberty starts, the pupils have become much stronger and proficient in the use of their fine muscles. Socially, pubescents can be very trying; their aggressiveness in their search for independence and freedom from parental domination is evidenced by their search for support from peers and peer groups. They show their longing for love and affection in crushes, in hero worship, and in their sensitivity to hurts and rejection. Their thinking begins to shift to include formal operations and the higher mental processes. After puberty, these advances continue, although there may be a slight plateau in intellectual development for a year or two. The young people complete their adolescent growth spurt, outgrow their adolescent awkwardness, continue their loyalty to peer groups, sustain their moodiness and unpredictable social behavior, and maintain their experimenting with abstract concepts and formal thinking.

By the high school years, most boys and girls have progressed from early adolescence to adolescence. They are for the most part physically mature, heterosexual, and approaching maximum mental efficiency, although they are still dominated by adolescent behavioral codes as they strive to set up their own moral and social folkways with emotional flightiness and otherworldliness.

One should not be dogmatic in describing the characteristics of any of these stages of development. Individuals vary in their development not only from one another but in their *own* physical, mental, social, and emotional development as well. Nowhere is the uniqueness of individuals more evident than in their growth and development.

SUGGESTED READING

Adelson, Joseph, *Handbook of Adolescent Psychology*. New York: John Wiley & Sons, Inc., 1980.

Biehler, Robert F., and Jack Snowman, *Psychology Applied to Teaching*, 4th ed. Boston: Houghton Mifflin Company, 1982.

Berzonsky, Michael D., *Adolescent Development*. New York: Macmillan Publishing Co., Inc., 1981.

Cohen, Stewart, and Thomas Cominsky, eds., *Child Development: Contemporary Perspectives*. Itasca, Illinois: F. E. Peacock Publishers, Inc., 1977.

Elkind, David, and Irving B. Weiner, *Development of the Child*. New York: John Wiley & Sons, 1978.

Gander, Mary J., and Harry W. Gardiner, *Child and Adolescent Development*. Boston: Little, Brown and Company, 1981.

Gibson, Janice T., and Phyllis Blumberg, *Growing Up: Readings On the Study of Children*. Reading, Massachusetts: Addison-Wesley Publishing Co., 1978.

Grinder, Robert E., *Adolescence*, 2nd ed. New York: John Wiley & Sons, Inc., 1978.

Johnson, Mauritz, ed., *Toward Adolescence: The Middle School Years*, Seventy-ninth Yearbook of the National Society for the Study of Education. Chicago: The University of Chicago Press, 1980.

Kaplan-Sanoff, Margot, and Renee Yablans-Magid, *Exploring Early Childhood: Readings in Theory and Practice*. New York: Macmillan Publishing Co., Inc., 1981.

Langer, Jonas, *Theories of Development*. New York: Holt, Rinehart and Winston, 1969.

Lipsitz, Joan, ed., *Barriers: A New Look at Young Adolescents*. New York: Ford Foundation, 1979.

McNally, D. W., *Piaget: Education and Teaching*. New York: International Publication Service, 1975.

Meier, Blanche Garner, *Changing: The Psychology of Adolescence*. St. Louis, Missouri: The C. V. Mosby Company, 1982.

Mosher, Ralph L., ed., *Adolescent's Development and Education*. Berkeley, California: McCutchan Publishing Co., 1979.

Papalia, Diane E., and Sally Windkos Olds, *Human Development*, 2nd ed. New York: McGraw-Hill Book Company, 1981.

Reilly, Robert, and Ernest Lewis, *Educational Psychology: Applications for Classroom Learning and Instruction*. New York: Macmillan Publishing Co., Inc., 1983.

Rice, F. Philip, *The Adolescent Development, Relationships and Culture*, 3rd ed. Boston: Allyn & Bacon, Inc., 1981.

Ripple, Richard E., Robert F. Biehler, and Gail A. Jaquish, *Human Development*. Boston: Houghton Mifflin Company, 1982.

Sahler, Olle Jane Z., and Elizabeth R. McAnarney, *The Child from Three to Eighteen*. St. Louis, Missouri: The C. V. Mosby Company, 1981.

Thornburg, Hershel D., *Development in Adolescence*, 2nd ed. Belmont, California: Brooks/Cole Publishing Company, 1982.

Williams, Joyce Wolfgang, and Marjorie Stith, *Middle Childhood: Behavior and Development*, 2nd ed. New York: Macmillan Publishing Co., Inc., 1980.

POST TEST

Multiple Choice (*Circle one.*)

1. One's readiness to learn depends upon one's
   a. maturity.
   b. background.
   c. attitudes.
   d. all of the above.
   e. all of the above, plus other factors.

2. Which statement is most true of developmental tasks?
   a. Developmental tasks are imposed on children by adults.

   b. Everyone must complete his developmental tasks at a particular age.

   c. Developmental tasks are prescribed by the school curriculum.

   d. Developmental tasks should be completed by a certain time in life, or they may never be completed.

3. One's general tendencies to behavior are the result of
      a. inheritance.
      b. learning.
      c. experience.
      d. natural drives, plus learning.

4. According to this module, conscious learning usually is most closely associated with
      a. problem solving.
      b. reflex activity.
      c. simple conditioning.
      d. pure trial and error.

5. Boys' and girls' ability to understand differs from adults because
      a. the basic process of learning differs at these age levels.
      b. children lack experience.
      c. the IQ increases with age.
      d. children are less curious than adults.

6. At the primary grade level, one can expect pupils to
      a. be very hardy.
      b. be strongly interested in sex.
      c. find it hard to focus on fine print.
      d. have excellent eye-hand coordination.

7. Girls typically reach puberty at age
      a. 9-10.
      b. 11-12.
      c. 13-14.
      d. 15-16.

8. During the preadolescent period, young people make two important shifts in their moral development. One of them is a shift toward
      a. greater dependence on authority.
      b. literal acceptance of rules and laws.
      c. moral realism.
      d. moral relativism.

9. The peer groups of middle-grade children are usually
      a. very formally organized.
      b. of minor importance in pupils' lives.
      c. sex-segregated.
      d. heterosexual.

10. By the sixth grade, the average pupil's mental development has reached the point that he can readily understand
    a. concrete concepts.
    b. abstract concepts.
    c. both concrete and abstract concepts.
    d. his own feelings.

11. The average age for the occurrence of puberty in males is
    a. 10-11.
    b. 12-13.
    c. 14-15.
    d. 16-17.

12. A male who matures before his male age-mates will have
    a. greater social adjustment problems than early-maturing females.
    b. greater social adjustment problems than late-maturing females.
    c. greater social adjustment problems than late-maturing males.
    d. fewer social adjustment problems than late-maturing males.

13. An adolescent's expectations for himself are largely defined by the
    a. peer group.
    b. family.
    c. school.
    d. culture.

14. Adolescent females are generally
    a. better than adolescent males in verbal ability.
    b. poorer than adolescent males in verbal ability.
    c. better than adolescent males in mathematical ability.
    d. poorer than adolescent males in social ability.

15. Intelligence
    a. increases steadily until about the age of fifteen.
    b. decreases steadily after the age of seventeen or eighteen.
    c. peaks sharply at about age fifteen.
    d. remains relatively constant through childhood and adolescence.

16. The major intellectual change during adolescence is the change
    a. from a formal operational mode of thinking to a concrete operational mode of thinking.
    b. from a concrete operational mode of thinking to a formal operational mode of thinking.
    c. in verbal ability.
    d. in the ability to perceive spatial relationships.

17. Of the changes in our world that have occurred since World War II, probably the one most closely related to adolescent social and emotional problems is the change in the

    a. natural environment.
    b. educational system.
    c. political system.
    d. family structure.

18. Students who come from deprived sociocultural environments are generally oriented toward
    a. self-expression.
    b. achievement.
    c. creativity.

19. Which is *not* a source of frequent conflict between adults and adolescents?
    a. Contradictions between expected behaviors and rewards.
    b. Inappropriate or unrealistic behavioral expectations.
    c. Rapid changes in the patterns of intellectual development.
    d. Peer-group behavioral codes.

20. The peer group provides for the early adolescent *all* of the following *except*
    a. opportunities to practice social skills.
    b. rewards for acceptable social behavior.
    c. "belongingness" needs-fulfillment.
    d. frequent cross-sexual social contacts.

INVOLVEMENT EXPERIENCES

1. Observe pupils in kindergarten, elementary, middle and high schools. Try to spot the physical and social characteristics of the various age groups.

2. Try to remember how you felt about things when you were a seventh and eighth grader. What were your principal interests? What your greatest concerns? What were your favorite activities? What did you dread most? What about school appealed to you? What did not?

3. Think back over your high school years. What were you like? What were your interests, concerns, abilities, favorite activities, fears, etc.? How did you differ from your middle school self?

4. If you can remember your younger years, ask yourself the same questions about your elementary school years. An informal free-for-all discussion with your colleagues about your likes as elementary, middle, and high school pupils might help you to better understand your pupils-to-be.

5. Set up a list of the behavior you think you ought to expect of your pupils. Discuss your list with your fellow students. Do you seem to be expecting enough? Or do you expect too much?

6. How do you think you might be able to utilize students' basic needs or developmental tasks in your teaching? What steps would you take to make sure that their basic needs and developmental tasks do not counteract your teaching goals?

7. If you find that pupils are not interested in learning what you wish to teach, what might you do? List several things you might do to encourage them to select goals compatible with yours.

8. Observe public school classes. What do the most effective teachers do to make their classes successful?

9. Think back over the past years. Did some of your teachers have problems with discipline? As you remember it, what seemed to cause these problems? In your experience, what seems to make the difference between a poorly motivated and well-motivated class? Discuss this matter with your peers.

10. What could you do to find out if pupils are ready for the lessons you wish to teach? If pupils are not ready, what do you propose to do about it? Discuss this problem with your peers.

MODULE
8

Tests and Measurement

Summative and Formative Evaluation / Criterion-Referenced and Norm-Referenced Instruments / Types of Instruments / Criteria for Evaluating Instruments / Validity / Reliability / Usability / Objectivity / Standardized Tests / Interpreting Standardized Tests / Teacher-Made Tests / Test Construction / Scoring Tests / Marks and Marking

The first-edition version of this module was written by Janice R. Boone, Dean, School of Professional Studies, Jersey City State College. It has been revised and updated for this edition.

RATIONALE

Academic testing is a fundamental part of the teaching-learning process. It is used not only as a basis for ranking pupils at the termination of the teaching-learning process, but it can be, should be, and is used to guide teaching, to aid in the development of curricula, to aid in the assessment of needs and differences, to evaluate progress, and to motivate learning. Psychological tests, standardized achievement tests, and teacher-constructed tests are all frequently used in achieving the ends just mentioned. It is necessary for a beginning teacher to have a working knowledge of testing and test construction in order to be able to select standardized tests in a realistic and rational fashion, and in order to develop tests that accurately measure the learning that has occurred in the classroom. Therefore, the primary aim of this module is to improve your basic familiarity with the subject of academic testing and with the vocabulary commonly used in relation to testing. In addition, it is intended to heighten your awareness of why and how mistakes are made in the construction of classroom tests, and to provide some guidelines for the construction of one's own classroom tests.

SPECIFIC OBJECTIVES

Upon completing your study of this module, you should be able to

1. Explain summative evaluation, formative evaluation, norm-referenced testing, and criterion-referenced testing.
2. Define *validity*.
3. Explain the various forms of validity.
4. Define *reliability*.
5. Define *usability*.
6. Differentiate between reliability and validity.
7. Name the basic methods of determining reliability.
8. In your own words, explain the term *normal curve*.
9. Explain why a distribution of test scores might be *skewed*.
10. Define the term *mean*.
11. Compute a mean for a set of scores.
12. Define the term *mode*.
13. Find a mode for a set of scores.
14. Define the term *median*.
15. Find a median for a set of scores.
16. Define *standard deviation*.
17. Compute the standard deviation for a set of scores.
18. State the purpose of "standard scores."
19. Computer z scores and T scores for a set of scores.
20. Define *percentile score*.
21. State at least two disadvantages of testing and grading.
22. Construct a test in your subject-matter area which follows the guidelines in this module.

MODULE TEXT

Measurement and evaluation are used in the schools for a number of different reasons. For example, one measures or evaluates to assist in pupil guidance, to rank pupils' success or achievement, to motivate pupils, to guide teaching, to evaluate methods and procedures of teaching, and to provide instruction for pupils.

Summative and Formative Evaluation

Not all measuring instruments are equally serviceable for these various purposes. The effectiveness of an evaluation is therefore dependent on the suitability of the measuring instruments used in the evaluation process. For instance, evaluation may be either summative or formative. Summative evaluation sums up the results of instruction and the progress of the group. It is the sort of evaluation we use to determine marks, to judge the success of instruction and the effectiveness of the curricula. It takes place after the student has finished the unit, course, or curriculum. Formative evaluation, on the other hand, takes place as the unit, course, or sequence progresses. It is used as a tool of diagnosis, as the basis for remediation, and to indicate students' strengths and weaknesses so that teachers may build on the pupils' strengths and correct their weaknesses before the instruction ends. Formative evaluation is aimed at small portions of the unit, course, or curriculum, so that teachers can make subsequent instruction more beneficial to individual pupils.[1] For these reasons, summative evaluation is more likely to be *norm referenced*, while formative evaluation is likely to be *criterion referenced*.

Criterion-Referenced or Norm-Referenced Instruments

In general, according to Ebel, criterion-referenced tests and norm-referenced tests differ from each other in four major ways:

1. Criterion-referenced tests are used to determine which specific objectives individual pupils have achieved, while norm-referenced tests are used to determine the pupils' overall knowledge of the subject.
2. Norm-referenced tests are used to determine a pupil's standing in the group, while criterion-referenced tests indicate pupils' attainment of specific instructional objectives.
3. Norm-referenced tests cover a large amount of subject matter; criterion-referenced tests concentrate on a limited number of objectives.
4. Norm-referenced tests are used to indicate "a student's degree of success in learning"; a criterion-referenced test is used to make sure that the student learns certain things.[2]

---

[1] Benjamin S. Bloom, J. Thomas Hastings, and George F. Madaus, *Handbook of Formative and Summative Evaluation of Student Learning* (New York: McGraw-Hill, 1971), p. 20.

[2] Robert L. Ebel, *Essentials of Educational Measurement*, 3rd ed. (Englewood Cliffs, New Jersey: Prentice-Hall, 1979), p. 11.

Types of Instruments

Not only do measuring instruments differ as to purpose, they also differ in kind. Among the various forms commonly used by teachers are standardized tests, objective-type tests, essay tests, rating scales, checklists, sociometric devices, and performance tests. In this connection we should remember that, in spite of the arguments of uninformed amateurs, neither essay tests nor objective-type tests are necessarily better than the other. Each has its uses. Which type of test one should use for any particular teaching-learning situation depends upon the situation. Table 8-1 compares some of the plusses and minuses of these two types of tests.

TABLE 8-1
Comparative Advantages of Objective and Essay Tests*

	Objective Test	*Essay Test*
Learning outcomes measured	Efficient for measuring knowledge of facts. Some types (e.g., multiple-choice) can also measure understanding, thinking skills, and other complex outcomes. Inefficient or inappropriate for measuring ability to select and organize ideas, writing abilities, and some types of problem-solving skills.	Inefficient for measuring knowledge of facts. Can measure understanding, thinking skills, and other complex learning outcomes (especially useful where originality of response desired). Appropriate for measuring ability to select and organize ideas, writing abilities, and problem-solving skills requiring originality.
Preparation of questions	A relatively large number of questions needed for a test. Preparation is difficult and time consuming.	Only a few questions are needed for a test. Preparation is relatively easy (but more difficult than generally assumed).
Sampling of course content	Provides an extensive sampling of course content, because of the large number of questions that can be included in a test.	Sampling of course content is usually limited, because of the small number of questions that can be included in a test.
Control of pupil's response	Complete structuring of task limits pupil to type of response called for. Prevents bluffing and avoids influence of writing skill. However, selection-type items are subject to guessing.	Freedom to respond in own words enables bluffing and writing skill to influence the score. However, guessing is minimized.
Scoring	Objective scoring that is quick, easy, and consistent.	Subjective scoring that is slow, difficult, and inconsistent.
Influence on learning	Usually encourages pupil to develop a comprehensive knowledge of specific facts and the ability to make fine discriminations among them. Can encourage the development of understanding, thinking skills and other complex outcomes, if properly constructed.	Encourages pupils to concentrate on larger units of subject matter, with special emphasis on the ability to organize, integrate, and express ideas effectively. May encourage poor writing habits if time pressure is a factor (it almost always is).
Reliability	High reliability is possible and is typically obtained with well-constructed tests.	Reliability is typically low, primarily because of inconsistent scoring.

* Norman E. Gronlund, *Measurement and Evaluation in Teaching*, 4th ed. (New York: Macmillan, 1981), p. 139.

Criteria for Evaluating Instruments

No matter which type of measuring instrument one decides to use, one must be concerned with the quality of the specific instrument one selects. Fortunately, even though there is great diversity in the format and construction of various measuring instruments, there are several basic standards which any measuring instrument should meet. These basic criteria for assessing the quality of evaluative instruments are validity, reliability, and usability.

Validity

Validity is the degree to which a measuring device actually measures what it purports to measure. All procedures for determining test validity are concerned with the relationships between performance on the measurement device and other observable facts about the characteristic being measured. The procedures for assessing validity have been classified into four categories: content validity, predictive validity, concurrent validity, and construct validity. A fifth category, face validity, is not validity in the technical sense. Face validity refers to a superficial type of authenticity, that is, whether or not a test "looks valid" or "looks as though it measures what it is intended to measure" to the subjects who take it or to untrained observers. Face validity should not be dismissed as insignificant, however. If test content appears to be irrelevant or silly, it may result in poor cooperation, resistance, and criticism. Cooperation and performance are usually much better if a measuring device appears to be relevant and believable.

Content Validity

Content validity is concerned primarily with the adequate sampling of the area of material or behavior to be measured. Content validation is commonly used in evaluating achievement tests and should be used by classroom teachers for all tests which they develop. In order to insure a high degree of content validity, the content area to be tested must be carefully analyzed to make sure that all major aspects of the content are adequately covered. This can be and should be done before the test is used. The sources a teacher may use to check the content include general and performance objectives, lesson and unit plans, textbooks, workbooks, and related materials. By comparing the items comprising a measuring device with the curriculum to which a child has been exposed, the teacher can usually determine with some degree of accuracy whether or not the measuring device is valid.

Content validity can also be determined by an empirical method, that is, the validity is checked by comparing the results obtained by the students to some other external success criterion.

Predictive Validity

Predictive validity refers to the effectiveness of a test or measuring device in predicting degree of future success. Test scores are checked against subsequent performance. This type of validity is most frequently used on tests for hiring, for discriminating for admission and placement, and for detecting potential personality disorders.

Concurrent Validity

The relationship between test scores and other criteria of success obtained at approximately the same time is referred to as *concurrent validity*. For example, test scores could be correlated with overall scholastic average to provide an index of concurrent validity. Concurrent validity is relevant to tests which are used to diagnose existing status rather than to predict future success.

Construct Validity

The construct validity of a test is the extent to which the test measures a theoretical trait or construct. Examples of these theoretical traits include intelligence, anxiety, and fluency. They are generally broader, less well-defined, and more abstract than those traits or skills previously mentioned. Construct validation involves the accumulation of data from a variety of sources.

Guidelines for Securing Validity

There are several things a teacher can do to make classroom tests more valid.

1. Before the teaching of the unit, determine the objectives of the unit, define them as specific pupil behavior, outline the unit content, and draw up a table of specifications that will show the objectives, the content, and the number or weight of the test items to be given in each area.
2. Build the test when the unit is being constructed.
3. Be sure that you test all the objectives in proportion to their importance. Following a table of specifications should ensure that the test has the proper balance.
4. Be sure the items are of the proper degree of difficulty. Include some easy items for the slowest pupils so they will not be discouraged and not try. Arrange the items from easiest to most difficult so as not to discourage the less bright.
5. Be sure the instructions give pupils all the information they need in terms they can understand.
6. Be sure the items are clearly worded. The reading level must not be too difficult; the grammar, vocabulary, and usage must be appropriate for your purpose.
7. Avoid trick questions.
8. Aim several items at each objective.
9. Design questions to fit the objectives they are to test. Do not overuse memory questions; rather, use questions that call for the kind of behavior the objectives call for.
10. To avoid confusion, use only a few types of items, and group items of each type together.
11. Be sure that the test scores are not affected by such irrelevancies as reading ability, writing skill, and the gift of gab.

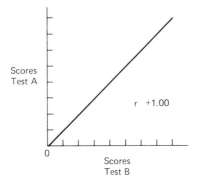

FIGURE 8-1 Diagram Representing a Perfect Positive Correlation.

Reliability

The reliability of a test refers to the consistency of scores obtained by the same individuals on different occasions or with different sets of equivalent items. Other terms that are synonymous with reliability are *dependability* and *stability*. Among the factors that will affect consistency of test scores are temporal stability (the degree to which scores on a test are affected by the random daily fluctuations in the condition of the subject or of the testing environment), the particular items included in the test, and the homogeneity of those items.

The determination of the reliability of a test involves the technique of correlating two independently derived sets of scores. The correlation is usually expressed in terms of a correlation coefficient, whose statistical symbol is r. Essentially, a correlation coefficient expresses the degree of correspondence between two sets of scores. If there is a perfect positive relationship between two sets of scores, as in Figure 8-1, r would have a value of +1.00. This would be the case if all students were to achieve the same relative standing on both tests—that is, the same student would get the highest score on both tests, another student would get the lowest score on both tests, another student would be ranked fourth on both tests, and so forth. The closer the distribution of scores approaches the diagonal depicted in Figure 8-1, the higher will be the positive correlation.

If there is a perfect negative relationship between test scores, as in Figure 8-2, r would have a value of -1.00.

This would be the case if all students were to achieve the opposite relative standing on two tests, that is, if the student who was ranked highest on Test A were to be ranked lowest on Test B, and vice versa. It should be noted that the distribution in this case follows a diagonal from the upper left to the lower right, and is in the opposite direction from the diagonal in Figure 8-1. A negative correlation is as useful to test users as a positive correlation, but we are conditioned to desire positive relationships. A zero correlation indicates the complete absence of correspondence between scores.

There are three basic methods for determining the reliability of an instrument. The method used least often is the *test-retest*. In this method, the same test is used twice on the same group of students, and the two sets of

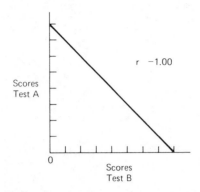

Scores
Test A

r −1.00

0

Scores
Test B

FIGURE 8-2   Diagram Representing a Perfect Negative Correlation.

scores are correlated. There are disadvantages and limitations to be considered when using this method for establishing reliability. The major disadvantages are concerned with the timing of the retest. If the retest is given too soon, immediate remembering, or a practice effect, may modify test scores. If too long a time elapses before retesting, major learning may occur inside or outside the classroom.

Another type of reliability is *equivalent-form reliability.* Students are tested with two parallel forms or equivalent forms of a test at the same time, or over a short period of time. The forms must be equivalent in content, difficulty, types of items, and so forth. One major limitation is that it is extremely difficult to make parallel or equivalent forms of the same test.

The most practical and commonly used method of establishing reliability is the *split-half method.* From a single administration of one form of a test it is possible to divide the responses to items on that test into two equivalent sets. A number of methods of division of responses are possible, but the most common (and adequate for most purposes) is to find the scores of the odd and the even items of the test. By doing this, one gets two sets of scores, the odd and the even, and a correlation can be made between the two. The most often used formula for establishing reliability is the Spearman-Brown formula. This particular conversion formula is discussed in most elementary statistics textbooks.

Several factors affect the reliability of a measuring instrument, and a number of them have already been mentioned briefly. Basically they are of four types.

1. Factors having to do with test construction, e.g.,
    lengths of test
    clearness of directions
    physical characteristics of test
    ambiguity of test items.
2. Factors having to do with scoring the test, e.g.,
    objectivity of test
    key's accuracy.
3. Factors having to do with test administration, e.g.,
    physical conditions (light, heat, noise, etc.)
    time allowed

directions of test administrator

supervision of the test.

4. Factors having to do with the students, e.g.,

their motivation

their attitudes

their physical condition

their emotional condition.

As a rule, the more these conditions are built into the test and the testing situation, the more reliable the test results will be.

Usability

The term *usability* means the degree to which a test can be used with the minimum expenditure of time, money, and energy. A synonym for usability might be *practicality*. There are many standardized tests available which are not practical for use by the classroom teacher because they are too expensive, are too difficult to administer, or are too difficult to interpret or score.

Objectivity

Objectivity is an *ingredient* in reliability. In testing, objectivity refers to the reduction of chance and error in scoring. Obviously, the less chance there is for error when scoring the test, the more likely the test is to be reliable. Thus multiple-choice tests are more likely than essay tests to be objective. For this reason, multiple-choice tests, true-false tests, and the like, are often called objective tests. Perhaps it would be better to call them objective-type tests.

Standardized Tests

The basic reasons for using a standardized test are to measure the differences among individuals and to measure the differences in knowledge, behavior, interests, emotions, and so on in an individual over a period of time. Standardized tests serve a variety of purposes. One of the reasons that standardized tests were developed, in fact, was to identify feeeble-minded children. The detection of intellectual deficiencies is still a major function of testing. Other applications of standardized testing include the detection of personality deviation, discrimination for placement, selection for employment, selection for educational and career placement, and selection and classification of military personnel. It is important for teachers to be familiar with the basic standardized tests with which they may be confronted during their teaching careers. These tests can be divided into three basic groups: general intelligence tests, attitude and personality tests (including projective tests), and interest and aptitude tests.

General Intelligence Tests

General intelligence tests are designed to be used in a wide variety of situations, and generally provide a single score or measure of intellectual level. Numerous tests that measure intelligence are available, and most of them relate reasonably well with each other.

The term *mental test* first appeared in an article written by Cattell in 1890, and it described a series of tests which were administered individually to measure such things as muscular strength, reaction time, memory, and so forth. Ebbinghaus, at about the same time, developed a series of tests in arithmetic computation, memory span, and sentence completion, and he discovered that there was a correspondence between at least one of these tests and scholastic achievement. Ferrari, Kraeplin, Oehrn, and others were similarly involved in attempting to show correspondence between various behavioral, physical, and intellectual traits with scholastic achievement or potential. In 1905, Binet and Simon prepared a series of tests to be used in the identification of retarded or slow students in response to a request from the French government. They included a series of sensory and perceptual tests, and numerous tests which dealt with verbal ability. It is upon this series of tests that almost all later intelligence tests have been based. In the 1908 revision of the Binet-Simon tests, the idea of "mental age" was introduced. Because the concept of mental age was easily grasped, intelligence testing gained great popularity.

Numerous translations and variations of the Binet-Simon tests were made. The most famous of these was made by Terman at Stanford University in 1916, and is known as the Stanford-Binet Intelligence Scale. It was in the Stanford-Binet test that the term *intelligence quotient* (IQ) was used for the first time. The intelligence quotient is a numerical ratio between mental age (as defined by the tests) and chronological age. The formula

$$IQ = \frac{MA}{CA} \times 100$$

was used in the interpretation of test scores for the late 1930s until the early 1960s. The scores of the Stanford-Binet and of most major intelligence tests are now usually reported in terms of deviation IQ scores.[3] The Stanford-Binet has been revised a number of time, most recently in 1960. Revision of a test or series of tests can cause a number of problems, even though frequent test revision is desirable to keep test content up to date.

The Stanford-Binet is a highly reliable individual test of intelligence; it is used primarily for diagnostic purposes with children who have demonstrated atypical learning behaviors or difficulties. This test places very heavy stress on verbal ability, and is culturally loaded (to a certain extent) to favor middle-class suburban children. One of the major disadvantages of the Stanford-Binet is that although it provides a score of general ability, it does not provide indices of differential development of various kinds of intellectual development. Other disadvantages are that it, along with other individual tests of intelligence, must be administered, scored, and interpreted by a highly trained tester. In addition it is extremely time-consuming, and not suitable for use on adults.

The Wechsler Intelligence Scale for Children (WISC) and the Wechsler Adult Intelligence Scale (WAIS) have been very widely used in recent years.

---

[3] Derived scores based on the use of standard deviation. They are described in a later section of this module.

They are similar to the Stanford-Binet, and have many of the same limitations, that is, expert testers are required, many props are needed, and they are lengthy and time consuming. Both WISC and WAIS do, however, tend to discriminate better for giftedness. In addition, both verbal and performance scores can be reported separately, and comparisons can be made between the various subtests.

Group intelligence testing was developed as a response to the need to be able quickly to classify military recruits, during World War I, according to their general intelligence. Information of this type was used to classify men for branches of the military, specialized training programs, officer training programs, and to reject or disqualify incompetents. The Army Alpha (a paper and pencil group intelligence test) and the Army Beta (a nonlanguage test for use with the foreign-born and illiterate) were released shortly after World War I for civilian use. These tests served as models for a wealth of group intelligence and achievement tests which were developed after their release. The major group intelligence scales used in connection with the public schools include

1. California Test of Mental Maturity.
2. Henman Nelson Tests of Mental Ability.
3. Kuhlmann-Anderson Tests.
4. Lorge-Thorndike Intelligence Tests.
5. Terman-McNemar Test of Mental Ability.
6. School and College Ability Tests (SCAT).
7. Scholastic Aptitude Test (SAT).
8. Graduate Record Examination (GRE—a combination of intelligence and achievement tests).
9. Miller Analogies Test.
10. College Entrance Examination Board tests (CEEB—frequently called the College Boards).
11. Numerous subject-matter achievement tests produced by textbook and test publishers.

Interest and Aptitude Tests

In addition to intelligence and achievement tests, there are a number of other devices available to teachers and school systems which are useful for diagnostic and counseling purposes. Among these are the vocational aptitude and interest tests. One of these, a battery of tests used especially for the counseling of high school students and for noncollege adults, is called the Differential Aptitude Test (DAT). It includes tests of verbal reasoning, numerical ability, abstract reasoning, space relations, mechanical reasoning, clerical speed and accuracy, spelling, and the use of language. The Strong Vocational Interest Blank furnishes an index of interests of people in seventy-five different occupations. By comparing students' expressed interests with those on the Strong occupational cross section, the teacher or counselor can gain valuable insight about the students and can guide them into careers and vocations where the probability of their success is greatest. The Kuder Preference Record is similar to the Strong VIB. The major difference is that it divides all interests into nine general categories which are associated with various job clusters.

Personality Tests

There are a number of personality tests now available for use by school psychologists and counselors which can provide valuable information for teachers. They are used primarily for students who have displayed serious adjustment and/or learning problems. In addition to paper and pencil tests, drawing tests, and rating scales, personality or emotional problems are also evaluated with situational tests and projective techniques. Among the more well known personality tests are the Minnesota Multiphasic Personality Inventory (MMPI), the Rorschach Inkblots, the Thematic Apperception Test (TAT), the California Psychological Inventory, and many others. Critical reviews of the various psychological tests may be found in the *Mental Measurements Yearbooks*, edited by O. K. Buros.[4]

Selecting Standardized Tests

Assuming that a school district feels a need to conduct a standardized testing program, a number of things can be done to insure that the program functions as intended. The most obvious steps to be taken by the people who select the tests to be used are an examination of data which relate to reliability, validity, and usability. In addition, those who will be selecting the tests should consult with those who have used a variety of them, in order to get their personal opinions about the quality of the tests. The *Mental Measurements Yearbooks*, which have already been mentioned, should be consulted. When the list of possible tests has been narrowed sufficiently, test manuals should be requested from the test publishers, and evaluated thoroughly. The final step in determining which standardized test to use involves obtaining a sample set of the tests under consideration. After careful examination of the sample set, which usually includes a copy of the actual test, a manual, and a scoring key, it is usually relatively easy to make a final decision.

Interpreting Standardized Test Scores

A basic knowledge of descriptive statistics is necessary for the interpretation of standardized test scores. The statistical concepts that are most important for teachers are the normal curve, measures of central tendency, measures of variability, and derived scores.

Normal Curve

The normal curve is one that is bilaterally symmetrical, with a single peak in the center (Figure 8-3). Most distributions of physical or behavioral traits on aptitude and intelligence scores will closely resemble the normal curve.

[4] O. K. Buros, *Mental Measurement Yearbook* (Highland Park, New Jersey: Gryphon Press), various dates.

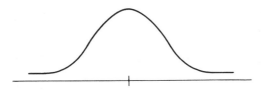

FIGURE 8-3   Normal Curve.

Most of the scores will cluster in the middle of the curve, and the curve will be bell-shaped.

The distribution of scores may not be normal, however, for any number of reasons. When this is the case (Figure 8-4), the distribution curve is said to be *skewed*. When test scores are skewed to the left, as in *A* in Figure 8-4, the implication is that the particular test had a "floor" that was too high for the population being studied. In other words, the test did not discriminate properly at the lower end of the spectrum (perhaps it was too hard). The opposite would be the case in the skewed distribution in *B* of Figure 8-4 (perhaps it was too easy).

It is conceivable, however, that a skewed distribution might be desirable. If, for example, a test-giver wished to pinpoint gifted individuals in a randomly assorted population, a test with a high floor would be administered, in order to discriminate only in the upper level of that population. Conversely, if one wished to pinpoint students with very low ability, one would use a test with a very low floor. A majority of individuals from a randomly assorted population would score well on this kind of test, and a distribution curve that is skewed to the right would be the result.

Measures of Central Tendency

Groups of scores can also be described in terms of central tendency. A measure of central tendency provides a single score which characterizes the performance of a group of individuals and their scores. The best known and most used of the measures of central tendency is the "average" or the *mean* (*M*). The mean is the sum of a group of scores divided by the number of scores. It is expressed mathematically by the formula

$$M = \frac{\Sigma X}{N}$$

where M is the mean, X is the raw score, N is the number of scores, and Σ

A   B

FIGURE 8-4   Skewed Curves.

(pronounced *sigma*) means the sum of or to add. The mean is the most useful of the measures of central tendency, because it is used in the computation of other statistics, and because it tends to give a more accurate picture of central tendency than do the median and the mode. When we compute a mean for the following set of raw scores (X = 2, 6, 7) with the formula,

$$M = \frac{\Sigma X}{N}$$

$$M = \frac{2 + 6 + 7}{3}$$

$$M = \frac{15}{3}$$

we find that the mean for this particular set of scores has a value of 5.

The mode is the score that occurs most frequently in a distribution of scores. The mode can be determined by inspection and is thus the easiest to use of all the measures of central tendency. In a normal distribution, the mean and the mode would be the same or nearly the same. The mode can be misleading in skewed distributions, however. For example, in this set of scores (X = 90, 20, 40, 50, 90, 70, 90), the mode is 90 but the mean is only 64.3.

The median of a set of scores is the point that bisects the distribution of scores when the scores have been arranged in order of magnitude. In other words, it is the midpoint of a set of scores. If there is an odd number of scores, the median is the middle score. If there is an even number of scores, the median is a point between the two middle scores. When a particular score is obtained by more than one student, the median is more difficult to determine. Any elementary statistics textbook will provide an explanation of the method to be followed in this case. The median is a useful measure because it is easily understood and because it characterizes a skewed distribution more realistically than does the mean. Consider the following set of scores (X = 10, 15, 20, 25, 80). The median score in this case is 20, but the mean is 30. The occurrence of an unusually high score tends to mislead one when one attempts to generalize about performance and considers only the mean score.

Measures of Variability

Although measures of central tendency deal with the clustering of scores, measures of variability refer to the spreading out of scores. The most obvious method of reporting variability is in terms of the range between the highest and the lowest of a set of scores. The range is useful because it is easy to understand and is easily found. The range does not, however, tell us about the variability between the scores that are between the two outer limits.

The standard deviation ($\sigma, s,$ or SD, depending on the material being used) is the most usable and the most important measure of variability. The stan-

TABLE 8-2
Calculation of Standard Deviation

X	M	(X – M)	(X – M)²
33	23.6	9.4	88.36
28	23.6	4.4	19.36
24	23.6	.4	.16
23	23.6	– .6	.36
22	23.6	– 1.6	2.56
21	23.6	– 2.6	6.76
20	23.6	– 3.6	12.96
18	23.6	– 5.6	31.36
189 = Σx			161.88 = $\Sigma (x – M)^2$

$$M = \frac{\Sigma X}{N} = \frac{189}{8} = 23.6$$

$$\sigma = \sqrt{\frac{\Sigma(X – M)^2}{N}} = \sqrt{\frac{161.88}{8}} = \sqrt{20.24} = 4.5$$

dard deviation·for a set of scores can be computed with the formula

$$\sigma = \sqrt{\frac{\Sigma(X - M)^2}{N}}$$

where X is one raw score, M is the mean for a set of scores, and N is the number of scores in the set. Although it may appear complicated, the calculation of the standard deviation of a set of scores is relatively simple. For example, suppose we wished to calculate the standard deviation of the following set of scores X = 20, 22, 33, 18, 21, 28, 24, and 23). The first thing one must do is prepare a table with the headings $X, M, (X – M)$ and $(X – M)^2$, as in Table 8-2. The second step involves listing the individual scores under column X, as indicated. The third step involves determining the mean (M) and placing that figure in column M, as shown in Table 8-2. For this particular set of scores, the mean is 23.635, and it has been rounded off to 23.6. The figure, 23.6, then is placed under the column labeled M. The fourth step involves subtracting the mean from each score and placing the resulting figure in the column labeled $(X – M)$. The fifth step is to square each entry in that column and then to enter the result in the column labeled $(X – M)^2$. The sixth step is to add the last column. In the example in Table 8-2, $\Sigma (X - M)^2$ is equal to 161.88. The seventh step involves substituting these values into the original formula, performing the indicated operations, and then finding the square root. The standard deviation in this example is approximately 4.5.

The greater the value of the standard deviation, the greater is the variability of the scores. The standard deviation is closely related to the normal curve. As indicated in Figure 8-5, approximately 68 per cent of all scores in a normal distribution will fall between the points from one standard deviation below the mean (-1σ) to one standard deviation above the mean ($+1\sigma$); ap-

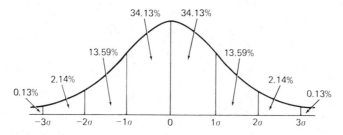

FIGURE 8-5   Per Cent of Cases Falling Within Standard Deviations in a Normal Curve.

proximately 34 per cent of scores will fall between the mean and a point either 1σ above or 1σ below; approximately 13.5 per cent of scores will fall between $+1\sigma$ and $+2\sigma$, or -1σ and -2σ; and a very small proportion of scores, approximately 2 per cent, will fall between $+2\sigma$ and $+3\sigma$ or -2σ and -3σ.

Derived Scores

When interpreting standardized tests, one must usually distinguish between raw scores and derived scores. A *raw* score refers to the actual number of correct responses tabulated when a test is scored according to the directions in the test manual. A *derived* score is a raw score that has been treated, converted, or manipulated to facilitate interpretation. Among the common derived scores are percentile rank, standard scores, deviation IQ scores, and age-grade scores. Correspondence between the normal curve, standard deviations and the common derived scores are portrayed in Figure 8-6.

Percentiles

Percentile scores are expressed in terms of the percentage of persons in a sample or distribution who fall below a given raw score. It is an easy concept to grasp, and thus has attained popularity. The percentile is any one of 99 points which divide a sample or distribution into one hundred groups of equal size. A percentile rank of 50 indicates that a student has performed better than 50% of the people who have taken the same test. The fiftieth percentile corresponds to the median, and in a normal distribution, to the mean also. *Do not confuse percentiles with "percentage scores"* which are simply raw scores expressed in terms of the percentage of correct responses.

Percentiles show where an individual stands in the normative sample, and are useful in comparing an individual's own performance on different tests. They are easy to compute, are universally applicable, can be used on any type of test, and can be used both for adults and children. Since they are considerably easier for lay people to understand than are standard scores and their derivatives, percentile scores have become more popular than other scores among test makers. According to Ebel, percentile scores are the best all-around means of presenting normative information.[5]

[5] Robert L. Ebel, *op. cit.*, p. 334.

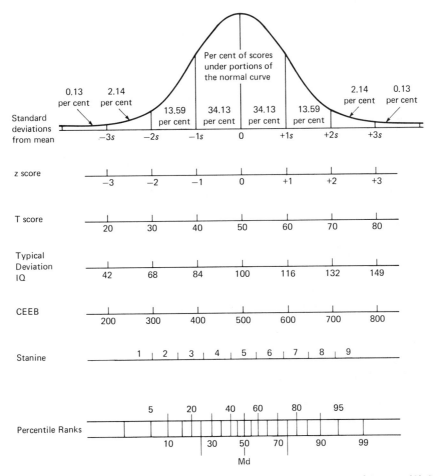

FIGURE 8-6   A Normal Curve Showing (1) Percentage Distribution of Scores, (2) Standard Deviations, (3) z Scores, (4) T Scores, (5) Deviation IQ Scores, (6) College Entrance Examination Board Scores, (7) Stanine Scores, and (8) Percentile Ranks.

Standard Scores

Standard scores are used to express one individual's distance from the mean in terms of the standard deviation. The basic standard score is the z score, which can be calculated with the formula

$$z = \frac{X - M}{\sigma}$$

where X is a particular raw score, M is the mean for a set of scores, and σ is the standard deviation for that set of scores. Stated another way, the z score is used to express one individual's difference from the "average" performance of a whole group, divided by the "average" difference for the whole group. Using the set of raw scores in Table 8-2 we can compute the z score for any particular individual. For example, the individual who obtained a raw score of 24 would have a z score of .088. This figure is derived by simply substituting known values into the formula for calculating z scores ($X = 24$, $M = 23.6$, and $\sigma = 4.5$). A positive z score indicates that the individual raw score is above the mean, a negative z score indicates a raw score below the mean, and a z score of 0 indicates that the raw score is at the mean.

The T score provides exactly the same information as the z score. The difference is that decimal fractions and negative numbers do not occur in the T score. T scores are computed with the formula

$$T = 10z + 50.$$

The T score for the previously mentioned problem would be 50.88, because $T = (10)(.088) + 50$.

The Army General Classification Test (AGCT) score and the College Entrance Examination Board (CEEB) score are also based on the z score. The CEEB, for instance, is computed by the formula

$$CEEB = 100z + 500.$$

Stanine scores[6] are another variation of scores based on standard deviations. Stanine scores consist of nine one-half standard deviation bands centering on the mean. They can be computed by the following procedure.

1. Find the mean of the raw scores.
2. Find the standard deviation of the raw scores.
3. Measure ¼ standard deviation down from the mean and ¼ standard deviation up from the mean to establish the limits of stanine 5 (the middle stanine).
4. Find the limits of stanine 1 through stanine 4 and for stanines 6 to 9 by measuring down or up one half standard deviation for each stanine.

Interrelationships between the standard scores may be observed in Figure 8-6.

Deviation IQ Scores

Deviation IQ's are not really intelligence quotients but standard scores. According to recommendations of the American Psychological Association, these scores should have a mean of 100 and a standard deviation of 16. Thus a deviation IQ of 116 would mean that a person scored one standard deviation above the mean on the intelligence test concerned. Unfortunately, not all test makers have used the same standard deviation. Some use 15; others use greater or lesser values. It is therefore imperative, when comparing and interpreting intelligence scores, to know not only the IQ's reported, but also to know the standard deviations for the particular test.

Teacher-Made Tests

Measuring academic achievement is an important part of the classroom teacher's job, and as such it is imperative that teachers develop the same degree of expertise in this area as they do in the various other aspects of teach-

---

[6] From standard nine.

ing. Teachers have always measured the extent to which pupils have mastered subject matter, but the development of the science of classroom testing did not really begin until the early 1900s.

A classroom testing program actually serves a number of purposes, but many of them do not receive the attention they deserve. Tests are administered primarily to discriminate among students, that is, to rank them in order of success, achievement, or lack of it. Tests are also used to guide teaching and planning. For example, if most of the students fail to respond appropriately to an item or group of items on a test, the implication is that the question was a poor one or that the teaching and planning for teaching was not appropriate for the group. Tests are also used to serve a guidance function, to motivate students, and to provide instruction. For students and parents, tests provide information which enables them to set realistic short- and long-term goals; tests help the teacher in detecting, defining, and describing students' educational needs; and they provide information that is extremely valuable in the restructuring of curricula.

Classroom tests and testing programs can and do occasionally have disadvantages or negative side effects. For example, test programs may impede the teaching process by so dominating the school program that instruction becomes totally geared toward tests. This domination is sometimes particularly harmful when standard tests are used as an integral part of the school system's evaluation program. Tests can become, in the eyes of the students, just a series of opportunities to fail, and teachers are likely to corrupt their courses and teach for the test so as to be sure that their pupils do well. Similarly, passing tests and getting good marks may become so important to pupils that they are concerned only with marks and not with learning. Cheating and unethical or immoral attitudes often result from overemphasis on testing and test results too. Sometimes testing can interfere with pupils' wholesome growth in other ways. Tests can also be harmful to pupils when they are used to categorize pupils as successes or failures, or when test results are considered the final word on a child's abilities, aptitudes, and prospects, or when they are the only means of communication between the school and the home.

Test Construction

Test construction should begin when the planning for teaching is being done, and should be properly based on the formulation of well-defined and explicit performance objectives. Only when a teacher clearly describes the terminal student performance desired can fair evaluation of achievement or mastery of subject matter occur. In addition to clearly stating performance objectives, the teacher, when constructing a test, must take pains to insure that the emphasis of the test parallels the emphasis of the planning and teaching. For example, a mathematics test should not include only problems dealing with the determination of the slope of a line if the major emphasis in planning and teaching has been the solution of maximum-minimum type problems.

The essay test and the objective test are the two types most frequently used in the schools. The tests have a number of similarities and differences. Some of their characteristics are listed in Table 8-3.

When selecting the type of test to use, the teacher should consider the characteristics listed in Tables 8-3. In addition, the teacher should remember that it is usually advantageous to present objective tests when many students are in the group, when the teacher wishes to use the test again, when a high degree of impartiality and objectivity in scoring is necessary, and when speed and efficiency are necessary. Essay tests are more likely to be useful when the teacher is most interested in pupils' attitudes, as opposed to their knowledge of content, and their communication skills. Because of difficulty in correcting them, essay tests are much more usable for testing small groups than large ones.

Essay Tests

Numerous classifications have been made of the types of essay questions. For our purposes, it will suffice to say that there are two basic types—the short-answer essay question, which is usually well-defined in terms of its structure and requirements, and the more open-ended, discussion-type question, which requires the students themselves to supply the structure and organization. The latter type is frequently used to explore attitudes and tendencies to modes of action. In addition, the latter type of question lends itself to the evaluation of creativity, and to skills relating to the use of judgment.

It is important to provide some direction or focus for either of these two types of questions. The kinds of directional words that are most often used include *compare, contrast, differentiate, summarize, outline, describe, explain, interpret*, and so on. Questions should be drafted carefully. If there is any possibility of misinterpretation of the directional words, they should be

TABLE 8-3
Characteristics of Essay and Objective Tests

Essay	Objective
Student organizes his own responses with minimal restrictions.	Student operates on an almost completely structured task.
Student uses his own phrases, words, and expressions in responding.	Student selects the correct response from a limited number of alternatives, or recalls a very short answer.
Student responds to a very few items.	
Student spends most of his time thinking and then writing.	Student responds to a large number of items.
	Student spends most of his time reading and thinking.
Quality of test is largely determined by person doing the grading.	Quality of test is determined by the test constructor.
Test is relatively easy to build.	
Test is very difficult to grade.	Test is very difficult to build.
Test encourages bluffing.	Test can be graded quickly and easily.
Test can be used to measure the achievement of goals which are measurable by a written test.	Test encourages guessing.
	Test can be used to measure the achievement of goals measurable by a written test.
Test can be used to encourage pupils to learn (facts, concepts, principles, and so on).	Test can be used to encourage pupils to learn (facts, concepts, principles, and so on).
Test can be used to stimulate either convergent or divergent thinking.	Test can be used to stimulate either convergent or divergent thinking.

defined. The questions should be worded in such a way that clues are given about the structure of the expected answer, unless it would be contrary to the objectives of instruction (particularly in relation to attitude development). Care should be taken to insure that all questions can be answered in the time period available. Time guidelines should be suggested if more than one essay question is used. Generally, it is a good idea to require that all students answer the same questions.

Objective Tests

There are two basic types of objective questions—the free-response type and the limited-response type. The simple recall question (a supply-type item that requires a student to furnish a word, phrase, or sentence) and the completion question (a supply-type item, which consists of a sentence or sentence series in which important words or phrases have been omitted) are both examples of the free-response type question. Alternative-response questions (true-false, and variations), matching questions, and multiple-choice questions are examples of the limited-response type, in these, students are presented with a limited number of alternatives from which they must select the most appropriate or most correct response.

Simple Recall Items. The simple recall type of question can be written as a statement or as a question, as in the following case.

_____ 1. Name the first president of the United States of America.
_____ 2. Who was the first president of the United States of America?

Care should be taken to insure that the item is stated in terms that are sufficiently specific, thus avoiding ambiguity and/or confusion. An example of a question that is not sufficiently specific is

_____ Who discovered America?

The question is unsuitable because too many responses are acceptable; the student may become confused while trying to determine which response is desired by the teacher.

Completion Items. Completion questions can be written in either interrogative or statement form. In a completion question, it is important that the teacher remember to ask for the important information, and to retain the key words which are necessary for the student to know what is required in the answer. For example, the following question does not provide sufficient information for students to respond with any degree of assurance.

1. _____ and plagioclase are the two most common
_____.

As stated, the question is meaningless to the general science student. If, however, the question is revised to read

2. The two most common feldspars are _____ and
_____.

the student is directed immediately to a specific group of minerals; by merely including the word *feldspar*, the student may respond with some degree of confidence and some likelihood of success.

There are several guidelines the teacher should follow in the construction of completion items. They include

1. Write the item as a short-answer question and then turn it into a completion item, if it seems desirable.
2. Avoid using phrases and sentences copied from "the book."
3. Try to write items for which there is only one correct answer.
4. Avoid indefinite, ambiguous statements.
5. Ask for important information; avoid asking for trivia.
6. Write the items so that the blanks appear at the end of the statement.
7. Use only one blank for the entire response, not a blank for each word in the response.
8. Make blanks all the same length so as not to give away the length of the response expected.
9. Beware of items that can be answered from general intelligence or common knowledge.
10. To make scoring easy, place the blanks in a straight column at the right or left side of the page.

Alternative Response Items. The alternative response or limited-choice item is a recognition-type item in which each question provides a choice between two or more alternatives, of which only one is correct. True-false, matching, and multiple-choice questions are the most common. All of these have minor variations.

The basic true-false item permits only one of two possible responses. It consists of a statement about which a judgment or evaluation of veracity must be made. In constructing true-false items, the teacher should first make a listing of true statements. These can then be changed to a false statement usually by altering a single word or short phrase. During the course of any given period of time, the quantity of true items and false items should be nearly equal, but any single test may be loaded in either direction. Figurative language and complex sentence structure should be avoided. Words such as *all, every*, and *impossible* should be avoided, because statements which include them are usually false. Conversely, words such as *generally, often*, and *sometimes* are used with statements that are true. The teacher should avoid giving unintended clues. Also, statements should not be lifted directly from the textbook.

Matching Items. The matching item is one of recognition, and consists, usually, of two columns (a stimulus column and a response column). The student is instructed to select the correct answer from the response column in reply to each stimulus item. Each group of matching items included on a test should be homogeneous, that is, all items under the stimulus column should be grouped under one category, and the same should be true of the response column. For example, the following matching items for a science test should be subdivided into two matching sections.

_____	1. metamorphic	a. mammalia
_____	2. frog	b. monite
_____	3. sedimentary	c. granite
_____	4. igneous	d. reptilia
_____	5. dog	e. slate
_____	6. rattlesnake	f. agnatha
		g. sandstone
		h. amphibia.

The preferred arrangements for these items would be

Rock Types   **Rocks**

_____	1. metamorphic	a. granite
_____	2. sedimentary	b. monite
_____	3. igneous	c. slate
		d. sandstone

Animals   **Class**

_____	4. frog	a. mammalia
_____	5. dog	b. reptilia
_____	6. rattlesnake	c. agnatha
		d. amphibia.

In the first example, there are only rock types and the names of common rocks to be associated. In the second example, there are only common animals and the class names of those animals. As a rule, there should be more items in the second column than there are in the first so as to minimize answering by elimination. It is usually a good idea to list responses in alphabetical order; and all items for a matching section of a test should be on the same page.

Multiple-Choice Items. The multiple-choice question is a recognition-type of item, which includes a stem word, phrase, or question, and at least three (preferably four) possible choices for response, of which only one is correct. Multiple-choice questions, although difficult to write, are very popular because they are subject to less ambiguity than are other types of test questions. In constructing multiple-choice questions, the teacher should first explicitly state the concept or idea that is to be embraced in the question. The next step is to divide that statement into two parts, the stem, and what will be the correct response. Other responses that appear to be related to the correct response should be formulated. Care must be taken to insure that these other responses do not completely fulfill the requirements of the question stem, that is, that there is only one correct response in the group of responses from which the student must choose. The correct responses should be placed randomly in sets of responses, in order to avoid the appearance of a pattern. As a rule, the stem should be worded in the form of a complete question rather than as an incomplete statement, because the former more clearly defines the problems and indicates the teacher's purpose. Care should be taken to avoid the use of inadvertent clues. For example, all responses should be of approximately the same length.

Preparing the Directions. When constructing any test it is imperative that the teacher write clear, concise directions for the students. There should be no confusion as to what they should do, where they should write an answer, or whether they should write a word or a letter. It is usually helpful to write a sample question and correct response each time a new type of question and new sets of directions are introduced. When conducting a test, it is important to keep students informed of the time they have left to complete the test. Students need to be able to pace themselves.

Scoring Tests

Scoring Essay Tests

When scoring essay tests, the teacher should first decide precisely what is to be evaluated, that is, learning of subject matter, concepts, and principles; literary style; writing mechanics; uniqueness; or some combination of these and others. If an essay test is to be evaluated for more than one factor, separate scores should be given for each factor.

Before evaluating and scoring essay tests, the teacher should decide what points or concepts need to be included in a response in order for that response to be considered minimally acceptable, acceptable, good, or excellent. It is a good idea to make a checklist of the ideas or concepts, and to make a point-value determination for each. In an essay question with a total value of ten points, for example, the student might receive two points for each of four major concepts included in the response, and one point for each of two minor points included.

All the answers to a particular question should be evaluated and scored before the teacher moves on to another question. Scoring is usually more objective, as a result. If possible, the tests should be evaluated by independent scorers. In addition, the tests should be scored as anonymously as possible.

Scoring Objective Tests

Objective tests are quite easy to score once one has a key. If the test answers have been arranged in a column, as we suggested earlier, all one has to do to make the key is to fill out the correct answers on an extra copy of the test. Then simply place the test key alongside the test being corrected, and check the correct and incorrect answers. You may find it easier to cut off the text of the test so that the key will be a strip which can be placed along either side of the test answers. Probably the most satisfactory way to score the test is to mark all the right answers and total them up to get the raw score. Some teachers prefer to mark only the wrong answers. Some, however, mark both.

Marks and Marking

Assigning marks to tests is not so easy as it might appear at first glance. To date, no one seems to have invented a marking system that pleases everyone. The standard A–B–C–D–F marking systems seem to hide more than they reveal; they make no allowance for individual differences; and they are overly influenced by irrelevancies, according to critics. Attempts to substitute pass-fail systems, mastery systems, and the like, have not been received enthusiastically. A mastery procedure that shows promise is the practice, adopted by some schools, of indicating pupils' progress by checking off the units or subunits as pupils master them. (See Figure 8-7.) This system may be combined with an estimate of the pupils' progress—noted, for example, by *Excellent, Good, Average*, or *Below Average.* Systems of this sort are usually criterion-referenced. Other systems report individual progress in elements of the various subjects. For instance, a report card in West Hartford, Connecticut indicates an assessment of the pupils' achievement in the various phases of the unit concerned; for the unit on decimals it provides information on the pupil's growth in basic development, addition and subtraction of decimals, and so on.

Marks on individual tests are usually a matter of the teacher's judgment. Even criterion-referenced marking systems are based on someone's judgment on what the criteria for successful completion should be. Attempts to provide objectivity in marking and grading by using the normal curve of probability and other devices have not proven satisfactory. The normal curve does not apply to most classes, because most classes are not normal. Derived scores such as stanine scores may be more satisfactory. The old-fashioned faith in per cent scores has been largely a fiasco.

Probably the most satisfactory approach for assigning marks is to decide which raw score you will accept as an indication of mastery (or of excellent, good, or satisfactory achievement), and then to assign marks accordingly. Marks of this type can be combined by averaging to give unit marks and term marks, as in the following example. In this example, we have recorded all marks in terms of A–B–C–D–F, and decided to base our marks on daily work,

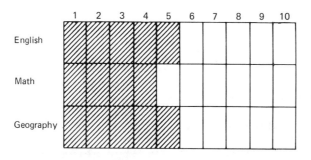

FIGURE 8-7   Units Completed.

25 per cent; papers and themes, 50 per cent; tests; 25 per cent. We then follow these steps:

1. Assign numerical values to the letter marks, to wit, A=4; B=3; C=2; D=1; F=0.
2. Combine the daily work marks. Assuming that the pupil had earned the daily marks, A, B, C, A, and A, the computation would be

$$
\begin{array}{rl}
A = & 4 \\
B = & 3 \\
C = & 2 \\
A = & 4 \\
A = & \underline{4} \\
 & 17:5 = 3.40
\end{array}
$$

3. Next, average the themes and papers. In this case, there are three themes and one major paper, which is equivalent to four themes which gives us the equivalent of seven themes in all.

Theme	B = 3	3
Theme	C = 2	2
Theme	B = 3	3
Major paper	A = 4 x 4	16
		24:6 = 3.43

4. Next, combine the test scores. In this case, we have only one unit test in which the student achieved an A.

$$\text{Unit Test} = 4$$

Now combine the averages.

Daily work = 3.40	3.40
Themes = 3.43 x 2 =	6.86
Test = 4	4
	14.46:4 = 3.62

The final mark is 3.62. If we assume that an A includes scores from 3.6 to 4.0, the term mark or grade is A.

The same basic procedure can be used to combine scores recorded as standard scores, T-scores, and the like.

SUGGESTED READING

Ahman, J. Stanley, and Marvin D. Glock, *Evaluating Pupil Growth: Principles of Tests and Measurement*, 6th ed. Boston: Allyn & Bacon, Inc., 1980.

Bertrand, Arthur, and Joseph Cebula, *Tests, Measurement and Evaluation.* Reading, Massachusetts: Addison-Wesley Publishing Co., Inc., 1980.

Bloom, Benjamin S., George F. Madaus, and J. Thomas Hastings, *Evaluation to Improve Learning.* New York: McGraw-Hill Book Company, 1981.

Ebel, Robert L., *Essentials of Educational Measurement*, 3rd ed. Englewood Cliffs, New Jersey: Prentice-Hall, Inc., 1979.

Gronlund, Norman E., *Measurement and Evaluation in Teaching*, 4th ed. New York: Macmillan Publishing Co., Inc., 1981.

Mehrems, William A., and Irvin J. Lehmann, *Measurement and Evaluation in Education and Psychology*. New York: Holt, Rinehart and Winston, 1978.

TenBrink, Terry D., *Evaluation: A Practical Guide for Teachers*. New York: McGraw-Hill Book Company, 1974.

Tuckman, Bruce N., *Measuring Educational Outcomes: Fundamentals of Testing*. New York: Harcourt Brace Jovanovich, Inc., 1975.

Wilhelms, Fred T., ed., *Evaluation as Feedback and Guide*. Washington, D.C.: Association for Supervision and Curriculum Development, 1967.

POST TEST

On the line to the left of each statistical symbol listed in Column A, write the letter of the statistical term in Column B that is associated with that symbol. Each term in Column B may be used once, more than once, or not at all.

Column A

_____ 1. σ
_____ 2. r
_____ 3. M
_____ 4. X
_____ 5. T

Column B

a. mean
b. standard score
c. correlation coefficient
d. standard deviation
e. median
f. number of scores
g. mode
h. raw score.

Match the terms listed in the left hand column with the definitions in the right hand column. Definitions may fit more than one term and terms may have more than one definition.

_____ 6. Stanine Score
_____ 7. Raw Score
_____ 8. Percentage Score
_____ 9. Standard Score
_____ 10. Percentile Score

a. $100z + 500$.
b. Derived score that indicates the distance from the mean in standard deviations.
c. A, B, C, D, or F Marks.
d. Number of items scored correct.
e. Per cent of items scored correct.
f. Percentage of pupils who fall at or below a given raw score.
g. Band of scores covering one half a standard deviation.

Match the words in Column A with the definitions in Column B. The terms may have more than one correct definition.

	Column A	Column B
_____	11. Mean	a. Measure of Central Tendency.
_____	12. Mode	b. Measure of Variability.
_____	13. Median	c. Arithmetical Average.
_____	14. Standard Deviation	d. Midpoint of a set of scores.
		e. In a set of scores the score that occurs most frequently.

Select the best response to each question or statement which follows and place the letter of that response in the space provided.

_____ 15. The degree to which a test actually does what it is intended to do is called
    a. reliability.   b. usability.
    c. validity.   d. dependability.

_____ 16. The relationship between test scores and other criteria of success obtained at approximately the same time is referred to as
    a. temporal stability.   b. concurrent validity.
    c. predictive validity.   d. equivalent reliability.

_____ 17. The consistency of scores on a test obtained by individuals on different occasions is referred to as
    a. test reliability.   b. test validity.
    c. predictive validity.   d. temporal usability.

_____ 18. The split-half method is a method for determining
    a. test reliability.   b. predictive validity.
    c. temporal stability.   d. concurrent validity.

_____ 19. Which of the following is of *least* importance when selecting a standardized test?
    a. ease of administration.   b. cost.
    c. ease of scoring.   d. attractiveness of format.

_____ 20. The formula for computing the mean of a set of scores is
    a. $M = \dfrac{\sigma X}{N}$ b. $M = \dfrac{N - X}{N}$ c. $M = \dfrac{\Sigma X}{N}$ d. $M = \dfrac{\Sigma N}{X}$

_____ 21. What T score would be the equivalent of the mean of any set of scores?
    a. 0   b. + 100   c. + 50   d. + or - 1σ.

_____ **22.** Which of the following is a normal curve?

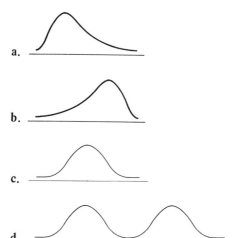

a.

b.

c.

d.

_____ **23.** Which of the above curves indicates that the test may have been too easy?

_____ **24.** Which of the above curves might be useful when one is attempting to pinpoint pupils with high ability?

_____ **25.** For purposes of diagnosis it would be best to use
    a. summative evaluation.
    b. norm-referenced test.
    c. criterion-referenced test.
    d. a skewed test.

_____ **26.** Overemphasis on testing is a problem in some schools because it
    a. may encourage cheating.
    b. cause teachers to corrupt their courses and teach for the test.
    c. may interfere with children's wholesome growth.
    d. all of the above.

The next six questions will be based on the following set of raw scores. In your calculations, *round off the mean to the nearest tenth.*

Elizabeth	29	Matthew	23	Lucas	25
Jennifer	28	Claire	28	Steven	28
Amanda	24	Maggie	24	Brian	26
David	26	Michael	27	Daniel	31

_____ **27.** What is the mode for this set of scores?
    a. 28.0   **b.** 26.4   **c.** 8.0   **d.** 26.5

_____ **28.** What is the median for this set of scores?
    a. 26.5   **b.** 28.0   **c.** 27.0   **d.** 26.4

_____ **29.** What is the *mean* for this set of scores?
  a. 26.5   **b.** 28.0   **c.** 27.0   **d.** 26.4

_____ **30.** What is the standard deviation for this set of scores?
  a. 0.66   **b.** 4.00   **c.** 8.00   **d.** 2.27

_____ **31.** What is Amanda's z score?
  a. 2.27   **b.** $-$ 2.27   **c.** 1.05   **d.** $-$ 1.05

_____ **32.** What is Elizabeth's T score?
  a. 79.0   **b.** 61.0   **c.** 1.1   **d.** 2.27.

INVOLVEMENT EXPERIENCES

  1. Look up some tests in Buros' *Mental Measurement Yearbook.*[7] What does Buros tell you about these tests?

  2. Compare a unit test with the objectives or content of the unit. Offhand, does it seem to be valid? Does it seem to test what was to be taught, in the proportion in which it was to be taught?

  3. Ask a guidance person or psychologist to show you and explain some of the standardized tests being used. Find out how these tests are used. Which tests do the people you asked use, and why did they select these?

  4. Ask a teacher to show you the raw scores on a unit or course test. How are the scores distributed? Are the scores spread out, or are they bunched together? Are they skewed? If so, how? What is the median score? the mid score? What is the mode? Do the mode, mid score, and mean coincide? What is the standard deviation? What A–B–C–D–F marks would you give on the basis of this distribution?

  5. Look at the objectives and content of a unit you might teach. Are there objectives or content that you feel would be best tested by the use of essay-test questions, by objective-type questions, or by performance tests? Why do you feel that particular types of test items are more suitable for testing these objectives or content?

  6. Try your hand at writing essay, objective-type, and performance-type questions. Ask your colleagues to criticize your questions. Are your questions clear and unambiguous? Do they actually test the skills and knowledge you wish to test for?

[7] O.K. Buros, op. cit.

MODULE
9

Social Problems: Culture, Society, and Education

Nature of Culture / Subcultures and Social Class Structure / Culture of the School / The School As a Social Institution / Socialization and Group Dynamics

The original first-edition version of this module was written by Michael P. Cutrona, Wagner College. It has been revised and updated for this edition.

RATIONALE

Perhaps the most dramatic occurrence in our twentieth-century United States, overshadowing all else, even two world wars and a major depression, is the emergence of our country as a mass society. There are few students of American civilization who would disagree with this statement.

Neither would many of them deny that the transformation has been accompanied by growing pains. Recent years have seen a period of strain and stress, of flux and change. Not only has the country become a mass society, it has also become a highly technological one. Small, well-knit communities and businesses have become sprawling, impersonal conglomerates in which it seems impossible to be someone of importance or to make one's impact felt. Values, too, have changed. Many people, old and young, look with suspicion on the rock-ribbed virtues of their elders. Sincerely held and highly prized national ideals are scorned by many as hypocrisy. Some of these growing pains are caused by the diversity of our population. Ethnic and racial minority groups who feel that they have not been treated fairly now demand a place in the sun. No longer are they willing to put up with institutions which they believe have not been responsive to their needs and rights. Their attempts to force the larger community to remedy their grievances have led to unrest, conflict, and, in some cases, to rapid realignments of values, customs, institutions, and agencies. To many Americans, it seems as though one cannot count on anything anymore. Yet it may well be that these changes, and others associated with them, are signs of the beginning of a new cultural awakening, heralding the advent of a new, better, and more democratic social order.

We find ourselves living in a time when policies, strategies, and developments change almost daily. The schools, too, are in the midst of great changes. New educational ideas come and go faster than educators can implement them. In such an atmosphere, there is great danger that school people will exhaust themselves by chasing will-o'the-wisps. To keep themselves oriented, educators must share in the broad perspective of contemporary American society and come to grips with the dynamics that are the mainstream of society. By so doing, they can perhaps offer some degree of continuity for education.

It follows, then, that educators who wish to be competent must understand our culture and society as well as our schools. One cannot assess what is happening, or judge what should happen, in education without a firm foundation in the schools' sociological roots.

This foundation can be laid through the study of educational sociology, which is the study of society and society's vehicle for transmitting and preserving the attitudes of society. Of course, sociologists share the responsibility for interpreting American civilization with educators, psychologists, political scientists, economists, and historians. Each of these disciplines, through its unique contributions, helps to strengthen our understanding of what makes the American society tick. Even though there may be sharp differences in their findings, taken together, these studies present an integrated view of the current American scene. Educational sociology attempts to present such a view.

Therefore, in the following modules (9 through 12), we shall try to present, briefly, the integrated view of society, culture, and the school that we believe to be so indispensable for you.

In this module, we shall focus upon several concepts for the understanding of factors that have helped to shape and change our schools: the nature of culture; subcultures and social-class structures; the culture of the school; the school as a social institution; socialization and group dynamics. These areas are interrelated—each one helps to shape the direction of the others. By presenting the parts separately, we hope to show you these concepts in detail, and bring out their basic unity—in this way helping you to broaden your understanding of the societal aspects of education.

Your aims in studying this module should be (1) to discover how all of these components interrelate; (2) to understand the implications of each in terms of educational issues; (3) to picture how they may relate to the kinds of teaching situation you may some day find yourself in; and (4) to discover how they may relate to the kinds of learning situation you already may have participated in.

SPECIFIC OBJECTIVES

Upon completing your study of this module, you should be able to

1. Define *culture*, and to name and illustrate at least two important sub-elements of the concept.
2. Define (or explain) similarities and differences among culture traits, culture complexes, and cultural patterns.
3. Cite seven characteristics of culture.
4. Explain (or define) the concepts of *norms* and *values* as they relate to society.
5. Cite at least two examples of a *belief* and two examples of a *value.*
6. Cite three examples of norms.
7. Distinguish between folkways, laws, and mores as they relate to society.
8. Explain *ethnocentrism* and *acculturation* as two forms of cultural cohesion.
9. Cite four examples of social-class stratification.
10. Cite three criteria for determining social class.
11. Cite five examples of subcultural distinctions.
12. Define *class consciousness*, and describe socially significant dimensions as traditionally related to schooling.
13. Cite three examples of power elites.
14. Define *power* as an aspect of social organization.
15. Draw a diagram illustrating the concept of hierarchical structure.
16. Cite four examples of the culture of the school.

17. Cite four examples of educational reforms that can change the culture of the school. Describe how the teacher, student, and community have encouraged reform.
18. Cite why socialization is an important function of the school as an agency of society.
19. Cite the purpose of group dynamics in schools.
20. Cite four examples of the goals of group dynamics in the schools.

MODULE TEXT

Nature of Culture

In every society, no matter how simple or complex, we discover standards, norms, customs, values, beliefs, and conventional ways of behaving that to a large degree structure the way of life in that society and shape the behavior and preferences of its members. These behavior-shapers are usually apparent along economic, aesthetic, social, ethical, and political lines.

In every society also, the individual acquires a certain set of normative behaviors from childhood on, whether he wishes to do so or not, and whether or not he is aware of this happening. These behaviors may fluctuate from society to society and from era to era, but they represent a process through which the social heritage, or, as it is often called, the culture, is passed on from generation to generation.

Culture

Man is not only a social animal; he is also a cultural being. Culture is not an easy concept to define. By culture, we mean the patterns and products of learned behavior, as well as the material objects of the society and the artifacts produced. Usually, culture is divided into two categories: (1) material culture, which is composed of man-made objects or tools—the technology of a group of people, and (2) nonmaterial culture, consisting of the etiquette, language, food preferences, religious and moral beliefs, knowledge, attitudes, sentiments, values, and customs passed down from generation to generation. Culture is thus largely abstract, although made up of fundamentally concrete examples of human reality.

The culture of one people may look very different from the culture of another. They display different behaviors and share different meanings. The material goods of a society, for example, are not complete in themselves; along with fashion and design, they carry meanings associated with their function.

"Thus, private automobiles have a different meaning in the United States than in China. In China, private cars do not exist; in Russia they are the possessions of a privileged few and a symbol of elite status; in the United States they are the possessions of all but the poorest underclass, evidence of private property that is available to the masses.[1]

[1] Mark A. Chesler and William M. Cave, *Sociology of Education* (New York: Macmillan, 1981), p. 3.

Researchers generally agree that the key to the nature of culture is lodged in man's own mind, for his ideas are the mainstream of culture. Furthermore, the nature of culture is the result of language. Man is the only living creature capable of communicating symbolically and storing his social heritage for transmission to new generations. Because of language, man can build upon the past; he does not have to start a new way of life at each new birth.

In a limited sense, cultures are all alike in that they solve the common problems of human beings. They do this, however, in different ways. Each culture provides its people with a means of communication (language). Each determines who wields power and under what circumstances power can be used (status). Each provides for the regulation of reproduction (family), and supplies a system of rules (government). The rules may be written (laws) or unwritten (custom), but they are always present.

Patterns of Behavior

Culture consists of continually changing patterns of learned behavior and the products of this behavior. Learned ways of doing things usually follow patterns. For instance, in reading this module, your reasons for reading it, the attitudes and feelings you have toward reading or for reading, and many other behaviors are interrelated. It would be difficult, indeed, to isolate one unit of behavior. Understandably, then, behavior is patterned or fitted together in a relationship between the behaviors of people when they are in contact. Many learned behaviors in one person's life have complementary behavior in the life of someone else—in, for example, husband-wife behavior, parent-child behavior, teacher-pupil behavior. In another sense, cultural learnings are the products of behavior. As experiences are impressed on a person, he changes and his behavior changes. We learn our behavior from others; they, in turn, learned from others, and so on, ad infinitum, until we get back, eventually, to the point of origin of a particular way of behaving. The illustration of the "looking-glass self" has been used to describe this process. Children begin to "see" themselves by perceiving how others treat them, developing an image or picture of themselves consistent with how they feel they are treated by others. Over time, young persons develop a coherent concept of "the self," a concept developed by peering into the "looking glass" of others' behavior.[2]

The concept of the "significant other" is another term used to describe this process. Young people are regarded as seeking the approval of other people who are close and important to them. In order to get this approval, young children do what they think these significant others want and expect. By so doing, the children learn appropriate ways of behaving within a family or culture. Over time, the combination of many "significant others" grows into one of the "generalized other," whereby children imagine on the basis of their past experience what other people or what society at large expect of them.[3]

---

[2] Ibid., p. 5.
[3] Ibid.

Traits

Sociologically, if we were to break down culture into its smallest parts, we would find these parts to be culture traits. A culture trait may be an object such as a pin (material culture trait) or an attitude or feeling (nonmaterial culture trait). Culture traits usually have a history. For instance, a button on the lapel of a coat may have been invented because it was needed to pull the coat around one's neck for warmth. In the course of time, the usefulness of this technique for keeping the neck warm may have vanished. However, the culture trait (the button) survives, and may be recycled from the original functional use to a nonfunctional ornamental value.

Mobility

Culture traits are mobile; they tend to spread among people over long distances, geographically. A case in point is the domesticated horse. Some believe that the horse was first domesticated in the Near East. Yet today, the use of the domesticated horse has spread to almost every portion of the world. With the world becoming smaller each day because of mass transportation and communication, culture traits may now be more mobile than ever before in history.

Complex

Culture traits tend to form clusters, called *culture complexes.* An example is the American game of baseball. The baseball complex involves not only material culture traits such as uniforms, bats, balls, shoes, gloves, a field, a stadium, and so on, but it includes also nonmaterial traits such as the rules, customs, folkways, and even superstitions that surround the game. One could list a multitude of culture complexes in modern society which are ever changing and ever being reshaped.

Patterns

Culture complexes also tend to form clusters called *culture patterns.* It is these culture patterns that help us to distinguish one culture from another. Among the culture patterns that identify our American democracy, for instance, are universal education, assembly-line technology, and Judeo-Christian ideals. Similarly, a culture pattern closely identified with India includes Hindu worship.

Common Characteristics

Culture has great variability (no two cultures are alike), but certain charactersitics run through all cultures. These are

1. Cultural behaviors are learned.
2. Cultural behaviors are organized into patterns.
3. Cultural patterns are taught by people and are passed on from one generation to another.
4. Cultures have material aspects and nonmaterial aspects.
5. Cultures are uniformly shared by the members of the society.
6. Cultural behaviors become a way of life.
7. Cultures are continually changing.

Collective Consciousness

Collective consciousness is what accounts for the order in any society. The ideas, sentiments, and habits that its members hold in common, the core of the culture, and its universals form the glue that binds a society together. Individuals assimilate consciousness from society. It exists apart from the individual, although it is carried in the minds of individuals; it existed before the individual was born, and it will live on, perhaps with only slight alteration, after the individual dies. This consciousness has a coercive nature, for society can change individuals much more readily than individuals can change society.

Society

Culture involves people. When we add this human ingredient, we have a society: a group of people who have lived together long enough to become organized into a unit. The behavior pattern of the culture determines the organization of the persons in the society. Insofar as we can tell from our present system of knowledge, human society seems to be unique in relation to those of other animals, because it possesses cultural elements in its social structure—for instance, norms and values. Ants, for instance, exhibit remarkable group behavior. However, they do not create, transmit, or share ideas, and so presumably do not have norms and values in their societies. Only man possesses this potential, because of his linguistic capacities.

Norms

Norms represent the rules governing the behavior in a society. They are the blueprints or designs for living. They prescribe patterns of behavior that are necessary in order to maintain social order and interaction in any society, and are transmitted through a socialization process. Norms transform men into cultured beings.

Values

Values are the purposes that utilize the norms within a cultural context. Because life is of value, there are norms which assure the preservation of life; for example, the ethics of medicine and laws forbidding killing. Because babies are of value, there are norms upholding the principle of legitimacy. Some values and norms are so important that they are hallowed by religion and made sacred. A classic example is the sacred cow of India.

Mores, Folkways, and Laws

Sociologically, we distinguish three different kinds of norms: mores, folkways, and laws. One of the best examples was given by William Graham Sumner.

> The mores are social ritual in which we all participate unconsciously. The current habits as to hours of labor, meal hours, family life, the social intercourse of the sexes, propriety, amusements, travel, holidays, education, the use of periodicals and libraries, and innumerable other details of life fall under this ritual. Each does as everybody does . . . The great mass of folkways give us discipline and the support of routine and habit. . . .

The mores have the authority of facts. The mores come down to us from the past. Each individual is born into them as he is born into the atmosphere, and he does not reflect on them, or criticize them any more than a baby analyzes the atmosphere before he begins to breathe it. Each one is subjected to the influence of the mores, and formed by them, before he is capable of reasoning about them. Some . . . want to argue in favor of polygamy on grounds of expedience. They fail to obtain a hearing. Others want to discuss property. In spite of some literary activity on their part, no discussion of property, bequest, and inheritance has ever been opened. Property and marriage are in the mores. Nothing can ever change them but the unconscious and imperceptible movement of the mores. Religion was originally a matter of the mores . . . Democracy is in our American mores. It is a product of our physical and economic conditions. It is impossible to discuss or criticize it. . . . The thing to be noticed in all these cases is that the masses oppose a deaf ear to every argument against the mores. It is only in so far as things have been transferred from the mores into laws and positive institutions that there is discussion about them or rationalizing upon them.[4]

As implied in this quotation, *mores* are basic and important behaviors (ideas or acts of people), such as wearing clothes, monogamy, loyalty. Mores are usually enforced through fear of social ostracism rather than legal sanctions. *Folkways* are less rigidly enforced by society than mores. As behaviors, they are often taken for granted because everyone participating in the society knows them. Mode of dress is an example of a folkway. Is the person dressed appropriately, and in good taste, for the situation? Folkways today represent a broad range of behaviors which vary according to region, situation, age group, and so on. Though mild pressures to conform to folkways are applied by groups, especially adolescents, few consider these to be serious in terms of moral code. Some patterns of behavior remain undefined, such as preferences, rituals, and other meaningless survivals. *Laws* represent written rules which seek to enforce norms consistently. They usually represent a normative pattern or an attempt to ensure morality.

To understand the normative quality of behavior that reflects purposes, goals, and values, let us consider the hippies. Although the hippies sought to rebel against established norms, they created a predictable alternative pattern of culture. Though unconventional, they developed a distinct lexicon that was transmitted and recycled from group to group. The hippie culture, although a revolt from the system, was based on specific values and aspirations. From these elements, the hippies created common mores and folkways which served as guides for daily living. Interestingly, their norms did not always separate them from the larger society, even though they were in conflict with traditional norms (indifference to money, indifference to matrimony, views about sexual activities).

There are many kinds of subgroups within the larger society. These subgroups may be based on ethnic (Irish, Italian, Polish), religious (Catholic, Protestant, Jew), or regional factors (North, South, urban, suburban, and rural). In general, the people of a certain subculture share certain commonal-

---

[4] William Graham Sumner, *Folkways* (New York: The New American Library of World Literature, Inc., 1960), pp. 68, 80, 81. Originally published by Ginn and Company, 1906.

ities not held by other American groups. Language differences—for example, dialects, slang, occupational jargon, ethnic terms, and accents, and differences in form and structure—are examples of these subcultural group commonalities. Ethnic backgrounds result in differences in mores and folkways, such as family-living practices, dress, medical practices, and religious ideologies. Geographic differences influence housing practices, uses of clothing, food preferences, and so on.

Ethnocentrism and Acculturation

In discussing normative patterns, we should note two forms of social adaptation that produce a high level of cultural cohesion, that is, the acceptance of these adaptations tend to make the society more solid. These adaptations are *ethnocentrism* and *acculturation*. Ethnocentrism is a tendency for members of a group to think of their cultural patterns as the best, most desirable, and most acceptable. Monogamy, for instance, is an ethnocentrism. We Americans automatically accept this as good—we do not think to question its value. Such ethnocentric beliefs give us security and structure by telling us how to behave, and what is expected of us. Through cultural adaptation, they help us to feel a sense of permanence. Ethnocentrism, however, can also become the seed from which prejudice blossoms. Differences resulting from ethnicity, race, religion, and so on produce conflicts. Ethnocentrism makes it difficult for men to understand and appreciate diversity.

Acculturation, on the other hand, is a process of cultural modification. In the process of acculturation, norms are altered to conform partially with new standards and values. New cultural elements guide the behavior. Persons come to understand and appreciate the newly discovered ways, even though some characteristics of older normative forms may be retained.

Complex Nature of Culture

Recognizing that the nature of culture is a complex totality of man's way of life, sociologists have placed special importance upon norms and values. Sociologists often study attitudes in an attempt to gain an understanding of why man behaves as he does. Changing relationships in a society between groups—racial, ethnic, or otherwise—can be explained in part as changes in ideas and meanings, values and norms. Man's behavior in all respects is not instinctive; it is normative. It is unlike the behavior of the goslings born in an incubator and raised in the isolation of a laboratory, who will automatically and accurately carry out elaborate courtship dances when they grow to adulthood even though they have never seen such rituals performed. These creatures are biologically prewired to carry out this behavior. Norms are agreed-upon behavior patterns that give order to society—they provide blueprints of our mores and folkways. Human beings build their own world and pass that world on to their children. Whereas other animals inherit a world through genetics, human beings learn a world from adults and from the continuing experience of the environment.

However, norms do not function perfectly, and therefore conflicts may arise, especially in rapidly changing societies. There are times in our society when an individual's norms conflict: the demands of a job may make it difficult for a man to fulfill his responsibilities as a father, for example. Also, cultural perspectives may differ between one subgroup and another within the same society. The nature of culture points up the fact that there are cultural similarities and differences, though most men tend to feel that their culture is the best. The study of subcultures and social classes in this context is an example of this contrast. Sociologists go beyond the concepts of the social self and culture; they include the aspect of social organization within the realm of culture. Social structure is thus a consequence of the complex interrelationship between man's social roles and diverse human groupings.

Subcultures and Social-Class Structure

"Frequently we Americans claim that we live in a classless society. But there are social classes in the United States, and Americans are well aware of class distinctions. Although they may not ever use the words 'social class,' Americans show the true state of affairs when they point out that someone 'is of that East Malaria gang' or 'She is in the Indian Hill Country Club set.'[5] "

Subcultures and Classes

As we have seen, subcultures differ from one another in various ways—race, creed, ethnicity, and occupation. Similar subcultural differences may exist among social classes; however, some of these class distinctions seem to be disappearing, and there is considerable doubt whether other alleged class differences ever were real.[6] Theoretically, at least, the behavioral norms of lower-, middle-, and upper-class people are not the same. Among these class differences are variations in behavioral norms regarding emotional expression, discipline methods, attitudes toward education, sex, religion, and status goals. Middle-class Americans, for instance, are said to be more apt to value a life style based upon long-range goals, future gains, and achievement, lower-class Americans, on the other hand, are said to favor more immediate goals. (If this alleged lower-class attitude is valid, it may be the result of poverty rather than a true difference in class attitude, however.) Similarly, middle-class persons are said to favor the use of cognitive methods of disciplining their children, that is, psychological punishment, such as emotional restraint; and lower-class families are said to prefer overt measures, such as physical punishment.

In the larger context of race, it might be said that native Americans, Hispanic subcultures, and a sizeable percentage of blacks do not find such core values as liberty, freedom, and justice operating for them in society. Many minority individuals proclaim that they have personally experienced and suffered through the disparities that exist between the rhetoric generally associated with these core American values and the actual behavior that is manifested.

[5] Leonard H. Clark, Raymond L. Klein, and John B. Burks, *The American Secondary School Curriculum* 2nd ed. (New York: Macmillan, 1972), p. 106.

[6] Some experts have challenged the theory of class differences. In any case, it is quite dangerous for teachers to make assumptions about specific individuals or groups, based on supposed class differences.

Linton[7] explains the differences that exist among subcultures by using the terms *specialties* and *alternatives. Universal* patterns of culture consist of those cultural elements about which among the members of that society there is no doubt. *Specialties* are those elements held in common only by a particular group within the society who exist as a distinctive collection of similar people. They are alike, these people, because they perform the activities of the particular group to which they belong. Medical doctors, for example, differ in some respects from the rest of society, as they have certain common attributes (such as, technical language, scientific interests, and so on) which they share with other members of the medical profession only because they too are medical people. Teachers, actors, news-media personnel, professional athletes, and the like have their own trade secrets and idiosyncrasies that set them off as viable groups. Most members of society, however, know how to contact these specialists, know what their functions are, and know what the effect of the specialist's activity should be. The universals and specialties of a culture make up its core. The *alternatives* described by Linton are those perhaps new and different things that are peculiar to a group and that are not shared by the culture at large. They include "such things as the unique habits of a family, the diverse doctrines of individual religions, the ideologies of competing political organizations, and widely differing theories of education. In every case individuals are offered a choice of behavior and ideas."[8] When alternatives are socially significant, they compete for a place in the core of the culture. Universals and specialties can be eased out of the cultural core and can become alternatives. They may remain as alternatives, or they may eventually pass out of the culture and be forgotten.

Hierarchical Organization

In speaking of social classes, we can use terms such as *levels, structure, hierarchy*, and so on, but the sociologist uses the term *social stratification* to describe similarities and differences among the classes. This term includes class level and other socially significant dimensions. Kahl[9] discussed seven dimensions of social class:

1. Prestige. Some of the people in the community have more personal prestige than others; other people look up to and defer to them.
2. Occupation. Some occupations are more prestigious than others, e.g., the professions, management and other occupations that are well paid and require special talents or training.
3. Possessions. Some people are richer than others.
4. Social Interaction. People interact with people of their own kind and not with others they may consider above, below or different from them.
5. Class Consciousness. Some people think of themselves as belonging to distinctive social groups, e.g., as working class, as management, as professionals.

[7] Ralph Linton, *The Study of Man* (New York: Appleton-Century-Crofts, 1936).
[8] Rodman B. Webb, *Schooling and Society* (New York: Macmillan, 1981), p. 58.
[9] J. Kahl, *The American Class Structure* (New York: Holt, Rinehart & Winston, 1957).

6. Value orientations. People's values differ. People identifying with certain social groups tend to share the same values and beliefs.
7. Power. Some people are more powerful than others. They can control the actions of other people.

These dimensions combine to determine social class. They are seldom found in isolation. In fact, they are more likely to be interdependent, interacting with one another. For instance, of the three characteristics, education, occupation, and wealth, by which social classes are most commonly defined, wealth (or possessions) and occupation are likely to be closely associated. Similarly, certain "higher" occupations are likely to be associated with high educational attainments. The total impact of the education, occupation, and wealth of oneself and one's associates would undoubtedly tend to make one class-conscious; that is, aware of oneself as a lower class, middle class, or upper-class person.

Power

Power is an indispensable factor in hierarchical social stratification. Power, or the ability of some persons to produce effects on others, has always been one of the aspects of social class that has caused social divisions. It has also caused unrest, which may result in the altering of social-class distinctions presently operating in our political, economic, civic, and educational life.

Although to many it seems more "American" to deny the existence of socioeconomic distinctions, the existence of powerful groups and individuals (political, military, and corporative) within communities is real. Differences in social class do exist in the community: Certain groups are considered "the elite," and others are the "John Doe's—Mr. Citizens." It is the elite who are in the controlling positions and who can affect, through their activities, the standards, norms, and values of the larger society.

The study of power, then, is an important means for understanding the social organization of culture and its various social strata. Power has been defined in a wide variety of ways: "power-influence-control-authority-leadership,"[10] "the capacity or potential of persons in certain statuses to set conditions, make decisions and/or take actions which are determinative for the existence of others within a given social system;"[11] "decisions men make about arrangements under which they live;"[12] a "power participation in the making of decisions [about] the policies which other persons are to pursue . . . participation . . . is an interpersonal relation."[13]

Power, then, implies actual behavior with intended effects. In part, it can serve to meet one of the cultural requirements of most societies—ordering the relations of the people. It is exercised by many subcultural elites, the

[10] R. Agger and D. Goldrich, "Community Power Structure and Partisanship," *American Sociological Review*, 23:383 (Aug. 1958).
[11] R. Schultz, "The Bifurcation of Power in a Satellite City," in M. Janowitz, ed., *Community Political Systems* (New York: The Free Press, 1961).
[12] C. W. Mills, *Power Politics and People* (New York: Oxford University Press, 1963).
[13] J. H. Lasswell and A. Kaplan, *Power and Society* (New Haven: Yale University Press, 1950).

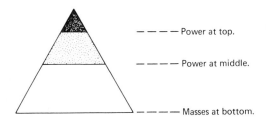

FIGURE 9-1 The Power Structure Hierarchy.

most highly organized of which are the economic, political, and military elites. "The techniques of the power elites determine the activities of power in the short run, but the basic culture and structure of a society will determine the actualities (outcomes) in the long run."[14] Thus, as we begin to analyze power, we see that the structure of the society determines the kind of influence the elites will exert on the culture.

A hierarchical approach to the power structure is relatively simple to understand. Graphically, it looks like a triangle. (Figure 9-1). A few people at the top make the major decisions, dominate economic movements, and generally set the norms or standards of the "mass" society.

This type of organization has given rise to many power elites. The most prominent are the three previously mentioned (economic, military, and political). Let us look at each of them more closely.

Economic Elite. Businessmen and those who generally control the "excessive wealth" constitute an important elite in that they influence issues affecting production, consumption, and the distribution of wealth. On economic issues, they represent a diverse set of interests. For instance, a war or a tariff may be of benefit to one kind of business, as it raises defense spending or increases the production in certain industries, even though it may not be beneficial to the majority of the people. Consequently, the economic elites may attempt to exert power so as to influence government policy. Thus, defense industries exert pressure on government expenditures; business interests exert pressures on governmental regulatory commissions; industrial unions exert pressures on government so that legislative acts are passed; commercial interests exert pressure through mass-media communication; and businessmen exert pressure for direct participation in government by seeking public office. Each of these examples illustrates how the interests of an elite exert power, which may affect the lives of the mass society along economic and other lines.

Military Elite. A second important powerful elite is the military elite. Contemporary military leaders are often like corporation executives, though the military organization's goals and logic differ from that of business. "The military style of life strives to produce an internally cohesive community

[14] A. Rose, *The Power Structure* (New York: Oxford University Press, 1967).

(subculture); at the same time, it thwarts social integration with civilian society . . . behavior of the military in the United States is still deeply conditioned by its social isolation."[15] The important role of the military elite in American life has little to do with efforts to gain power over civilian life, or to an alleged willingness of the economic elite to use the military as allies in the quest for power. Rather, the military elite serves a more active role—in international affairs and foreign policy, in military technology, and in governmental bureaucracy. As an elite, it seems somewhat split between the economic power forces and the political factions of the society.

Political Elite. The political elite represents perhaps the most concentrated base of power in the United States. Some of this is understood by the American people because of the formal structure of the political-governmental structure (voting, political campaigns, political parties, government structure, and so on), and because it is taught in schools in social studies. However, the informal structure of politics (the inner workings of political parties or relationships, pressures and motivations of candidates) is unfamiliar to the average citizen. Even highly educated people may not truly comprehend the power process if they have not studied the political process or have not actively participated in politics. The public becomes involved in local and state parties, national party organizations, and personal political organizations, however. To some degree, people who are differentiated from the masses by virtue of their interest in something or someone do become more fully aware of the informal aspects of power. Yet, the pressure that can be exerted by the groups to which they belong is often directed by more powerful forces—the larger organization or the person who has a reputation and power in the community at large.

Though these elites may be dominant powers in American society, and the majority of people, individually, may be powerless, manipulated, and passive, the participation of organized groups working for special interests has served to exert pressure and to offer challenges to the powers that be. The issues of community control, accountability, and equality of opportunity serve to illustrate the power of organized groups. Thus, the hierarchical power structure of social class can be influenced by nonhierarchical groups who seek participation and a redistribution of power.

From this brief critique, it should be apparent that people have developed complex behavioral organizations for structuring the conduct and the attitude of the mass society. The salient issues of the power-oriented substructure of American society have had dramatic effects upon the culture of the school and upon the role of the school as a social institution.

Culture of the School

As we stated earlier in this module, men develop and direct the culture of a society through diverse organizations. In addition, man maintains his culture through education. From birth to death, the individual is indoctrinated with

[15] M. Janowitz, *The Professional Society* (New York: The Free Press, 1960), pp. 204–205.

the folkways of the group and the patterns inherent in the group's social class and position—powerless or powerful. In turn, these ways are passed on, with alterations owing to time and need, to other generations. As people create their culture, they have the capacity to change it. Changes in occupational trends, social interaction among groups, social consciousness, value orientations, and use of power can cause great unrest. Evidence of such unrest in our own culture can be seen in the events of the sixties and early seventies, which brought about great, even traumatic, changes in our society and in the direction of our culture.

Social Unrest and the School

Even though a society constantly needs to improve its institutions and make relevant its beliefs, change in cultural tangibles is usually a slow and labored endeavor. At present, public confidence in our society appears to be very low, and is accompanied by disillusionment with promises for change. During this era of change—which may go down in history as the "age of unrest"—the power structure has been under the attack of reformers acting in the name of "relevancy." In this attack, social-activist elements of our society propose changes that would have been branded anti-American or unconstitutional only a few decades ago. Among the recommended changes are such educational reforms as the abandonment of public education[16]; the establishment of black schools and bilingual schools in lieu of integrated schools; political and economic reforms as a prerequisite for better schools; schools run by students; schools without formal subjects; and a variety of forms of alternative schooling. Innovations such as team teaching, educational television, programmed instruction, differentiated staffing, educational vouchers, and performance contracting have been initiated, and continue to be tried. Critics confront us with examples of instances in which, they claim, the existing system of public education has failed; and, they claim, alternatives such as street academies, freedom schools, experimental high schools and colleges, and schools without walls have succeeded.

What we are observing seems to be a great concern for the culture of the school and the effects that expanding unrest are exerting on it. The sharpness of the resulting issues suggests that the organizational structure of American society is undergoing tremendous strains.

Social strains such as those we have just described do not occur in isolation. Our schools are experiencing the combined effects of the changing culture of the community, the power elite, and the impact of pressure groups who are seeking to come to grips with the broad implications of participating in twenty-first century American society.

The School's Role

There can be no doubt that the unrest we have been witnessing will affect the culture of the school. For too long schools have resisted change. Furthermore the kind of school system a society maintains depends upon its culture, for the school is an agent of the culture with a tripartite function. It serves as

---

[16] Ivan Illich, *Deschooling Society* (New York: Harper & Row, 1971).

(1) a social institution; (2) a cultural transmission vehicle; and (3) a clearing-house for ideas, attitudes, and ideologies. In a complex culture such as ours in the United States, the school's role is to present selected elements of the stored cultural experience in concentrated form so that each individual can acquire elements of the culture that might not be acquired through more in-formal ways. It is this function that has encouraged the larger society to ex-amine how the school operates in transmitting culture.

Upon examination, we find that, like the family or peer group, the school has its own unique, self-contained social system. It is, in effect, a subculture of its own with its own subcultural values—ways of behaving and thinking. Frequently these subcultural values—its traditions regarding the function of the school—indicate a cultural lag in the school. Schools are concerned mainly with transmitting the core of the culture to students. Educators who go beyond the cultural core for course material are sometimes surprised at how quickly the reaction to the controversial topic they have introduced spreads beyond the classroom and into the community.

Core values of a culture taught uncritically predispose the school to the danger of ethnocentrism. When American values are presented as if they are inherently superior to any other values (only because they are American), we transmit an inaccurate picture of ourselves. We retard our ability to evaluate our culture and hence our ability to improve it. The current movement to promote thoughtful criticism of our core values is not only compatible with democracy, but it is also an essential ingredient of the democratic spirit.

Certainly, activist behavior has been a significant development in our age. Many contemporary educational issues concern the role of the school with respect to the larger issues which, however, lie outside the school's capacity to provide rational change. The school is not separate from the society at large and cannot isolate itself from participation in dealing with these issues. (Although, in some circles, simple dissension or withdrawal from established ways has been increasing.) Because American society seems to be character-ized by constant change, and its institutions, such as the schools, seem to be under pressure to change, the culture of the school—its activities and social interactions—in spite of its resistance to change, has been reflecting changes in pedagogical thought.

Middle-Class Orientation

Traditionally, the culture of the school, particularly its physical plant, curriculum, personnel, and values, has been predominantly middle class. In it authority has rested in the hands of adults—teachers and school administra-tors. Children have been clearly subordinate, as the formal aspects—rules, graded classrooms, and time schedules—attest. Many aspects of school life have been isolated from real life. Teachers have been left with the respon-sibility for determining the curriculum and carrying out the teaching functions, without much input from the community. Being middle class themselves, teachers have held middle-class values in high esteem, and, with community approval, incorporated these values into the curriculum, their teaching, and, insofar as they could, the school milieu.

Presently there is reason to believe that there may be a retreat from the middle-class orientation. For example, elementary and secondary schools seem to be moving away from the achievement-status orientation so typical of the middle class. At present, the trend seems to be to focus on the individual person's needs, interests, and abilities. Also, the school seems to be becoming less formal. All in all, it seems that the culture of the school is being brought closer to the culture of the community; therefore, perhaps in the future, inconsistencies and irrelevancies, such as cultural lag, may be avoided.

Geographical Variation

Across the nation, schools vary in cultural orientation because of the geographical area they serve. Such regional variation is necessary and desirable. The incorporation of special folkways and customs into the school program is part of the school's role as a socializing agent. In this way it can enhance the cultural acceptance of subgroups into the large society. Furthermore, it is axiomatic that the culture of the school must incorporate the attitudes and values of students and community as well as of teachers in order to fulfill its educational roles.

The School As a Social Institution

In addition to maintaining a culture of its own, the school is a social institution. As such it inherits recognized normative patterns of behavior. Like the church, it develops and maintains these normative patterns. As Hertzler has noted

> Institutions are defended, often at great cost of life and resources because they come to reflect society's image. They define its aspirations and its moral commitments; they are the source and receptacle of . . . unique identity . . . The institutionalized modes of . . . defining responsibility, transferring power, raising children . . . are developed in order to satisfy specific needs. But like the habits of an individual, they have the indirect consequence of committing the society to an integrated system of values. Taken together these valued institutions reflect the ethos of the culture, its peculiar way of self-fulfillment.[17]

It follows, then, that certain social institutions such as the school are indispensable to human society. In the United States, schools are a basic and universal agency in community life. Like every other institution, schools reflect societal purposes and goals which change and are constantly compromised.

As an institution, the school of today seems to be in crisis, partly because of changes in students and faculty. For example, the opening up of college enrollment to individuals of all social classes, coupled with financial assistance programs to minority students, has been somewhat traumatic. In the process of offering to the many a privilege once reserved for the middle and upper classes, the schools of higher learning have had to adapt to diversity because of the emergence of a variety of new and challenging student subcultures. The rapid assimilation of these new styles of life at the university level

[17] J. Hertzler, *American Social Institutions* (Boston: Allyn & Bacon, 1961), p. 84.

will no doubt trickle down to the elementary and secondary school levels and to the society at large. The results of this movement may dramatically affect class differences and the role of the school in society.

That the influence of the school should have great impact on society as a whole should not be surprising. Historically, the function of the school as a social institution has varied, depending on the subculture being served. For instance, the upper and middle classes often valued the school's social aspects more than its intellectual ones. To them it was not so much learning that mattered as membership in the right school and right fraternity or sorority, and perhaps participation in athletics and festive affairs. However, in all social classes we find the need for preparing youth for occupational pursuits. Consequently, schools have always been both vocationally and academically oriented. The prep school and college were greatly valued by upper- and middle-class parents because they might provide their children with contacts that would serve them well in their business and professional as well as social lives to come.

In many schools, the traditional practice has been to provide vocational education for the economically less fortunate and to reserve academic education for the wealthy who could afford to stay out of the job market until they finished college. This practice seems to be vanishing. Perhaps this change is the result of differences in student orientation. As we have already seen, students today represent change and diversity. Faculty, too, reflect diverse orientations, many teachers having come from the working and lower classes. This new breed of teachers is not content to perpetuate the "ivory tower" tradition. They seek, rather, to bring the school into social action. Moreover, we find teachers becoming both sympathetic to the youth culture, and hence more activist. Teacher negotiations, collective bargaining, and even strikes to gain economic advantages and power exemplify the changing character of the school as an institution.

School Organization

In any discussion of the school as a social institution, it is important to focus on its organization and to analyze what is happening to its leadership.

The organization of the school has traditionally been much like the hierarchical social structure previously mentioned in this module. In this type of organization, authority flows from the top down through the various levels to the pupils at the bottom. (Figure 9-2) At the top of the structure is the school board. In some communities, board members are appointed by the mayor and in others they are elected. As the representative or agent of the community, the school board is charged with the responsibility of deciding on school policy, selecting school administrators and other personnel, and setting up school budget plans. Theoretically, at least, the school board acts in the interest of the community.

The second level of this hierarchy is that of the superintendent and other administrative personnel such as principals, supervisors, and directors. Traditionally, these administrators acted as middlemen between the school board and the faculties and staff. The next level is that of the teachers and other staff members. Here we find teachers of various sorts, as well as nonteaching

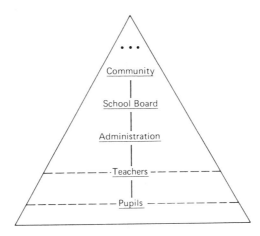

FIGURE 9-2 Diagram of Typical School Organization.

personnel such as special-services professionals, psychologists, social workers, learning-disability consultants, and guidance personnel. At the base of the structure are the pupils who are the "clients" of the school.

Unrest of Parents, Teachers, and Students

Although this type of flow of authority, from top to bottom of the hierarchy, has long been accepted in our schools, recently it has become a source of dissension. For one thing, students have questioned the commitment of those in leadership roles. For another thing, students are themselves seeking greater roles in decision making. In particular, many feel that they should have a hand in determining the direction of the curriculum and in setting school policy. In short, they want power.

In challenging the hierarchal power and social structure of the school, students have pointed out many sources of irrelevancy. For instance, they have focused on school dress codes and on curriculum content, which they consider to be archaic. They have also pointed out the importance of direct participation in policy making in lieu of indirect forms of participation, such as student councils. Students also point to society and to the occupational market places which continually put increased demands on them. The school as an institution cannot isolate itself from these issues. The students are reinforcing the idea that cooperative problem solving is necessary. They wish a stronger role in thinking out problems of classroom operation and school policy. The reaction to student activism has been varied. To some, student-activist groups represent those who wish to encourage reform in the schools. To others, however, student groups are viewed as nonconformist and unconstructive.

Unrest among disenchanted and frustrated students, coupled with the new militance in teachers, has placed school leaders in troubled waters. The unrest among faculty and students has traveled into the communities. Thus, parents and the community—who were supposedly represented by the school board at the top of the hierarchy—have now themselves become vocal. This movement reflects a trend for interest groups to seek participatory roles. Today, serious questions come from the community regarding the selection of personnel, curricula, budget spending, and overall relevancy of the school. As community unrest builds in momentum and lay participation increases, school boards, administrators, and teachers will directly feel the elimination of old established ways. The school, as a social institution, will change to become consistent with the culture of the community.

Socialization and Group Dynamics

Socialization

In every society, as children grow up, they accumulate certain appropriate skills and knowledge and so become productive members of the social system. This process is called *socialization*. Through socialization in our society, the school as an agent of the society orients the individual toward those attitudes, values, and beliefs that society considers important.

Sociologically, there is an interdependent relationship between society and the individual. It is this relationship that makes socialization as a process so important. When something interferes with this process, the consequences may be serious for the society in that we may have individuals who are not social—for example, the autistic child. In discussing this concept, it should be noted that socialization is a process that continues throughout the life of a society and a person. Therefore, our tendency to view the process of education as terminating with a diploma or degree, or after a stated period of time, is sociologically inconsistent. Because individuals are dependent upon a social context throughout their entire lives, the school has the responsibility to go beyond formal concentration on socialization during school hours; the school should help each individual grow in the ability to apply the social ideas he has learned to various other social contexts. In our times of change and turmoil, this is indeed an important goal.

Whereas socialization is a continual life experience, varying situations call for desocialization and resocialization, that is, the abandonment of useless skills and the adoption of new skills and knowledge. In this process, the importance of the group as an interacting unit is crucial. This fact leads us to a related concept—group dynamics.

Group Dynamics

The great emphasis on the school as an interacting and functioning institution has placed attention on the concept of group interaction and group dynamics. In our society, the group is a major force in determining and shaping the behavior of its members. The greater the group's unity, the greater its influence. Pedagogically, we cannot truly understand individuals unless we study their functioning in groups.

Group dynamics in the school should seek to "promote effectiveness in leadership, independence of thinking, the ability to resolve problems democratically, the ability to formulate clearly defined goals, the willingness to assume responsibility and initiative, and consideration of and sensitivity to the views of others without sacrifice to one's own ideals." All of these behaviors

Social Problems: Integration, Poverty, Delinquency, Crime, Mobility

Racism and Segregation / Integration and Poverty / Dropouts, Delinquency, and Crime / Demographic Shifts, Mobility, and Expanding Population / Trends for the Eighties

The first-edition version of this module was written by Michael P. Cutrona, Wagner College. It has been revised and updated for this edition.

RATIONALE

All educational systems serve their respective societies. Thus social, economic, and political relationships of the educational sector mirror closely those of the society of which they are a part. Major societal values and concerns are reflected in the schools. When the larger society is not clear about its values or priorities, these uncertainties usually surface in the schools.

Through the years, schools have been concerned less with promoting social change than with socializing children into the existing lifeways. This posture has resulted in the emergence of schools as conservative institutions that generally lag many years behind social trends and movements.

Advocates of rapid social change have complained about this "lag" between the social world and the schools. Critics have decried the ignoring by the schools of social injustice, of the abuse of human rights, and of the misuse of the earth's resources. In their vocal attacks upon society to force quicker action, they have often chastised the school for its apparent lassitude in the areas of overpopulation problems, inequitable distribution of wealth, and a whole host of similar social issues. In many instances, the schools have been expected to achieve the impossible task of doing something about problems that are indigenous to the larger society. Problems such as racism, vandalism, integration, and inequality of opportunity, which are socially caused and socially perpetuated, have been looked upon by some as solvable if the school would apply itself vigorously to their solution. The school as an institution, powerless to control problems of such enormity, has sometimes been used as the scapegoat.

The decade of the 1960s, with the Vietnam War on the international front and the violent internal social upheaval on the domestic, badly shook the self-confidence of America as a nation. By the latter part of the 1970s, however, fair-minded people everywhere could see that the country was serious about pursuit of its values and zeal for achieving dignity for all people around the globe. The goal was especially for equal opportunity in education for all of the children of all of the people in this country.

In the 1970s the biggest newsmakers in the world of education were not the educators, but the U.S. Supreme Court, the Congress, and the federal executive departments. With their more than one hundred federal aid programs, U.S. Government officials guided, influenced, and sought to control local education to an extent that could hardly be measured or comprehended either by educators or the public. Similarly during this period the states tried to reform their local educational systems. At least twenty-five states attempted to revamp the school finance procedures within their states so as to eliminate the differences in educational opportunities between rich and poor districts. At the close of the decade the results of these federal and state efforts were still unclear. Nevertheless, although the research data on some of the projects were disappointing, there seemed to be evident a more conscious striving for excellence in most districts as indicated by attempts for establishing accountability, particularly in the area of a basic and thorough education for all youngsters.

Discussion in this module will focus upon some of the social problems of the decade. The purpose of the presentation is to help you assess the enormity of the problems addressed by society and to appreciate the powerlessness of the school to effect any spectacular modifications on the broad scope. The module will focus upon some research-findings emerging from this troubled period. It provides helpful guidance for the decade of the 1980s.

SPECIFIC OBJECTIVES

Upon completing your study of this module, you should be able to

1. Define racism.
2. Discuss the change from "melting pot" to "great boiling pot" in our multicultural society.
3. Distinguish between *de jure* and *de facto* segregation.
4. Describe how the "self-fulfilling prophecy" pertaining to academic success or failure operates.
5. Explain the significance of the WASP (White Anglo Saxon Protestant) designation in cultural assimilation.
6. Discuss the impact on urban education of the out-migration of middle-class whites and the in-migration of Southern blacks and Hispanics.
7. Explain the process and effect of stigmatization of the poor in our society.
8. Cite several instances in which forced busing was utilized to effect integration.
9. Describe some of the effects of the Civil Rights Movement on American society.
10. Cite at least four arguments against such busing that have been utilized.
11. List at least five findings included in the Coleman Report that relate to the variables contributing to what students learn in schools.
12. Describe how magnet schools and change of patterns in school organization were expected to alleviate the problem of segregation.
13. List at least four of the seven research findings regarding teaching behaviors and attitudes that have been found to correlate consistently with students' gains on academic tests.
14. List at least ten of the most significant characteristics of school dropouts among the twenty-five quoted from Cervantes.
15. Cite some of the research evidence in support of alternatives in schooling that promise success for efforts in the decade of the 1980s.

MODULE TEXT

Racism and Segregation

Within the sociologist's concept of culture discussed in Module 9, there are included those aspects of man's behavioral existence identified as attitudes and aspirations. These ingredients influence man's decisions and modify beliefs and values upon which interactions in society are based. In a multicultural society like ours, these cultural attributes control the amount of prejudice and discrimination exercised by the white and nonwhite races. These attributes also explain the relationships that exist between have and have-not residents.

How people of diverse racial, religious, and ethnic backgrounds can manage to dwell together in peace within the same geographical areas is the critical problem confronting all societies in the contemporary era. In the technological society of the United States, however, in the 1970s the problem erupted into a struggle by the minority groups which had undergone the most in corroding failure, psychological inhibitions, and economic hardships, to crash into the more rewarding orbit enjoyed by the majority White Anglo-Saxon Protestant level. Early sociologists coined the term *melting pot* to describe the process whereby this fusion of many diverse cultural and ethnic groups was to take place. But events of recent years seem rather to indicate that the term *great boiling pot* might have been a more descriptive appellation, since the result appears to have been of components moving apart—disjointed, discriminatory, and prejudiced—rather than fusing.

The notion that one's own racial stock is superior is defined by the American Heritage Dictionary as *racism. Segregation* is defined as "the policy and practice of imposing the social separation of the races." Based on these definitions, racism and segregation are contradictory to the melting-pot concept and to the principle of pluralism and multiethnic society. In practice, however, one can see the existence of these two contradictory elements in all aspects of American social, economic, political, and, hence, educational processes.

To many minorities, particularly to Blacks and Hispanics, the urban school system has become a racist institution, reflecting the values, attitudes, and bigotries of the larger, white, American society. In their view, the general policies of school systems, the teachers' attitudes, the insensitivity in general of school personnel toward minority children, and the lack of systematic effort for genuine integration of the total educational system corroborates these allegations. Accusers point to the containment of various ethnic minority children in a substandard system as an expression of the majority's will to provide separate and unequal education for racial minorities. Whether these allegations are true or false, it is apparent that the flight of the white, middle-class majority to the suburbs, and an increase in minority population in the big metropolitan centers, have caused the isolation of races and seclusion of racial minorities into *de facto* segregated systems. In addition, on the local levels practices and policies such as the following have encouraged segregation and have effectively separated races: (1) gerrymandering of school attendance zones that keeps separate races in selected schools; (2) building of new schools or the expanding of old ones in areas that preserve segregation; (3) organizing grade levels in order to keep the balance of races in accordance with a desired level.

The exclusion and containment of minorities have led to surges of protest, in both violent and nonviolent forms, to demonstrate discontent with the imposed limitations and support for the struggle for equal opportunity and treatment. Some people, either from culturally induced convictions or for psychological reasons (such as their fear for job security), are unprepared to face the challenges of minority demands and therefore offer active or passive resistance. The struggle for equal rights has brought the attention of many to the fact that a multicultural, multiracial society cannot survive without mutual respect, understanding, and a mutually receptive atmosphere in which there is appreciation of the positives in a diversified culture.

Problems relating to race, say the social scientists, come about not because of the physical differences among the races but by the recognition and significance accorded to the differences.[1] In schools, the visible minority children are handicapped precisely because many persons, including a sizable number of teachers, remain convinced that physical characteristics are "intrinsically related to moral, intellectual, and other non-physical attributes. It is as if racial identity were a summarizing variable from which all kinds of inferences could be drawn about a child's capacity to learn, potential achievement, future success in life, and so on."[2] Recent research documents indicate that race is a powerful factor in determining the level of expectation that teachers set for children. Social-status characteristics that can be inferred from the appearance of the child in the classroom precondition the teachers' judgment about the capability of the child to achieve. Teachers expect less of lower-class children than they do of middle-class youngsters. This is the phenomenon of the *self-fulfilling prophecy*, which is particularly relevant to the visible minority child because of the inclination to stereotype minorities, especially blacks, as of lower social class.

The practice of making invidious distinctions between persons on the basis of race is not limited to people who are basically evil, hateful, and malicious. Quite to the contrary, persons who make such judgments are frequently well-meaning, gentle, and caring people. Consequently, when they are confronted with the notion that they themselves may be engaging in racist behavior, their reaction is usually one of stunned disbelief and of personal resentment. Their lack of awareness results from the legitimacy and social approval that racism has been given. Practices that are institutionally legitimized are accepted. Few question them. Even those against whom discrimination is directed accept these practices when they are given legitimacy. And so the difficult problem of racism continues to becloud the horizon for educational improvement.[3]

---

[1] John Jarolimek, *The Schools in Contemporary Society* (New York: Macmillan, 1981), p. 87.
[2] Ibid., p. 88.
[3] Ibid.

The explosion in the sixties of angry black Americans revolting against existing prejudice and discrimination evidently shocked the nation out of complacency. Racial disorders brought cities to a new dawning of fear, bewilderment, and the need for serious search for ways to change. Perhaps the greatest fear was that the prophecy of the Kerner Commission on Civil Disorders would be realized.

> This is our basic conclusion: Our nation is moving toward two societies, one black, one white—separate and unequal.[4]

Integration and Poverty

The Poor

Historically, race relations in our country have been dominated by white people in an almost caste-like society. Early in the eighteenth century, White Anglo-Saxon Protestants established their dominant cultural pattern. They conquered the American Indians, the Spanish-speaking peoples of the Southwest, neighboring provinces, and several outlying islands. As immigration increased in the nineteenth century, they became alarmed lest their manner of life would be disrupted by the impact of foreign cultural groups. Gradually it became routine for them to believe that non-Anglos transplanted inferior modes of living and perpetuated low-class folkways that did not mesh with the prevailing culture. These people did not or were not allowed to assimilate. Many of those who did make their way into society were forced to settle for a position in the lowest stratum of social acceptance.

All societies have some form of stratification among their peoples simply because people are rewarded differently for various status positions. The class system may be less apparent in some societies than in others, but some form of social differentiation that ranks individuals on the bases of the statuses they occupy is found everywhere. The lowest stratum of social class, that powerless group sometimes referred to as the "underclass", ever since has stubbornly resisted all efforts to find and eliminate the root cause of their problem. The oppressed status of minority peoples, in our society as well as in others, then seems to be a direct result of social arrangements. The question, "Is American society responsible for not only creating but, more important, of maintaining the subordinate position of minority peoples?" has recently been posed with increasing vigor. Herbert Gans suggests that the answer to this question is yes. He notes

> Poverty ... may well satisfy a number of ... functions ... the existence of poverty ensures that society's "dirty work" will be done ... [i.e., menial jobs—low wages], the poor ... subsidize the affluent [i.e., domestic work, child care for wealthy] ... poverty creates jobs ... that serve ... the poor and protect the rest of society from them ... the poor buy goods others do not want and thus prolong the economic usefulness of such goods ... the poor can be identified and punished as alleged or real deviants in order to uphold the legitimacy of conventional norms ... the poor have a

---

[4] O. Kerner, *Report of the National Advisory Committee on Civil Disorders* (New York: E. P. Dutton & Co., 1968), p. 1.

direct cultural function [i.e., music and art-blues] . . . adopted by the more affluent . . . poverty helps to guarantee the status of those who are not poor . . . the poor help to keep the aristocracy busy, and justify its continued existence . . . the poor being powerless can be made to absorb the costs of change and growth in American society [i.e., urban renewal, etc.] . . . the poor facilitate and stabilize the American political process . . . the poor pay all.[5]

Poverty, opportunity, and race can hardly be discussed in isolation. Though there are poor whites and poor nonwhites, the literature abounds with examples of the dilemma of the blacks. A major problem is that of coping with and adjusting to increased urbanization which had its roots in the post-World War II migration of the blacks from rural to urban settings. Contributing factors were high concentrations of blacks in the core cities and the retreat of whites to the suburbs; inadequate housing; decaying city neighborhoods; poor jobs; low income; inequality of educational opportunity; substandard municipal services; racism and oppression caused by the social-class structure; and the social-authority structure existent in our society.

This out-migration of whites to the suburbs and the in-migration of blacks and other nonwhites from the rural South and Caribbean islands to an impoverished job market in our cities produced even greater poverty; and it lessened the likelihood of their assimilation into the mass society. Thus, the isolation and segregation of the poor minorities increased. To some degree, the poor were trapped in a situation in which opportunities for economic, educational, occupational, and political advancement were limited. Industries had become so advanced that unskilled jobs were at a premium. It was difficult to get into craft unions, and opportunities for special technical training apprenticeships were difficult to secure. Consequently, the poor males often remained unemployed for long periods of time, and often left their families to secure unskilled migratory work.

Educationally, our free and democratic society has preached the maxim that educational opportunity is open to all, and that education is the way to achieve social-economic mobility. In 1966, Coleman's findings, however, revealed that our schools were largely segregated.[6] According to this report, the majority of poor children were nonwhite, and were attending schools in which 90 to 100 per cent of the children were nonwhite. The report noted that the inner-city children (blacks and other nonwhites) attending disadvantaged or ghetto schools had less favorable access to important facilities, and had insufficient supplies and textbooks. And the report stated that, overall, their education was of a lower level of quality than that of their white counterparts. This situation is in part the result of the white middle-class abandonment of the urban public schools upon their exodus to the suburbs. The isolation and separateness of the urban ghetto school has powerful effects on the achievement, motivation, and self-concepts of poor children.

The majority of Americans have long entertained negative opinions of the poor. Those people existing in poverty, especially those receiving public as-

[5] Herbert Gans, "The Uses of Poverty: The Poor Pay All," *Social Policy* (July–August 1971), 20–24.
[6] James Coleman, *Equality of Educational Opportunity* (Washington, D.C.: U.S. Government Printing Office, 1966).

sistance, appear to have been stigmatized as deviant and undesirable. Subtly, the sociologists inform us, over time the majority appears to free itself from the obligation of treating the stigmatized minority with politeness or with trust. "Because of pity, disgust, or fear the 'normal' individual feels little obligation to be attentive to the stigmatized individual's definition of the situation."[7]

In the schools, the results of this stigmatization can clearly be seen. Children of poverty generally experience their first long-term contact here with middle-class adults. Their tender age and comparative powerlessness make them particularly vulnerable to the stigmatizing assumptions of their teachers. The ideals that, despite differences in ability and family background, each child should be equally deserving of respect, equally worthy of membership in the school community, and equally entitled to develop unique potentials, certainly do exist in the attitude of the professional staffs of the schools. But side by side with this uplifting attitude also exist negative attitudes about poor adults. When a teacher then has difficulty teaching the children of the poor, it becomes an easy matter to label them as unreachable and to blame their home life as the cause. Unfortunately, the labeling has the debilitating effect of causing the stigmatized individuals to believe the definition that "normals" assign to them. This labeling renders it more difficult for them to change their orientation toward success. Once individuals have internalized the stigma they have been assigned, they can erase it only with great difficulty. They develop, among other things, coping strategies designed to protect themselves against the pain of negative evaluation by others. They make belittling remarks about themselves, for example, and they denigrate their achievements; they publicly declare themselves as incompetent before anyone else has a chance to do it. Teachers frequently refer to such children as having low self-concepts. This label suggests that the trouble resides within the child; it tends to ignore the significant part that the school has played in the self-depreciation process.[8]

Growing up in severe poverty ill prepares children for what they face in school. What goes on in the microworld of the family profoundly affects how children perceive and experience in the macroworld beyond the home. The actual extent to which teachers' expectations account for students' performance is not clearly known as yet, but numerous studies do reveal that teachers generally favor students whom they perceive as high achievers and give short shrift to those whom they believe to be slow learners. Research cited by Webb[9] shows that teachers call on the "low expectation group" less frequently to recite; are more publicly critical of such pupils; have fewer positive interactions and shorter exchanges with them; pay less attention to their comments; reinforce their behavior inappropriately; and wait less time for their answers to the teacher's questions.

The phenomenon identified as the self-fulfilling prophecy appears to be relevant in the relationship between teachers and children of the poor. This concept as described by Merton consists of "a false definition of the situa-

[7] Rodman B. Webb, *Schooling and Society* (New York: Macmillan, 1981), p. 373.
[8] Ibid., p. 375.
[9] Ibid., p. 376.

tion evoking a new behavior which makes the original false conception come true." In other words, the prophet-teacher cites the actual course of events as proof that the original diagnosis was right from the very beginning. Thus, a teacher's expectation that low-poverty students will fail will increase the likelihood of their poor academic performance.[10]

Despite governmental support for innovations designed to improve the quality of education in low-income area schools, few attempts have been startingly successful. In fact, numerous educational critics have come to feel that the public schools have, in the main, strengthened social class lines and increased racial stratification. Though we may have moved from *de jure* segregation, we have evidently not yet abandoned *de facto* segregation nor effected the type of urban schooling that minimizes the effects of family poverty.

Poverty continues to be a problem in all areas of the country for large numbers of families. In general, the poverty rate seems to be declining in the South as compared with other regions of the country. However, the South still has the highest percentage in the country of families who are economically impoverished.

Integration

In the years since the Brown decision of 1954, in which the Supreme Court of the United States ruled that in the field of public education the doctrine of separate but equal has no place, and that separate educational facilities are inherently unequal, integration as an issue has moved through several different phases. Most of the 1950s were devoted to determining whether unequal educational services were associated with segregation of staff or students. This was evidenced by dozens of political actions and activist movements in cities and suburbs. This phase seemed to be mainly one of stimulating interest groups to study the issue.

Next, during the years from 1959 through 1968, segregation of schools was chiefly dealt with by prescription. Studies and investigations into the qualifications of educational staff, the physical facilities, and the achievement failures of segregated schools indicated that the situation required immediate attention, in the form of change. Plans for change were outlined, but racial segregation in the schools was firmly entrenched along with economic segregation, subcultural conflicts between the school and the culture of the community, and teaching-learning discontinuities. At this phase of the segregation dilemma, ideologies were basically solution- or accommodation-oriented. Proposed solutions ranged from immediate desegregation to balanced programs, and black separation.

Desegregation began in the urban North, and involved many varieties of experiments to break the race barrier. Desegregation or integration of schools was approached as a separate problem. In order to secure passage of effective change or prescriptive measures mandated by the Brown decision, Congress responded with the adoption of five civil rights acts—those of 1957, 1960, 1964, 1965, and 1968. These five measures aimed at speeding up desegregation of schools where *de jure* segregation was obvious.

[10] Ibid., p. 377.

During this phase, strides were made in desegregating hotels, restaurants, housing, trains, and schools. To speed up integration, the Civil Rights Movement used freedom rides, marches on Washington, court decisions, and other kinds of demonstrations. These actions precipitated two immediate reactions: white backlash, and the incorporation of many working class blacks into the movement, thus strengthening it.

However, by the mid-sixties, rising frustration had replaced the earlier optimism. Civil rights laws did not promote jobs, housing, educational training or vocational opportunities. Compensatory projects for the disadvantaged appeared to have little impact upon raising opportunity levels. As a result, the issues of inadequate living conditions, work, and *de facto* segregation had become more pressing. Black frustration was starkly revealed by the Watts riots during the summer of 1965, in Los Angeles. The following year, Congress passed the Open Housing law, which forbade discrimination in the sale or rental of houses or apartments. This issue had been a breeding ground for violent reactions by minorities.

Radical black leaders such as Malcolm X (a Black Muslim), Stokeley Carmichael, Huey Newton, and Eldridge Cleaver (a Black Panther) encouraged direct confrontation regarding racism. Black power, they maintained, was the only solution to black problems. On the other hand, older black leaders, such as Roy Wilkins (Congress of Racial Equality) and Dr. Martin Luther King, Jr., rejected the use of violence and advocated the nonviolent route to change. Despite this difference in their leaders' strategy, the slogans "Black is Beautiful" and "Black Power" were quickly accepted by the nonwhite community. These terms implied community control of ghetto schools, self-respect, and racial pride.

Blacks, along with other nonwhite and economically poor groups, have no doubt benefited socially from the human rights laws, civil rights laws, and desegregation of employment opportunities, public facilities, and other aspects of public life. However, there are many tangible effects they have not yet experienced. Now, in the eighties, we are in a new phase in the struggle for racial equality and integration. In this phase, emphasis is on education. Despite federal compensatory inputs, however, and federal spending in low-income areas, and government-sponsored research, there are many indications that total integration for racial equality will be a long time coming.

In 1979, the National Institute of Education reported on a three-year project that examined life in several desegregated schools. These studies showed that life within these schools is still based on racial distinctions. Both social patterns and instructional practices separated blacks and whites and, in effect, resegregated the schools. For instance, students developed special names for members of the opposite race that symbolically separated them, and students congregated regularly in special places where members of other groups were not welcomed. In these ways, students maintained their boundaries symbolically and spatially.[11] Certain instructional policies such as ability grouping, or "tracking" students into "advanced," "average," and "basic" groups also served to separate students along racial lines. These social

---

[11] Ibid., p. 424.

and instructional forms of resegregation may account for the minimal impact of desegregation on the achievement and attitude of students.

Busing

One solution attempted for the problems caused by *de facto* segregation was the busing of black students from all-black neighborhoods to schools that were closer to all-white in student population. Events in recent years underline both the complexity and the touchiness of the forced busing issue. In spite of the numerous court decisions that mandate forced busing, resistance to it is still great. And so we find referenda that condemn busing, statements by politicians that withdraw support for busing, an attempt to amend the United States Constitution in order to stop busing, riots over busing, and attempts to overturn the law in the courts.

In order to understand the busing problem fully, it is essential to examine the historical roots of pupil-busing schemes. School busing dates back to at least 1869, when Massachusetts passed legislation authorizing public funds for the busing of children to and from school. (Of course, at that time the "buses" were horse-drawn vehicles). This legislation was soon followed by similar legislation in Vermont, Maine, and New Hampshire. By World War I, nearly all states had compulsory education laws that necessitated pupil transportation in rural areas using the consolidated school plan. It is now common practice in both rural and urban areas in every state of the Union, whether or not desegregation plans are involved. In addition to being used for transporting rural youth to consolidated or centralized schools, the buses are used to take handicapped children to special schools, to transport pupils to educational parks, to carry pupils to private and parochial schools, as an alternate to double sessions, and for field trips and curriculum excursions. Thus we see that busing has traditionally been used to equalize educational opportunity.

Historically, then, pupil transportation has been an accepted practice. According to U.S. Department of Transportation figures, in January 1972, 42.2 per cent of all school children in the United States were being bused to and from school. An analysis of their statistics reveals that the number of children being bused had increased 5 per cent during the preceding decade and that 60 per cent of all the children in Michigan, West Virginia, Kentucky, Missouri, North Carolina, Idaho, and Oregon traveled to and from school by bus.

Busing in order to eliminate racial imbalance in the schools has come about as a direct result of the U.S. Supreme Court's 1954 decision in *Brown* v. *Board of Education, Topeka,* which overturned the old doctrine providing for separate but equal facilities for the black and white races. This decision has been followed up by a number of other court decisions that have mandated enforced busing in order to desegregate the schools. Let us consider some of these decisions.

In Detroit, (1974) the U.S. District Court ordered full integration of all schools. Busing was the alternative means selected for this purpose (*Bradley* v. *Miliken*). In Richmond, Virginia (1968) a district court ordered the consolidation of schools in Henrico and Chesterfield Counties. The court ruled in favor of multiracial schools (*Green* v. *New Kent County*). In Denver, Colorado (1970) the courts ordered desegregation of all schools, open enrollment and compensatory education programs as alternatives to segregation (*Keyes* v. *Denver*). In Pontiac, Michigan (1970) the courts found that the intention to build new schools was perpetuating segregation and ruled in favor of busing for racial balance (*Davis* v. *Pontiac*). Perhaps the most publicized of the decisions during the mid-seventies were those of U.S. District Court Judge W. Arthur Garrity, Jr., who, after ordering the desegregation of the Boston schools, took strong steps to be sure that desegregation was carried out in spite of the opposition of the Boston School Committee, school officials, and groups of irate citizens. In 1976, in a far-reaching decision, the court decided that pupils in Delaware must be bused across district lines in order to desegregate schools in the Wilmington area.

As the foregoing comments imply, there has been much resistance to the court-ordered measures for desegregating the schools. In March 1972, a Florida State referendum condemned busing. President Nixon, while affirming his belief in integration, opposed busing as an alternative to racial balance. His plan was to seek to upgrade the neighborhood-school concept, revise attendance zones, and increase federal spending for schools by two and a half billion dollars. Some members of Congress had become so concerned that they proposed the so-called Ashfield, Bloomfield, Green Amendment (anti-busing amendment) to the United States Constitution that would prohibit the Commissioner of Education from using federal funds for the purpose of overcoming racial imbalance in the schools. In Boston, feelings ran so high that attempts to bus black students into the South Boston white enclave led to much violence and rioting, and in the summer of 1976 there were plans for appealing to the United States Supreme Court for relief from Judge Garrity's decisions. President Ford's basic attitude was similar to President Nixon's. On May 29, 1976, he announced that he had "directed the Attorney General to continue an active search for a busing case which would be suitable for judicial review of current case law on forced school busing" and had asked the Attorney General "to accelerate his efforts to develop legislative remedies to minimize school busing".[12] During the campaign for the 1976 Presidential Election, other candidates of both parties took much the same line.

In general, the arguments against school busing included such rationalizations as (1) busing is against the American tradition; (2) the neighborhood school is more desirable than the consolidated school; (3) bus-riding is bad for children; and (4) busing is too expensive. Most educators consider these arguments to be myths, or at least half-truths, that cloud the real issues. Still the arguments pro and con continue. The number of proposals for busing and other measures for integrating the schools continues to grow, even though the skeptics on busing claim that it is not a viable alternative until housing patterns and economic patterns are altered. To date, there has been little research done which supports busing on the grounds of improvement in academic skills, self-esteem, or racial tolerance. Although in 1970 James S.

[12] *The New York Times* (May 30, 1976), p. 1.

Coleman was contending that we have not succeeded in providing equal opportunity through school inputs alone or through capital expenditure, the realization that outside educational resources and exposure to achievement can help deprived children by enriching their school experience, necessitates that alternatives for integraton be pursued.[13] Minority students, he discovered, generally enter school at an academic disadvantage. The gap separating minority and majority achievement scores widened as students progressed through school. Although differences were found between black and white schools, the disparities were small and not always in favor of white schools. Class size, per-pupil expenditures, school facilities, and varied curricular offerings had virtually no impact on academic achievement. Of all the variables that contributed to what a student learned in school, the most critical was found to be the influence of the home. Coleman found that disadvantaged students were more likely than their advantaged counterparts to believe that they were unable to affect their environment. These students felt that what happened to them was more a matter of luck than a matter of planning and effort. Positive fate-control attitudes showed the strongest relationship to achievement at the sixth-grade level and above. In 1975 and 1976, Coleman suggested that perhaps forced busing may do more harm than good. One result, he believed, might be white flight from the urban areas. Other sociologists and educationists took issue with this contention, and many pages in educational journals (for example, *Phi Delta Kappan*, February, 1976; *Harvard Educational Review*, Winter, 1976) were devoted to debating the effects of busing.

In March of 1981, two legislators in the national Congress sponsored a bill setting "reasonable limits" on the powers of the courts to order busing. These limits were set according to minutes and miles. For example, "a court could not order a student bused farther than five miles or longer than fifteen minutes by bus beyond the school nearest his home."[14] It appears that getting such legislation through the House will not be easy. House Judiciary Committee Chairman Peter Rodino (Democrat–N.J.) has always opposed legislation that restricts the authority of the courts to decide constitutional questions involving civil rights. Some legal experts have already said such a bill would be unconstitutional. Despite all the sound and fury coming from legislators faced with nasty busing disputes in their own states, the power to settle questions still resides in the courts, not in Congress.

Certainly the issue of race and the multiracial school will not soon disappear. Other solutions to the problem of *de facto* segregation have been tried, including voluntary integration, the creation of magnet schools, and the change of school organization.

Voluntary Integration

In the voluntary integration attempts, school districts encouraged both black and white parents to send their children voluntarily into schools where integration did not occur naturally by virtue of the local housing pattern.

---

[13] James S. Coleman, *op. cit.*
[14] "Washington Report," *Phi Delta Kappan*, 62:550 (April 1981).

White parents bused their children into city schools that were in all-black neighborhoods, and black children were bused to suburban areas that were all white.

Magnet Schools

The idea of the magnet concept was to attract students regardless of race to particular schools in which high quality programs, perhaps specializing in a certain area, had been established. Parents throughout a district were given the opportunity to examine the programs at these schools and to send their youngsters to the one that most impressed them. The high quality of the programs was expected to prove attractive enough to draw the attendance of white youngsters whose parents would be willing to enroll them in magnet schools in traditionally black neighborhoods.

Reorganization Schemes

Still another system that was attempted was the reorganization of the grades housed in any school building. Instead of the traditional K–6 organization, some districts changed to a K–2, 3–4, 5–6 scheme. Some schools, for example, might have only grades one and two (in such a building, there might be as many as ten or twelve separate first-grade and second-grade classrooms); others might have only grades three and four; and so on. Because within any given neighborhood attendance boundary there are not a sufficient number of first- and second-graders to fill an entire building, the youngsters must be brought in from a much wider attendance area.

Dropouts, Delinquency, and Crime

The stark realities of statistics reveal that within our credential-oriented society, approximately one fourth of our young people do not complete high school, and that one of every nine children is referred to juvenile courts for acts of delinquency before the age of eighteen. Both the dropout and delinquent find themselves in social and economic disarray; and when these two factors combine for one individual, the person stands in double peril.

The Dropout

Research has identified a number of reasons why children drop out of school. Actually, dissatisfaction with school is usually only a part of a larger picture of discontent encompassing the student's overall view of himself in relation to his world. The disadvantaged child, for instance, often finds himself incompatible with a school in which the curriculum and teachers represent the dominant middle class. If the fault lies in the school, even if the dropout is encouraged to return to school, he will soon drop out again.

Dropouts often fail to perceive any value in education. This negative attitude toward school may be the result of lack of relevancy in the school curriculum, teacher failure in motivational techniques, or community, group, or family attitudes toward schooling. Such negative attitudes can be a serious obstacle to success in school. Lack of orientation toward education seems to be a considerable factor in the talent loss resulting from the dropping out of pupils who have a high potential.

Closely related to the dropout-problem are such problems as under-achievement, attitudes toward schooling, the inability to conform to school expectations, attendance problems, limited or underutilized cognitive resources, and emotional instability. Self-rejection on the part of the under-achiever in academic areas, coupled with self-acceptance behavior in non-academic areas, may further complicate this picture.

Dropouts and Delinquency

Dropouts and delinquency are often observed in combination. Study of this problem underscores the fact that failure in school is often related to delinquency. Moreover, there is mounting evidence that many of the causative factors of this phenomenon are school-based. The school experiences of the delinquent are likely to have been negative. Often the delinquent's grades show repeated failures; he is often overage or oversized for his grade level; his attitudes are often charged with oppositional feelings; he is likely to have changed schools frequently; and his attendance is erratic. Because the delinquent and the dropout find the curriculum to be achievement-oriented, and are unable to cope with it, they find themselves trapped educationally. Consequently, their motivation declines and negative feelings grow. As their motivation declines, their achievement and skills fall off, and they fall farther and farther behind. Leaving school as soon as the law allows permits this type of student to escape from a frustrating and degrading experience.

When one examines the profile of juvenile delinquents and dropouts, one often finds many similarities—usually in terms of personal make-up. Because their intellectual resources and aptitudes are underutilized, anxiety is often high, and their need to defy authority is important. Their social adjustment often reflects impulsiveness and distrust. Their personalities seem characterized by strong suggestibility, egocentrism, and self-indulgence. Their goals are usually immediate; long-range planning is rare. Often the home milieu of the delinquent and dropout is characterized by contradictory social norms, broken family units, economic stress, deteriorated neighborhood residence, inadequate supervision during the formative years, and indifferent parental relationships. In school, failure, repeated and multiplied by truancy, discipline problems, and unclear perspectives of the future are prevalent.

In large urban centers, the average daily attendance hovers around fifty per cent of secondary school enrollment.[15] Black students of all ages tend to drop out (or to be pushed out) of school almost twice as often as white students in the post seventeen-year-old grouping,[16] and students of lower income groups fail and drop out more often than students of higher income groups. These youngsters have a much more negative view of our economic system than do white youngsters,[17] and are more likely to feel that our form of government needs to undergo major change.

[15] Mark A. Chesler and William M. Cave, *Sociology of Education* (New York: Macmillan, 1981), p. 253.
[16] Ibid., p. 267.
[17] Ibid., p. 273.

As one might expect, these young people have a history of poor home conditions, and of personal, social, and emotional problems. Specifically, the potential or actual dropout, according to a report by Lucius F. Cervantes,[18] is unhappy at school:

He is at least two years below level in reading or mathematics at grade seven;
> performs below his potential academically;
> has low marks in school;
> fails at least one year, most frequently the first, second, eighth, or ninth;
> often skips school or arrives late;
> seldom, if ever, participates in school functions and extracurricular activities;
> has frequently moved from school to school;
> is often in disciplinary trouble;
> does not feel that he really is welcome or belongs in school.

He also has difficulty at home, for instance:
> There are more children at home than the parent(s) can adequately take care of and control.
> The parents are inconsistent in displaying affection and maintaining discipline.
> The home life is unhappy.
> He has no father, or an ineffectual one.
> The educational level of the parents is low.

His emotional and social aspects leave much to be desired.
> He has few family friends and some of these may be "problem units," i.e., divorced, deserted, delinquent, dropouts.
> His parents do not approve of his friends.
> His friends do not like school.
> His friends are much older or much younger than he.
> He resents authority of any sort—home, school, or any other type.
> He requires immediate rewards and finds it difficult to wait for deferred gratification.
> His image of himself is weak.

As Cervantes' list implies, delinquency is not so much the result of rebelling against society, as it is an attempt to find a way to make a place for oneself. A Mobilization for Youth statement presents this fact very well:

> much delinquent behavior is engendered because opportunities for conformity are limited. Delinquency therefore represents not a lack of motivation to conform but quite the opposite: the desire to meet social expectations itself becomes the source of delinquent behavior if the possibility of doing so is limited or nonexistent.[19]

In this vein, it is postulated that delinquent and dropout-patterns are related to discrepancies between the students' behavior, the expectations of the school, and the lack of opportunity in the community. Federal action in the Johnson Administration's War on Poverty, delinquency, and crime utilized this lack of opportunity paradigm. Mobilization for Youth was perhaps

---

[18] Lucius F. Cervantes, S. J., *The Drop Out: Causes and Cures* (Ann Arbor, Michigan: University of Michigan Press, 1965).

[19] Mobilization for Youth, *A Proposal for the Prevention and Control of Delinquency by Expanding Opportunity* (New York: Mobilization for Youth, Inc., 1961), pp. 44–45.

the largest nationwide effort to pursue social institutional change. Although the demonstration project fell short of its goals, it underscored the school's role in dealing with the dropout and delinquency problem: The school must work in concert with all community agencies and resources. In this manner, it can do much to reduce the problem which threatens a large segment of our youth.

Delinquency and Crime

Much of the crime that we read about—and which inflates our crime statistics—is organized crime. Criminal activities have penetrated small businesses, large corporations, and even high governmental offices. Corruption has touched the branches of government at all levels, as the Abscam and Watergate scandals point out only too well. Crime and corruption, of course, are common in the working class also. Businesses claim losses in tremendous amounts from theft in supermarkets and department stores. Many blue-collar or white-collar workers, though they may use a different approach, are involved in criminal activities.

Public reaction to crime has been largely one of fear. During the sixties, people trembled through the summer race riots and ghetto lootings. A few years later, street crime seemed to be on the increase. Muggings and robberies cleared the streets at night. During the seventies, there was a great concern over campus disorders and crime in the streets, and it is impossible to predict what future fears will be. Regarding crime, however, and the public's reaction to it, we see considerable uncertainty. Whatever the reactions, demands for law and order will no doubt remain a permanent aspect of our response to cultural unrest. This sort of response will probably apply to youth, especially because they have reacted to our social disorganization with varied forms of activism.

Like most of society's other problems, the problem of crime and delinquency involves some sobering realities. It is a fact that a great deal of crime occurs in urban areas, and that much of the crime is committed by juveniles and blacks. But while such cities as Boston, Detroit, Chicago, Kansas City, Miami, Memphis, and Portland, Oregon reported decreases in school crime in the year after firm-tough policies began, suburban communities noted for good schools and quality education were "being scandalized by physical assaults and threats against teachers and students."[20] School authorities emphasize that "a high proportion of violent incidents are perpetrated by non-student intruders, who have easy street access to many schools.[21] It is also a fact that many city crimes do involve juvenile delinquents, and the increase in drug use may be related to this increase. Crimes include assault, rape, robbery, burglary, larceny, and motor vehicle theft. Placing the problem in perspective, juvenile delinquency and crime as an issue involve the social structure of our society. Both conservative and liberal views of this issue tend to agree that poverty and racism have contributed to criminal activities. Within the ghetto, many disadvantaged people who commit crimes also tend to be the victims of crimes. To them, criminal behavior has become a way of sur-

[20] *U.S. News & World Report* (May 21, 1979).
[21] Ibid.

vival and an emotional release from frustration. Thus, imperfections in the social equilibrium may, in effect, push some people toward crime. Some analyses of this issue blame our social and economic institutions for this imbalance. Robert Morgenthau has written:

> We . . . find persons who publicly denounce crimes of violence while privately committing more . . . socially acceptable white-collar crimes . . . There is, moreover, a national tendency to enforce the law against crimes of violence more rigorously than against the more sophisticated white-collar crimes.[22]

Public response to crime, especially in relation to juvenile delinquents, may represent biased perceptions. It is most important for society to attempt to manage this problem equitably—on all levels, for all classes, and for all individuals.

The School—a Social Habitat

Certainly, if the school can do anything to prevent dropouts, delinquency, and crime, it should. All schools face, to some degree, the persistent problems of lack of motivation, school failure, delinquent behavior, vandalism, and stealing. Unfortunately, many teachers resist change, especially in terms of curriculum revision. Although the special-services approach, which uses psychiatrists, psychologists, social workers, child-care specialists, and counselors, is often used for solving problems of dropouts and delinquency, it is likely to be a futile effort. One reason for this failure is that the problem is the result of factors rooted not in the psyche or the family, but in the social system of the school. The social milieu of the school is often foreign to the youngsters. Its network of interpersonal relationships very much depends on the schools' own culture or social system, which often seems to have little relevance to the needs of the students. In slow-moving, slow-changing schools, students begin to judge this milieu, and find it lacking. Student unrest, dropouts, and delinquency are the result. Involvement of students in policy making and curriculum revision may be one way to revamp a milieu that students find irrelevant, immaterial, and, in the final analysis, worthless and even cruel.

What power does a student have when caught up in an irrelevant, inefficient, dull, school environment? He can rebel, he can drop out, or he can accept it. The student who is a possible dropout needs a program that identifies his needs and allows him avenues for effective release and self-awareness. In preparing such programs in order to prevent delinquency and dropouts, schools must

1. Break through age barriers between youth and adults.
2. Provide a positive climate for the nonachieving student.
3. Be staffed by authentic teachers, whom students trust.
4. Achieve greater differentiation of curriculum to ensure a meaningful school program.
5. Encourage early detection of possible delinquents, and attempt to alter the development of these behaviors.

[22] Robert Morgenthau, "Equal Justice and the Problem of White-Collar Crime," *The Conference Board Review* 8:20 (1969).

6. Have adequate counseling services available.
7. Work closely with the community they serve.

Without active involvement of the school as a community agency, the community can have little effect on its delinquency and dropout problems. However, by mobilizing the school and community forces and having them work in concert, much can be done to prevent and control the social problems toward which many of our youth move.

Demographic Shifts, Mobility, and Expanding Population

Since World War II, Southern blacks have migrated North in great numbers. By far the largest influx of black migrants has been in New York State, where almost 400,000 settled during the 1960s. Another group, the Puerto Ricans, also have found our urban areas a haven, and they have migrated steadily since the late 1940s. The migration is expected to continue, probably because of the pull of supposed opportunity in the larger cities of the North. This pattern of poor and unskilled blacks and Puerto Ricans moving into urban areas, especially into New York City, has had important ramifications: increasing welfare costs, deterioration of existing housing stock, and urban density. At the same time, the quality of municipal services and other social amenities has decreased. This problem is being aggravated presently by the influx of refugees and illegal aliens from the Caribbean and Latin-American countries.

Urban Orientation

During the past fifty years, America has become an urban-oriented society, with most of its citizens living and working in metropolitan centers. In 1920, thirty per cent of the American population was living on farms, but by 1970 the percentage had dropped to 4.8 per cent, and the total number living on farms had dropped to 9,712,000.[23]

As people have left the farms, especially in the Southern rural areas, they have moved to burgeoning metropolitan centers. Recent population growth has been greatest in satellite areas and in suburban communities surrounding large urban centers. However, demographers, educators, and urbanologists have noted that whereas the major increase in the movement of blacks has been into urban centers, the major white middle-class population increases have come in other areas defined as semiurban: satellite and suburban communities.

The core-cities have continued to grow, but they have taken on the educational and social onus of having to accommodate an influx of the poor, the old, and the socially deviant. As Perel and Vairo note, "for the most part, the departing middle-class citizens have been replaced if at all by poor Southern Negroes, Puerto Ricans and Mexican-Americans. . . . There is even a tendency for middle-class persons to move from the core of the city to its outskirts, even when they do not remove themselves into the suburbs."[24]

[23] Shirley Boes Neill, "Demographers' Message to Education," *American Education.* **15**:6–11 (January/February, 1979).
[24] W. Perel and P. Vairo, *Urban Education: Problems and Prospects* (New York: David McKay, 1969), pp. 15–25.

One result of contemporary mobility and population trends has been the development of new centers of population. Especially noticeable has been the growth of communities close to new business establishments that are involved in defense and aerospace activities, and to vacation and retirement areas suitable for the affluent and aging elements of the population.

As a result of these migrations, today the urban environment is one of the least desirable environments for human habitation. It is polluted, congested, expensive, unsafe, and decaying—in a state of perpetual major crisis, fighting for its very survival. Presently, our cities stand a good chance of becoming a no-man's land. By middle-class standards, many city residents are deviants, aberrations from the cultural norm in that they are members of minority groups, poor, and sometimes old.

In the schools,

"nearly 25 per cent of all children with language handicaps that impede their educational progress are in the urban schools; city schools have unusually high numbers and concentrations of students eligible to participate in compensatory, bilingual, and desegregation programs; proportionately more handicapped children receive services today in urban school systems; and the education and training of teachers and administrators in urban settings are not commensurate with the dramatic changes in demography brought about by migration of persons into and out of urban centers."[25]

The children in the ghettos continue to eat lead-filled paint and plaster, and the youth continue to be brutalized by their experiences in the schools of the inner city and the community. The aged succumb to malnutrition and to other poverty-linked diseases. Ways must be found and priorities reestablished to help the inner-city community to become a fit place in which to reside and learn.

Minorities

Many youngsters enrolled in school do not speak English as a first language. At home they may speak Vietnamese, Czech, Polish, French, Cantonese, Japanese, or some other tongue. However, the vast majority of young people who do not speak English as a first language speak Spanish. These Hispanics are by no means uniformly distributed across the country. Spanish-speaking children of Mexican descent are common in the schools of California, Arizona, New Mexico, and Texas. Spanish-speaking children of Cuban-born parents are common in many schools in Florida. Spanish-speaking children of Puerto Rican ancestry are common in New York State, particularly in the schools of New York City.

From a small core of perhaps 100,000 in the 1940s, the Spanish-speaking Puerto Rican group has risen to over one million in population. Although American citizens, Puerto Ricans, because of their language and their predominantly Spanish culture, are still considered foreigners by many. Young Puerto Ricans entering into the "new world" of the American city soon discover that in this setting their cultural conflicts are intense. Thus caught within their own ethnic diversity, their internal conflicts may soon cause them to turn upon themselves or their own groups. Adaptation for young

---

[25] Shirley Boes Neill, op. cit.

Puerto Ricans is not easy. They quickly realize that to adapt well depends upon having a job, being a male, having more education, being young, and being white. Although migrants are generally hopeful about achieving their occupational aspirations, and although they realize that success in America depends upon education, a higher percentage of Puerto Rican children leave school in states like New York than any other ethnic group. For Puerto Ricans of the "white" group, assimilation into the main population appears to be merely a matter of time; those of mixed or Negro groups appear to face a more formidable problem.

The major problem faced by blacks and Puerto Ricans living in the United States proper is becoming increasingly one of coping and adjusting to the big city. It is presently estimated that almost one half of all American Negroes live outside the South, mainly in the inner-city ghettos of Northern cities from which the white middle class has fled. In these ghettos, where schools are substandard, homes are substandard, and housing is in disorder, the effect of racial isolation on the schools is frightening, according to the U.S. Riot Commission.

Trends for the Eighties

During the frustrating decade of the 1960s, public school educators, the federal government, and the major foundations tried a multitude of change models based upon diffusion and dissemination. Research follow-up in the early 1970s revealed, however, that public education had resisted all of those efforts and had remained largely unchanged. It now seems clear that the schools in the decade of the 1980s, by using the concept of alternatives, can achieve what previously proved so elusive. Recent reports indicate an intriguing relationship between alternatives and declines in school violence, vandalism, and disruption. By the late 1970s, alternative public schools were generally perceived as "the single most agreed upon recommendation of educators for the resolution of school vandalism and violence,"[26] even for schools serving students who have been labeled as "hard-core" offenders. Research has consistently shown

(1) A high positive correlation between small school size and low teacher/student classroom ratios and reduction of school crime. Since many alternative schools have fewer than two hundred students, they are better able to treat students individually.

(2) The importance of "significant others" in influencing behavior; it also verified the presence of positive, caring, and more student-centered faculty members in such schools.

(3) A relationship between poor academic achievement and disruptive or delinquent behavior, both in school and out. Effective alternative schools have been designed precisely to provide academic success to youngsters who are far below grade level in reading and who have rarely experienced success in school.

[26] Robert D. Barr, "Alternatives for the Eighties," *Phi Delta Kappan*, **62**:571 (April, 1981).

(4) Success in the area of enhancement of self-concept. Since most discipline-problem and drop-out students have low personal esteem and a negative self-concept, progress in this area is almost a prerequisite for success in other areas. The most promising development is that "it is probably practical and possible to implement some of the policies and practices of the alternative school programs (that have been demonstrated so effective in dealing with violence and vandalism) in traditional, conventional high schools."[27]

We now know that people learn in different ways. When schools are able to develop programs designed to meet individual needs, impressive gains occur. We now know that all children do not need fifty-minute classes and standard textbooks; some do not even need teachers. Some students learn best in individualized learning carrels; others learn best outside of school. Some students need a desk, visual aids, dictionaries, and libraries; others do not. Some students need rigorous structure to learn; others demand maximum flexibility. "It is quite likely that public education will continue to move away from a single, monolithic educational program for all students and toward a diverse system of educational alternatives in the schools and in the community."[28] The eighties may well become the decade of school diversification for public education.

SUGGESTED READING

Banks, James A., *Teaching Strategies for Ethnic Studies*, 2nd ed. Boston: Allyn & Bacon, Inc., 1979.

Blumberg, Rae Lesser, *Stratification: Socioeconomic and Sexual Inequality.* Dubuque, Iowa: William C. Brown Company, Publishers, 1978.

Cave, W. M., and M. A. Chesler, *Sociology of Education.* New York: Macmillan Publishing Co., Inc., 1981.

Clark, Kenneth, *Dark Ghetto.* New York: Harper & Row, Publishers, 1965.

Coleman, J., *Equality of Educational Opportunity.* Washington, D.C.: United States Government Printing Office, 1966.

Cuban, Larry, *To Make a Difference.* New York: Macmillan Publishing Co., Inc., 1970.

Dentler, R. et al., *The Urban R's.* New York: Praeger Publishers, Inc., 1968.

Fitzpatrick, J., *Puerto Rican Americans.* Englewood Cliffs, New Jersey: Prentice-Hall, Inc., 1971.

Glazer, Nathan, *Affirmative Discrimination: Ethnic Inequality and Public Policy.* New York: Harper & Row, Publishers, Inc., 1976.

Green, Robert L., *The Urban Challenge: Poverty and Race.* Chicago: Follett Publishing Co., Inc., 1977.

Kerner, Anne O., *Report of the National Advisory Committee on Civil Disorders.* New York: E. P. Dutton & Co., Inc., 1968.

Lawler, James M., *IQ, Heritability, and Racism.* New York: International Publishers, 1978.

Moynihan, D., and N. Glazer, *Beyond the Melting Pot.* 2nd ed., Cambridge, Mass.: M.I.T. Press, 1970.

[27] Ibid., p. 572.
[28] Ibid., p. 573.

Social Problems: Political and Social Ideologies

Democracy and Education / Contemporary Political Ideologies / Capitalism and Education / Socialism and Education / Communism and Education / Fascism and Education / World Peace and Understanding

The first-edition version of this module was written by Michael P. Cutrona, Wagner College. It has been revised and updated for this edition.

RATIONALE

The major social changes of the twentieth century have been associated with ideological movements in politics. Changes in the social classes and in the power exerted by various strata of society, the "narrowing" of geographical distance between nations since the advent of air travel, and the vast shifts in territorial controls by various world powers are among the occurrences that have influenced political-social systems. Political ideology seems to be an omnipresent element in human interactions. Both peaceful times and the violent conflicts are experienced in the context of some ideology—whatever it may be.

In studying various social perspectives of education, it is of particular interest to focus on the conservative, liberal, and radical alternatives. Their postulates about the State and its institutions, such as the schools, raise many questions regarding the concepts of democracy, freedom, and public responsibility.

The role of education in a society is influenced by the society's ideology. Rightly or wrongly, the state exercises a great influence on our daily lives in such areas as education, health, welfare, transportation, and housing. Consequently, any teacher of future citizens has an obligation to consider such questions as: What right do some men have to govern others? Is that right unlimited, or are there certain things no government should do? How far should the state intervene in matters of education and public welfare?

Government is the machinery through which any state maintains itself in power. It differs from other social institutions, such as the family, the church, or fraternal organizations, in being able to enforce its policies through police action. The precise point at which force is used depends on the ideology of the government in question. The more authoritarian the government, the more easily it can resort to force. A democratic state tends to use coercion only as a last resort. Even so, where there is society, there must always be law. And, we might add, there must be law enforcement. When the social system changes, education adjusts—sometimes voluntarily, and sometimes by force.

We can differentiate among a variety of contemporary ideologies—capitalism, socialism, communism, and fascism. The rationale behind each of these is somewhat different; however, each represents an attempt to reconstruct society or the world according to planned "social blueprints." In the West, there are many who postulate a decline of orthodox ideology for its own sake. As the world community evolves and as international problems rise to prominence, nationalistic drives will be increasingly subtle. The Industrial Revolution, with its technological and scientific advances, made it possible to influence life by appealing, ideologically, to the public in many nations of the world. This influence still continues, but the milieu has changed.

In this module, we shall investigate the significance of democracy as a sociological concept, and compare it with the major contemporary ideologies which can affect education—or, more specifically, the schools.

In this module, we shall focus upon several concepts which it is necessary to grasp if one is to understand the relationship between major contemporary political-social ideologies and education.

The seven areas listed on the title page are important because of the relationship of the political ideologies to the concepts of democracy, nationalism, academic freedom, and the overall sociological role of the school in society. Professionals in education are teaching students for the future. In doing so, education must broaden its perspectives regarding the international political scene.

Your aim in studying this module should be (1) to understand how each of these seven components relate to each other; (2) to be able to discuss some of the implications of each ideology in terms of educational issues; and (3) to be able to project how these implications may relate to future curricula or to the teaching situations you may encounter.

SPECIFIC OBJECTIVES

Specifically, at the conclusion of your study of this module you should be able to

1. Define freedom and explain its importance in education.
2. Explain the concept of democracy as it relates to education.
3. Define *academic freedom* and cite three examples of this concept.
4. Cite two examples of educational practices that violate the concept of academic freedom.
5. Cite three conditions that can place academic freedom in jeopardy.
6. Write a paragraph describing how teaching can be a subversive activity.
7. Cite at least four reasons why students have been inspired to seek academic freedom.
8. Describe ways in which students demonstrate academic freedom in schools.
9. Write a paragraph explaining the historical roots of academic freedom in education.
10. Cite two similarities and two differences between applied academic freedom at the university and public school levels.
11. Define the term *indoctrination* and explain its role in democratic education.
12. Explain the differences and similarities between *indoctrination* and *teaching for democracy*.
13. Define the term *political ideology*.
14. Cite three elements or views by which a political ideology can be characterized.
15. Define and explain the conservative political-social perspective and its implications for social institutions such as schools.
16. Define and explain the liberal political-social perspective and its implications for social institutions such as schools.

17. Define and explain the radical political-social perspective and its implications for social institutions such as schools.
18. Define the term *capitalism* as a political ideology.
19. Cite four examples of applied capitalistic ideology.
20. Write a paragraph describing capitalism in an industrial society.
21. Cite five educational implications of the capitalistic principle in the schools.
22. Define the term *socialism* as a political ideology.
23. Explain the similarities and differences between controlled capitalism and socialism.
24. Define the concept of *Fabian socialism* and cite an example of its proposed application to society.
25. Write a paragraph describing the American Socialist Party.
26. Cite three examples of socialistic principles in education.
27. Define the term *communist* as a political ideology.
28. Cite the names of two major architects of the communist system.
29. Define and explain the term *dialectical materialism.*
30. Discuss the means by which communist ideology inculcates itself on society.
31. Cite three educational implications of the communist principle in the schools.
32. Cite four examples of how communist ideology perceives the role of education.
33. Define the term *fascist* as a political ideology.
34. Cite three countries which have accepted fascist ideologies, and cite two political leaders that are associated with this system.
35. Discuss the concept of national socialism as an aspect of fascist ideology.
36. Cite three educational implications of fascism in the schools.
37. Discuss the role of nationalism in terms of international understanding and world peace.
38. Write a paragraph explaining the implications of modern political-social ideologies on world affairs and peace.
39. Cite three international bodies that attempt to establish coexistence among nations of varying ideologies.
40. Describe the role of education for public responsibility in the world community.

MODULE TEXT

Democracy and Education

Freedom is one of the perennial goals of human civilization and one of the primary measures for gauging cultural progress. As such, it has been an important goal of education. The citizens of the city-states of ancient Greece were taught the discipline of free men. Stoicism in Roman civilization was concerned with making men inwardly free. Jews and Christians through the centuries have sought to impart the truth in order that men might be liberated from the bondage of sin and ignorance. The scientific progress of the past four hundred years has been based on the ideal of the freedom of inquiry . . . Modern history has been marked by the growing recognition that liberty belongs not to a privileged class but to all men. Most of the social revolutions and re-formations of recent centuries have sought to expand political, economic, religious, and personal freedom. In these movements, education has played an important part.[1]

In this quotation, Phenix emphasizes that a person's freedom is related to the structure of the culture in which he resides. Hence, we cannot have freedom if society holds men in political-social bondage. In the United States today American culture supports freedom in at least five ways.

1. The state is not considered as an end in itself but as a means for the attainment of human ends. The basic function of the state is to secure "the greatest happiness of the greatest number." It enables every citizen to make the fullest use of his own capacities without restricting the right of fellow citizens to do the same.

2. All men possess certain inalienable rights. Whether or not other particular societies recognize them, these rights are universal and belong to all men, irrespective of race or class or creed. These rights (life, liberty, and pursuit of happiness) derive not from society but from human nature itself. Hence, the people are entitled to change any government that infringes upon their rights.

3. The more freedom we enjoy, the more responsibility we have to assume. Every political order must exact duties from its members if it would maintain stability and guarantee progress. In many ways our democratic society ideally demands more individual responsibility than do authoritarian societies.

4. Our democracy preserves and enhances individual freedom. To be free is to be uncoerced. Democratic theory sees the greatest threat to freedom in the arbitrary exercise of state power. It therefore restricts the role of government to a minimum interference in the lives of individuals. This view rejects the authoritarian tenet that the individual becomes free only by accepting social responsibilities. Rather it insists instead that men are freest when left alone. Give every man the opportunity rationally to pursue his own happiness and it will be found automatically to coincide with the greatest happiness of all.

5. In our democracy, all men are legally regarded as equal. However widely men may differ in their attributes, they are all equal in their common humanity, which differentiates them from other living things. As individuals, we cannot all hope for the same income, the same house, or the same intelligence. But we have the right to expect equality of treatment in certain very important respects—equality before the law, equality of political rights, equality of educational opportunity, and equality in matters of physical and economic well-being.[2]

[1] Philip Phenix, *Philosophies of Education* (New York: John Wiley & Sons, 1967), p. 122.
[2] George F. Kneller, ed., *Foundations of Education* (New York: John Wiley & Sons, 1963), p. 192.

Public education has long been considered necessary for the survival of the conditions of freedom; but freedom of society cannot persevere without freedom in the schools. Thus, our society has extended our freedoms of press, speech, lobby, and religion to include freedom to learn and teach. Americans have firmly believed in the cultivation of free education and in the power of every citizen to achieve an American Dream. For this reason, the individual is of prime importance. John Gardner noted, "As long as we are true to our deepest convictions as Americans, a concern for the individual will be a central theme in our consciousness. But concern for the individual is not enough. Free men must see their goals at two levels—the level of the individual and the level of the society."[3] The aims of a free people can be seen in the richness of diversity among men. We have long recognized that this ideal underscores the dimensions of academic freedom.

Academic Freedom: An Ideal and a Challenge

In order to preserve our freedoms and to encourage independent judgments, our society has exercised a resistance to censored official opinions or ideologies. To this end, academic freedom (freedom to teach and learn) has become one of our principal educational doctrines. One's concept of freedom, of course, varies according to one's political-social ideology and one's educational objectives. Before exploring education in relation to capitalism, communism, socialism, and fascism, we must explore the effects of the concept of academic freedom.

Academic freedom as an ideal today is in sharp contrast with the ideals of our historical past. For example, Sir William Berkeley, Colonial Governor of Virginia (d. 1677) once stated,

> Thank God there are no free schools or printing . . . for learning has brought disobedience and heresy into the world, and printing has divulged them . . . God keep us from both.

Today, academic freedom is viewed as necessary in order to transmit knowledge without bureaucratic intervention. It is, in effect, an educational form of civil liberty, maintained in the belief that the search for truth is so important that it must not be restricted, no matter how controversial its findings may be. Academic freedom is derived from this postulate as one of the responsibilities of scholarship.

The nature of controversial material has offered a challenge to the concept of academic freedom. Though the scholar would leave his work open to scientific scrutiny, many have encountered bitter response from the citizens. Yet, the scholar recognizes that the introduction of controversial matters appropriate to the subject under study serves to stimulate the inquiring mind. On the other hand, the use of the prerogatives of academic freedom to support preconceived purposes or nonacademic causes interrupts the educative process, and has been the source of much public concern (especially during the years of the Viet Nam conflict). The point at issue, of course, concerns

---

[3] John Gardner, *Excellence: Can We Be Equal and Excellent Too?* (New York: Harper & Row, 1969), p. 145.

the relevancy of opposing ideas to the betterment of the individual and the society.

Democracy implies faith in human intelligence. No society is infallible. Nevertheless, when the correctives that mark a flexible democracy—the ballot, the amendment, and judicial review—are used by an informed electorate, that electorate must be trusted to solve its own problems intelligently. Of its very nature, democracy esteems intelligence and truth, limiting neither the exercise of the one nor the search for the other. To the extent that men are allowed to remain ignorant or irresponsible, democracy is in danger.

By restricting governmental intervention in the spheres of religion, press, speech, and assembly, the First Amendment to the American Constitution recognizes that the state must not obstruct men in their quest for truth. It also recognizes what many have been inclined to forget, that no one person or party or organization has a monopoly on the truth. Democracy, therefore, implies freedom to dissent. The right to be wrong warrants the same protection, if not always as much respect, as the right to be right. Indeed, the right to be wrong can be defended on grounds of expediency as well as of principle, if only for the fact that it is not always possible to know in advance which views are right and which are wrong.

Periods of unrest, including wartime, economic instability, and social disorder, have on occasion severely tested our belief in this democratic educational principle. The fear, for example, of an anti-American political foothold developing in our society made academic freedom a target for those infected with social paranoia in the 1950s when McCarthyism flourished alarmingly.

The notion of teaching as a subversive activity seems to have provoked many subtle questions regarding academic freedom. The issue here really focuses on the distinction between *freedom* and *license*. For instance, some extreme positions on an issue may not imply academic license, but other extremes may border on anarchy or tyranny. Some extremists, both radical and conservative, deny to others the freedom that they demand for themselves. In order to judge claims for academic freedom, one must be cognizant of both the framework in which the idea is presented and its ramifications.

In a democracy, policies are formulated through consensus and majority vote. A person may disagree with the actions of the government, but he accepts them because he knows they are approved by others, and he is confident that the limits set by the government are best for the majority of people. In so doing, however, he reserves to himself the right to call for changes in the law. Obedience to the law is the foundation of liberty. The right to change the law is its guarantor. Indeed, public debate is the method of democracy. The child in school in a democracy must be led to realize that it is not enough simply to assert his own opinion; he must ground it in factual knowledge and be able to persuade others of its validity. The teacher likewise may not impose his views but must state what they are, and why, and should encourage students to make up their own minds individually.

Citizens are not to be uncritically fixed in their ways but must be intelligently flexible and prepared for change. Thus the school should encourage the child to look at a problem from all sides, to suspend final judgment until all the evidence is in, and, even when he has judged, to be prepared to change his mind, should later events prove him to have been mistaken. This does not mean that teachers should sponsor hesitance and indecision. The open mind is not the empty mind. Rather, the teacher should seek to cultivate balanced minds that can make decisions based on certainty or on reasonable probability without confusing the two.

Academic freedom extends to the student and his learning experience. During the sixties and seventies we witnessed a national student movement against attempts to limit the extent of students' educational exposure. At the college level, secondary school level, and at certain elementary levels, students refused to be included in what is often referred to as the "silent majority." Students demanded the same privileges given to the scholar. If we are true to our own ideal, we must accept their petition. Postman and Weingartner noted,

> it is reasonable to assume that most of us would include something about what is called the "democratic process," and how Americans have valued it, or at least have said they valued it. Therein lies a problem: one of the tenets of a democratic society is that men be allowed to think and express themselves freely on any subject, even to the point of speaking out against the idea of a democratic society. To the extent that our schools are instruments of such a society, they must develop in the young not only an awareness of this freedom but a will to exercise it, and the intellectual power and perspective to do so effectively. This is necessary so that the society may continue to change and modify itself to meet unforeseen threats, problems, and opportunities. Thus, we can achieve what John Gardner calls an "everrenewing society."[4]

Faith in the free expression of ideas does not mean that all ideas are good or equally appealing. It means that in order to discover what is good, we have to consider all kinds of ideas, some better than others. It is not difficult, it would appear, to entertain ideas that confirm our prejudices. The real test is whether we can allow and even listen to ideas we dislike.

In addition to opposition to curricular content, students continue to attack discipline practices, dress codes, racial practices, pollution, and a score of other immediate issues—all on the grounds of academic freedom. In their student publications, they voice opinions on current issues, bureaucratic practices, and the alleged dehumanizing forces of our social milieu. Although they may at times demonstrate poor judgment or bad taste in their student publications and activities, they must still be provided with these constructive avenues of expression. Where schools have denied these avenues or reacted negatively to student pressures for academic freedom, the schools have been challenged in the courts (*Tinker v. Des Moines*, 1969; *O'Brian v. United States*, 1968).

Where students' freedom to learn, to form associations, to assemble, and to participate in setting goals have been opposed, confrontation has arisen. Unfortunately, such response often mobilizes radical student behavior, and

---

[4] Charles Weingartner and Neil Postman, *Teaching as a Subversive Activity* (New York: Dell Publishing Co., Inc., 1969), p. 1.

instead of securing the liberty the students want, the response causes public indignation.

Toward Truth

Intellectual curiosity can be observed in almost every youngster who enters school. But somehow, the milieu at home or in school often seems to inhibit this natural curiosity. Restraint can stifle curiosity. Yet, it is only through inquiry that people can learn to discriminate in their thinking. Therefore, academic freedom is necessary in a democratic society, because it encourages the people to think and allows individuals to become articulate citizens. Without academic freedom, advancement in science, art, and technology would undoubtedly be curtailed. The countless accomplishments that have revolutionized our society in recent decades have evolved because we live in a free society. If one accepts democracy over other forms of political-social application, then academic freedom must be considered as inseparable from education.

The historical roots of academic freedom can be traced to the Greeks. The Athenian State approved of one's being philosophically free to think, despite the political affairs of the society. In medieval times, universities—the feudal system notwithstanding—were able to secure a remarkable degree of academic freedom, but this freedom was sharply reduced during the Reformation. At that time, the religious conflicts and consequent high feeling narrowed academic freedom to the point that authorities administered loyalty oaths and established other controls. These controls remained until approximately the eighteenth century, when secular schools began to emerge. As the religious and political state controls diminished, freedom of thought increased.

Academic freedom at the university level was common during the nineteenth century. This was not true in the lower-level schools. In the early part of the twentieth century, academic freedom in higher education continued to operate, but in the public school it was somewhat limited. During the forties and fifties, fears that teachers might be engaged in subversive activities, or that they might be disloyal, severely restricted academic freedom in a number of instances.

Public school teachers have always enjoyed less academic freedom than university professors. Curricular patterns in public schools were designed to aim toward the learning of information, and not toward inquiry into social issues. Also, in order to gain community support, often schools were forced to avoid controversial issues; and, of course, at the elementary school level there is less need to present controversial material than on the secondary or college levels, although academic freedom is essential at all levels. Teachers in the public schools, because of the age of their students and the degree of autonomy they enjoy, must tailor their application of this free and democratic concept to the circumstances.

In America, we have experienced constitutional challenges in the area of civil liberties. In its desire to guarantee the free, unobstructed flow of knowledge, our present generation seems more enlightened than our forebears. Although many Americans would choose to abridge civil liberties in school and university settings, the restriction of such basic rights as academic freedom is hardly a palatable solution for twentieth-century man.

Toward Democracy

Academic freedom includes, according to some, freedom from indoctrination—even indoctrination for democracy. This type of thinking upsets many traditionalists; their fear is that democracies may fail to teach their young the democratic ideals upon which democracy depends for its existence. According to the Traditionalist viewpoint, the support of democracy is the prime objective of the schools. Because our culture holds democracy to be the best way of life, they maintain that the schools must transmit this belief to their students. This position leads to a conflict over whether or not one can teach democracy by using authoritarian methods—methods diametrically opposed to democratic ideals. A different version of the question is, Can democracy be preserved without authoritarian indoctrination?

The Progressivist and Liberal reply to this kind of query is that democracy can be saved only by the application of democratic principles and ideals in the teaching-learning process. In a democracy, they say, the teacher must respect the student's intellectual integrity and capacity for independent judgment. Thus, although teaching for democracy may require teachers to provide basic concepts and postulates, it does so not to indoctrinate, but only to provide the student with a foundation on which to analyze issues with intelligence and depth.

Contemporary Political Ideologies

When we look at today's world and the purposes of the educational systems in changing cultures, we discover that a major purpose of education in any society is to transmit the basic tenets of the political-social system to every member of the society. These tenets, which make up the accepted political ideology, represent the body of interrelated ideas that create the conditions that influence the society's social structure and institutions—for instance, the schools, home, church, and the media. These institutions integrate the viewpoint of the local political ideology into their value systems.

As they develop, new nations may either follow existing ideological and educational patterns or they may develop new ones. Basically, three choices are available to them:

1. To accept the basic concepts of democracy and its attendant beliefs in the value and worth of each individual as a person and potential citizen; the right of all individuals to an education designed to prepare them to use their competencies and talents in meeting and solving problems as they arise, with the hope that solutions developed will result in improving the way of life for all; government of, by, and for the people; and respect and tolerance for peoples of all religions, all races, and all nations.

2. To accept totalitarianism (e.g. communism) and all it entails—the shaping of people to the ends determined by the party; government by and

for the party in power; intolerance for, and ruthless rejection of, individuals, peoples, and nations that do not accept its point of view or fit into its pattern; and education as a means of developing the competence and talents of individuals to serve the purposes of the party.

3. To attempt to develop a form of government and plan for education based on their own unique philosophy and culture, supplemented where desirable by the best and most defensible concepts evolved by other nations or groups of nations.[5]

The school then, as one of society's more important institutions, draws its values and perspective from the political ideology of the society. Because in our society conservative, liberal, and radical political ideologies vie with each other, and because normative social behavior is determined by valuations of specific elements of these perspectives, it follows that conservative, liberal, and radical elements are fundamental to the continuum of viewpoints that make up the social reality within the school.

Conservatives

Present-day conservative perspectives are rooted in classical nineteenth-century English liberalism. In general, conservative viewpoints regarding the role of government are that it should be limited to the traditional, established practices and values; they usually reject untested proposals for change. Conservatives are strongly partial to the private businessman, and seem very much concerned about inefficiency in government. Conservatives take a dim view of government interference with personal liberties. They favor noninterference with natural law, a traditional pattern of social life, and a well-ordered system of social classes within society; they are strong in support of private ownership—private enterprise being equated with freedom. In the exercise of political judgments, conservatives generally rely on the principle of precedent.

Liberals

The liberal perspective, though somewhat unclear sociologically, has also evolved through historical experience. As a political perspective, it seeks freedom in politics, social relations, and personal life. As a political-social ideology, it represents opposition to restrictions and privileged associations. It is not limited to the thinking of a single scholar, as some radical viewpoints are, but represents a broad sweep of opinion by thinkers who in many ways are pragmatically oriented. Liberals tend to seek logical, pragmatic solutions to remedy societal problems.

Liberal and conservative conceptions of social reality are not fundamentally different, but these two perspectives do differ remarkably in the manner in which they deal with problems. This difference stems primarily from their analyses of the State. As the liberals see it, the State should be held accountable to the people, especially in regard to change, and all groups should

---

[5] James A. Johnson, Harold W. Collins, Victor L. Dupuis, and John H. Johansen, *Introduction to the Foundations of American Education* (Boston: Allyn & Bacon, 1973), p. 122.

be represented in government. As Domhoff has noted, three dimensions of government are favored by the liberal perspective: (1) government responsibility to redistribute income; (2) government regulation of private factors when consumer preferences are affected; and (3) government provision for essential social services that cannot be provided for by private sources.[6]

Radicals

Conservative and liberal viewpoints both differ markedly from the radical perspective. Neither the conservative nor the liberal view of the State intends that government serve only one class of people; radical views do. Contemporary radical perspectives of society are based, in part, on the works of Karl Marx. Their analyses of society have evolved from a dynamic syntheses of paradigms partially based on historical considerations.

The radical perspective challenges the mode of economic production in modern society. It questions the organization of labor and productive activity as it relates to private ownership, or the dominating factors of impersonal markets as exemplified in the capitalistic system. It favors unorthodox revolutionary methods for bringing about change. It holds that the State's role is to service a controlling class in a stratified society. The State, then, should not only provide the members of the elite with services; it should also protect the society's system of institutional organizations by supporting the power of the ruling class. As the radicals see it, present political-social systems are irrational. Society is faced with dilemmas because of the structure of its institutions. These dilemmas can only be solved by a radical restructuring of the existing institutions. As they envision it, the ideal society will be a milieu in which man is both free to develop as a human being and simultaneously to cooperate with his fellow man in the development of the total socialist scheme.

Capitalism and Education

Capitalism as an economic philosophy was born in eighteenth-century Europe, and then spread to America and the rest of the world in the nineteenth century. Today it is the dominant ideology of Western civilizations. As a political-social system, it freed individuals from the religious and economic constraints of earlier periods. In its classic form it can be defined simply: it is the private ownership of products, private production for profit, private control over property, and private wage contracts for workers. In this form, it provides motivation for acquisition, competition, and planning for long-range profits. As an economic system, it moves beyond production of goods for the market; labor itself becomes a commodity, because production and the accumulation of money for the purposes of acquiring material goods places each person in the marketplace. So long as the individual does not violate the society's penal code, his freedom is unlimited. Consequently, the productive activity of the individual is self-motivated and self-governed, and the accumulation of capital produces enormous increases in social produc-

[6] G. Domhoff, *Who Rules America?* (Englewood Cliffs, New Jersey: Prentice Hall, 1967).

tion and wealth. Increases in productive capacity lead to still greater increases, partly because the introduction of technological innovations breeds new innovations which in turn cause increased competition for markets and profits.

In some ways, capitalism as a concept can be said to have evolved from the onset of the industrial era. As it pertains to industry, capitalism is a system under which the means of production, including the industrial plan, tools, raw material, and acquisition of property, may be owned by private persons. However, under capitalist philosophy, ownership is conditional. Provisions in the laws provide for the protection of the masses from absolute rights of ownership. The owner's use of property, for instance, may be scrutinized in terms of the interests of other people, that is, in regard to pollution, ecology, public safety, and so on. Moreover, in the capitalistic system, certain property, such as roadways, rivers, and harbors, must remain public. For instance, if tolls are required for the upkeep of properties, the tolls should be collected by the State.

Central to the political beliefs of capitalistic ideology is the notion of non-interference with natural human activity. The general welfare, progress, and social order are considered best maintained by freeing the individual from constricting political controls. Although democracy is not necessarily equated with capitalism, democracy in the Western world has been basically capitalistic.

The capitalistic (and democratic) concept of individual autonomy presupposes an educational system that encourages individuals to acquire the motivation and capacity to solve problems, take risks, and assume responsibility for their own success or failure. The capitalist social system makes it possible for one to select freely the particular goals or style of life that seem most desirable. This kind of civil liberty makes our democratic society possible. Applied to education, capitalism supports the principles of universal human liberty, equality of educational opportunity, natural law, personal freedom, and academic liberty. Despite certain inequalities in personal wealth and income which the capitalist economy creates, its educational system provides a pathway for social mobility. This produces a widely scattered distribution of resources in the society.

1. Private enterprise is valued because it gives opportunity for the creative potentialities of the entrepreneur or of corporate management. It gives entrepreneurs the largest measure of freedom in working out their work destinies, because the opportunities of sharing in the profits provide the best stimulus for individual effort.
2. Production of goods is valued as a prerequisite to economic well-being. The drive toward more efficient and increasing production is very important.
3. The sanctity of contract and respect for property are valued as the foundation for orderly and dependable economic relations.
4. The economic well-being of the individual person is valued as the cornerstone of a sound economy, and is the essential foundation for a full and rounded individual life. It is frequently defined in very simple material terms.

5. The profit system is valued because only where profits are made can private enterprise long continue. The profit system is modified or limited by the entry of government into the economy through laws and regulations.

Socialism and Education

A wide variety of definitions and paradigms have accumulated under the banner of socialism as a political-social ideology. As an economic system, socialism seeks an egalitarianism in which private ownership is permitted within a collective order. Thus, major societal resources would be publicly owned and operated, but minor resources would be privately owned. In other words, the State (and not private industry or enterprise) would operate industry for the public benefit and so would reduce the danger of abuse to the working class.

As a system, socialism has been applied in the form of a controlled capitalism in which large segments of a country are under government control, as in England. Another socialistic system, democratic socialism, has been presented as an alternative to capitalism. Democratic socialism asserts that any form of economic dependence or exploitation through the use of power (for instance, corporate monopolies) infringes on individual liberty. In this vein, democratic socialism rejects communism because of the emphasis on dictatorial powers of the State, which subordinates individual freedom.

Other varieties of socialistic philosophy include Christian socialism and Fabian socialism. In the former, we find a nineteenth-century revival of religious ethics as they relate to social justice and man's behavior. In its economic application, it seeks to emphasize equalizing resources to help the poor elements of society. "Each man should be his brother's keeper." Somewhat similarly, Fabian socialism, very much in the tradition of Karl Marx, insisted that all persons must share in the society's abundance. Thus, the nineteenth-century English Fabian Society sought the redistribution of wealth in a manner that would benefit society at large rather than private investors. Both of these political philosophies viewed society's democratic processes as evolutionary in nature.

In the United States, the Socialist Party has been a successful minority on the political fringe. It has seldom elected a candidate to a major office, but many of its viewpoints have become widespread. As an illustration, this party provoked serious consideration of the concepts of a minimum wage, fair-housing laws, fair-employment practices, social security, and the forty-hour work week before they were established by our majority parties. Being in a moderate left position, the Socialist Party considers itself mainly a propaganda group today.[7]

One finds that the factors that tend to align socialism with democratic conditions are reflected in its position on education. Like other political-social movements, socialism seeks power and so would like to see its philos-

[7] G. T. Thayer, *The Farther Shores of Politics* (New York: Simon & Schuster, 1968), p. 447.

ophy of a collective order deeply rooted in the tradition and culture of the school. As it attempts to reorganize the social system, even though with a democratic twist, socialism hopes to eliminate the stratification of people— which so greatly influences living conditions. Therefore, socialists would like to extend educational opportunities, vocational training options, and available health services. However, the price for this extension of public benefit would be the inhibition of private ownership, private control, and the provision of services for self-profit. Because the socialist ideology envisions change as evolutionary and rejects violent revolution, civil disorder, and radical reform activities, under socialism the schools would serve as the incubator for the eventual realization of the socialist scheme. Every student should be educated according to ability, not according to social position or capacity to pay. Children from lower-income groups should not only be taught to ply a trade but also to realize themselves as people. To this end, the school leaving-age should be raised, so that teenagers are not sent into the world half-educated during the most impressionable years of their lives. Young people at work should be given the opportunity to pursue their education part-time. Since education is a lifelong process, the government should actively promote adult education. Public support and the widespread acceptance by the "people" are essential to the socialist vision for a secured social order. In their view, education is the means by which to seek such support and acceptance.

The history of socialist philosophic splits and the variety of Marxist clichés that have plagued the socialist ideology seem responsible for its political-social lack of success. The socialist philosophy has never been supported by large segments of the society, not even by large segments of the labor force or the working classes.

Communism and Education

Of all the architects who charted the blueprint of socialism, Karl Marx and Friedrich Engels stand out as the major draftsmen. It was their thinking and writing that led to the transition from nineteenth-century socialism to modern communism, which nowadays is one of the largest branches of the socialistic tree. The basic economic and social postulates of communism, as set forth by Marx and Engels, were developed in the midst of the Industrial Revolution, when the labor force became the massive working class. These postulates assume, among other things, that both social classes and the State will eventually disappear; that the interests of capital and labor are incompatible; that because of the exploitive nature of capitalism, the differences between capital and labor are insoluable; and that disorganization, violence, and revolution are necessary in order to resolve this conflict.

Marx's theory of communism was derived from close study of historical, economic, and political-social data, plus a conviction that man must be capable of determining a system superior to capitalism. Communism is materialistic, declaring that matter exists independently of ideas. It maintains that the mind has emerged from matter, is dependent on it, and only mirrors reality. Communism insists that all events form part of a gigantic, evolving pattern, propelled by the continual conflict of opposing forces. This Hegelian concept, which claims that all phenomena can be explained in terms of a duel of opposites, is known as the *dialectic.* Hence, communist philosophy often is referred to as *dialectical materialism.* Thus, according to communist dogma, man's socialization is determined by material causes.

It follows, then, that under communism the productive forces of society determine the society's form of government and social ideology. Marx asserted that man's ideas change as his social existence changes. Thus, social systems, by virtue of their own evolution toward maturity, destroy themselves through the process of changing. Marx attributed this destructive element to material conditions. As a result of this element, he contended, capitalism would cause its own end, because capitalism creates class-consciousness and a stratified social order, in which the seeds of class conflict and destruction are inherent.

The communist system focuses on class conflict as a vehicle for radical change. Marx and Engels directed their ideas toward the worker in the *Communist Manifesto* (1848). According to Hammen

> The contents of the Manifesto had little that was new or original. It was a synthesis of accepted or widely current ideas, impressions, prejudices, fears, hopes, historic and economic concepts. It harnessed much that was familiar in the service of revolution to overthrow the existent. Its impact was strongly emotional. Therein lies its strength and appeal. Humanity is asked to accept a supposedly inevitable conflict of classes, social warfare and the inhumanity of revolution, all in the name of humanity and with the promise of higher humanity. It asked for a war to end all warfare.[8]

Communists assert that their ends can be achieved only by overthrowing existing social conditions. Where liberalism sees the basis of society in the individual, Marx found it in the class. The individual, he declared, was a product of his class, and class molded morality, tastes, and conduct. Revolutionary or radical alternatives call for the taking over of political power by the working class when the government elects to establish a thoroughly socialist society. In creating a communist society, they believe in the words of Che Guevara.

> We are doing everything possible to give work this new category of social duty and to join it to the development of technology, on the one hand, which will provide the conditions for greater freedom, and to voluntary work on the other, based on the Marxist concept that man truly achieves his full human condition when he produces without being compelled by the physical necessity of selling himself as a commodity . . . We will make the twenty-first century man . . . [9]

Communists view education from the vantage point of their belief in a classless society. Conceivably, such a society would be able to create schools characterized by a humanistic educational administration, with freedom from publications produced by profit-making corporations. In such a system the schools would be owned and controlled by the government. Communis-

---

[8] O. J. Hammen, *The Red 48'ers* (New York: Charles Scribner's Sons, 1969), p. 171.
[9] J. Gerossi, "The Speeches and Writings of Che Guevara," in D. Gordon, ed., *Problems in a Political Economy* (Lexington, Mass.: D. C. Heath, 1971), pp. 8–9.

tic teachers would use teaching strategies based on impersonal technical knowledge free from so-called political slants.

Because of their belief in a classless society, the communists feel that within the communistic educational framework high values can be preserved and developed. Capitalistic school systems, they charge, cannot build and maintain high values, because their efforts are nullified by class stratification, depressions, war, and general moral decay. Communism, on the other hand, can achieve a more responsible art, science, literature, and education, they believe. Of course, in a communistic society, they maintain, the educational efforts would emphasize the welfare of the masses.

To understand the dialectical relationships between freedom and order, independence and dependence, majority rule and minority rights, and human liberty and slavery, one must understand the communist beliefs: that the source of freedom is communism and that truth is communist dogma. According to the communist ideal, every classroom must serve the communist cause by being a vehicle for indoctrination and for the advocacy of communistic ideas. In this way, pedagogy can serve as an instrument for nationalizing their ideology. It follows, then, that academic freedom is anathema to the communist. When communist faith is served up as the basis for freedom, individuality, and liberal education, free enterprise in learning cannot be tolerated.

Educational standards in communist countries apply throughout the nation; they do not, as in America, vary from state to state. Controls are drawn up according to national rather than to local specifications, so that pupils everywhere have the same choice of subjects. There must be no waste of human resources, such as communists claim exists in Western societies, where students allegedly are educated as individuals regardless of the tasks society expects of them. Instead, all available talent is carefully measured, pooled, and steered along approved channels. The emphasis on planning and coordination is found at all levels of the educational system. Schooling is free at all levels, with higher education conditional on ability and political reliability.

In general, we may summarize the communist belief as follows: (1) capitalism fails to fulfill the promise of material and spiritual abundance because of the class-structure of the socio-economic milieu; (2) education means a cooperative communal effort of parents, students, and teachers in all age groups in the society; (3) educational opportunity in a class society is a myth; and (4) genuine education can occur only in a society that is free from prejudice, cultural and economic bias, and inhumane social conditions. In countries where this ideology has predominated, we find, however, that there seems to be a contradiction between the philosophy and the pragmatic implications of this ideology.

Fascism and Education

Fascism, which became for a time the ruling philosophy of Spain, Italy, and Germany, is a mixture of controlled capitalism and rigid socialism. Both Benito Mussolini and Adolph Hitler described it as *national socialism.* Although fascism, superficially, does seem to be socialistic, it is distinct from socialism in that instead of serving the whole society it serves only a small, powerful, wealthy elite. A basic premise of fascism is that the interests of the nation override the interests of individuals.

As an economic system, fascism is less systematic than the other ideologies we have discussed. In the quest for power, it is almost unpredictable. Emphasis is on military supremacy, political deception, and the notion that to be ethical implies weakness. Fascist ideology accepts conflict as a natural goal. Aggression is viewed as a source of strength, and harmony is viewed as a myth. This antipacifism, which places war over peace as the milieu for unleashing man's creative energies, is clearly reflected in the historical accounts of Mussolini's Italy and Hitler's Germany. On the one hand, fascism represents the concept of a central State which embodies idealism as the prime ethical idea. In fascism, man is assumed to belong to a higher spiritual order, and materialism is thought of as vulgar. On the other hand, national socialism divides national life into the elite and non-elite. In Nazi Germany, for instance, the people were ranked as superior or inferior, with a leader at the top. This system of ranking culminated in a fanatical racism in which the Aryans were conceived to be almost godlike Teutonic heroes, and the Jews and Slavs were thought to be fit only for death or slavery.

Fascism declares that the good of the individual is inseparable from that of the nation. The individual can develop as a person only to the extent that he dedicates himself to an end greater than himself—the national will. In Western democracies, the citizen acts cooperatively and sometimes even competitively as an independent individual within the group or community. Under fascism, the person ceases to be separate and identifies his own incomplete personality with the complete personality of the state. Fascism also rejects the democratic ideal of equality. Men, it declares, are inherently unequal, and the nation must select its leaders from the natural aristocracy of the race. The purpose of the state is to enhance the supremacy either of a particular race (according to National Socialism, it was the Aryan race and its elite, the German people) or culture (in Italy, an Italian hegemony descended from the Roman Empire). Deriding the decadence of bourgeois democracy and the vacillation of the intellectuals, fascism extols the values of courage, discipline, devotion to duty, and respect for tradition. Fascist education simplified the relation of student and teacher and obviated some of the disciplinary problems that often arise in the democratic West. The individual student became one among a well-defined community of students. The purpose of the teacher was the same as that of the individual and the class. The fascist teacher had to be trained carefully since he was not simply the child's advocate but also the servant of the state. More than a scholar, he had to be a natural leader, capable of arousing the admiration of his pupils and inspiring them with the conviction that there was no greater honor than to serve their country. In his hands, subject matter had to be illuminated with ideology.

Fascist ideology asserts that self-discipline is more important than happiness; reverence for the State is more important than personal freedom; and that radical or ethnic origin, regardless of socialization within the culture, determines worth. Thus, this system denies a meaningful existence to people who are not members of the elite. The State is presumed to be above criticism: the superior power elite are ordained to rule the masses. Although the fascist states of Mussolini and Hitler were defeated during World War II, today we still find many examples of fascist ideology in fringe-group politics of the international arena and in post-Franco Spain.

Just as the fascist political-social system denies all spheres of the personal in art, science, literature, and politics, so too it denies academic freedom. Education and scholarship have no claim to freedom from political authority and censorship. Individual contributions in these areas are viewed as expressions made possible by the fascist whole. The individual is subordinated, controlled, and under national scrutiny. In its extreme interpretation, all contributions to art, science, philosophy, education, or sociology are created only by members of the superior race, that is, Aryan, in the Nazi State. Members of all other races are viewed as receivers. Therefore, schools are segregated and educational opportunities are controlled by factors beyond the individual's capacity to alter.

World Peace and Understanding

All of the modern political-social ideologies presented in this module were designed and propagated through the efforts of scholars. At the center of each ideology we find the concept of "power" (that is, the resources with which to pursue a goal), and varied references to a "democratic" concept. Each ideology attempts to legitimize itself by nationalizing itself. Simply, there is an interplay between the ideology, or system, and power.

Western political ideologies have used the schools to propagate a secular ideological faith in the system; academic freedom and democratic commitment are in a pivotal position. In America, we find a decline of ideological theses, at least in the orthodox sense, as the postindustrial era has witnessed a solution or near-solution to our major social problems. Opportunity, organized labor and industry, public welfare, governmental authority, and the economic system of the society are committed to democratic and capitalistic constitutional systems. Bell noted

> Few serious minds believe any longer that one can set down "blueprints" and through "social engineering" bring about a new utopia of social harmony.[10]

Nationalism and World Peace

In an expanding context of international politics, the concept of nationalism has a great impact on world peace. Despite political ideologies, peaceful relations among nations depend upon economic, social, and political cooperation or coexistence. An inability to develop a world order (for instance, international law) may bring about the demise of some newly developed or neonationalistic nations. Nationalism—a concept that provides sovereignty to any group who wishes it—is probably an error, even though there is no established international order.

Our post-industrial triumphs in nuclear science have presented the interna-

[10] Daniel Bell, *The End of Ideology* (New York: Collier, 1961), p. 397.

tional community with the threat of annihilation of the human race because of the power-plays of certain political ideologies. International developments, such as formalized agreements, disarmament policies among world powers, international councils, regional and world organizations (the U.N., NATO, Common Market) have had only a limited impact upon the aggressive activities of nations.

Throughout the nations of the world, the schools are vehicles for transmitting nationalistic loyalties and for cultivating national ideas. The decline of direct indoctrination of ideologies is considered healthy for world peace and understanding. National problems are quickly becoming international in scope, and it is important that the people of all nations understand this. No nation can afford to allow nationalistic feelings to obscure the need for an open mind about the international community of people.[11] The education of all nations must prepare youth to be both citizens of the nation and citizens of the world. An appropriate goal for mankind in each nation would be to make a real contribution to long-range solutions of worldwide problems.

The schools of any nation tend to reflect the culture, values, and norms of the mass society. Unfortunately, in some nations the schools have been used to exploit the national ideology for its own sake. In such situations, the ideology can become a serious threat to world peace and understanding. The ethics which some political systems disavow may serve as the only vehicle for achieving a workable international peace.

Education and Public Responsibility

Our country faces many moral and political challenges. When examining the educational implications of the various political ideologies, one cannot help but wonder, "What does constitute morality and public responsibility?" Adlai Stevenson asserted

> All politics is made up of many things—economic pressures, personal ambitions, the desire to exercise power, the overriding issues of national need, and aspiration. But if it is nothing more, it is without roots. It is built on shifting, changing sands of emotion and interest. When challenged, it can give no account of itself. When threatened, it is in danger of collapse . . . Today, when the threat and challenge to free society seem more total and powerful than ever before, it is not a political luxury or fruitless pedantry to re-examine our fundamental principles. I think it more likely to be the condition of survival.[12]

In education as in politics, our conception of the role and character of the enterprise is changing rapidly. Although there are many fundamental threads that run through American education and withstand the effects of time, we are no longer dealing only with hierarchal transmission of knowledge— teacher to student. Today we are developing nonhierarchal educational approaches that feature lateral transmission of knowledge to the members of our society. With these approaches, people learn from each other, and from our mass media, as well as from teachers. As our conception of teaching and

---

[11] K. Boulding, *The Meaning of the 20th Century* (New York: Harper & Row, 1965).

[12] Adlai Stevenson, "Politics and Morality," in C. S. Fletcher, ed., *Education for Public Responsibility* (New York: Norton, 1961), p. 21.

learning continues to evolve, one notion that is gaining strength is that education should be equated with public responsibility.

Truth and brotherhood must stand as the hallmark of any ideology if it is to influence national morality in the educational enterprise. Indeed, the consequences of ideologies that deny, scorn, or distort the concepts of truth and brotherhood are inhibitory to human welfare. An example is the manner in which the communist ideology equates brotherhood with a communal destiny for society rather than with public responsibility for independent free behavior. The foregoing statements are not mere generalizations: The major world powers are storehouses of harnessed political energy. Without truth and brotherhood, these storehouses of energy may explode.

Energetic nationalistic drives cannot help but spill over into world affairs. The restlessness of some world powers, especially the anticapitalist factions, has made isolationist philosophies impossible. Thus, the schools must play a major role in preparing our young people for a future which may never see national isolation again.

The vivid truth is that in our new and emerging world society, regardless of political-social ideology,

> No one will live all his life in the world into which he was born, and no one will die in the world in which he worked in his maturity.[13]

SUGGESTED READING

Apple, Michael, *Ideology and Curriculum.* London: Routledge & Kegan Paul. 1979.

Bell, Daniel, *The Coming of Post-Industrial Society.* New York: Basic Books, Inc., Publishers, 1973.

Bowles, Samuel, and Herbert Gintis, *Schooling in Capitalist America: Educational Reform and the Contradictions of Economic Life.* New York: Basic Books, Inc., Publishers, 1976.

Demhoff, G., *Who Rules America?* Englewood Cliffs, New Jersey: Prentice-Hall, Inc., 1967.

Duberman, Lucille, *Social Inequality: Class and Caste in America.* Philadelphia: J. B. Lippincott Company, 1978.

Edwards, R., M. Reich, and T. Weisskopf, *The Capitalist System: A Radical Analysis of American Society.* Englewood Cliffs, New Jersey: Prentice-Hall, Inc., 1972.

Fantini, Mario, M. Gittell, and R. Magat, *Community Control and the Urban School.* New York: Praeger Publishers, Inc., 1970.

Gordon, D., *Problems in Political Economy.* Boston: D. C. Heath & Company, 1971.

Gregor, A., *Contemporary Radical Ideologies.* New York: Random House, Inc., 1967.

Gross, B., and R. Gross, *Radical School Reform.* New York: Simon & Schuster, Inc., 1969.

Hall, Edward T., *Beyond Culture.* Garden City, New York: Anchor Books, Doubleday & Company, Inc., 1977.

Ianni, Francis A., ed., *Conflict and Change in Education.* Glenview, Illinois: Scott, Foresman and Company, 1975.

Karabel, Jerome, and A. H. Halsey, eds., *Power and Ideology in Education.* Part 2: "Education and Social Selection." New York: Oxford University Press, 1977.

[13] Margaret Mead, "A Redefinition of Education," *NEA Journal*, 48:15–17 (Oct. 1959).

Leiser, Burton M., *Liberty, Justice, and Morals: Contemporary Value Conflicts*. New York: Macmillan Publishing Co., Inc., 1973.

MacIver, R., *Academic Freedom in Our Time*. New York: Columbia University Press, 1955.

Masannat, G., and G. Abcarian, *Contemporary Political Systems*. New York: Charles Scribner's Sons, 1970.

Mosteller, Frederick, and Daniel Patrick Moynihan, eds., *On Equality of Educational Opportunity*. New York: Random House, Inc., 1972.

Rich, J. M., *Challenge and Response*. New York: John Wiley & Sons, Inc., 1974.

Sherman, Robert R., and Joseph Kirschner, eds., *Understanding History of Education*. Cambridge, Massachusetts: Schenkman Publishing Company, Inc., 1976.

Sieber, Sam D., and David E. Wilder, eds., *The School in Society*, Part 2: "Socialization and Learning." New York: The Free Press, 1973.

POST TEST

Multiple Choice (*Circle one.*)

1. Freedom for the individual is dependent upon certain conditions, such as
   a. the structure of the culture.
   b. academic freedom.
   c. the political ideology.
   d. the attitudes of the people.
   e. all of the above.

2. Academic freedom in a democracy encourages people to make independent judgments, resist censorship of knowledge, and
   a. indoctrinate for capitalism.
   b. teach controversial issues.
   c. reject official dogma or opinion.
   d. all of the above.
   e. none of the above.

3. Freedom to enjoy academic liberty has been challenged under certain conditions, such as
   a. periods of social unrest.
   b. during wartime.
   c. during economic crisis.
   d. when freedom becomes license.
   e. all of the above.

4. Historically, academic freedom as a concept can be traced to the Greek Athenian State, to medieval universities, and to
   a. the Reformation.
   b. the eighteenth-century Church of England.
   c. the English university system.
   d. the nineteenth-century university.
   e. the autonomous scholar.

5. The schools can reinforce the structure of democracy *best* by
   a. indoctrinating for democracy in teaching.
   b. applying democratic principles in teaching.
   c. seeking to reinforce traditional ideals.
   d. teaching the great freedoms of America.
   e. none of the above.

6. Political ideology represents a body of interrelated ideas which, in the social arena, are referred to as radical, conservative, or
   a. racist.
   b. right wing.
   c. left wing.
   d. nationalistic.
   e. liberal.

7. Which statement is *most* correct?
   a. Conservative perspectives express the desirability of the traditional pattern of social life, including a class-strata system.
   b. Conservatives look favorably upon government regulations of industry for consumer protection.
   c. Conservative ideology views change as an essential quality of social life.
   d. Conservatives are usually pragmatists.
   e. Conservative ideology represents the forces behind most economic policy changes for the working classes.

8. Liberal perspectives seek
   a. radical reform.
   b. historical bases for seeking change.
   c. group representation and State accountability.
   d. a Marxist philosophy.
   e. none of the above.

9. Liberal and conservative perspectives of social reality are not basically in disagreement except in their
   a. analysis of change.
   b. socio-economic representation.
   c. views regarding democracy.
   d. approach to solving problems.
   e. committment to people.

10. Radical analyses of society engender an ideology which challenges
    a. the existing economic system.
    b. the organization of labor.
    c. the function of government.
    d. the role of education.
    e. all of the above.

11. The dominant political ideology in the free West is
    a. liberalism.
    b. communism.
    c. socialism.
    d. nationalism.
    e. capitalism.

12. As a political system, capitalism freed the individual from economic and religious bondage. In its practical application it emphasizes private enterprise, private owner-ship, and
    a. decentralized government.
    b. labor power.
    c. private profit-making.
    d. controlled competition.
    e. none of the above.

13. Capitalism evolved as a predominant concept because of
    a. the industrial era.
    b. production accumulation.
    c. the overflow of raw materials.
    d. the modern era.
    e. the free-enterprise system.

14. Educationally, the application of capitalist ideology is observable in its encourage-ment of civil liberties, academic freedom, free selection of goals, and
    a. scientific law.
    b. equal educational opportunity.
    c. academic quality.
    d. unusual individuality.
    e. all of the above.

15. Democracy as a concept can be observed in which ideology?
    a. Socialist.
    b. Communist.
    c. Fascist.
    d. Capitalist.
    e. Controlled capitalist.

16. In a socialistic system, collective order for egalitarianism would, in concept,
    a. allow the State to operate industry for public rather than private profit.
    b. reduce class stratifications.
    c. be a form of controlled capitalism.
    d. not be adverse to democratic ideas.
    e. all of the above.

17. In America, some accepted current practices that may have had socialist ideological roots are
    a. social security.

  b. minimum wage.
  c. equal housing.
  d. equal employment practices.
  e. all of the above.

18. Within the framework of collective order, socialistic educational literature claims to desire
  a. free enterprise.
  b. an individualistic educational system.
  c. broad extensions of educational opportunity.
  d. deschooling society.
  e. none of the above.

19. Socialistic ideology, like others, seeks power and change. This system would approach this goal by
  a. violent revolution.
  b. radical social reform.
  c. control of the State economy.
  d. nationalizing ideas for widespread acceptance.
  e. unifying conservatives and liberals.

20. Communistic ideology as a branch of socialistic thought was charted mainly by
  a. Karl Marx.
  b. Karl Marx and F. Engels.
  c. R. Zeitung.
  d. Pierre Joseph Proudhon.
  e. Moses Hess.

21. Among the main postulates of communist ideology, one finds that
  a. labor and capitalism are exploitative.
  b. revolution is necessary.
  c. communal order is natural.
  d. pacifism is a vulnerable behavior.
  e. all of the above.

22. The communist position, that man's social reality is determined by material sources which mirror physical reality, is called
  a. metaphysics.
  b. productive reality.
  c. existentialism.
  d. dialectical materialism.
  e. all of the above.

23. The educational effort of the communist order, according to Marx, would
  a. emphasize the promise of materialism for the masses in communal order.
  b. seek freedom in physical and moral reality.
  c. be spiritually superior to capitalism.

    d. all of the above.
    e. none of the above.

24. The teaching strategy, according to communist ideology, would emphasize
    a. humanistic techniques.
    b. philosophic tradition.
    c. impersonal technical knowledge.
    d. all of the above.
    e. none of the above.

25. Historically, three countries have been associated with the ideology of fascism: Italy, Germany, and
    a. France.
    b. Greece.
    c. Spain.
    d. Israel.
    e. Cyprus.

26. Which statement is *most* correct?
    a. Fascism is synonymous with racism.
    b. Fascism is a system which regards power as a central feature of national politics for the elite.
    c. Fascism, like other ideologies, was planned along systematic social-economic goals.
    d. Fascist ideology is a mixture of socialism, communism, and controlled capitalism.
    e. Fascist philosophies place the masses in a central role.

27. Prominent European proponents of fascism, according to history, are
    a. Franco and Martinez.
    b. Churchill and Landsbury.
    c. Lenin and Trolla.
    d. Hess and Argus.
    e. Hitler and Mussolini.

28. Schools under fascist ideology would create conditions in which the masses are dealt with by
    a. identifying abilities and grouping people.
    b. controlling overt behavior.
    c. segregating people.
    d. identifying people by genetic criteria.
    e. none of the above.

29. A central concept in every political ideology is
    a. economy.
    b. education.
    c. indoctrination.
    d. freedom.
    e. power.

30. Nationalism as it relates to education must
   a. reconstruct isolationist ideology.
   b. prepare our youth for a future of international conflicts.
   c. instill capitalist-democratic ideals in the youth.
   d. make a contribution to long-range world implications.
   e. none of the above.

INVOLVEMENT EXPERIENCES

1. Many application forms for teaching positions ask the candidate to state briefly his philosophy of education. Write your philosophy of education, discussing classroom management, teaching methods, discipline, and utilization of the community.

2. Visit a board of education meeting, or a meeting of an *ad hoc* citizens' committee preparing a report for the board. As you listen to the various speakers, try to identify the basic philosophic position of each. If there is a conflict in the group, examine the various proposals to see if the root of the problem is not in fundamental differences in philosophy.

3. Discuss with some of your classmates the rationale (pro and con) for the inclusion of the following offerings in the high school curriculum: driver training, diversified occupations, home economics, welding, physical education, athletics, electronics, typing.

4. In the above discussion, include the ways in which traditional education viewed tests and assignments of grades. Do these views coincide with your views? Do the traditional views differ from the views used in schools today? What techniques of discipline would be utilized by the teachers from each of these schools of thought?

5. Try to arrive at an understanding of what is meant by "educating the whole child." Do you accept this position as a legitimate goal of American schools?

6. In the light of the functions of the school discussed under the various headings presented in this module, appraise the experiences you had in your high school. Would you now describe your experiences as commendable reflections of the democratic way of life? If not, which heading would they best fit under?

7. List some ways in which you will try to help your students in your classroom absorb democratic principles. Do not fail to address yourself to the dilemma of freedom and license as applied to the curriculum content, school performance, and student behavior.

8. Many school systems distribute to teachers bulletins containing statements of the school's functions. Collect one or more of these bulletins, and critically appraise the statements made in the light of the contents of this module.

9. Talk with a school administrator regarding such problems as student protest, student governance, drugs, sex education, and contemporary values. Try to come away with a frame of reference to use with your students when you begin to implement your beliefs about education in your classroom.

MODULE
12

Impact of Change

Dynamics of Change / Changing Attitudes and Values / Science, Technology, and Industrialism / Mass Society and Vertical Mobility / Futuristics

The first-edition version of this module was written by Michael P. Cutrona, Wagner College. It has been revised and updated for this edition.

RATIONALE

Widespread change is occurring today in the structure and functioning of American society. Hopes for reform are high and action is apparent. All about us, innovations in theory and practice are increasing. Change is abounding.

Boulding, in 1966, noted:

> One thing we can say about man's future with a great deal of confidence is that it will be more or less surprising. This phenomenon of surprise is not something which arises merely out of man's ignorance, though ignorance can contribute to what might be called unnecessary surprises. There is, however, something fundamental in the nature of our evolutionary system which makes exact foreknowledge about it impossible, and as social systems are in a large measure evolutionary in character, they participate in the property of containing ineradicable surprises.[1]

Conjecture about the future and the study of change as it occurs are among the most important and yet most difficult aspects of the scientific study of society. The emergence of the United States as a mass society, with its vast technology, has underscored the importance of planned change. It is for this reason that an understanding of attitudes of behavior must be pursued.

When the astronauts landed on the moon, the planets, and indeed the individual countries of the world, were brought closer; the earth became smaller. This event precipitated an awareness that world cultures may be brought into a more intimate relationship, and that the future development of society—for both developed and underdeveloped nations—would be affected.

The transformation we have been observing is scientific, cultural, technological, economic, religious, philosophical, social, and political. Attitudes that reflect resistance to change may be signs that one is avoiding reality. Furthermore, in the few decades between now and the twenty-first century, educators may find themselves in still more uncomfortable times. Traditional views and practices are increasingly more difficult to maintain. Levels of educational and vocational preparation are in flux. We are forced to reexamine education and ask the question, "What is our goal?" Reactions to change will bring our social interactions into a new posture. Life in the mass society, with its speed, competitiveness, and abounding knowledge, will place great demands upon mankind. Attitudes and perceptions will either clarify our understanding of changing cultural products or permit paradoxical generalizations to result in conflict.

No wonder the study of values, attitudes, technological impacts, social dynamics, and changing social functions stands at the forefront of socioeducational dilemmas. These dilemmas are amplified because the rate of change in so many aspects of modern life is much more rapid than in any previous eras of the world's history. It is because of this speed that it becomes increasingly

---

[1] K. E. Boulding, "Expecting the Unexpected: the Uncertain Future of Knowledge and Technology," in E. Morphett, ed., *Prospective Changes in Society by 1980* (Denver, Colorado: University of Colorado, 1966).

difficult to study change. Nevertheless, the planning for change is necessary if we are to set as our destination the farther shores of world cultural interaction.

In this module we shall study four areas which must be understood if you are to understand the concept of change, especially as it relates to attitudes and functions in an evolving mass society. These areas are

The Dynamics of Change.
Changing Attitudes and Values.
Science, Technology and Industrialism.
Mass Society and Vertical Mobility.

The significance of these four areas results from their response to change. The impact of change and its effects upon a mass society and its institutions precipitate onto the people and the educational system. An overview of change, attitudes, and technology cannot help but highlight implications for the future. The final section of the module speculates about some of the changes the future may bring.

Your aim in studying this module should be to understand and to be able to discuss with proficiency the implications of each area in terms of society and education; to be able to relate these to educational issues at the forefront of current thought; and to appreciate how an understanding of these issues can help you in the planning of educational strategies.

SPECIFIC OBJECTIVES

Specifically, upon completing your study of this module, you should be able to

1. Explain *change* as a sociological-educational concept.
2. Cite three examples of changes in society.
3. Describe why it is important to understand the dynamics of change.
4. Cite three major sociological concepts involved in cultural change.
5. Define the concept of *diffusion.*
6. Define the concept of *invention.*
7. Define the concept of *cultural lag.*
8. Define what is meant by *attitude.*
9. Write a paragraph explaining attitudinal changes, and cite an example.
10. Explain and define how attitudes are learned.
11. Cite four factors that tend to influence an attitude or trend.
12. Cite at least five trends that vary by age, social, demographic, and economic groups.
13. Write a statement describing what is meant by educational trends.
14. Cite at least four educational changes that are occurring.
15. Discuss the issues relating to the measurement of attitudes.
16. Cite three methods used to study attitudes.
17. Describe the importance of the semantic-differential technique in the measurement of attitudes.

18. Explain the concept of *progress* in relation to science and technology.
19. Write a statement describing the role of science and technology in an institutionalized culture.
20. Define *technology*, and cite an example of how the schools have improved upon methods of teaching by using scientific or technological knowledge.
21. Cite four examples of how science and/or technology have affected the basic routines of daily life.
22. Cite four examples of how the technological revolution has affected or modified cultural attitudes and values.
23. Define *industrialism*.
24. Cite at least three similarities between the school structure and the structure of an industrial situation.
25. Explain what is meant by a "mass society."
26. Explain how goals are changing within a mass society.
27. Define and describe what is meant by *vertical mobility*.
28. Cite three examples of vertical mobility.
29. Describe the outlook for the future of vertical mobility as a concept in a mass society.

MODULE TEXT

Dynamics of Change

In the three short decades between now and the twenty-first century, millions of ordinary, psychologically normal people will face an abrupt collision with the future. Citizens of the world's richest and most technologically advanced nations, many of them will find it increasingly painful to keep up with the incessant demand for change that characterizes our time. For them, the future will have arrived too soon.[2]

The study of change is necessary for understanding major concepts of society, social dynamics, and culture. Change is the most obvious and frequently studied aspect of human society, as the abundance of federally funded research, and textbook and periodical literature, shows. The planning and implementation of change is perhaps the least understood of social phenomena. Any student of change will confront disagreement among the major theorists. The end result, to date, has been an abundance of ideas, paradigms, and hypotheses—unrelated, often conflicting, and very complex. There are reasons for this state of paradox, for the nature or dynamics of change may imply either organization or disorganization.

Change is an obvious condition of living. It occurs in its most basic form through evolutionary transformations over long periods of time. It may occur in a complex form, apparently without order, almost overnight—such as in the overthrow of governments. It may differ for varying subcultures, age groups, socioeconomic, or demographic groups. Change is difficult to define, identify, and delineate.

In social science, the study of change is often limited to time and social

[2] Alvin Toffler, *Future Shock* (New York: Random House, 1970), p. 9.

variables that may influence the significance of inferences drawn from the sociological data. This type of traditional study, despite its limitations, helps in our understanding of the nature of human group behavior (that is, the behavior, attitude, and beliefs of gangs, peasants, drug users, hippies, and so on). However, a clear-cut identification of precisely what has changed, how the change occurred, and what changes may be forthcoming is extremely difficult. A thorough understanding of changing social phenomena must include a study over a long period of time and in a variety of social and cultural contexts.

In the study and understanding of change, it is important to maintain sociological, psychological, scientific, and lay perspectives. Too often, we tend to limit our own capacity to deal with change, because we are incapable of synthesizing variability, instability, and a lack of order or organization in our own pespectives of cultural phenomena. Thus, it is possible that some theories of change, as we presently understand them, are weak because of their particular scientific preoccupations. Studies of change in educational sociology seem to occupy a pivotal position between the classical study of change and modern applications of change strategies.

Reasons for Change

Margaret Mead has noted

> I see two main reasons for these changes in organizational life. One has been implied earlier in terms of changes taking place in society, most commonly referred to as the population and knowledge explosion. The other is more subtle and muted—perhaps less significant, but for me profoundly exciting. I have no easy name for it, nor is it easy to define. It has to do with man's historical quest for self-awareness, for using reason to achieve and stretch his potentialities and possibilities. I think that this deliberate self-analysis has spread to large and more complex social systems, to organizations. I think that there has been a dramatic upsurge of this spirit of inquiry over the past two decades. At new depths and over a wider range of affairs, organizations are opening their operations up to self-inquiry and analysis. This really involves two parallel shifts in values and outlooks, between the men who make history and the men who make knowledge.[3]

Change reflects our society's capacity to evolve and to seek survival. Although man's capabilities in science and technology are gaining control over his environment, man must seek to maintain intimate ties with the behaviors of his human tribe.

When man reached the moon, he marked the beginning of a new human era. This technological breakthrough necessitated an attitudinal breakthrough for humanity. Man could no longer seek isolation from the world cultures at large. Change, technological or cultural, can be both threatening and hopeful. If we examine history, we will find that all great changes have caused deep concern and some anxiety. The changes our society has been experiencing are a combination of scientific, cultural, technological, social, psychological, philosophical, economic, and political realities. The realities of our human

---

[3] Margaret Mead, *Cultural Patterns and Technical Change* (Paris: UNESCO, 1953), pp. 570–571.

ecology are confronting society with some of its most acute problems. Resistance to change would not necessarily facilitate a constructive transformation of our culture. In education, the effects of those advocating traditional values versus those advocating more controversial ideas perhaps illustrate the discomfort that imminent change can cause. Our society is taking a hard look at itself, and especially, its educational system. Collective survival of a culture depends upon this vehicle of cultural transmission—the schools. As the demands for change continue and increase in volume, we shall witness more reorganization—some meaningful, some suspect.

Cultural Change

When addressing ourselves to change as a concept, we are interested in human behavior. Consequently, in this discussion we must return to the concept of culture. What are the causes, nature, and consequences of change in man's ideational world? Can cultural changes occur without an immediate impact upon aspects of the social system? Will changes in one area of human social organization precipitate changes in other areas? These questions lead us to three major sociological processes involved in change: diffusion, invention, and cultural lag.

Diffusion. The term *diffusion* relates to the process that occurs when different cultures merge or borrow cultural traits. Technological advancements and the establishment of international organizations are typical vehicles for diffusion. Sometimes the combination of cultural elements may lead to a new and entirely different cultural pattern. Perhaps the most significant example of diffusion in the contemporary world is the movement of non-Western societies toward the adoption of Westernized culture patterns and artifacts.

Inventions. Inventions are represented by the technological innovations of our industrialized societies. Inventions and innovations in our communications and transportation systems have been responsible for making the world a smaller place in which to share knowledge, beliefs, and cultural tools. Technological innovation and invention have precipitated changes in our cultural and social order. For example, changes in the work week, leisure time, and the worker's role have influenced modes of family and community life.

Cultural Lag. An important aspect of change dynamics is referred to as *cultural lag;* it is characterized by a lapse in time between a technological change and its accompanying social and/or cultural acceptance. Although some inventions have produced changes which radically altered the larger society, some people are reluctant to make full use of them. An example is the invention of the typewriter and the social or cultural lag which followed with respect to the acceptance of women typists. Schools, too, have been reluctant to change. In the usual course of events there is a lag of fifty years between the development of an invention and the institutionalized use of the change in school practices.

As we have mentioned, the study of change is a complex one, involving relationships among demographic, cultural, and social forces. It reflects the perplexing position of modern sociology, which seeks to be scientific and at the same time humanistic in its interpretation of change. It is with this orientation that we shall begin to explore change in the attitudes, values, and technology of our mass society.

Changing Attitudes and Values

By definition, an *attitude* is a tendency to act in some manner toward a person, structure, or idea. In simple terms, attitudes amount to likes or dislikes and interests or disinterests; they can be private or shared. They are cultural in nature and, as a rule, are formulated through the socialization process. Once formulated, they in turn often influence further socialization.

Change, attitudinally speaking, can be understood in the context of trends. Thus, in recent years a great number of attitudes are "returnees" to the social scene, especially attitudes concerning law and order and reactions to social changes. Many individuals are uncomfortable with some new social trends and so cling tenaciously to traditional views about society. However, whether one approves or not, when man developed procedures by which to harness energy or to prolong life through artificial methods, technology created change. As these advances show, we have both increased our potential for survival and at the same time threatened it. Therefore, the need for careful analysis and collaborative attention to the problems that face our society is paramount.

Attitudes Are Learned

Attitudes are *learned*—there is no other way by which a person can develop acquired preferences (which is what attitudes are). Even the form of our tendencies to act that are associated with the drives for food and sexual expression is acquired. Although the physical requirements of these drives may be met satisfactorily with any physical stimulus, our preferences or attitudes determine the acceptability or unacceptability of the stimulus; these preferences are learned through socialization.

It is difficult to trace the origin of an attitude, or the circumstances under which an attitude was learned. In fact, often a particular attitude seems so fundamentally a part of a person's behavior that it is difficult to conceive of the behavior ever having been other than it is. Actually, attitudes are usually acquired over a relatively long period of time as a result of different kinds of experiences. The most dramatic case in point involves racial attitudes.

Attitudes and attitudinal change and trends tend to cluster about members of a group. It has been pointed out, in Module 9, that in the course of growing up in a group with a common culture, an individual ordinarily acquires the attitudes that prevail in that culture. The principal illustration given in Module 9 is that of ethnocentrism.

Membership in a group may limit the opportunity for an individual to arrive at conclusions that are counter to the prevailing attitude of the group. In fact, when individuals deviate from the social norm behaviorally, they are likely to become the target of criticism and discipline. In this way, group membership produces cultural pressures that may influence attitudinal behavior. In order to be an accepted member of a group, one needs to maintain attitudes and behaviors consistent with those of other participating members of the group. Often these group attitudes, behavior, and notions are unconsciously transmitted. For this reason, many individuals act as though they were conforming, even when they entertain personal attitudes that are quite different from their overt behavior. Consequently, if one focuses on any particular group, similarities in attitude and related overt behaviors will be evident. Concepts such as *beauty, important, valuable, right,* or *ugly, unimportant, worthless,* or *wrong* are also to a large degree culturally defined among members of the group.

Youth Trends

The values and attitudes of youth are salient aspects of their environment. Whether an individual's personal goals and his potentialities are consistent with these values and attitudes or not, the individual knows that his behaviors are gauged by the standards of his group, and are continually being judged by the group (for instance, by approval, disapproval, notoriety, or public personal rejection). In other words, for our youth, much as for adults, socio-cultural contexts influence trends and changes in attitudes. This is extremely significant in both school and nonschool contexts; the overt attitudes may be altered by virtue of the setting. For example, a youngster may display one attitude to his peers in the neighborhood, yet on the same subject, display a different attitude to adults. In other words, as the student might say, "He gives them a line."

Intensive study of attitudinal trends includes, of course, an analysis of youth culture. As the result of lowered voting ages, young people today may participate more fully in influencing the direction of our future than was possible only a few years ago. Through their voting privilege, they may become more active in exerting influence on trends. Even their apathy and consequent neglecting to vote may influence future developments. Moreover, the rapid assimilation of youths' ideas into the mainstream culture has tended to influence attitudes about youth. As young people realize that their voices are heard and their advice attended to, the young will, no doubt, increase their involvement, formally and informally.

Trends in clothing, life style, educational philosophy, and ideas about culture reflect attitudes which vary by social, economic, demographic, and chronological age group. Often, these personal or specific group attitudes may conflict with other social expectancies. This conflict often reveals itself through ambivalencies. Parents, for example, sometimes act in a fashion by which they lose the respect of their children. But their children have learned that, according to traditional values, they must respect their parents. How can one respect someone whose actions are not respectable? Most persons resolve this sociological conflict by keeping their attitudes to themselves. However, this commonly observed manner of coping with changing trends does not entirely resolve the conflict. It may reinforce unrealistic stereotypes about young people or adults; it may produce hypocrites; or it may influence, unconstructively, opinion on matters that deal with whole groups, for instance: "all young people are hippies," or, "all older people do not understand the times."

Conventional stereotypes, one of the most significant means by which society standardizes attitudes and indoctrinates people, inhibit trends. This standardization is especially unfortunate when the stereotype is inaccurate. If we can accept the premise that human beings secure their attitudes from their experiences, it is inconceivable that even vicarious stereotyping can be avoided. One problem facing us today is the misrepresentation of information; this can profoundly affect the formulation of attitudes because our advanced communication technology makes it possible to transmit this to the masses.

Education Trends

Changes in trends have had their effects upon education. Many educators are uncomfortable about changes in the educational process and cling to their traditional views. The concept of accountability, and the demands for a clear, objective look at education are examples of a change in attitude. Sacrosanct ideas about education and employment opportunities are now suspect. Attitudes ranging from advocation of alternative forms of schooling to scrapping the whole educational system are commonplace today.

As old assumptions are discarded, the schools must accept a change in posture. The average age of students will change as schools are opened up to communities; grading systems will undergo recycling as evaluation processes are changed; the teacher-student role will be altered; and structural changes in the operation of schools will be modified. A change in stance for the teacher—from that of a repository of knowledge to that of a facilitator of learning how to liberate knowledge—is occuring now. These necessary alterations will not be contained in the schools. Because the school is the "transmission belt" for the culture of the mass society, changes along these lines will no doubt have a broad-based effect on the society at large. Moreover, these changes will cross ethnic, religious, social, demographic, economic, age, occupational, educational, and philosophic lines. Productive possibilities will evolve, as has always happened in the societies of our historical past.

Measurement of Attitudes

Attitudes are among the most difficult aspects of socialization to understand; nevertheless, they are the most important aspects of cultural behavior, and must be studied. A persistent problem facing the scientist is how to measure attitudes or attitudinal changes. Superficially, it may appear relatively simple to determine an individual's attitude through the person's verbal behavior. Research has shown, however, that individuals may be unwilling to reveal their attitudes, and that one's attitudes may vary according to the situation. Some attitudes are learned from direct experience, but others, such as stereotyping, develop from vicarious encounters. Attitude changes may be gradual and unconscious, or they may be the result of individual or group planning. Consequently, many approaches must be used to study and measure attitudes. One approach, the study of public attitudes and opinion by polling, questionnaires, or opinionaires, has become controversial. Another approach, also controversial, involves the use of attitude tests, scales, and inventories. Lately, social scientists, intrigued with the problem of measuring attitudes, have sought methods of empirical measurement.

Since 1957, the semantic-differential technique for studying attitudes has captured the imagination of the sociobehavioral scientist. This technique, first developed by Osgood, views the language process within an individual as being an interaction between two parallel systems of behavioral organization: sequences of events and sequences of the communicative product. It is the communicative product—verbal or written—which is observed. In light of the evident reliability of this technique, its use in the study of attitudes may close some of the gaps in our knowledge about attitude change.[4]

Science, Technology, and Industrialism

Examination of the history of research, the basis of science, reveals that when paradigms change, the world itself changes. Led by new paradigms, scientists adopt new interests and look into new places, and, more important, their discoveries and inventions reshape the familiar into a new and different world.

Sociotechnical Progress

The most influential aspect of the dynamics of change in the modern Western world has been the concept of progress. The idea of progress as we think of it today was little developed by our Roman and Greek predecessors in civilization. Earlier social and cultural epochs supposed that nonsecular factors—that is, the gods—controlled man's destiny. This belief made the contemporary notion of progress inconceivable. The future was in divine hands. With the birth of modern times at the end of the Middle Ages, massive alterations in Western man's cultural, social, political, religious, and scientific attitudes took place. Man no longer waited for divine providence to act, but attempted to control his own destiny. "The Lord helps those who help themselves," became the guideline. As science developed the techniques for influencing change, progress was proven to be a natural and essential part of human survival. Improved living conditions, growing populations, falling death rates, better technological knowledge, and other changes resulted. Progress influenced social dynamics.

Science and Technology: An Aspect of Institutionalized Culture

We live in an age of science and technology which pays rewards in human improvement. Science has become a formalized trial-and-error procedure in which the scientist (1) sets up a hypothesis; and (2) tests it to prove its fallaciousness or workability. Primitive societies have no science, even though they do have practical knowledge; for example, they are skilled at mapping out travel areas and well understand agriculture, animal life, trade winds, ocean currents, and climates. Although this knowledge represents a basis for

---

[4] C. E. Osgood, and J. Snider, *Semantic Differential Technique* (Chicago: Aldine Publishing Company, 1969).

the physical sciences, primitive peoples have not formalized it into a system involving scientific principles.

Science as an organized system of knowledge has changed the world for twentieth-century man. The more science helps man to understand the world in which he lives, the more he becomes aware of how much there is to know. We can only speculate as to the future developments still to be made in aerospace, energy, sound, and movement.

Science satisfies man's curiosity about the nature of things. But, too, it provides the foundation knowledge by which men reconstruct the world in which they live. When we consider science as being the instrument for the step-by-step conquest of the environment, we are defining man's technology. By *technology*, we mean the industrial arts and techniques for converting raw materials into cultural objects. It is typified by the world of machine methods and industry, which has become an increasingly important aspect of modern culture. In education, teaching machines, audiovisual technological equipment, and innovative learning devices have become popular examples of modern technology.

The power of a society is measured by its technology and life style. The United States, the Soviet Union, and the Republic of China represent three world powers. The people living in these countries enjoy a standard of living which is consistent with their technology, and which is in many ways superior to nations of lesser resources.

Changing Life Styles

Science and technology influence the basic routines of life. For instance, increased technology can affect the work week, sleep patterns, and recreational styles of people. Since the invention of the electric light, television, telephone, automobile, airplane, and so on, we have become more nocturnal and more widely traveled than in previous times. Rapid communication, new capabilities for the storage and immediate retrieval of knowledge, and the widespread institutionalization of innovative apparatus are changing our patterns of life.

The technological revolution of the twentieth century has also served to modify other areas of human behavior. The abundance of automobiles has broken down our notions concerning the proper observation of the Sabbath. Radio and television have altered church-attendance patterns by broadcasting church services of many denominations. Speed of travel has influenced safety. Technology has changed domestic life. Family or home industries are few; most people spend their working day away from their home. Children often have only limited contact with their parents' occupation. Technology has influenced women to join the work force in larger numbers. Leisure time has increased, and "technological man" today can enjoy more time for recreation. Men no longer need to spend most of their energy in working solely to provide the physical needs of life.

Industrialization

A far-reaching result of science and technology is industrialization. Industrialization is characterized by a skewed structure: relatively few hands can generate a large amount of production. Production is mechanized, assembly-line, and massive. The work output of employees in an industrialized situation is dependent upon their skill in a technical operation and upon the efficiency of the machines and the system. Culturally, mechanization opens up the labor market to more people. With new operations and changed demands, the orthodox, homebound existence of past times is eliminated. The impact of industrialization appears to be worldwide. We cannot predict all the changes it may bring to the life style of men and women throughout the world, but we can safely assume that the changes will be enormous.

Because technology and science provide the means of analyzing and dealing with the world, these are at the focal point of cultural change. Technology requires that man change in all spheres of life. Receptive attitudes toward innovation are important in the development of new cultural tools and in the sharing of cultural traits. Probably the great advancements made in the Western world have been, in part, a result of the remarkable tolerance for technological change which has been characteristic of Western peoples. In the industrial situation, the old quickly becomes obsolete. Thus, an attitude favoring change in technological devices undoubtedly influences attitudinal tolerance, which then carries over into the culture of the mass society. Because of its technology, Western society's fatalistic attitude about the future has been replaced by the belief that through technology and science life can be made better.

The Schools: An Industrial Era

Science, technology, American capitalism, and attitudes toward change are powerful determinants of social behavior. The vast changes in society are reflected in the transformation of schools from elitist institutions educating a select group to systems for educating all people. During the period when America was making the adjustment from agrarian to industrial life, educational goals were designed to prepare the student for life by teaching everyone in the same manner, irrespective of whether the student was to follow an academic or a laboring existence. This period perpetuated the "work ethic" and emphasized social Darwinism, which holds that man's life in its struggle with nature is analogous to his biological life, and therefore only the fit survive to acquire advanced schooling or to accumulate worldly possessions.

The progressive movement, which dawned in the earlier part of this century, encouraged a new view of education. From diverse origins—child-centered educators, social reformers, and psychological specialists—several trends developed. Subject matter was no longer considered to be of importance for its own sake; it was important only for its relevancy to the life of the total child. The educational emphasis changed from preparation for adulthood to stress on each child's benefiting to his maximal potential at each developmental stage. Subject matter was tailored to the child. Programs were planned to motivate pupil interests and to bring about active involvement in solving problems and in creativity. Thus, progressive theorists introduced new curricular arrangements that, once implemented, would change the teacher's role from that of an expositor of knowledge to a facilitator of learning—a movement very much current today. Stress was placed on basic needs and competencies. It was held that no single group of subjects could guarantee desired outcomes, but that a variety of experiences was required.

Another progressive trend was the recognition that the majority of youth in the industrial society would not plan to attend college and would therefore need to acquire marketable vocational-technical skills. Progressive schools represented a great diversity of methods; their spirit of change and experimentation was remarkable. In some school systems, these trends were considered too radical and were abandoned. Nevertheless, the impact of progressive education in the industrial era was substantial.

The Schools: A Postindustrial Challenge

Many economically prosperous countries, including the United States, have entered what many sociologists consider to be a postindustrial era. Whereas the industrial age, prior to the late 1940s, required the use of many people to perform tasks related to mass production, automation has changed all that. The development of computers has made possible important advancements in technology, undreamed of only a generation ago: advances in machinery,engineering, space exploration, medicine, and so on. Furthermore, the postindustrial society has been thrust into the space age. In addition to meteorological and scientific information, space exploration has afforded man a new perspective on his world and on his place in the vast universe. These remarkable changes in our world—solar energy, mass production, and computers—have created new demands in the development of educational systems for a postindustrial age. Not only have these technological advances caused a rapid growth of knowledge, but they have also altered the competencies required for living and making a living. Many a worker, still in the prime of life, is finding his occupational skills obsolete, for instance. These changes have had a great impact upon the manner in which people relate to each other—their attitudes, values, and beliefs. As Alvin Toffler states in *Future Shock*, too great changes in too short a time are disorienting, because they do not allow people enough time to adapt properly. Because the present rate of change will no doubt accelerate, we need to develop educational practices that can meet this need of the time in which we live.

One of the many serious educational problems in this postindustrial era has been the lack of intelligent generalists, those who can bridge the gaps between the various specialties which have evolved in our science and technology. It is estimated that technical information doubles every ten years. There are one hundred thousand technical journals available now, and the number doubles every fifteen years. In the field of medicine alone, over three hundred thousand journal articles are published yearly. As our knowledge increases, there is a need for a coordination and capsulization of significant information in order that it can be easily transmitted to the masses. Without such coordination and capsulization, the curriculum (content) of our schools cannot be made either meaningful or relevant to the pupils.

Confronted with such change, it is not surprising that educators' attempts to provide models for change in our schools have floundered, have been confused and disoriented, and have resulted, in some cases at least, in the community and teachers refusing to accept the changes.

New Educational Reform

Most of the new educational reformers can be classified as *neoprogressives*, for their essential ideas are not greatly different from those of the earlier progressives. However, the earlier progressives strongly believe that the "good society" so valued progress that desirable change would be inevitable; the neoprogressives seem to be skeptical about the inevitability of change, especially in the schools as they presently exist. Both in and out of public schools, the neoprogressives have devoted much consideration to the affective correlates of human development. They have been concerned with providing more equal opportunities for the disadvantaged. Moreover, the neoprogressives of this postindustrial era have shown less concern about updating or changing curriculum than on developing strategies of overcoming school conditions which, they believe, alienate creativity by virtue of their similarity, organizationally, to the industrial situation. These reformers have highlighted, far better than any other group in educational history, the extent to which bureaucratic school systems may be alienating and dehumanizing institutions. They have offered valuable insights into teaching practices, classroom organization, and methods by which teachers can improve upon their role. They have introduced alternatives to standard educational practices as models for new types of education. Finally, they have provoked free discussion about the future of education, and have launched a widespread promotion for change.

The unique features and demands of a postindustrial society present many problems to the people of the world as we approach the twenty-first century. Imagine how greatly the scope of our problems in the United States would be magnified if they were spread worldwide!

Future Shock: Future Aims

Educational aims are the by-products of the culture of the society in which they will be applied; aims cannot be stated in isolation of social conditions. What is meaningful and feasible today may not be ideal for tomorrow. One important contribution of the reform movement of the sixties was that we saw the possibility of teaching students to grasp basic principles and concepts of the various fields of study so that with this understanding they could seek modes of inquiry which might help them to deal with the knowledge explosion.

Because vast changes have occurred within a short time span, perhaps one generation, people must be taught to deal with change. Students need to understand the reasons for the changes they see and experience, and to be aware of the areas in which change may be the greatest. They must learn the social consequences of change and how to acquire the kind of education that will enable them to find a meaningful way of life.

Obviously, this is a tall order for any school. However, many school programs meet with a lack of success because they leave unresolved problems and conflicts which, in many ways, may be related to the concepts we have discussed. A considerable part of this problem is that change can assault one's attitudinal system, leaving it shaken, and, indeed, in a state of shock. One of the critical tasks of the educator is to prepare students for conditions that do not presently exist by presenting ideas about the future to the students. This kind of planning and coordination is likely to bring about a firmer grasp of future trends and directions.

Mass Society and Vertical Mobility

Changing Functions

Most of you who read this module have become sensitive to contemporary human relations and are already aware of the massive social reorganization in progress around us. You are also well aware that Western society has been transformed into a "mass society." In the transformation, probably the most oversimplified but fundamental feature is the growing homogeneity and conformity of role functions. To some degree, individualism is retarded in a mass society because audiovisual technology influences and conditions desires, and rewards conformity.

Mass communication, production, and distribution tend to standardize people. Some of the standardization is economic and is the result of concentrations of influence. Curiously enough, however, Americans, perhaps because of their sensitivity about being "brainwashed," and perhaps because of their perceptions of the future evolution of our technology, and the beginning of post-industrial society, are growing less similar each day.

Changing Goals

When we consider mass society, exemplified by increasingly urbanized, modern, and technical environments, we must also consider how the other half lives. The so-called underdeveloped areas, which are essentially rural and derive their survival from agriculture, represent a challenge to the world powers. These countries have minimally sophisticated governmental or political systems, and their people appear largely untouched by the politico-economic considerations of the mass society. Educational opportunities are often absent, and most individuals seek sustenance for the "here and now." However, the technical countries of the world have viewed as a prime goal the spreading of technical knowledge to these countries, as a means of aligning these countries on their side—for economic as well as for world political reasons.

Mass society, where it has developed or where the concept has been introduced, affects different people differently. The concepts of "the American way of life" or the "Industrial Revolution" are descriptive terms, but they cannot be translated literally. The mass societies of yesteryear, today, and tomorrow are changing entities, with altered roles and goals. One of the interesting social realities of this period of history has been the massive vertical movement of people.

Vertical Mobility

In mass societies, status changes occur as the result of socialization, education, and income changes. The basic difference between class and caste societies rests on this point. Within a mass society there are many social elevators. Every social institution in mass society provides elevators that move upward from one rank to another. Once a person establishes himself, opportunities for his special skill can help him to climb. He may climb via the church, via business, via the educational system, or via social activities—without formalized institutional opportunities. Nevertheless, in a massive, competitive society, vertical mobility is a difficult endeavor, because there are always others who seek the same goal.

The public school system is a widely utilized elevator for vertical mobility. Through the school system, each individual is provided with an opportunity to attain social movement. Although a lack of wealth may be an inhibiting factor to some in the attainment of higher training and education, many can work their way through school, and some are provided with a government financial subsidy. Climbing the educational ladder is a means of achieving economic and social status, for educational achievements open up opportunities within mass society.

For many individuals seeking vertical mobility, the teaching profession has provided the vehicle. McGuire and White note:

> Teaching as a profession appears to involve upward social mobility for at least 40 per cent of those who enter the field. Only one in five, however, come from upper lower-class backgrounds. Some of lower status origin apparently achieve an upper middle-class way of life; others, although upward mobile, attain only a lower middle status in their community. . . . About three of every four of the persons in education seem to follow an upper middle-class pattern of living and more than a third come from such family backgrounds.[5]

Vertical mobility by profession, income, or socialization varies from one part of the country to the other. Within mass societies, there is a great deal of movement—up and down. With this vertical movement in an open-class system, people are required to change their places within the social group. New status means new roles or functions, and new goals. This is essentially what climbing the ladder of success in America means.

Outlook for Vertical Mobility

The masses of people in Western society believe that a democratic way of living forbids the class stratification that would inhibit vertical mobility. Yet, the process of stratification by virtue of attained competencies is always going on. Because of the inequities of opportunity that have prevailed in our mass society, some sociologists have expressed great concern about the future of vertical mobility. Other sociologists regard vertical mobility as quasi-mobility, for corporative or higher economic interests seem to control the uppermost points of the socioeconomic pyramid. In a class system, where boundaries exist, a check must be kept to ensure the permeability of the boundaries by individuals. Status differences in a democratic society are an aspect of the human relationship; a society is democratic to the extent that it allows the individual to move from one stratum to another, regardless of family heritage. It is imperative that we resist this challenge to the ideal of vertical mobility, if the American dream is ever to be attained.

[5] C. McGuire, and G. D. White, "Social Origins of Teachers in Texas," in *The Teachers Role in American Society*, Yearbook #14, the John Dewey Society (New York: Harper & Row, 1957), pp. 36, 37.

Futuristics

We have said that discoveries and inventions reshape the familiar into a new and different world. This fact is particularly evident today. The postindustrial society resulting from recent changes and new changes to come will undoubtedly be very different from what we have known since the impact of the Industrial Revolution of the late eighteenth century. Changes already take place so rapidly that we can no longer follow the lead of Scarlett O'Hara, the heroine of *Gone With the Wind,* who in moments of great stress procrastinated by saying "I'll think about that tomorrow." Just what the world will be like in the future we do not know. Let us look at some of the changes forecast by futurist scholars.

The End of Mass Society

Evidently the mass society we discussed in the previous section is coming to an end. In the words of Toffler:

> The "mass society" theorists are obsessed by a reality that has already begun to pass us by. The Cassandras who blindly hate technology and predict an ant-heap future are still responding in knee-jerk fashion to the conditions of industrialism. Yet this system is already being superseded.
>
> To denounce the conditions that imprison the industrial worker today is admirable. To project these conditions into the future, and predict the death of individualism, diversity and choice, is to utter dangerous clichés.
>
> The people of both past and present are still locked into relatively choiceless life ways. The people of the future, whose number increases daily, face not choice but overchoice. For them there comes an explosive extension of freedom.
>
> And this freedom comes not in spite of the new technology but very largely because of it. For if the early technology of industrialism required mindless, robot-like men to perform endlessly repetitive tasks, the technology of tomorrow takes over precisely theses tasks, leaving for men only those functions that require judgment, interpersonal skills and imagination. Super-industrialism requires, and will create, not identical "mass men," but people richly different from one another, individuals, not robots.
>
> The human race, far from being flattened into monotonous conformity, will become far more diverse socially than it ever was before. The new society, the super-industrial society now beginning to take form, will encourage a crazy-quilt pattern of evanescent life styles.[6]

Demassification will require new social arrangements. Workers and families will be more independent. Family groupings will probably follow no set pattern. If anything, they will probably be less child-oriented. Perhaps they will be stronger units, however, because adults, freed from the office and factory, will perhaps be spending more time at home.

Society seems to be becoming less materialistic. Evidently it is beginning to recover from the obsessive belief that bigger is better. Presumably future citizens will be more interested in appropriate size than in bigness, and in quality rather than quantity. Perhaps this change will usher in a no-growth society. Certainly the world no longer has sufficient resources to support

[6] Alvin Toffler, op. cit., pp. 301–302.

bigger populations, larger bureaucracies, more enormous governments, greater industries, and immense waste.

If present trends continue, it appears as though our civilization is becoming individualized and customized. Technological developments make it so easy to customize goods and services to individual specifications that standardization is becoming obsolete. Assembly lines and mass-production techniques are no longer necessary. Instead, employers are able to introduce flex-time schedules for their workers. In such arrangements, workers are freed from the lock-step of fixed working hours. Rather, they set up individual work schedules that let them work at hours congenial with their personal schedules and preferences. Many people will be able to work at home as the use of home computers and computer terminals spreads. Do-it-yourselfers will produce their own goods at home. The rise of these *prosumers* (Toffler's name for people who produce materials for their own consumption[7]), if Toffler is right, spell the end of the split between production and consumption brought about by the Industrial Revolution. The goods produced by these prosumers will of course be built to their personal specifications—another example of standardized products being replaced by individualized products.

The information media are also becoming more customized. Mass media, newspapers, and magazines, are rapidly being replaced by specialized sheets serving special groups; for example, special magazines for campers, motorcyclists, or van owners, and suburban and exurban throw-away newspapers. Even the domination of the airwaves by the major networks is being overthrown by the birth of narrowcasting—narrow spectrum telecasting by cable television and by satellite arrangements aimed at special audiences.

The World of Work

A new industrial revolution has upset the world of work. The twentieth-century corporation, with its top heavy bureaucracy, line-and-staff hierarchy, and assembly-line technology, is rapidly becoming obsolete. Not only are corporations finding it necessary to demassify, diversify, and customize, but they are also being compelled to aim at more than just the economic bottom line. Society is holding them responsible for environmental, social, informational, and moral impacts. On every side, they are being coerced by social pressures and governmental regulations. These pressures become more complicated and onerous as businesses and business organizations become more transnational. Corporate structures are being forced to become matrix-styled; instead of pyramidal, single-purpose organizations, they are becoming multi-purpose, many-product institutions in which decision making is segmented, diversified, and decentralized and production is individualized, customized, non-repetitive, non-standardized, and non-faction-oriented.

New technologies are revolutionizing both products and processes. The new work world will feature electronic technology, manufacturing in space, development of oceanic industries and food production, and genetic industries. Biology-based industries and agricultural innovations will probably re-

[7] Alvin Toffler, *The Third Wave* (New York: Bantam, 1981), chapter 20.

place our present manufacturing and chemical technology in a biotechnological revolution. Computer technology is already being used to solve problems that were unsolvable only a few years ago. The age of dependence on fossil fuels will end. Both fossil and nuclear fuels will undoubtedly be replaced by new types of renewable energy already on the scene.

Governmental Changes

National governments seem not to be working well in many parts of the world. Problems arising from bilingualism, homerulism, and decentralization are common the world over. Nations such as Canada are faced with separatist movements. Others are faced with private armies and terrorist groups such as Italy's Red Brigade. Our own government in the United States is finding it difficult to cope with the activities and demands of the various splinter- and special-interest groups. Regionalism is developing in the larger nations as it becomes evident that interests and problems associated with the various regions are not always compatible with those of other regions or the nation as a whole. Perhaps because of the decentralization and dispersion of production and economic activity, economic policies in large nations need to be regionalized. What is good for the Southwest is not necessarily good for the Northeast!

Other trends downgrade the nation states. Transnational corporations, associations, and unions spread their loyalties beyond national borders. Television and radio beam information and propaganda all over the world, without regard for national boundaries. The world is becoming a matrix organization consisting of many kinds of suborganizations—political, economic, social, and cultural—that work for and against each other. Inter-governmental agencies such as OPEC (The Oil Producing and Exporting Countries), The Common Market, The Organization of American States, and the International Atomic Energy Agency dominate international relationships. Presumably the number and strength of such organizations will grow as the world gets smaller and more complex. Globalism as an ideology is beginning to be common. Its proponents claim to represent the interests of the entire globe— not one nation, region, or bloc of nations.

Education

According to Harold G. Shane and the 132 experts on education and the future that he and his colleagues interviewed for a Phi Delta Kappa jubilee project, education in the future must also be customized.[8] Equal opportunity in education, they say, does not mean the same education for everyone. Rather, education should increase human differences so that all students can make the most of their potentials. To this end, school programs will have to be made more flexible, and pupils will have to be more effectively motivated and protected from the pernicious influences of the mass media. Schools will have to feature action learning in the community and greater involvement of parents and lay people.

If the experts are right, the curriculum of the future will feature lifelong

[8] Harold G. Shane, with M. Bernardine Tabler, *Educating for a New Millenium* (Bloomington, Indiana: Phi Delta Kappa Educational Foundation, 1981), pp. 134–135.

learning. It will have to be much more flexible, to reflect the changing needs of the community and its people. It must without dogmatism acquaint all pupils with the lessons of the past. It should give pupils opportunities to develop their individual talents optimally, without exposing them to unreasonable pressures. All pupils should become reasonably proficient in communication, mathematical, and thinking skills. They should learn to understand at least one foreign language and to detect false advertising, "political double talk," and propaganda. Rather than being exposed to many electives, pupils should be required to learn essential content. They need to learn how to improve the human conditions, to choose alternative futures, to recognize the present threat to the biosphere, and to understand the human geography of the earth's cultures. So that education may be successful in these missions, the teachers and administrators and community members must become aware of advances in the knowledge of human growth and development. This awareness should be worldwide, for educational needs are worldwide.

In sum, there is great need "for a reasonably paced and continuous transformation based on the best features and present practices recast and supplemented by the demands that the . . . future will impose."[9] This is a large order, but not an impossible one.

Since no one knows exactly what the future will be, education for the future should (1) inform boys and girls what alternatives the future may hold, (2) teach them ways in which to influence the future toward the alternatives they prefer, and (3) teach them how best to cope with whatever the future holds. To carry out missions of this sort, Allain[10] recommends that units and courses in futuristics be included in the curriculum. In these courses or units, students could study alternative futures: those that are possible, those that are probable, and those that are preferable. Students would thus become knowledgeable about what may happen, what is most likely to happen, and what they can do to bring about the future they deem most preferable.

SUGGESTED READING

Beeghley, Leonard, *Social Stratification in America: A Critical Analysis of Theory and Research.* Santa Monica, California: Goodyear Publishing Co., Inc., 1978.

Bennis, Warren, ed., *American Bureaucracy.* New Brunswick: New Jersey: Transaction Books, 1970.

Bredemeier, Mary, and Harry Bredemeier, *Social Forces in Education.* Sherman Oaks, California: Alfred Publishing Co., Inc., 1978.

Edinger, Lois V., Paul L. Houts, and Dorothy V. Meyer, eds., *Education in the 80's: Curricular Challenges.* Washington, D.C.: National Education Association, 1981.

Feather, Frank, ed., *Through the 80's: Thinking Globally, Acting Locally.* Washington, D.C.: World Future Society, 1980.

Gordon, D. M., *Problems in a Political Economy.* Lexington, Massachusetts: D. C. Heath & Company, 1971.

[9] Ibid., pp. 138–139.

[10] Violet Anselmini Allain, *Futuristics and Education* (Bloomington, Indiana: Phi Delta Kappa Educational Foundation, 1979).

Post Test
Answer Key

Module 1

1. b, d	2. a, c	3. b, d	4. a, d	5. b
6. a	7. b	8. a	9. a	10. b
11. c	12. a	13. b	14. c	15. a
16. a	17. c	18. a, b	19. b	20. a, b
21. b	22. d	23. b	24. b	25. a
26. c	27. a	28. b	29. c	30. c

Module 2

1. a, b	2. b, c	3. a	4. b
5. a	6. c	7. a, c	8. c
9. a, c	10. a, d	11. d	12. b, c
13. a, b	14. a, c	15. a	16. a, b
17. a, b	18. a, b, c	19. b	20. c
21. a, b, d	22. b	23. a	24. d
25. a, b, d	26. a	27. d	28. e
29. c	30. b, d	31. a	32. e
33. c	34. c	35. a, b, e, g	

36. Cognitive
    Affective
    Psychomotor

37. Their complexity.

38. They spell out exactly what the pupil is to be able to do after the learning is completed.

39. Schools should mind their own business. People who try to do everything end up doing nothing well. Therefore they should concentrate on teaching the academic subjects they call the "basics."

40. Yes.

Module 3

1. Epistemology.

2. The critical evaluation of human experience.

3. It deals with the goals of life.

4. The systematic and logical study of life and the universe to frame a system of general ideas by which the sum total of human experience can be evaluated.

5. Correspondence.

6. Empiricism.

7. Socially useful.

8. Axiology.

9. The development of the whole person; becoming socially effective.

10. The transmission of the knowledge of civilization necessary for one's intellectual development.

True or False

11. False. Philosophy articulates the principles by which we live and provides a necessary basis for evaluating human existence.

12. False. Any position on the nature of man influences the aims of education.

13. False. Leads to a teacher-centered classroom wherein the teacher plans according to known truth, and leads by example.

14. True. However, it is more difficult to employ sound methods in a classroom where memorization, drill, and obedience are stressed.

15. False. The student must develop from within, but in a social setting.

Module 4

1. Instrumentalism.

2. Dialectical Materialism.

3. The Dialectic.

4. Objective to the spectator.

5. Mind.

6. Metaphysics.

7. The individual over society.

8. Epistemology.

9. The Idealists.

10. Pragmatism.

11. Progressivism.

12. Individual development.

13. Progressivism.

14. Universally approved.

15. Every level of activity, cooperatively.

16. True.

17. True.

18. False. Teacher must plan for the acquisition of facts.

19. True.

20. False. Rights are always social, never individual.

21. False. True of communism.

22. False. Social benevolence is not limited to any one philosophy.

23. True. Everything is under State control.

24. True.

25. True.

26. True. Perfectibility of the student is assumed in the effort to mold the mind.

27. False. This is democratic theory based on the rights of the person.

28. True.

29. True. Philosophies differ only on the emphasis of this goal.

30. False. Idealism.

Module 5

1. d	**2.** b	**3.** c	**4.** b	**5.** c
6. b	**7.** a	**8.** a	**9.** b	**10.** b
11. d	**12.** b	**13.** d	**14.** b	**15.** d
16. d	**17.** b	**18.** c	**19.** c	**20.** a
21. b	**22.** c	**23.** b	**24.** d	**25.** a

Module 6

1. c	**2.** c	**3.** d	**4.** d	**5.** d
6. c	**7.** b	**8.** a	**9.** c	**10.** d
11. d	**12.** c	**13.** d	**14.** b	**15.** a
16. d	**17.** b	**18.** d	**19.** a	**20.** a
21. c	**22.** b	**23.** a	**24.** d	**25.** d

Module 7

1. e	**2.** d	**3.** d	**4.** a	**5.** b
6. c	**7.** b	**8.** d	**9.** c	**10.** c
11. c	**12.** c	**13.** a	**14.** a	**15.** d
16. b	**17.** d	**18.** b	**19.** c	**20.** d

Module 8

1. b	**2.** c	**3.** a	**4.** b	**5.** b
6. g	**7.** d	**8.** e	**9.** b	**10.** f
11. a, c	**12.** a, e	**13.** a, d	**14.** b	**15.** c
16. b	**17.** a	**18.** a	**19.** d	**20.** c

21. c	22. c	23. b	24. a	25. c
26. d	27. a	28. a	29. c	30. d
31. d	32. b			

Module 9

1. e	2. e	3. c	4. c	5. a
6. e	7. b	8. c	9. c	10. a
11. b	12. d	13. e	14. a	15. e
16. b	17. c	18. b	19. d	20. b
21. a	22. c	23. c	24. a	25. d
26. b	27. a	28. b		

Module 10

1. e	2. c	3. d	4. d	5. b
6. b	7. e	8. d	9. a	10. e
11. b	12. c	13. c	14. d	15. e
16. a	17. c	18. e	19. b	20. c
21. e	22. d	23. b	24. d	

Module 11

1. e	2. c	3. e	4. d	5. b
6. e	7. a	8. c	9. d	10. e
11. e	12. c	13. a	14. b	15. d
16. e	17. e	18. c	19. d	20. b
21. e	22. d	23. a	24. c	25. c
26. b	27. e	28. d	29. e	30. d

Module 12

1. d	**2.** e	**3.** a	**4.** b	**5.** c
6. a	**7.** e	**8.** b	**9.** a	**10.** b
11. d	**12.** b	**13.** e	**14.** a	**15.** d
16. a	**17.** e	**18.** e	**19.** b	**20.** e
21. c	**22.** b	**23.** b	**24.** d	**25.** c